Teesdale's Special Flora

Special Flora

Places, plants and people

Margaret E. Bradshaw

WILD*Guides*

PRINCETON
UNIVERSITY
PRESS

DEDICATION

To S. Max Walters

Published by Princeton University Press,
41 William Street, Princeton, New Jersey 08540
99 Banbury Road, Oxford OX2 6JX
press.princeton.edu

British Library Cataloging-in-Publication Data is available

Library of Congress Control Number: 2022951309
ISBN 978-0-691-25133-2
ISBN (ebook) 978-0-691-25134-9

Printed in Great Britain

10 9 8 7 6 5 4 3 2 1

Contents

Foreword

Teesdale's Special Flora

Upper Teesdale has been revered by generations of British naturalists and for good reason. As the author Dr Margaret Bradshaw clearly points out here *"The Teesdale Assemblage is unique. Nowhere else in the UK do these particular species grow together in a comparatively small area."*

With seventy years' experience in the area, Dr Margaret Bradshaw may be the latest in a long line of botanists drawn to the plant communities of Upper Teesdale but the publication of this important book is particularly timely. A recent survey has revealed that this unique flora has markedly decreased in both quantity and distribution over the last forty years.

'Teesdale's Special Flora' looks at the why as well as the what, and provides valuable context on the area. There is much here for both the professional botanist and the layperson, not least through the identification guide with its excellent photographs of plants that do not always advertise their presence.

Perhaps unusually for a botanist, the author comes from a farming background, having originally grown up on a mixed farm on the Yorkshire Wolds. This has clearly informed her thinking on the relationship between animals and plants along with her genuine interest in those who live and work on the land and their impact on Teesdale's special flora.

As a landowner, I have often seen Margaret at the local agricultural shows for she is well known to the farming community here. She is not shy about proffering botanical advice when asked or even when not, for the viability of rare plant populations is often dependent on land management practices by farmers in the dale. As discussed in the book, small changes in grazing regimes can have a profound effect on plant communities.

Margaret Bradshaw wrote in 2003 *"I have hope that the dale will support the largest number of rare plants in a limited space in Britain after I am gone for we hold in trust the country's oldest heritage in the Dale."* I see Teesdale's Special Flora as part of that legacy along with her establishment of the Teesdale Special Flora Research and Conservation Trust. This will bring huge benefits in providing essential data across the whole of the Tees catchment area in Upper Teesdale to enable this remarkable flora to be conserved for the future. Margaret has studied the flora of Teesdale in more detail than anyone else and over her long career has taught and encouraged new generations of botanists.

When I think of the special flora of Upper Teesdale it is of Margaret in her nineties striding across Widdybank, eyes fixed to the ground, with companions in her wake struggling to keep up. All about her are those big skies, the distinctive moorland air, and a vast seemingly empty landscape that is anything but desolate, for it hides the many botanical treasures that Margaret reveals here. Her boundless enthusiasm for the subject is infectious and I hope that this book will inspire future botanists to safeguard the populations of special plants that are now threatened.

Barnard,

The Lord Barnard DL

Preface

This book has had a long gestation of ten years, longer than that of an elephant! Its origin was a request put to me following a weekend meeting of the then English Nature Regional Botanists led by Dr Jill Sutcliffe. I find writing difficult so initially I turned down the request. But, after some thought and wondering who else might write it and how I would feel if someone else was the author, I agreed.

It is a very personal book, including a little of my origin on a farm on the Yorkshire Wolds. Yes, I am an 'incomer' as the locals would say. I appear to have had an inherited attraction to plants from my maternal grandmother. The first I remember were the beautiful flowers of Bogbean, and Water Mint with its very distinctive scent and, in the wood, Great Horsetail, all near Bradshaw's flour mill, once driven by a water wheel. At my first school I was given a buttercup to draw; my effort caused a stir amongst the teachers but no one explained why to me. At Bridlington High School, whilst my usual biology teacher was on sick leave, for one day a week I was taught by Miss Heafford who opened my eyes to the marvellous structures and life of plants. So, the die was cast in favour of plants over art or agriculture (75 years ago, what was offered to a girl at agricultural college other than learn to make cheese or keep poultry?).

At Leeds University I did a Joint Hons Degree in Botany and Zoology (it was wartime so a single subject course was not available). Encouragement there came from Dr H.G. Baker. The ecology course consisted of four large blackboards full of lists of plants taken directly from *The British Islands and their Vegetation* by A.G. Tansley (1939), in the neat hand-writing of Dr Arthur Sledge. Enough to put off any potential field botanist, but, not me.

In my second year I missed out on joining a small group of the staff, including Prof. Irene Manton, on a visit to search for special ferns in Teesdale, which made me wonder what was so special about the plants there. After graduating I became a teacher, first in Derbyshire for one year, then to Bishop Auckland to be within easy reach of Teesdale's special flora. Why it attracted and intrigued me I do not know. At school everybody knew where the 'Blue Gentian' grew in Teesdale, and pupils would bring in a baking-tin filled with moss and studded with Blue Gentian flowers – a local tradition. Bird's-eye Primrose was also familiar but it was not easy to find out what the other species were, nor where they grew. There was one book: *Teesdale* by Douglas M. Ramsden (1947) that did have an Appendix: *Flora of Upper Teesdale* with the times of flowering and their habitats. This was a start for weekend excursions by bus and foot. Fortuitously, the following year I met Dr S. Max Walters of Cambridge who suggested I look for *Alchemilla* species in Teesdale as he had found rare taxa there and offered to send his recent paper on the genus in Britain published in the *Proceedings of the Botanical Society of the British Isles* (BSBI) (Walters, 1947). I switched concentration to this critical group and eventually produced maps of the distributions of five of the nine species in Teesdale and Weardale including one new to Britain. I had become an active member of BSBI soon after meeting Max. Max was my support, inspiration and friend, and I stayed many nights with him, Lorna and their family in Cambridge, at Cory Lodge in the Botanic Gardens; and lastly in Grantchester.

The threat of a reservoir in Teesdale turned my attention back to the rare plants and the need for factual evidence of which of the rare species grew where below the critical, top-water-line of 1,603 ft (489 m) and crucially the percentage of the whole populations of key rare species on Widdybank Fell.

As the world knows, the case was lost and the Cow Green Reservoir was built. ICI donated £100,000 for research in Upper Teesdale. I obtained grants to finance two Research Assistants to do a phytosociological survey of Widdybank Fell and start studies of the population dynamics of several rare species; most of the plots were still being recorded in 2022. A smaller grant supported groups of volunteers, who spend three separate weeks each July mapping the locations of 25 rare species on the sugar-limestone grassland and some flushes on Widdybank Fell. This became the baseline record that was used by J. O'Reilly for comparison with his records of 2017–19.

I am aware that this book has many shortcomings – some critical taxa are not covered, *e.g. Taraxacum, Hieracium, Salix*, and some aquatic species: some sections written in the early years have not been revisited.

I wish to thank Lord Barnard and the Earl of Strathmore and Kinghorne for access to their Estates, and all other landowners, tenant farmers and gamekeepers who have allowed me to roam over much of Teesdale; also the currently named Natural England for access to the two National Nature Reserves, now combined into the Moor House-Upper Teesdale NNR: and Linda Robinson, Jeremy Roberts, Rod Corner for watershed records and botanical information of vegetation at the higher altitude of the Tees watershed – Cross, Little and Mickle Fells.

I almost succeeded in obtaining photographs of the species taken in Teesdale; apparently it is a rare botanist who likes to photograph aquatics, so thank you John Crellin. Many of the photographs are mine. I knew exactly the shot I wanted: some are historical and unrepeatable, *e.g.* the Cow Green area before flooding; plant communities that have evolved, *e.g. Sesleria–Calluna* heath ravaged by Heather Beetle; and short sedge-marsh overrun by tall rush species. I am grateful for the generous provision of photographs by Martin Rogers, Dave Mitchell, Jeremy Roberts and Geoff Herbert and several others whose names are attached to their pictures. I valued discussions with Ken Park (Researcher), Dennis Coggins (High Force Hotel), Ken Bainbridge (Langdon Beck Hotel), Alan Scott (farmer from Widdybank), Alec Tarn (farmer from Cronkley and Mickle Fells), George Horn (shepherd), John Wearmouth (gamekeeper), all no longer with us, and Christine Bell (farmer Cronkley Fell and Pasture). Thanks are also due to Ken and Mabel Bainbridge and Mary for their kindness to me over many years, and for their hospitality and forbearance when I filled the hotel and used the dining room for studies every evening (the table to be re-set for breakfast afterwards!) for three weeks in each July for almost five years, and Marion at the Youth Hostel. Does any reader remember those happy days?

My thanks to the Durham Wildlife Trust for permission to use the map in *The Natural History of Upper Teesdale* (2018) and to Ian Findlay for his input to the section on Weather and Climate on *pages 23–31*.

Lastly, I add my grateful thanks to Jill Sutcliffe, friend and editor, for her patience in staying with me and keeping **WILD**Guides interested in designing the book, and also for her many pages of contributions to this book.

Thank you, Jill.

Margaret E. Bradshaw MBE

Map of Teesdale

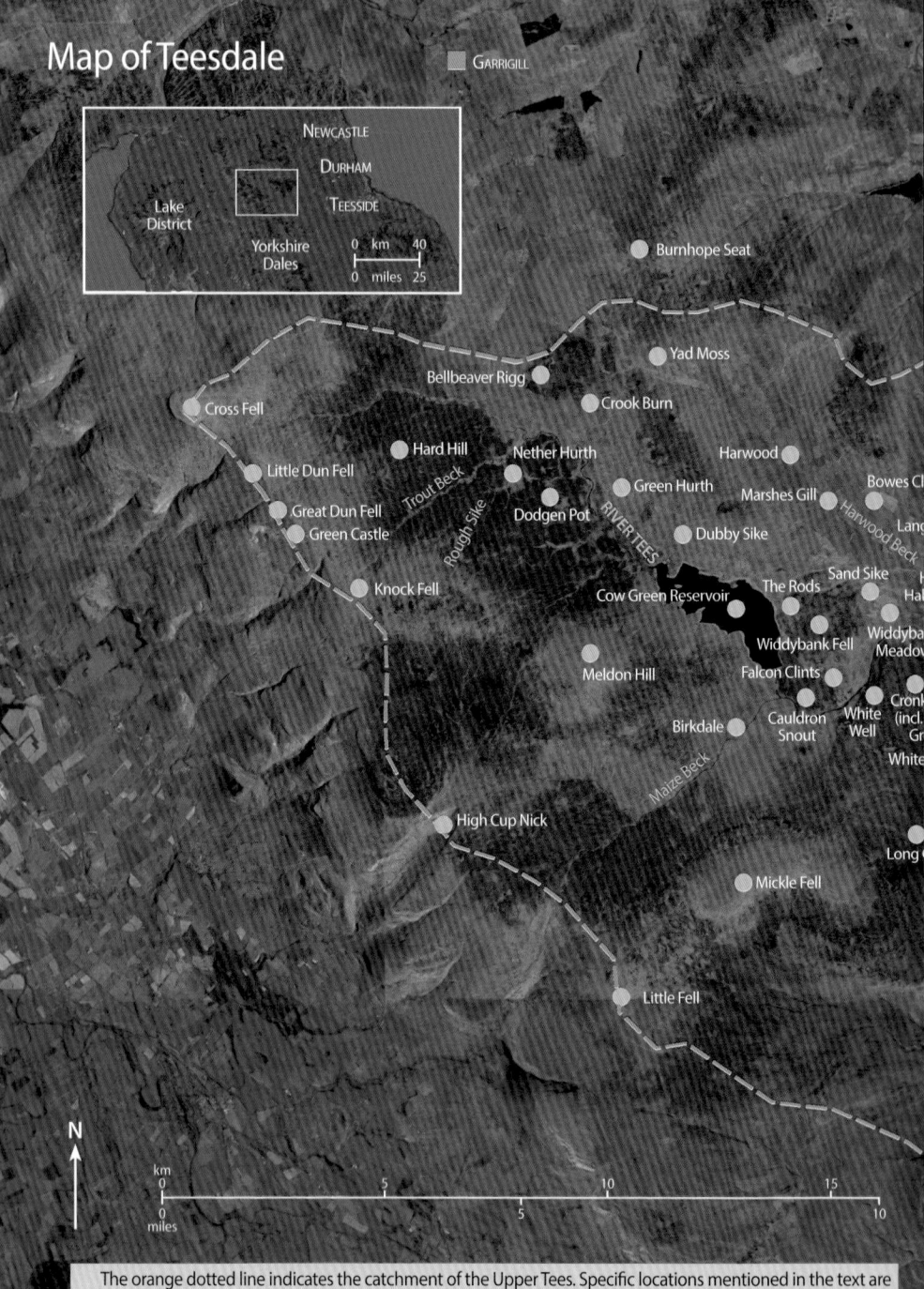

GARRIGILL

NEWCASTLE
DURHAM
TEESSIDE
Lake District
Yorkshire Dales

0 km 40
0 miles 25

Burnhope Seat

Yad Moss
Bellbeaver Rigg
Crook Burn

Cross Fell

Hard Hill
Nether Hurth
Harwood

Little Dun Fell
Green Hurth
Marshes Gill
Bowes Cl

Great Dun Fell
Trout Beck
Dodgen Pot
RIVER TEES
Harwood Beck
Lang

Green Castle
Rough Sike
Dubby Sike

Knock Fell
Cow Green Reservoir
Sand Sike
The Rods
Hal

Widdyba
Meadov
Widdybank Fell

Meldon Hill
Falcon Clints

Birkdale
Cauldron Snout
White Well
Cronl
(incl.
Gr

White

Maize Beck

High Cup Nick

Long

Mickle Fell

N

Little Fell

km
0   5   10   15
0   5   10
miles

The orange dotted line indicates the catchment of the Upper Tees. Specific locations mentioned in the text are indicated with a yellow dot, water courses are named in blue, and significant habitations are shown with an orange square. The *Gazetteer* on *page 277* gives the Ordnance Survey grid reference for each location. See also *page 17* for map showing the extent of the Moor House-Upper Teesdale NNR. *Map based on Google Maps.*

Stanhope

St John's Chapel

Fendrith Hill

Outberry Plain

ST-IN-TEESDALE

Ettersgill

Holm
ar

RIVER TEES

High Force

Low Force

Bowlees Visitor Centre

Newbiggin

Wynch Bridge

Ravelin/Brockers Gill

Park End Wood

Holwick Scar

RIVER TEES

Middleton-in-Teesdale

River Lune

Eggleston

Lunedale

Romaldkirk

Selset Reservoir

River Balder

Blackton Reservoir

Cotherstone

Hunder Beck

Barnard Castle

9

Introduction and significance of the Teesdale flora

To the author, Upper Teesdale means blue sky, white clouds and a landscape of many shades of green and brown, air like mountain spring water and a very special place of rare and fragile plants, plant communities and renewal.

Please halt, switch off radio, mobile phone, etc. Now look around at the sky…the landscape… the vegetation; now look again…what more can you see? Listen…what can you hear…what can you not hear? What do you smell…what can you not smell? What do you feel under your feet? Is it hard – is it soft – is it soggy – is it wet – is it dry? Remember and repeat all of these at home, in a supermarket carpark or town centre!

There is a core of vascular plant species traditionally known as the Teesdale Assemblage, and a halo of noteworthy plants. All are rare to some extent, one grows only here, and others are on the edge of their range in Britain. Here is my personal selection from among these special plant species.

This assemblage is unique; nowhere else in the UK do these particular species grow together in such a comparatively small area. It is generally understood that the majority of them are relics of a flora that was widespread in Britain at the end of the Ice Age, 12,000–15,000 years ago. Fragmentation of their original distribution patterns took place during the subsequent warmer, and later wetter, periods. These plants had originally formed a more or less continuous land cover up to then.

Just consider – from the evidence available – it is thought that some of these species have had a continuous presence in Upper Teesdale since the late glacial times. This means they are part of our oldest heritage and a good reason why these flowering plants should be treasured and protected. Many are small and fragile and the habitats in which they grow are themselves unstable: crumbly sugar-limestone, shallow stony streams, eroding river margins, soft damp marshes and cliffs, all of which can be easily damaged by trampling and climbing. Even closed, species-rich turf can be worn out, like a carpet. Therefore, great care is needed if they are to survive this century and beyond.

In 1950, I moved to County Durham, having heard that this place, Teesdale, had a particularly interesting flora. With no contact with anyone who knew these plants, it was not easy to discover the identity of this flora and where it grew. In his book Teesdale (1947), D. M. Ramsden aimed 'to give a picture of Teesdale' as it was in 1946, and included a list of the plants in an Appendix. So, with this list and a flora (pre-Clapham, Tutin & Warburg's *Excursion Flora of the British Isles*, 1959) I started to visit Wynch Bridge, Widdybank and Cronkley Fells at weekends, using the bus service to Bowlees (High Force in summer), thus reducing the great distances walked by those active explorers of the early 19th century. I well remember meeting two gentlemen in long gabardine coats at the east end of the sugar-limestone and trying in vain to get confirmation that the violet I was looking at was *the* Teesdale Violet and, on another occasion, that I had found the Dwarf Milkwort on Widdybank Fell, said at that time to be only on Cronkley Fell. My dedication to the plants of Teesdale really took off a year later when I was fortunate to meet the late Dr S. Max Walters who suggested, in characteristic style, that I might like to 'look at' lady's-mantles. That very first summer of 1951, with the luck of a beginner, I found a meadow species which he identified for me as new to Britain. This was an inspiring result given my ignorance of the classical localities for the recognized rarities and of botanising elsewhere in the dale.

Plant assemblages   An assemblage of plants is a collection of rare and local species, each strongly, sometimes exclusively, linked to an area. Other places that famously have particular botanical interest include the Brecks in Norfolk/Suffolk, Ben Lawers in Perth and Kinross, the Burren in Co. Clare, Ireland and the Lizard Peninsula in Cornwall. The species within the assemblage plants do not all grow in the same plant community, or even habitat, but within a defined geographic area. The members of the Teesdale Assemblage are to be found in a number of different habitats and plant communities; some occur in several, whilst others can be very specific and limited to one habitat, feature or locality. The species listed below form the core of the Teesdale Assemblage. These and the other species that can be considered to be part of the assemblage are the subject of species accounts in this book.

Why is the flora of Upper Teesdale so special?

Today, we know that the botanical 'hotspot' of Teesdale is home to a unique assemblage of plants in Britain, including the 21 notable taxa listed in the table *below*.

The only location in the world for one subspecies:		Page
Hoary Rock-rose	*Helianthemun oelandicum* ssp. *levigatum*	134
The only location in the UK for two species:		
Teesdale Sandwort	*Sabulina stricta*	145
Spring Gentian	*Gentiana verna*	156
Aalmost the only location in the UK for one species:		
Large-toothed Lady's Mantle	*Alchemilla subcrenata*	117
The only location in England for five species (although these also occur in Scotland):		
Scottish Asphodel	*Tofieldia pusilla*	177
False Sedge	*Carex simpliciuscula*	206
Alpine Foxtail (HIGH-LEVEL)	*Alopecurus magellanicus*	211
Alpine Forget-me-not (HIGH-LEVEL)	*Myosotis alpestris*	159
Sheathed Sedge (HIGH-LEVEL)	*Carex vaginata*	198
The northern end of the range of four species found in England:		
Horseshoe Vetch	*Hippocrepis comosa*	101
Hoary Rock-rose	*Helianthemun oelandicum*	134
Rare Spring-sedge	*Carex ericetorum*	200
Dwarf Milkwort	*Polygala amarella*	103
One of only four sites in the UK for one species:		
Teesdale Violet	*Viola rupestris*	124
One of only three sites for a hybrid in the UK:		
Teesdale × Common Dog-violet	*Viola × burnatii*	126
At, or almost at, the southern end of the range of the UK range for six species:		
Alpine Rush	*Juncus alpinoarticulatus*	183
Dwarf Birch	*Betula nana*	123
Shady Horsetail	*Equisetum pratense*	73
Alpine Bartsia	*Bartsia alpina*	166
Mountain Avens	*Dryas octopetala*	104
Marsh Saxifrage	*Saxifraga hirculus*	93
One of only two sites for one species in England:		
Shrubby Cinquefoil	*Dasiphora fruticosa*	110

So, Teesdale supports a mixture of plants not usually seen growing together. In Upper Teesdale there are plants that are at, or almost at, the **southern** end of their range in Britain and species that are at the **northern** end, as well as plants that have a distribution across the **north of England** and out to the **west of Ireland**. Nowhere else in Britain are so many species of different phyto-geographical patterns found together as in the comparatively small triangle of the catchment of the Tees from just east of Wynch Bridge to the tops of Cronkley and Widdybank Fells which, in turn, form the nucleus of the larger triangle comprising the head of Teesdale and the hills immediately surrounding it.

In 1868, J. G. Baker wrote of this area: "*There is probably no ground in Britain that produces so many rare species within a limited space as Widdy Bank Fell.*" He listed 32 acknowledged rarities from an area of approximately $10\,km^2$ (4 sq.mi.) of Upper Teesdale that is very well-known to botanists today. To many, this richness in rare and local species has remained a very valid attraction, but with the development of botany as a science, the original 'floristic' approach stimulated studies of greater depth and wider importance over the last century. Comparative plant geographical studies have shown that the Teesdale Assemblage is outstanding not only in terms of its British distribution, but also its Eurasian and total world-spread, representing a remarkable mixture of diverse phyto-geographical elements.

Table 1 (*opposite*) gives a short list of the Teesdale Assemblage plants (Matthews, 1955); a longer list that includes the Geographical Elements of all 96 species described in this book is in Preston & Hill (1997).

Thus, growing in Teesdale are northern and montane species, *e.g.* Alpine Bartsia and Mountain Avens, which are centred in the Alps and the Arctic, and others that are found predominantly in one region or the other – *e.g.* Alpine Foxtail in the Arctic, Spring Gentian in the Alps. Teesdale Sandwort and the more abundant Cloudberry are Arctic-Sub-Arctic, although the Teesdale Sandwort may now be extinct in the Alpine foothills thereby making Teesdale its most southern location. Also occurring on Widdybank Fell are Teesdale Violet, Rare Spring-sedge, Bird's-eye Primrose, Dwarf Milkwort and the Wrinkle-leaved Feather-moss – all continental northern species not particularly associated with high altitudes or high latitudes. Finally, and perhaps most remarkably, is the presence of the continental southern species Hoary Rock-rose and Horseshoe Vetch, at their most northerly and highest British locations.

The real significance of the co-existence of so many geographical elements is better appreciated when viewed in the context of the surrounding vegetation, which is characterized by such typically western European heath and bog species as Heather, Cross-leaved Heath and Bell Heather, Bog Asphodel, Heath Rush and Hare's-tail Cottongrass.

On a national scale, the distribution patterns of the Teesdale Assemblage show a similar diversity. For example, Widdybank Fell is the only location for Teesdale Sandwort and one of only three for the hybrid Teesdale Violet × Common Dog Violet, although the rarer parent, Teesdale Violet, is also known in three other localities on unaltered limestone or glacial-drift deposits. The Teesdale population of False Sedge far exceeds the sum of the populations in its only other British locations, which are in the Central Highlands of Scotland. Teesdale provides an unusually *low-altitude* location ($<540\,m$) at or near the southern end of the range of many northern and montane members of the Teesdale Assemblage. This is particularly so for Scottish Asphodel, for which there are no other extant records south of the Highland Fault.

Table 1 | The Geographical Elements in the Teesdale Assemblage of Flowering Plants
(Matthews, 1955)

CONTINENTAL SOUTHERN	
Hoary Rock-rose	Helianthemum oelandicum
Horseshoe Vetch	Hippocrepis comosa

CONTINENTAL NORTHERN	
Rare Spring-Sedge	Carex ericetorum
Northern Bedstraw	Galium boreale
Dwarf Milkwort	Polygala amarella

NORTHERN MONTANE	
Starry Lady's-mantle	Alchemilla acutiloba
Velvet Lady's-mantle	Alchemilla monticola
Large-toothed Lady's-mantle	Alchemilla subcrenata
Mountain Everlasting	Antennaria dioica
Shrubby Cinquefoil	Dasiphora fruticosa
Bird's-eye Primrose	Primula farinosa
Small-white Orchid	Pseudorchis albida

OCEANIC NORTHERN	
Thrift	Armeria maritima

ARCTIC-SUB-ARCTIC	
Rock Lady's-mantle	Alchemilla wichurae
Alpine Foxtail	Alopecurus magellanica

ARCTIC-ALPINE	
Bearberry	Arctostaphylos uva-ursi
Alpine Bartsia	Bartsia alpina
Dwarf Birch	Betula nana
Alpine Bistort	Bistorta vivipara
False Sedge	Carex simpliciuscula
Hoary Whitlowgrass	Draba incana
Mountain Avens	Dryas octopetala
Teesdale Sandwort	Sabulina stricta
Spring Sandwort	Sabulina verna
Yellow Saxifrage	Saxifraga aizoides
Marsh Saxifrage	Saxifraga hirculus
Scottish Asphodel	Tofiedia pusilla
Teesdale Violet	Viola rupestris

ALPINE	
Spring Gentian	Gentiana verna
Alpine Forget-me-not	Myosotis alpestris
Alpine Penny-cress	Noccaea caerulescens

With regard to the southern species, Teesdale provides an unusually *high-altitude* location (540 m) at the northern extremity of the range of the three species with southern affinities – Rare Spring-sedge, Hoary Rock-rose and Horseshoe Vetch. A fourth group consists of species mainly absent from Scotland and southern England but also found in western Ireland; it includes Spring Gentian, Shrubby Cinquefoil and Blue Moor-grass (very rare in Scotland). To this group also belong the three meadow Lady's-mantle species, Starry, Velvet and Large-toothed, which are almost confined to Durham county. Other notable rare and local species include Hair and Slender Sedges, Tall Bog sedge, Bog-sedge, Hoary Whitlowgrass, Variegated Horsetail, Three-flowered Rush, Spring Sandwort, Alpine Bistort, Yellow and Marsh Saxifrages and five species of moss. A further special feature of interest exhibited by several species is that taxonomically they are represented by local varieties in Teesdale.

Pigott & Walters (1954), curious to know why certain localities in Britain supported 'assemblages' of rare plants, analysed 20 locations where high frequencies of rare species occur today, and noted they had only two features in common – freedom from tree competition and relatively high base status of the soil, *i.e.* containing basic salts (*e.g.* lime). They listed seven groups of habitats which (it is reasonable to suppose) have continuously provided a soil of sufficient base status; since the end of the last Ice Age, and even in the warmest Forest Maximum period, they could never have carried closed woodland over their whole area. These groups are as follows:

1) mountains above the tree limit (which was higher than it is today) allowing high light intensity giving only partial shade;
2) inland cliffs and screes;
3) sea cliffs;
4) river gorges, eroded riverbanks, river shingles, alluvium, *etc*.;
5) sand dunes and dune slacks;
6) shallow soils over chalk and limestones, especially on steep slopes; and
7) certain marsh and fen communities, lake shores.

It is yet another remarkable character of Teesdale that no fewer than five (1, 2, 4, 6 and 7) of these seven groups of habitats are present, and these do support high frequencies of the rare species. Examples of all these five types can be found in the Tees Catchment. The highest parts of Teesdale comprise the 'mountains above the tree limit' habitat (Group 1) although, it is now known that there were scattered small trees on the summit of Cross Fell. These still support the Alpine Forget-me-not, Alpine Foxtail and Sheathed and Water Sedges. On inland cliffs and screes (Group 2) of Whin Sill and limestone from Scorberry Bridge to Cauldron Snout are Rock Whitebeam, Aspen (surely a relict species here), Common Juniper, Bearberry and many small herbs found also in other habitats – Alpine Cinquefoil (very scarce), Hoary Whitlowgrass, Mossy Saxifrage and Rock Lady's-mantle. The habitats of Group 4 are numerous by the Tees and its tributaries and support very many species. The shingle and rocks of the bed of the Tees are well known as the habitat of the Shrubby Cinquefoil, a species with a disjunct distribution in two arcs across Eurasia from its centre of origin in East Asia. The northern arc linking populations in western Ireland, Lakeland, Teesdale and Öland (Sweden) is of dioecious (separate male and female) plants, whilst the flowers of the southern are all hermaphrodite. These riverside sites are becoming increasingly important as modern refugia.

Large-toothed Lady's-mantle *MEB*.

Cross Fell summit polygons, A. V. Jones, *c.* 1969 *MEB*.

Shallow soil on sugar-limestone *MEB*.

Metamorphosed (sugar-)limestone rock and sand *TS*.

Eroded riverbank with **Water Sedge**, 2016 *MEB*.

Cliffs and screes, Holwick Scar *MEB*.

Short sedge-marsh *MR*.

A recent study of Globeflower in two areas, one just higher than the other, has shown that although the species is still quite widespread in the higher area, it is now virtually restricted to the banks of the Tees and near some small streams below High Force. Above High Force, river erosion of the drumlins has produced a fine series of habitats showing varying degrees of instability and colonisation. Undercutting by the river is just sufficient to maintain a state of instability, which prevents the development of a closed community – here, many of the rare species find a niche. Sites like this will have been continually available since the pre-forest period. When the course of the river has changed following catastrophic floods, new eroded banks have formed, although some older banks have become completely grassed over and without rare species. Others have been so strongly undercut that large lumps of loosely aggregated vegetation have slipped off the over-steepened slope, leaving an extensive bare face. These communities of the eroding drumlins are variants of the 'turfy marshes' (Group 7) which occur on the slopes and hollows in the undulating moraine deposits in Widdybank and Cronkley Pastures. Frequently these develop under the influence of trampling in the unstable zone below the springs and seepage-lines on the drumlins. The characteristic vegetation contains many small sedges (including Hair Sedge) and other Cyperaceae, with Spring Gentian, Bird's-eye Primrose, Common Butterwort, Lesser Clubmoss, Northern and Early Marsh-orchids and Scottish Asphodel. Here too, is Alpine Bartsia, a Durham species absent from the Cronkley area today. These habitats belong to Pigott & Walters' (1954) 'certain marshes' of Group 7. Finally, the other habitats belonging to Groups 6 and 7 are confined to, or mainly associated with, the sugar-limestone and flushes on the higher parts of Cronkley and Widdybank Fells. These support Spring Gentian, Mountain Everlasting, Hair Sedge, Alpine Bistort, Mountain Avens, Bird's-eye Primrose, Scottish Asphodel, False Sedge and many others.

Of equal scientific significance and interest is the mosaic of rare and common plant communities. Those with large numbers of rare species (rare communities themselves) are interspersed amongst vegetation characteristic of the British uplands and indeed the western seaboard of Europe, that is blanket bog and upland heath.

Fen, Wheysike House *MEB*.

The area, geology and soils

The area of interest covers the broad valley of the Tees in the North Pennines west of the north/south National Grid line NZ915 through the junction of the Balder and the Tees. It is bounded by the watershed on the south-west above the Eden escarpment, from the north side of the Balder to the watershed, then via Mickle Fell (797 m), Little Fell (753 m), High Cup Nick (550 m), Meldon Hill (767 m), the two Dun Fells – Great (842 m) and Little (848 m) – to the summit of Cross Fell (893 m) and on to the NW via Bellbeaver Rigg (620 m) and the watershed with Weardale in the north-east from Burnhope Seat (746 m), Fendrith Hill (696 m) to Outberry Plain (675 m) and the west side of Eggleston Burn to the Tees Fell, Cross Fell, Burnhope Seat and Fendrith Hill. The major tributaries of the Tees are the Maize Beck, Harwood Beck, the Lune, the Balder and the lesser Eggleston Burn, to the north.

The River Tees is unique in its upper reaches. It rises from the eastern slope of Cross Fell at approximately 760 m and, as a typical mountain stream, rushes down to Trout Beck Foot (530 m). Then, it meanders slowly like a lowland stream between drumlins to the top of Cauldron Snout, a gentle fall of only 36·6 m over eight kilometres (almost five miles) creating the Weel, now submerged in the Cow Green Reservoir. From there it cascades down Cauldron Snout (61·5 m fall over 180 m), and on to High Force (21 m vertical fall) and Low Force (5·5 m near-vertical fall) over a rocky bed often between hard rock cliffs and then under Wynch Bridge and between more drumlins and flood plains to Cotherstone and beyond. In places, the moraines are eroded into steep banks and in others shingle-beds have formed to the inside of bends. Two major tributaries join the Tees – the Maize Beck below Cauldron Snout and about six kilometres further on the Harwood Beck, and thence by numerous becks, burns and sikes. Between the meanders of these smaller streams mini-flood plains have formed. Since the building of the Cow Green Reservoir the flow of the river is more constant, but impressive spates still occur, especially when the Maize Beck

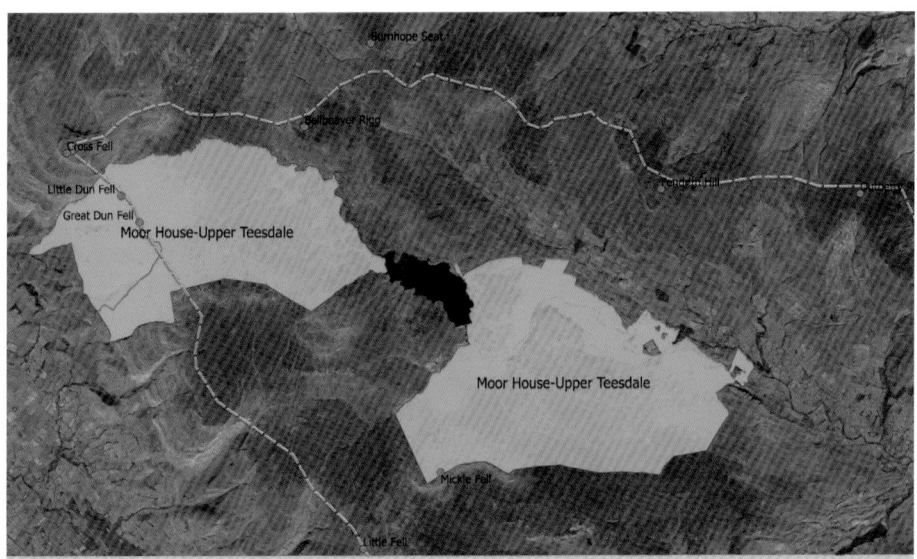

Map of Upper Tees catchment showing the Moor House-Upper Teesdale NNR. *Map based on Microsoft (Bing) Maps.*

17

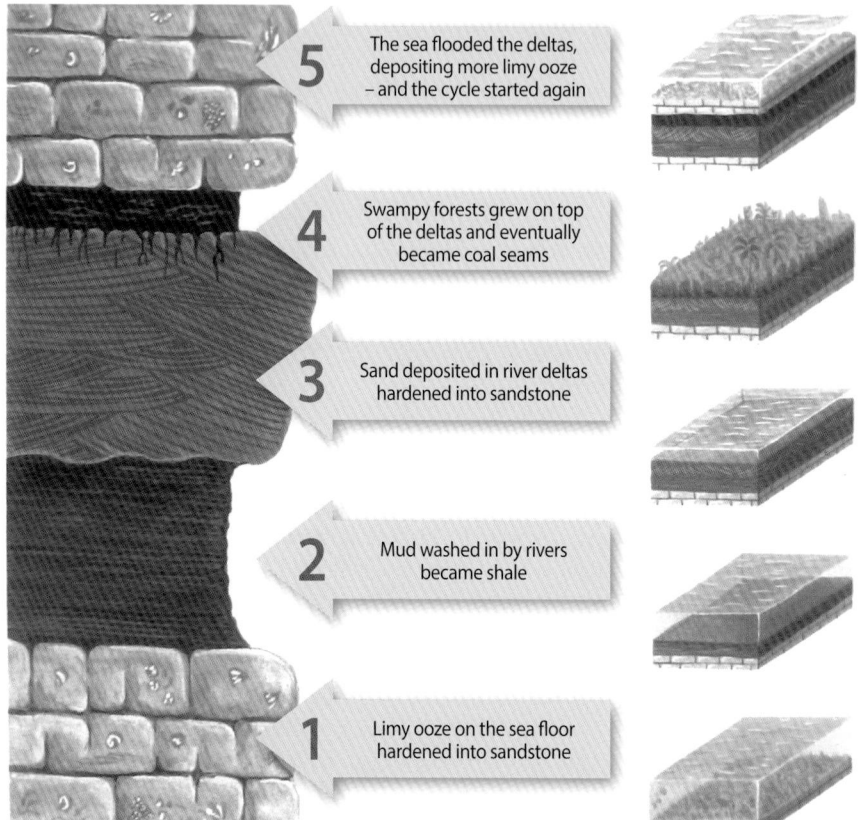

Typical Yoredale series of cyclical rock strata
(reproduced with permission from *Reading the Rocks* (*p. 13*), www.landscapesforlife.org.uk).

has received heavy rain when the reservoir is full and water overflows the dam, and also following periods of heavy, prolonged snowfall followed by a rapid thaw.

Geology

The Carboniferous lithostratigraphical classification of northern England, including the North Pennines, has endured some changes in recent years. Many make good sense and better assist the classification, correlation and description of these rocks. The bedrock (solid geology) of most of Upper Teesdale comprises from the lowest levels the Marsett, Melmerby, Alston and Stainmore formations within the Ravenstonedale, Great Scar Limestone Group and Yoredale Group. The Ravenstone Group contains the basal conglomerate and associated shales and sandstones seen at the foot of Falcon Clints and on Cronkley Scar. Under these is the Teesdale Inlier, a small exposure of the oldest rocks – the Ordovician (Palaeozoic) – near the Tees below Cronkley Scar; this is insufficient to be of floristic significance.

The Melmerby Scar and Robinson limestones are our local representatives of the Great Scar Limestone Group (characteristic of/and familiar in the Craven area) the former is the sugar-limestone of Widdybank and Cronkley Fells and the latter forms the skyline on the North side of the track to Birkdale south of Slapestone Sike. All of the remaining Carboniferous succession up to the base of the Coal Measures is now termed the Yoredale Group and is subdivided into the Alston Formation (beds between the top of the Robinson and the top of the Great Limestone) 18 m thick and prominently exposed on the north side as High Hurth Edge, and the Stainmore Formation from here to the base of the Coal Measures. Here are some very coarse sandstones, as on Cross Fell, but they are not the true Millstone Grit of the South Pennines.

The light-coloured Melmerby Scar Limestone, about 40 m thick in total, is a particularly pure limestone where the absence of carbon contributed to it being metamorphosed into crystalized marble known as sugar-limestone. This has been and is of great, botanical significance. It was split into lower thin and upper thick layers in the early Permian (radiometric dates *c.* 295 million years ago) by hot magma from the Earth's centre intruding into these rocks in northern England and gradually cooling to form the quartz-dolerite rock known as Whin Sill (quarried as whinstone). This igneous rock baked the adjacent rocks producing, for example, the famous metamorphosed limestone, known as sugar-limestone and mudstone/whetstone from small pockets of clay within the limestone. The North Pennine mineralization was emplaced very soon after the intrusion of the Whin Sill. The main pattern of faulting, with many of the conjugate pattern of faults occupied by mineral veins must post-date the Whin Sill emplacement/intrusion, but very soon afterwards, as in Teesdale, there are examples of North Pennines mineral veins that have been interpreted as having formed whilst the Whin Sill was very hot and cooling. The most important minerals include galena (lead sulphide), baryte (heavy spar), fluorite, which is scarce in Teesdale, and quartz – all of economic importance and some botanical significance. Also present are small quantities of pyrite ('fool's gold') and sphalerite (zinc sulphide, 'blackjack'). The Burtreeford Disturbance is

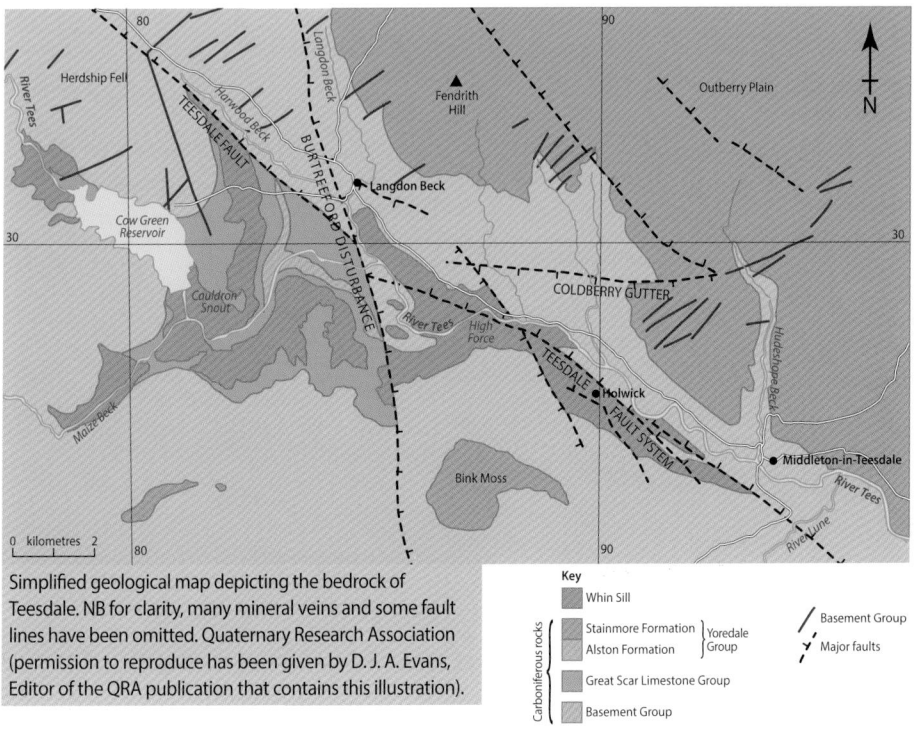

Simplified geological map depicting the bedrock of Teesdale. NB for clarity, many mineral veins and some fault lines have been omitted. Quaternary Research Association (permission to reproduce has been given by D. J. A. Evans, Editor of the QRA publication that contains this illustration).

Key

- Whin Sill
- Stainmore Formation / Yoredale Group
- Alston Formation
- Great Scar Limestone Group
- Basement Group

Carboniferous rocks

- Basement Group
- Major faults

a rather unusual north–south-orientated fracture zone where faulting was accompanied by some folding. There is plausible evidence for it being initiated pre-Whin Sill, but it has clearly moved again post-Whin Sill. This part of the Pennines is criss-crossed by many faults, resulting in the British Geological Survey 1:25,000 map no. 36, *sheet NY82* and *part of NY92 Middleton-in-Teesdale* (1974) being a fascinating mosaic of colour.

More recently in the geological timetable, successive glacial periods of the Pleistocene Great Ice Age covered the country's rocks with thick sheets of ice. When the ice of the final Ice Period melted, glacial drift had been deposited in successive occasions over all but the steepest slopes on the dip slope that is the Tees catchment area (Upper Teesdale). This is made of the ground-up remnants of only the local rocks (limestone, sandstone and Whin Sill and the shales which became clay) and minerals, as it is only in Baldersdale and to the east that there is evidence of glacial deposits from outside the area. Geologists claim the various blanket and basin peats as the youngest geological deposits. These are formed from plants, the most important being the Imbricate Bog-moss that can still be found in very small quantities on Widdybank Fell today. Depending on the topography the peat bogs lie mainly between approximately 455–670 m. At lower altitudes are lateral moraines and many drumlins easily seen in the floor of the dale below and above High Force and also evidence of a former course of the Tees, as can be seen in the photograph of Holwick Scar (*below*). These are of great botanical importance.

Holwick Scar *MR*.

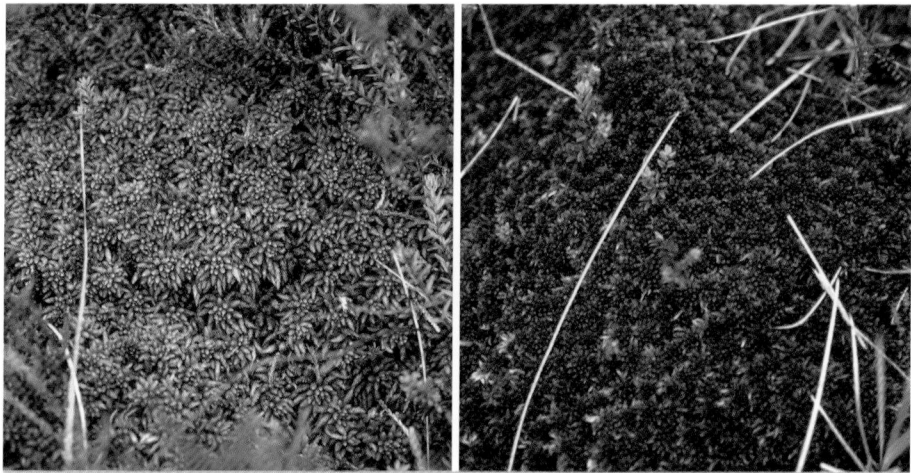

Two mosses from Widdybank Fell – both are relict species: Imbricate Bog-moss (LEFT) and Rusty Bog-moss (RIGHT) *both MEB*.

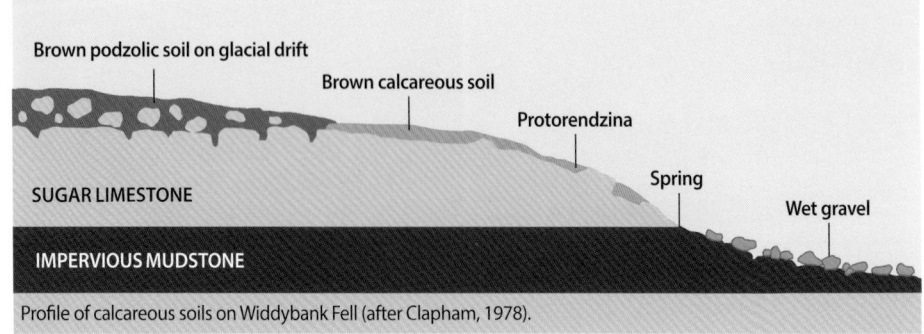

Profile of calcareous soils on Widdybank Fell (after Clapham, 1978).

Soils

On the exposed outcrops subject to erosion very shallow grey or almost black rendzina soils have developed. These differ from soils on unaltered limestone in the frequency with which they become dry and, if unprotected by vegetation, are subject to wind-erosion. In a strong wind I have experienced blown loose 'sand' to a depth of 20–30 cm on Cronkley Fell. Away from the eroding edges, the limestone is covered with various depths of glacial drift material. Where this is very shallow it is usually well-drained and greatly influenced by the limestone to give a brown loamy soil, known as a mull rendzina or calcareous brown soil. Earthworms are plentiful and attract Moles, which provide yet another cause of extensive surface disturbance. As the drift becomes deeper the influence of the limestone diminishes and brown podsolic soils develop. Where deep drift impedes drainage typical peaty gleys and organic soils are formed.

Where the metamorphosed limestone (sugar-limestone) rests directly on the impermeable dolerite, or there is a thin layer of metamorphosed mudstone within the limestone, springs emerge at the junction to form spring-heads and the calcareous water flows over the impermeable surface to form small or extensive areas of wet gravel – the so-called gravelly flushes. It is on these shallow rendzina soils that the rarest of the Teesdale species grow together: Teesdale Violet, Mountain Avens, Hoary Rock-rose, Rare Spring-sedge and in damper places False Sedge.

An issue under sugar-limestone onto Whin Sill rock. Widdybank Fell *MEB*.

Rendzina soils overlying sugar-limestone rock at Widdybank Fell *MEB*.

Weather and climate

AUTHOR'S NOTE: Most of this chapter appeared in *The Natural History of Upper Teesdale*, 5th edn. (2018) edited by Steve Gater. It was written by Ian Findlay, who gave me permission to include, modify and update it prior to the book's publication.

Manley noted that the mean May temperatures at the summit station were similar to the mean January temperatures in London and he considered the climate in Upper Teesdale similar to that at sea level in Iceland!

Introduction

The weather in Teesdale has changed since I started to visit nearly 70 years ago. As for the first 50 winters, these were 'proper winters' – cold with lots of snow and ice. For several years I remember seeing a patch of snow on Cross Fell that had lasted all summer. When I returned in 1998 after nearly 20 years in Devon changes were on the way; I did not believe the locals who said "*we do not get the snow and blocked roads we used to*" – they were almost correct, as can be seen from the data in Ian Findlay's outline.

Geographically, the Pennines are unique within England, because they are the only significant upland area that is not close to the sea. This fact has implications for the climate and, given that the River Tees has its source close to Cross Fell (the highest summit in the Pennine chain), Upper Teesdale has its own climatic conditions.

The dale is also unique in having more data and long-term weather stations than any other UK upland area. A continuous temperature record is available from 1931 (Holden & Adamson, 2001). Gordon Manley, of Durham University, began recording at Moor House at 550 m in the 1950s, using a hut close to the summit of Great Dun Fell (at 850 m, the second highest Pennine summit). Designation of the area as a Site of Special Scientific Interest (SSSI) in 1948, then as a National Nature Reserve (NNR) in 1952, led to Moor House being established as a Nature Conservation field station and daily recordings were made for almost 30 years.

Reservoirs built in Selset and Lunedale (1955) and Baldersdale (1960) took advantage of the heavy local rainfall and, despite strong opposition, Cow Green Reservoir was built in the late 1960s. Significant funding was provided for research to monitor any changes associated with the reservoir, including the effect such a large body of water might have on the micro-climate. A weather

High wind and snow *MR*.

Icicles in Teesdale *MR*.

Weather station at Widdybank Fell (510 m) *MR*.

Relocated weather station at Langdon Beck (370 m) *MR*.

station was set up on Widdybank Fell (510 m) for daily recording, the data being analysed by local universities and sent to the Met Office, which took over the recording in 1974. Records were mostly made by Ian Findlay until his retirement in 1996, when he relocated the weather station to his home at Hunt Hall Farm, Langdon Beck (370 m). He has continued recording ever since.

What are conditions like?

"We therefore form a conception of excessively windy and pervasively wet autumn, a very variable and stormy winter with long spells of snow cover, high humidity and extremely bitter wind, alternating with brief periods of rain and thaw. April has a mean temperature little above the freezing point and sunny days in May are offset by cold polar air, while the short and cloudy summer is not quite warm enough for the growth of trees. Throughout the year, indeed, the summers are frequently covered in cloud." GORDON MANLEY (Pigott, 1956)

This cool, wet climate has been central in dictating the range of vegetation and associated fauna in Upper Teesdale. Blanket bog, rare in a global context, is common above 500 m on the top of the limestone and other rock types. Climatic conditions allow some plant growth, but only partial decomposition of dead material, the latter forming peat to a depth of around 2 m.

At the altitudes of 350–800 m in the dale, the growing season is very short, even with 'the best weather', with implications for wildlife and hill farmers.

And the characteristic weather of uplands is the occurrence of extreme climatic events, such as the severe winters of 1916, 1940, 1947 (all with late winter and heavy snowfall); 1963 (prolonged snow cover and very cold); and 1978–79. Weather dictated the rate of farming practice, particularly up to 1960 when the horse was relied upon rather than the tractor. As late as 1979, the four-wheel-drive tractor was a rare vehicle in the dale.

For the past 25 years, the Environment Agency (EA) has asked all upland weather stations to record snowfall and to measure the depth and weight of snow, as well as rainfall during the winter. Such data are used in flood forecasting for the lowlands.

Records 1931 to 1999

Across this period the average temperature was 5·3 °C, ranging from -18·5 °C (31 January 1972) to 28·0 °C (4 August 1990). On 23 August 1976, at Widdybank Fell, the maximum temperature was 23·0 °C, followed by a minimum of –1·5 °C, a range of 24·5 °C. On average, there was some rain on

Extreme weather events

1976: A very dry, hot summer reaching 18·6 °C mean maximum in July and August. A wet autumn, with a total of 45·5 cm of rain (September 21·8 cm, October 23·6 cm). For the effect on two rare plant species and their response to the wet autumn see Case Study 9 (*p. 240*) This was followed by low temperatures, high snowfall and heavy drifting in November and December.

1978: Snowfall in late December and two days of blizzards to end the year.

1979: A dreadful winter. Four separate periods of blizzards for two or three days, and 129 consecutive days on cross-country skis to cross Widdybank Fell. Local roads were blocked for long periods, Birkdale Farm was cut off by snow from 28 December to 16 April, local schools were closed and people couldn't get out of the dale to their jobs. A very difficult time for the farming community.

1983: 8 July, following a thunderstorm a 1–1·5 m-high roll on Maize Beck, two more later and then a final roll in late July – four rolls within three weeks! Rain fell at the rate of 15·2 cm per hour, washing peat off high ground, destroying two bridges and washing away walls.

1985: Very wet (58·4 cm) in July and August, delaying hay making until September/ October (first use of big bales).

1986: Much freezing rain (30 cm) in January with several days of ice, nine days of blizzards and severe drifting in February, with a mean maximum temperature of −2·5 °C and a mean minimum air temperature of −6·4 °C. There was up to 35 cm of snow in February/March. Five different thermometer readings (maximum, air minimum, grass minimum, wet and dry bulb) were below zero for 31 days – a record. Total rainfall of 203·7 cm. One of the coldest months of the century.

1992: Severe gales on 2–3 January, average wind speed 60 mph over 2–4 hours (gusts 80 mph) caused severe tree damage at High Force and felled 700+ trees. Yet, unbelievably, later in the month seven days were completely calm!

1995: 10 cm of rain fell over 48 hours on 30–31 January. A rapid 7 °C rise in temperature triggered a sudden thaw of large amounts of snow on the fells, producing the biggest becks and River Tees since 1968. The Environment Agency issued flood warnings for the lowland areas.

Low rainfall totals for June, July and August combined (only 1·5 cm, the lowest on record), high sunshine totals and high temperatures (August mean maximum temperature 19·9 °C). Many areas with shallow soils were burnt out, Cow Green Reservoir was so low that the ruins of the mine shop and construction road were exposed in late summer. Did these drought conditions contribute to the huge decrease in the populations of the rare species that had occurred between 1983 and 2000 whilst the author was in Devon?

1996: The January sunshine total of 6·9 hours was a record low (the average is 35·0 hours for the month).

Fig. 1 | Weather data for Upper Teesdale 2000–19

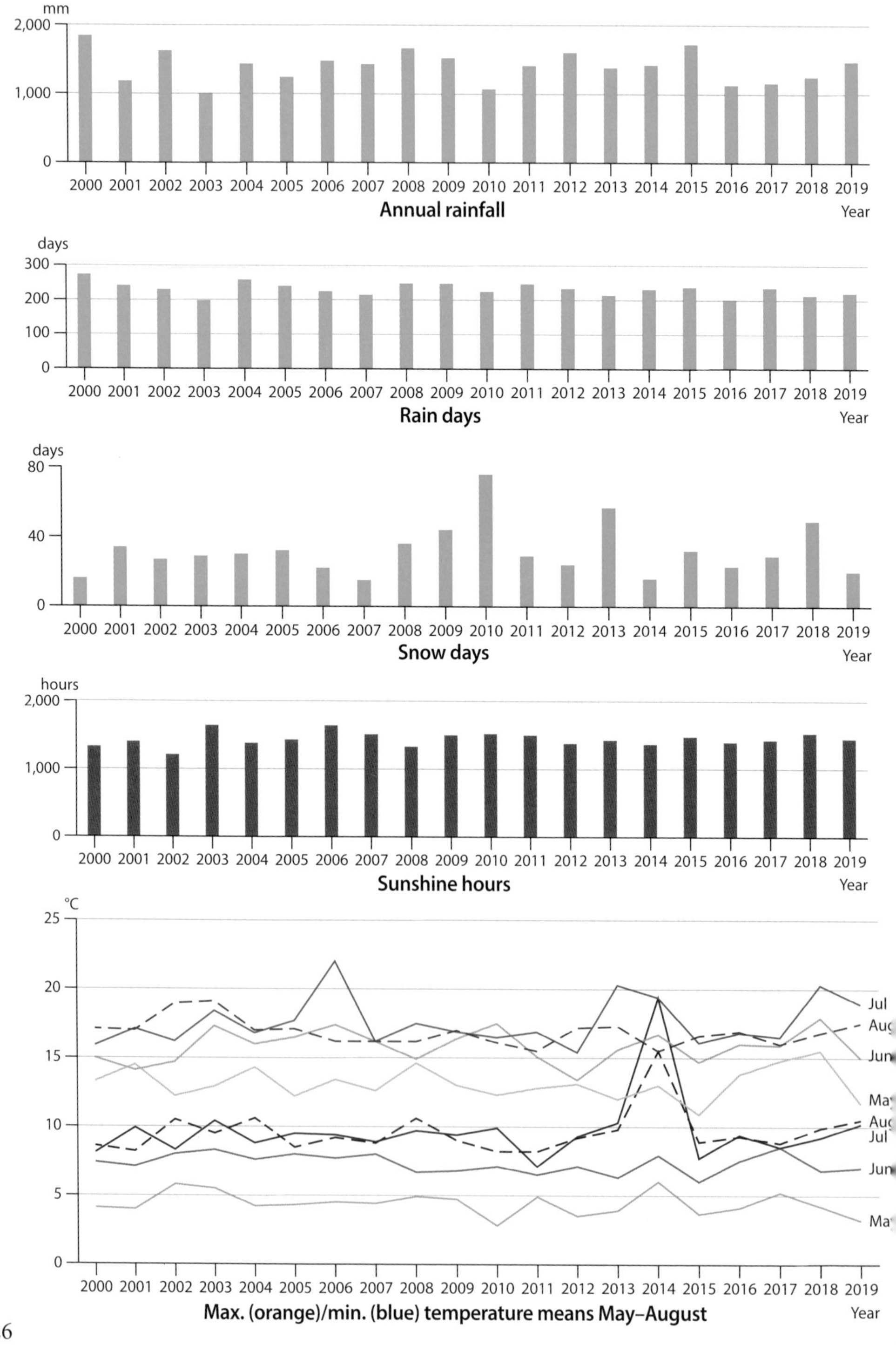

Annual rainfall

Rain days

Snow days

Sunshine hours

Max. (orange)/min. (blue) temperature means May–August

Table 2 | Weather notes for Upper Teesdale 2000–19

Year	Snow (1)				Temperature (No. of days > 20 °C}				Snow (2)			Notes
	J	F	M	A	M	J	J	A	O	N	D	
2000	2	9	5	–	2	3	1	1	–	–	–	RAINFALL very wet: November 307·3 mm; SUNSHINE below average
2001	9	9	15	1	3	2	9	4	–	–	–	RAINFALL average; very dry summer; SUNSHINE average
2002	5	6	15	–	–	–	2	7	–	–	1	RAINFALL dry: February 373·4 mm [record low]; SUNSHINE very low
2003	12	6	11	–	2	3	8	13	–	–	–	RAINFALL low; TEMPERATURE high; SUNSHINE high
2004	10	8	5	–	–	2	6	7	–	1	6	RAINFALL very wet: August 274·3 mm; SUNSHINE below average
2005	5	9	10	–	–	5	7	3	–	4	4	RAINFALL average; SUNSHINE average, but low in summer
2006	1	6	14	1	2	10	22	3	–	–	–	RAINFALL above average: December 335·0 mm; TEMPERATURE July very warm; SUNSHINE high: July 299.6 hrs [record high]
2007	6	4	4	–	–	4	–	2	–	–	1	RAINFALL very wet June and July
2008	7	1	7	3	2	1	6	–	1	3	14	RAINFALL very wet June, July and September
2009	13	14	1	–	2	7	3	1	–	1	15	RAINFALL very wet: November 432·5 mm [record high]
2010	27	17	1	–	4	7	2	1	–	6	25	RAINFALL below average; SNOWFALL very high January, February, December; TEMPERATURE very cold December (max 0·9 °C; min –5·4 °C), River Tees frozen with 15–20 cm of ice
2011	8	6	2	–	–	4	5	1	–	–	13	TEMPERATURE quick thaw January; SUNSHINE below average summer
2012	4	7	–	3	6	–	–	4	–	–	10	RAINFALL wet summer, autumn and winter; SUNSHINE low total: May 218·6 hrs, June 94·7 hrs [record low]
2013	15	14	22	5	1	–	19	5	–	–	1	RAINFALL average early year, wet end to the year; TEMPERATURE very cold March (max 2·8 °C; min –2·8 °C), very warm July; SUNSHINE June 269 hrs [2nd highest recorded]
2014	3	6	1	–	1	1	12	1	–	–	6	RAINFALL very wet January and February; very dry June (33 mm), July (38·1 mm), and September (15·2 mm) – total rainfall only 38 mm more than 2013
2015	12	13	1	–	–	3	4	1	–	3	3	RAINFALL 2nd highest post-2000: December (492·7 mm) – highest since 1968; SNOWFALL high number of snow days; TEMPERATURE above average winter, below average summer
2016	8	4	3	3	2	3	4	4	–	5	–	RAINFALL low; SNOWFALL recorded in 5 months for short periods; SUNSHINE average
2017	6	5	3	–	4	5	2	1	–	1	14	RAINFALL below average: very dry April and May, wet June–October; TEMPERATURE cold: December 14 snow days, 18 ground frost days, 17 air frost days
2018	14	15	15	4	6	8	21	3	–	–	1	RAINFALL very dry May and June; SNOWFALL above average; TEMPERATURE a lot of air and ground frosts
2019	9	3	3	2	–	3	9	8	–	–	3	RAINFALL very dry January, very wet June–September (>125 mm each month); thunderstorms July and August

244 days of the year and 45 days per year were considered to be foggy. The average number of days with air frost was 126 per year, with frost occurring in every month.

Records in the new millennium

Weather patterns from 2000 changed slightly, as the summary (*Table 2, p. 27*) shows. The figures on the following tables must be read with the understanding that they reflect the weather patterns only in Upper Teesdale, which covers large areas of the uplands varying in height from 350 m to 700 m. At these altitudes the growing season is very short. The facts and figures highlight that in any given year wildlife/farming has to cope with complex weather conditions.

The implication of change

Since 2000 the weather pattern has altered, with extremes of rainfall, sunshine and strong winds. Winters have had less snowfall and the period of snow cover is now measured in weeks, not months. Climate change is not new, but it does impact on the flora and other wildlife, and affects the farming year with implications for the farming community, flora and fauna.

Wet, open winters with a high rainfall delay ground warming in the spring, affecting invertebrate eggs and overwintering pupae, including those of moths, which provide food for the chicks of early nesting waders. Slow growth of vegetation delays suckler cows and their calves being turned out into pastures by two or three weeks, at extra feed cost to the farmer.

Table 3 (*below*) shows the occurrence of months with rainfall exceeding 14 inches (355·6 mm) – it seems to be getting wetter. This view is supported by very recent records of total rainfall and rain days over the three consecutive months of November 2015–January 2016 (*Table 4, below*).

Table 3 | Months with rainfall > 14 inches (355·6 mm)

Years	Months	Rainfall inches (mm)
1968–99 (31 years)	December 1994	14·3 (363·2 mm)
2000–16 (17 years)	February 2002	14·7 (373·4 mm)
	November 2009	17·0 (431·8 mm)
	December 2015	19·4 (492·8 mm)

Table 4 | Rainfall November 2015–January 2016

Month	Rainfall (mm)	Rain days
November 2015	11·5 (363·2 mm)	27
December 2015	19·4 (492·8 mm)	30
January 2016	9·2 (233·7 mm)	27

The vascular plants are in a dormant state in the winter, and their growth and flower-production can be affected by the absence of a really cold period. Even though wet, cold soils delay growth in the spring, the indigo spikelets of Blue Moor-grass, in particular, will be produced in March. Bird's-eye Primrose rosettes will be expanding and, by the end of the month, Spring Gentian and Teesdale Violet may be in flower. However, the latter two species flower best in May, when Rare Spring-sedge, Dwarf Milkwort and Bird's-eye Primrose will also be in bloom.

Rainfall is shown in *Fig. 2g* (*opposite*); any months falling below the highlighted level may be insufficient to maintain springs and flushes. Growth and flowering of Three-flowered Rush has been poor on the west side of Widdybank Fell in recent years, where most springs have been almost dry.

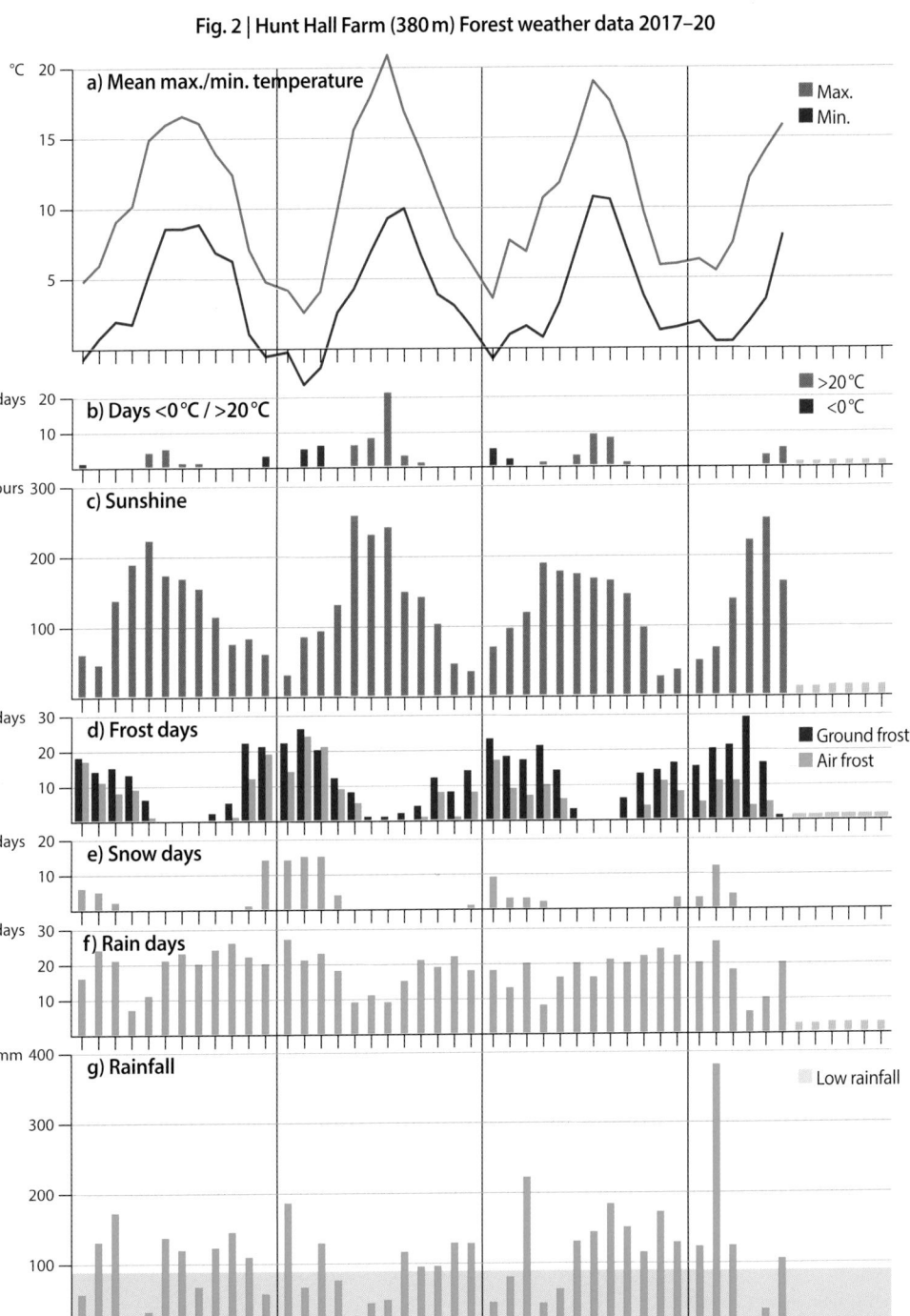

Fig. 2 | Hunt Hall Farm (380 m) Forest weather data 2017–20

Snow on the Sand Hill sugar-limestone escarpment; Red Sike in foreground *MEB*.

Slabs of ice with snow jammed into mouth of Slapestone Sike at the reservoir edge *MR*.

The year 2018 is noteworthy for the 'Beast from the East' and the hot, dry May, June and July. In recent years easterly winds have been more prevalent. On 21–22 February 2018, an easterly gale (48·7 mph at Hunt Hall Farm Met. Stn. (380 m)) swept from the Durham lowlands across the rising ground to Upper Teesdale, dropping its load of snow wherever the altitude decreased; consequently, the road in Forest-in-Teesdale was blocked and, on the side of Widdybank Fell facing the Cow Green Dam and Reservoir, a long, deep snowdrift covered most of the sugar-limestone escarpment and the very low temperatures caused the surface of the reservoir to freeze. Slabs of ice with snow accumulated around the reservoir margin to the depth of over a metre. January had been dry, as were April, May, June and July; the latter three months had six, eight and 21 days respectively of temperatures >20 °C and >200 hours of sunshine. This dryness and heat were very stressful for plants on the shallow, porous sugar-limestone and mineral soils, *e.g.* Hoary Whitlowgrass, and by mid-July Dwarf Milkwort plants were very flaccid; rain in August was too late, as records made on 9 September revealed that 19 of the 51 plants had died.

The following year (2019) started dry; the first two months together had only 122·9 mm of rainfall. April and May had only 104·0 mm. From June until the end of the year was wetter and June to August had three, nine, and eight days respectively with temperatures of >20 °C. The Dwarf Milkwort population gained one plant.

April and May 2020 were again dry (143·1 mm of rain) with 220·2 and 251·5 hours of sunshine respectively. Temperatures in May and June of >20 °C numbered three and five days respectively. At this time, grass and forbs grew little, meadows were short and, on Widdybank Fell, plants produced few flowers. Those that did completed their seed production early; by July the only conspicuous flowers were Common Rock-rose. The larger open Dwarf Milkwort plants had flowered comparatively well and shed their seed by July. In this species production of flowers is indeterminate, only ceasing when the plant is stressed by, for example, frost or drought. Whether or not the small terminal flower buds will open, only more observations will tell.

As a result of this hot, dry period, hay and haylage would be scarce and hence expensive, winter food would need to be bought from down the dale, or more stock than originally intended would have to be sold in the autumn. Fine, hot summers do not suit all residents in the dale, nor do mild winters; some plant species require a sharp frost and/or prolonged cold periods to stimulate flower initiation.

Periods of high rainfall caused a surge of Bracken growth on the lower fells, especially in Common Juniper woodlands, that cannot be managed by chemical treatment. This is associated with less snow cover and fewer frost days. Rush species spread extensively in pastures and wet ground areas in the dale due to less cattle grazing, but open winters and high rainfall do not help.

The Rabbit population is higher everywhere in Teesdale. On the fells, hard winters had previously kept them under control. Since the Foot-and-mouth Disease, fewer sheep graze the uplands, and on Widdybank Fell Blue Moor-grass and Glaucous Sedge can dominate areas to the detriment of the rare plants. A similar increase in Bog Asphodel puts sheep, particularly lambs, at risk because of the plant's high toxicity.

Heavy and sudden rainfall cause damage to road foundations and drains, cutting off the B6277 – the only access road running east to west in the dale. As the road is built on glacial till and runs close to the Tees, it is at risk from future extremes. The challenge for the future is to devise appropriate land management that will encourage the long-term survival of the highly valued Upper Teesdale flora and fauna.

Very dry **Hoary Whitlowgrass**, Widdybank Fell *MEB*.

High Force in spate *MR*.

Soft-rush in pasture *MEB*.

Discovery – four centuries of plant hunting in Upper Teesdale

AUTHOR'S NOTE: This chapter draws heavily on the Ph.D. thesis and published works of Dr Frank Horsman (see *pages 269–270* of *"References"*), material from which is used with his consent.

Introduction

Today, it is not easy to imagine the remote and wild nature of Upper Teesdale in the 18th century: tarmac roads ascend to 848 m on one side, 630 m on the other side, and to 510 m in the interior on the Cow Green Plateau. In 1792, the Hon. John Byng (Andrews, 1936) on his journey from Cotherstone to High Force, when approaching Middleton-in-Teesdale, recounted that "*…here we were stop'd by the Tees, who though not violent, nor stoney, afforded a wide, and no easy pleasant ford: but thro' it we must and did go…*" [a bridge was built *c.* 1817]. Even as late as 1803, in Garland's *A Tour in Teesdale* (Garland, 1803) it was said of the route out of Upper Teesdale "*It is practicable to pass over the Moors from Caldron Snout to Appleby…but there are many bogs, which you cannot avoid, and the very best of the road, till you get to Dufton, is along the stony channel of Maisbeck, or the edges of broken scars…*".

17th Century

The first published records of some Teesdale plants was made by John Ray in his *Catalogus Angliae* **11** in 1677 (Ray, 1677 in Horsman, 1995) namely: Red Currant, Shrubby Cinquefoil, Dwarf Cherry, Wood Vetch, Common Knapweed (*see p.161 op. cit.*) and Yellow Star-of-Bethlehem.

Ray wished to see the Shrubby Cinquefoil and was introduced to Ralph Johnson by the professional plant collector, Thomas Willisel, who knew the plant. Subsequently, Johnson became Ray's "great friend and expert in Natural History" (Horsman, 2021). Ralph Johnson (1629–95), native of the lower Tees, was a student at St. John's College, Cambridge and became the master at Darlington Grammar School and then the Vicar at Brignall, near the River Greta (Horsman, 1995). That Johnson knew the wild and remote parts of the dale is revealed by a fellow antiquarian,

Frank Horsman. July 2008 *RL*.

Ralph Johnson's Tomb, Brignal Church and (inset) the plaque that was attached to it by Frank Horsman *both MR*.

Christopher Hunter (1675–1757) who transcribed Johnson's papers and listed 15 plants that had been found by Johnson in Upper Teesdale.

Table 5 | Ralph Johnson's 17th Century list (after Horsman, 2011)

From further studies, Horsman (2011) concluded that it was Hunter who discovered the 'Teesdale rarities': Roseroot, "at High Cup Gill", Alpine Bartsia, Alpine Birch and Scottish Asphodel. He most probably saw these on his known visit in 1699, when he also wrote to Martin Lister FRS about his find of the Spring Gentian on Widdybank Fell. Unfortunately, neither Johnson's nor Hunter's records were placed in the public domain at the time and, therefore, it was as if they had never been made.

Name as in Stace, 2019 *part of the Teesdale Assemblage*	Name 'sufficient' to enable the reader to find the entry in Hunter's notebook	Common name
* Festuca vivipara (L.) Sm.	Gramen montanum	Viviparous Sheep's-fescue
* Galium boreale L.	Mollugo montana	Northern Bedstraw
Geranium lucidum L.	Geranium saxatile	Shining Crane's-bill
* Bistorta vivipara (L.) Delarbre	Bistorta minor	Alpine Bistort
* Chamaenerion angustifolium (L.) Scop.	Lysimachia speciosa	Rosebay Willowherb
Marchantia polymorpha L.	Lichen petraeus	a liverwort
* Dasiphora fruticosa (L.) Rydb.	Pentaphyllum fruticosum	Shrubby Cinquefoil
Asplenium ruta-muraria L.	Adiantum album	Wall-rue
* Sabulina verna (L.) Rchb.	Alsine pusilla	Spring Sandwort
Saxifraga stellaris L.	Cotyledon hirsuta	Starry Saxifrage
* Sedum villosum L.	Sedum purpureum	Hairy Stonecrop
Saxifraga hypnoides L.	Sedum alpinum	Mossy Saxifrage
Adoxa moschatellina L.	Moschatellina foliis	Moschatel
* Polemonium caeruleum L.	Valeriana graeca	Jacob's-ladder
Drabella muralis (L.) Fourr.	Bursa pastoris	Wall Whitlowgrass

18th Century

Following Ray's death in 1705 there was a pause in the search for plants. In the early part of the 18th century the second edition of *Britannia* (Camden, 1722) was published by Edmund Gibson. Here, in the account of County Durham, were mentioned: *Betula rotundifolia nana* Dwarf Birch "on a moss near Birdale [Birkdale]", *Pentaphylloides fruticosa* Shrubby Cinquefoil "below Egglestone Abbey" and *Tofieldia pusilla* Scottish Asphodel.

John Wilson (1696–1751), of Kendal, is credited with Alpine Bistort and Starry Saxifrage in 1744 (Baker, 1903). In 1777, Stephen Robson (1741–79) published *The British Flora* (Robson, 1777) in English using the Linnaean binomial nomenclature. This included 31 Durham rarities.

In the decades each side of the year 1800 the search for the specialities of the Teesdale flora was revived. Although many of these have been attributed to a Revd Harriman, Frank Horsman

(Horsman, 2005) has provided convincing evidence that William Oliver, apothecary and botanist of Middleton-in-Teesdale, was the true discoverer of many of the Teesdale rarities. Oliver was born in Hawick (*c*.1761–1816), apprenticed there to his grandfather, William Scott, a physician/surgeon, from whom he would have learnt the herbs or 'simples' to make their medicaments. He attended the Winter Medical School Sessions at Edinburgh University from 1780–83, and botanised with John Hope, Professor of Botany (1725–86). He would have possessed the *Flora Scotica* written in English (not Latin) by the Revd John Lightfoot in 1777. Thus, when Oliver arrived in Teesdale in 1783 he was already an experienced botanist and, in pursuit of herbs and when visiting his patients, would have encountered many of Teesdale's rare plants.

By a fortunate chain of connections, news of Oliver's discoveries reached two eminent Fellows of the Linnean Society – James Sowerby (engraver) and James Edward Smith (later Sir), who were illustrating and describing the flora in the 36 volumes of *English Botany* (1790–1814). Smith wrote the descriptions and always mentioned the name of the person who had sent in the specimen from which Sowerby had made his drawing. It so happened that the Revd John Harriman (1760–1831) became the curate in Eggleston in 1795 and botanised with Stephen Cleasby, surgeon apothecary of Barnard Castle, who knew Edward Robson, of Darlington, an Associate of the Linnean Society. Founded in 1788, the Linnean Society was the prestigious centre of eminent natural historians and of learning; membership was greatly coveted.

Harriman would have quickly made the acquaintance of Oliver – a fellow botanist – who had been in Upper Teesdale for over 10 years. Oliver took him there in 1796, apparently Harriman's only visit. The plants they gathered were sent by Harriman to Edward Robson (1763–1813) and thence to Sowerby and Smith. This is confirmed by the name on a sheet of Alpine Bartsia in Oliver's handwriting, and "-*Nr Middleton from Dr Oliver VIII 1796*" in that of Robson. Under the drawing of the species, Smith has written "*The wild recent specimens of this very rare plant, from which our drawing was taken, were gathered July 27,1796, near Middleton in Teesdale, Durham, by the Revd. Mr Harriman and Mr W. Oliver surgeon, of Middleton and sent to us by E. Robson…*". It was on that day that Harriman spotted the basal leaves of Spring Gentian.

Dwarf Birch on a moss near Birkdale *MEB*.

William Oliver's gravestone, Middleton-in-Teesdale Parish Church *MEB*.

Several of these early botanists were Quakers who, debarred from many learned professions, turned to the natural world. Many were related, so it is important to specify the first names and, where these are the same, to give the date of birth and/or death. Edward Robson (1763–1813) was the nephew of Stephen (1741–79) who wrote the first *British Flora* in English and the Backhouse father (1794–1869) and son (1825–90) were both called James.

In the herbarium of Edward Robson, Horsman found that Oliver had sent at least

The Reverend Harriman's Box Tomb, Croft-on-Tees *FS*.

19 specimens directly to Robson in August 1796. By the reverse route, Oliver learned of the plants not yet included in *English Botany*. In order to obtain these, he made a mutual agreement with John Binks, a miner and 'simpler' for druggists, whom he instructed what to look for and where he could find the plants. Before 1796, nothing is known of Binks, a man of 'gentlemanly appearance,' 'observant,' and 'intelligent'. He did the better-paid 'dead' work like sinking shafts from one level to another. Working four days a week in the mine, without family and smallholding, gave him two days to collect 'simples' to sell to the 'druggist' (chemist) during this time of famine, following two bad harvests and a very bad winter 1794–5. The earliest record of him in Middleton-in-Teesdale is 1796. Did he come from Derbyshire after the London Lead Quaker Co. sold its mines there in 1792 and leased new mines in Teesdale 1792–8? Horsman suspects he was local.

Oliver had been botanising in Teesdale since 1783 and had found a number of plants that he had been unable to identify – plants such as Spring Gentian, Shrubby Cinquefoil, Hoary Rock-rose, Alpine Bartsia – not in *Flora Scotica* – and Mountain Avens, not illustrated, until he met Harriman. Evidence shows that some plants were found by Binks, *e.g.* Yellow Saxifrage in Baldersdale of which it is written "*the bogs are yellow with this plant*", but there are some species where it is not possible to know which of the two – Oliver or Binks – first found a particular plant.

Horsman concludes that Harriman played no substantial part in the discovery of the rare plants, except as a go-between, citing plant specimens as "from *the Egleston area*" [*sic*] so that visitors would come to him first. Harriman also wrote that for the first two years (1796–7) he concentrated on sedges (Carices) and willows (Salices) and in the third moved completely to lichens.

In 1794, Edward Robson had printed a *Catalogus Plantarium rariorum circa Darlington sponte nascentium* (Catalogue of rarer wild plants around Darlington). That was succeeded in 1798 by his *Plantae rariores agro Dunelmensis indiginae*. These lists showed that most of the Teesdale Rarities had been discovered, or reported to Edward, during the period June 1794 to May 1798. Included was a list supplied by Harriman and Oliver. Although this is not extant, Horsman has reconstructed Oliver's List from a paper found in the Winch Correspondence in the Linnean Society Library, in which Harriman had marked 159 Vascular Plants as occurring "around Eggleston", including the 36 Teesdale Rarites shown in *Table 6 (p. 36)*.

As shown earlier, some of these plants had been discovered in Upper Teesdale in the 17th century, but there was no way that Oliver could have known of these records of Johnson and Hunter. Harriman's important contribution is defined by the fact that nothing was known of

Table 6 | List of Teesdale Plants in E. Robson's *Plantae rariores* supplied by Harriman and Oliver from 1794–98 (after Horsman, 2005).

Where the current scientific name is different, the name in Stace (2019) follows in brackets.

Orchis bifolia (*Platanthera bifolia* (L.) Rich.)	Lesser Butterfly-orchid
Satyrium albidum (*Pseudorchis albida* (L.) Á.& D. Löve)	Small-white Orchid
Ophrys cordata (*Neottia cordata* (L.) Rich.)	Lesser Twayblade
Malaxis paludosa (*Hammarbya paludosa* (L.) Kuntze)	Bog Orchid
Sesleria cerulea (*Sesleria caerulea* (L.) Ard.)	Blue Moor-grass
Galium boreale L.	Northern Bedstraw
Plantago maritima L.	Sea Plantain
Primula farinosa L.	Bird's-eye Primrose
Gentiana verna L.	Spring Gentian
Statice Armeria [sic] (*Armeria maritima* (Miller) Willd.)	Thrift
Juncus triglumis L.	Three-flowered Rush
Tofieldia palustris (*Tofieldia pusilla* (Michaux) Pers.)	Scottish Asphodel
Epilobium angustifolium (*Chamaenerion angustifolium* (L.) Scop.)	Rosebay Willowherb
Polygonum viviparum (*Bistorta vivipara* (L.) Delarbre)	Alpine Bistort
Rhodiola rosea L.	Roseroot
Micranthes stellaris (L.) Glasso, Banfi & Soldanao	Starry Saxifrage
Saxifraga aizoides L.	Yellow Saxifrage
Saxifraga hypnoides L.	Mossy Saxifrage
Arenaria verna (*Sabulina verna* (L.) Rchb.)	Spring Sandwort
Sedum villosum L.	Hairy Stonecrop
Rubus chamaemorus L.	Cloudberry
Potentilla fruticosa (*Dasiphora fruticosa* (L.) Rydb.)	Shrubby Cinquefoil
Dryas octopetala L.	Mountain Avens
Cistus marifolius (*Helianthemum oelandicum* (L.) Baumg. subsp. *levigatum* M. Proctor)	Hoary Rock-rose
Thalictrum alpinum L.	Alpine Meadow-rue
Trollius europaeus L.	Globeflower
Bartsia alpina L.	Alpine Bartsia
Thlaspi alpestre (*Noccaea caerulescens* (J. & C. Presl) F. K. Mey)	Alpine Penny-cress
Draba incana L.	Hoary Whitlowgrass
Cochlearia groenlandica (*C. pyrenaica* DC.)	Pyrenean Scurvygrass
Geranium sylvaticum L.	Wood Crane's-bill
Anthyllus Vulneraria [sic] L. (*Anthyllis vulneraria* L.)	Kidney Vetch
Carduus helenoides (*Cirsium heterophyllum* (L.) Hill)	Melancholy Thistle
Gnaphalium dioicum (*Antennaria dioica* (L.) Gaertner)	Mountain Everlasting
Pteris crispa (*Cryptogramma crispa* (L.) R. Br. ex Hook.)	Parsley Fern
Asplenium viride Huds.	Green Spleenwort

Oliver's botanical activities until he (Harriman) arrived in 1795. The role of Edward Robson in the discovery of the 'Teesdale rarities' had previously been totally overlooked. After Oliver's solitary work in discovering most of the Teesdale rarities, the only vascular plants that were thought to be awaiting discovery in Upper Teesdale were those that were critical and/or very rare. However, this was not so and at the end of the 18th century yet more species were found:

18th Century Discoveries post Robson's *Plantae rariores* list (after Horsman, 1998)

1793	Downy Currant *Ribes spicatum*: E. Robson
1796	Stone Bramble *Rubus saxatilis*: W. Oliver
1796	Cranberry *Vaccinium oxycoccus*: W. Oliver
1796	Bog Bilberry *Vaccinium uliginosum*: J. Binks
1796	Lesser Clubmoss *Selaginella selagnioides*: W. Oliver & J. Harriman
1796/7	Bog Orchid *Hammarbya paludosa*: J. Binks
1797	Mountain Pansy *Viola lutea* (as *V. tricola*): J. Harriman & W. Oliver
1797	Dioecious Sedge *Carex dioica*, Hair Sedge *C. capillaris*, Oval Sedge *C. leporina*, Flea Sedge *C. pulicaris*: J. Harriman
1798	Bearberry *Arctostaphylos uva-ursi*: J. Binks
1798	Small Cow-wheat *Melampyrum sylvaticum*: J. Harriman & W. Brunton (Tennant, 2008)
1798	Lily-of-the-valley *Convallaria majalis*: W. Oliver & J. Harriman
1798	Alpine Cinquefoil *Potentilla crantzii*: W. Oliver & J. Harriman
1798	Holly-fern *Polystichum lonchitis*: W. Oliver
1799	False Sedge *Carex simpliciuscula*: J. Dickson
1799	Broad-leaved Cottongrass *Eriophorum latifolium*: J. Dickson

19th Century Discoveries

As the Napoleonic Wars eclipsed the 'Grand Tour' the 19th century tourists were diverted to explore scenic areas at home, such as The Lake District and Upper Teesdale, aided by guide books such as *A Tour in Teesdale* (Garland, 1803). The botanical riches of Upper Teesdale began to be known amongst the botanical cognoscenti, in part due to the publication of *The Botanist's Guide through the Counties of Northumberland and Durham* that included 20 Teesdale plants (Winch, 1805). Many more botanists and tourists visited the area and hired guides to show them the sights and/or plants, thus helping a local profession to develop. The second edition of Garland's book published in 1813 contained *"a list of 28 flowering plants communicated by Mr. Oliver…."* The New Edition [revised 5th edn., 1848] some 35 years later contained 77 species supplied by a George Brown.

1801	Bog Orchid *Hammarbya paludosa*: J. Binks (Horsman, 1998)
1803	Marsh Saxifrage *Saxifraga hirculus*: J. Binks (Horsman, 1998)
1805	Melancholy Thistle *Cirsium heterophyllum*: N. J. Winch (Winch *et al.*, 1805)
1805	Tea-leaved Willow *Salix phylicifolia*: J. Harriman (Graham, 1988)
1810	Chickweed Willowherb *Epilobium alsinifolium*: J. Binks (Horsman, 1998)

At this time the two James Backhouses, father (1794–1869) and son (1825–90), from Darlington and York respectively, were active in Teesdale (Baker, 1903). James Sr., a nephew of E. Robson, was of delicate health as a young man, probably from working in a druggist's shop, and spent the summers of 1810 and 1811 exploring the botanical riches of Teesdale, often in the company of miner, John Binks. The 19th century botanists were great walkers covering 25–30 miles of upland country in one day, as do some today! Subsequently, he trained as a gardener at a nursery run by a Quaker family in Norwich and then acquired a nursery in York that he managed with his brother, Thomas, and later with his son, James Jr. Together, father and son visited Teesdale so frequently that at the High Force Hotel there was 'Mr Backhouse's Room'. At this time new discoveries continued to be made.

H. Adlard, sc

James Backhouse (Sr.) (1794–1869)

1810   Rock Whitebeam *Sorbus rupicola*: J. Backhouse Sr. (Horsman, 1998)

1821   Oblong Woodsia *Woodsia ilvensis*: J. Backhouse Sr. near Cauldron Snout (Horsman, 1990)

The account of the recognition of *Woodsia ilvensis* in Teesdale is well-known (Horsman, 1990). On seeing the illustration of a *Woodsia* in *English Botany* (1809) in 1821, Backhouse Sr. realised he had seen the fern near Falcon Clints several years earlier (maybe in 1811) and declared to his sceptical friends "*it is there, – I will go and fetch it*." The specimen is labelled in his handwriting "*Foot of Cauldron Snout, Teesdale. 1821, first found there*." Unfortunately, the species has been extinct in its original Teesdale sites since *c.* 1895, undoubtedly due to the thoughtless greed of botanists, *e.g.* "*At least one herbarium sheet collected from here shows eight whole plants collected as a result of a single visit*" (Graham, 1988). Plants grown from spores from Scotland and Wales were introduced to the areas of two former sites in Upper Teesdale in 1999 and 2000.

1829   Variegated Horsetail *Equisetum variegatum*: C. W. Trevelyan in Winch (1932) (Horsman, 1998)

1831   R. B. Bowman (Horsman, 1998) compiled the first British map of plant distributions in the North of England. The Upper Teesdale section of 1831 with additions in 1836 was annotated with the names of many rare species

1832   Alpine Willowherb *Epilobium anagallidifolium*: C. W. Trevelyan (Baker, 1903)

1842   Alpine Saxifrage *Micranthes nivalis*: J. Backhouse Sr. & Jr. (Backhouse, 1843). In VC 69 (Westmorland), usually included in the Teesdale Assemblage of rare and special higher plants

1842   Six hawkweeds (*Hieracium iricum, H. gothicum, H. pallidum, H. anglicum, H. crocatum, H. corymbosum*): J. Backhouse Jr. (Backhouse, 1884) [probably on Cronkley Scar or in High Force Gorge]

1842   Alpine Meadow-grass *Poa alpina*: J. Backhouse Jr. (Backhouse, 1884) [probably on Cronkley Scar or in High Force Gorge]

1843   Jacob's-ladder *Polemonium caeruleum*: J. Backhouse Sr. & Jr. (Backhouse, 1843)

1844   Shady Horsetail *Equisetum pratense*: J. Backhouse Jr. (Graham, 1988)

1844   Teesdale Sandwort *Sabulina stricta*: G. S. Gibson of Norfolk when visiting Teesdale with a group of Quakers led by the Backhouses (Horsman, 1990). First thought to be Snow Pearlwort *Spergula saginoides* (now *Sagina nivalis*), it was identified by Sir W. J. Hooker, of Kew Gardens, as Teesdale Sandwort *Alsine* (now *Sabulina*) *stricta*.

1852   Stemless Bird's-eye Primrose *Primula farinosa* var. *acaulis*: J. Backhouse Sr. & Jr. (Horsman, 1990)

1852 Alpine Forget-me-not *Myosotis alpestris*: J. Backhouse Sr. & Jr. (Horsman, 1990)

1852 Dwarf Milkwort *Polygala amarella*: J. Backhouse Sr. & Jr. (Horsman, 1990)

1861 Teesdale Violet *Viola rupestris*: J. Backhouse Jr. (Horsman, 1990)

1872 Alpine Bladder-fern *Cystopteris alpina*: R. Potter (Tennant, 1995)
      It is last known to have been seen and collected by C. E. Salmon in 1911 from the same locality. Despite extensive searching in recent years, David Tennant has failed to find it in Teesdale (Tennant, 1995; 2010).

1883 Tall Bog-sedge *Carex magellanica*: E.S. Marshall (In BSBI records)

1885 Bog-sedge *Carex limosa*: W. Foggitt (In BSBI records)

20th century discoveries

Perhaps, slightly surprising for such a well-worked area, 14 new species have been found in the 20th century:

1903 Alpine Rush *Juncus alpinoarticulatus*: G.C. Druce (Graham, 1988)

1903 Velvet Lady's-mantle *Alchemilla monticola*: A.E. Hume [In British Museum herbarium; identified by Wilmott] (Wilmott, 1922)

1905 Deergrass hybrid *Trichophorum ×foersteri*: T.J. Foggitt [In British Museum herbarium (specimen from Widdybank), identified by Swan] (Hollingsworth & Swan, 1999; Durkin, 2016) [See also 2009]

1913 Dark-leaved Willow *Salix myrsinifolia*: C.E. Moss of Cambridge (Graham, 1988)

1923 Alpine Cat's-tail *Phleum alpinum*: Wilson (Halliday, 1997) [vc 70 (Cumberland), outside the Tees catchment]

1924 Shining Lady's-mantle *Alchemilla micans*: G.C. Druce [In British Museum herbarium; identified by Walters] (Swan & Walters, 1988)

1927 Pale Forget-me-not *Myosotis stolonifera*: J.E. Lousley; identified by C.E. Salmon (Graham, 1988)

1933 Starry Lady's-mantle *Alchemilla acutiloba*: J.F.G. Chapple [In British Museum herbarium; identified by Wilmott] (Walters, 1949)

1942 Slender Lady's-mantle *Alchemilla filicaulis* ssp. *filicaulis*, herb. CGE: S.M. Walters & J. Allison (Graham, 1988)

LEFT: Five Quakers set out in Teesdale; RIGHT: First sighting of one of Britain's rarest plants – Teesdale Sandwort from J. Rawlins' book *An 1844 Pennine Way from Tees to Ribble: Five botanists walk from Crook to Settle*, published in 2016 by York Publishing Services Ltd.

1947   Rock Lady's-mantle *Alchemilla wichurae*: S. M. Walters (Walters, 1949)

1947   Clustered Lady's-mantle *Alchemilla glomerulans*: S. M. Walters (Walters, 1949)

1949   Rare Spring-sedge *Carex ericetorum*: T. C. Tutin (1949) herb. DHM (Graham, 1988)

1951   Large-toothed Lady's-mantle *Alchemilla subcrenata*: M. E. Bradshaw; identified by S. M. Walters (Walters, 1952)

1959   Alpine Foxtail *Alopecurus magellanicus*: D. Ratcliffe & A. Eddy (Ratcliffe & Eddy, 1960)

1965   Dwarf Birch *Betula nana*: re-found by T. C. Hutchinson (Hutchinson, 1966)

1966   a dandelion *Taraxacum pseudonordstedtii*: new species named by A. J. Richards (Richards, 1972)

1968   Water Sedge *Carex aquatilis*: H. C. Proctor; identified by A. C. Jermy (Graham, 1988 *pers. comm.*)

1970   Kidney Vetch *Anthyllis vulneraria* ssp. *lapponum*: M. E. Bradshaw

1979   Whorl-grass *Catabrosa aquatica*: F. J. Roberts (Roberts & Halliday, 1979)

The lady's-mantles were identified by Wilmot from material in the British Natural History Museum (BNHM). Large-toothed Lady's-mantle was found by the author on her first 'sampling' expedition after meeting Max Walters. Also, in the BNHM there is a sheet of four whole plants of a lady's-mantle collected by Druce in 1924 at Langdon Beck and subsequently identified by Walters as Shining Lady's-mantle. No plants of this species were found in Teesdale during the author's early searching in the 1950s, nor later.

Rare Spring-sedge was recognised by Tutin when looking for the Teesdale Violet with D. H. Valentine on Widdybank Fell.

Water Sedge was found by the Revd Hugh Proctor in 1968 in slack water by a small tributary on the north side of the Tees before the building of the Cow Green Reservoir destroyed the site (for later finds see below). The reservoir was first filled in 1972.

Dwarf Birch was re-found by Tom Hutchinson, the location fits well enough with the record of "on a moss near Birdale [Birkdale]" in Hunter's Notebook 1699 (Horsman, 2011) and "on a moss near Birdale [Birkdale]" (Camden, 1722).

Whorl-grass was found in 1979 by F. J. Roberts (*pers. comm.*) on the NE side of Little Fell (River Lune drainage into the Tees) and in 2005 on Mickle Fell by R. Corner, F. J. Roberts and L. Robinson.

21st century – more additions have been made:

In 2001, following the removal of sheep from the higher Teesdale fells because of the earlier serious outbreak of Foot-and-mouth Disease, the very short vegetation at the higher levels above about 615 m attained a size by which the erstwhile hidden species could be identified.

2005   Sheathed Sedge *Carex vaginata*: F. J. Roberts on Little Dun and Knock Fells (Corner, Roberts & Robinson, 2006). Other populations have been found on the Cross Fell to Mickle Fell range, as well as more Alpine Foxtail and Water Sedge found by R. W. M. Corner on the Cross Fell range, and more populations of the Alpine Foxtail, and Water Sedge *Carex aquatilis,* have been discovered.

2008   A Yellow-rattle *Rhinanthus minor* ssp. *monticola* on Widdybank Fell: M. E. Bradshaw; identified by A. Lean

2009   Northern Deergrass *Trichophorum cespitosum*: F. J. Roberts (Roberts, 2009) Northern Deergrass and the hybrid *T.* ×*foersteri* with Common Deergrass [see 1905] were both found by Roberts in Widdybank Pasture at about 430 m in Forest-in-Teesdale, and both at 490 m, two small tufts only, by M. E. Bradshaw with L. Robinson, on Valley Bog, near Moor House, at 553 m, in 2010.

2011 Rush hybrid *Juncus × surrejanus* in Forest-in-Teesdale at about 430 m: M. E. Bradshaw; identified by M. Wilcox (*pers. comm.*)

2014 Slender Sedge *Carex lasiocarpa* on Black Hill opposite Birkdale at about 450 m: J. O'Reilly, BSBI Meeting

2022 Dwarf Birch *Betula nana* on Cronkley Fell: by J. O'Reilly on 29th August

The future

It is highly likely that new finds of plants in Teesdale will continue to be made, particularly of species that are known on the west side of the watershed. This is exemplified, for example, by the following finds: Alpine Saxifrage and Alpine Meadow-grass found by P.S. Lloyd in High Cup Nick in 1964; Alpine Cat's-tail in Crowdundle Beck; and Field Fleawort on Mickle Fell. Field Fleawort as *Senecio campestris* is included in Baker (1903), p.83, no date or exact location is given. Halliday (1997), p.480, has "*1846 J. Backhouse on limestone outcrops 1200–1500ft. above Brough*," also "*Westmorland side of Mickle Fell* (T. J. Foggitt) *is presumably somewhere near Little Fell.*" In 2011, a search above Brough was unsuccessful (F. J. Roberts, *pers.comm.*). Field Fleawort is a plant of the chalk in SE England – could it be on Cronkley Fell along with Horseshoe Vetch, Dwarf Milkwort and Small Scabious?

A good knowledge of the mountain flora and a sharp eye are all that are needed by the plant hunter, plus determination, persistence and a fit body, as well as a notebook and/or camera. However, not only have changes in management resulted in the appearance of species hitherto not recorded in the area, climate change is sure to make its impact felt among this special relict community. Alas, many of this Teesdale Assemblage of rare and special plants have decreased in quantity and range during the 70 years the author has known the Upper Tees catchment area and the Moor House-Upper Teesdale NNR in the dale. It is management practices in the more immediate future that will determine their long-term survival, as much as climate change.

I am aware there are many omissions from the Teesdale Assemblage and noteworthy higher plants of the Tees catchment, especially of aquatics, ferns and hawkweeds.

A group recording plants at Maize Beck Scar *MWH*.

Communities and habitats of the Teesdale Assemblage

The members of the Teesdale Assemblage are to be found in a number of different habitats and plant communities. Some occur in several, whereas others are very specific to one habitat, *e.g.* sugar-limestone or riversides. Human beings have influenced all the habitats and communities over several millennia, so that most can only be described as semi-natural. There is no true wilderness, even though the upper reaches of Teesdale may appear wild and natural to many visitors.

The vegetation that gives special distinction to the flora of Teesdale is that associated with the metamorphosed sugar-limestone on Widdybank and Cronkley Fells. Although similar rock is to be found in small quantities on the metamorphosed Dalradian limestone in the Blair Atholl and Pitlochry areas of Scotland, where some of the 'Teesdale' plants also grow, the associated species are not identical. In the following, descriptions of each community reference the most appropriate National Vegetation Classification (NVC – *see opposite*).

Plant communities and habitats of the sugar-limestone

The most characteristic community occurring on the dry limestone areas is the close-cropped grassland in which the most commonly found plants are:

Sheep's-fescue	*Festuca ovina*		Eyebright	*Euphrasia officinalis* agg.
Blue Moor-grass	*Sesleria caerulea*		Fairy Flax	*Linum catharticum*
Quaking-grass	*Briza media*		Wild Thyme	*Thymus drucei*
Crested Hair-grass	*Koeleria macrantha*		Common Dog-violet	*Viola riviniana*
Carnation Sedge	*Carex panicea*			

Blue Moor-grass – Limestone Bedstraw grassland (CG9) on Widdybank Fell *DM*.

The National Vegetation Classification (NVC)

The NVC is a system of classifying natural habitat types in Great Britain according to the vegetation they contain. It comprises 286 communities, such as woodlands, grasslands, heaths, *etc.* and all their subtle variations. It was published by Cambridge University Press in the following five volumes:

Rodwell, J. S. (ed.) 1991. *British Plant Communities, Volume 1: Woodlands and scrub.*

Rodwell, J. S. (ed.) 1992. *British Plant Communities, Volume 2: Mires and heaths.*

Rodwell, J. S. (ed.) 1992. *British Plant Communities, Volume 3: Grassland and montane communities.*

Rodwell, J. S. (ed.) 1995. *British Plant Communities, Volume 4: Aquatic communities, swamps and tall-herb fens.*

Rodwell, J. S. (ed.) 2000. *British Plant Communities, Volume 5: Maritime communities and vegetation of open habitats.*

Information concerning the NVC and details of the codes, communities and associated species can be obtained from the JNCC website at https://bit.ly/38CDNFj.

Photographs and additional information about the species is available from the *Online Atlas of the British and Irish flora*, which can be accessed via https://www.brc.ac.uk/plantatlas.

The various plant communities are grouped into the following major categories (those highlighted in **bold** include communities that occur in Teesdale):

Code	Description	Number of communities
W	**Woodland and scrub**	25 (19 classed as woodland; 4 as scrub; 2 as 'underscrub')
M	**Mires**	38
H	**Heaths**	22 (within 6 subgroups)
MG	**Mesotrophic grasslands**	13
CG	**Calcicolous grasslands**	14
U	**Calcifugous grasslands and montane communities**	21
A	**Aquatic communities**	24
S	**Swamps and tall-herb fens**	28
SM	Salt-marsh communities	28
SD	Shingle, strandline and sand-dune communities	19 (16 classed as sand-dune; 1 as shingle; 2 as strandline)
MC	Maritime cliff communities	12
OV	**Vegetation of open habitats**	42

NVC communities and sub-communities in Teesdale, referred to in this book

Code	Constant (and associated) species
Woodland and Scrub	
W3	Bay Willow *Salix pentandra*–Bottle Sedge *Carex rostrata* woodland
W9	Ash *Fraxinus excelsior*–Rowan *Sorbus aucuparia*–Dog's Mercury *Mercurialis perennis* woodland
W9b	Ash *Fraxinus excelsior*–Rowan *Sorbus aucuparia*–Dog's Mercury *Mercurialis perennis* woodland, Marsh Hawk's-beard *Crepis paludosa* sub-community
W11	Sessile Oak *Quercus petraea*–Downy Birch *Betula pubescens*–Wood-sorrel *Oxalis acetosella* woodland
W19	Common Juniper *Juniperus communis* ssp. *communis*–Wood-sorrel *Oxalis acetosella* woodland

Code	Constant (and associated) species
Mires	
M1	Cow-horn Bog-moss *Sphagnum denticulatum* bog pool community (with Common Cottongrass *Eriophorum angustifolium*, Bogbean *Menyanthes trifoliata* and Feathery Bog-moss *Sphagnum cuspidatum*)
	[5 associated rare species: Bog Orchid *Hammarbya paludosa*, Brown Beak-sedge *Rhynchospora fusca*, Rannoch-rush *Scheuchzeria palustris*, Intermediate Bladderwort *Utricularia intermedia* and Golden Bog-moss *Sphagnum pulchrum*.]
M2	Feathery Bog-moss *Sphagnum cuspidatum*/Flexuous Bog-moss *S. flexuosum* bog pool community (with Cross-leaved Heath *Erica tetralix*, Common Cottongrass *Eriophorum angustifolium*, Round-leaved Sundew *Drosera rotundifolia* and Flat-topped Bog-moss *Sphagnum fallax*)
	[3 associated rare species: Bog-rosemary *Andromeda polifolia*, Tall Bog-sedge *Carex magellanica* and Golden Bog-moss *Sphagnum pulchrum*.]
M4	Bottle Sedge *Carex rostrata*–Flexuous Bog-moss *Sphagnum flexuosum* mire (with Common Haircap *Polytrichum commune*, Feathery Bog-moss *Sphagnum cuspidatum* and Flat-topped Bog-moss *Sphagnum fallax*)
	[2 associated rare species: String Sedge *Carex chordorrhiza* and Tufted Loosestrife *Lysimachia thrysiflora*.]
M7b	White Sedge *Carex canescens*–Russow's Bog-moss *Sphagnum russowii* mire, Water Sedge *Carex aquatilis*–Flexuous Bog-moss *Sphagnum recurvum* sub-community
M10	Dioecious Sedge *Carex dioica*–Common Butterwort *Pinguicula vulgaris* mire
M10b	Dioecious Sedge *Carex dioica*–Common Butterwort *Pinguicula vulgaris* mire, Quaking-grass *Briza media*–Bird's-eye Primrose *Primula farinosa* sub-community
M10c	Dioecious Sedge *Carex dioica*–Common Butterwort *Pinguicula vulgaris* mire, Hook-beaked Tufa-moss *Hymenostylium recurvirostrum* sub-community
M11	Common Yellow-sedge *Carex demissa*–Yellow Saxifrage *Saxifraga aizoides* mire [can merge into M10]
M16	Cross-leaved Heath *Erica tetralix*–Compact Bog-moss *Sphagnum compactum* wet heath
M16d	Cross-leaved Heath *Erica tetralix*–Compact Bog-moss *Sphagnum compactum* wet heath, Heath Rush *Juncus squarrosus*–Broom Fork-moss *Dicranum scoparium* sub-community
M17	Northern Deergrass *Scirpus cespitosus* (now *Trichophorum cespitosum*) [but since this species has now been split, the definition should be to deergrass sp. *Trichophorum* sp.]–Hare's-tail Cottongrass *Eriophorum vaginatum* blanket mire
M21	Bog Asphodel *Narthecium ossifragum*–Papillose Bog-moss *Sphagnum papillosum* valley mire
M26	Purple Moor-grass *Molinia caerulea*–Marsh Hawk's-beard *Crepis paludosa* mire
M32	Fountain Apple-moss *Philonotis fontana*–Starry Saxifrage *Saxifraga stellaris* spring
M37	Curled Hook-moss *Palustriella commutata*–Red Fescue *Festuca rubra* spring
M38	Curled Hook-moss *Palustriella commutata*–Common Sedge *Carex nigra* spring
Heaths	
H10b	Heather *Calluna vulgaris*–Bell Heather *Erica cinerea* heath, Woolly Fringe-moss *Racomitrium lanuginosum* sub-community
Mesotrophic grasslands	
MG3	Sweet Vernal-grass *Anthoxanthum odoratum*–Wood Crane's-bill *Geranium sylvaticum* grassland (with Common Bent *Agrostris capillaris* and Smooth Lady's-mantle *Alchemilla glabra*) [associated with well-drained permanent pastures and meadows. Localized community of northern England.]

Code	Constant (and associated) species
MG3b	Sweet Vernal-grass *Anthoxanthum odoratum*–Wood Crane's-bill *Geranium sylvaticum* grassland, Quaking-grass *Briza media* sub-community [associated with well-drained permanent pastures and meadows. Localized community of northern England.]
MG6a	Perennial Rye-grass *Lolium perenne*–Crested Dog's-tail *Cynosurus cristatus* grassland, typical sub-community
MG6b	Perennial Rye-grass *Lolium perenne*–Crested Dog's-tail *Cynosurus cristatus* grassland, Sweet Vernal-grass *Anthoxanthum odoratum* sub-community
MG8	Crested Dog's-tail *Cynosurus cristatus*–Marsh-marigold *Caltha palustris* grassland
Calcicolous grasslands	
CG8	Blue Moor-grass *Sesleria caerulea*–Small Scabious *Scabiosa columbaria* grassland
CG9	Blue Moor-grass *Sesleria caerulea*–Limestone Bedstraw *Galium sterneri* grassland
CG9a	Blue Moor-grass *Sesleria caerulea*–Limestone Bedstraw *Galium sterneri* grassland, Hoary Rock-rose *Helianthemum oelandicum*–Squinancywort *Asperula cynanchica* sub-community
CG9b	Blue Moor-grass *Sesleria caerulea*–Limestone Bedstraw *Galium sterneri* grassland, typical sub-community
CG9c	Blue Moor-grass *Sesleria caerulea*–Limestone Bedstraw *Galium sterneri* grassland, Flea Sedge *Carex pulicaris*–Carnation Sedge *C. panicea* sub-community
CG9d	Blue Moor-grass *Sesleria caerulea*–Limestone Bedstraw *Galium sterneri* grassland, Hair Sedge *Carex capillaris*–False Sedge *Carex simpliciuscula* sub-community (includes Heather *Calluna vulgaris* and Cranberry *Vaccinium oxycoccos*)
CG9e	Blue Moor-grass *Sesleria caerulea*–Limestone Bedstraw *Galium sterneri* grassland, Mossy Saxifrage *Saxifraga hypnoides*–Pyrenean Scurvygrass *Cochlearia pyrenaica* sub-community [ssp. *pyrenaica* is usually found on more basic soils than is ssp. *alpina*]
CG10	Sheep's-fescue *Festuca ovina*–Common Bent *Agrostis capillaris*–Wild Thyme *Thymus drucei* grassland
CG10c	Sheep's-fescue *Festuca ovina*–Common Bent *Agrostis capillaris*–Wild Thyme *Thymus drucei* grassland, Yellow Saxifrage *Saxifraga aizoides*–Bendy Ditrichum *Ditrichum flexicaule* sub-community
Calcifugous grassland and montane communities	
U4	Sheep's-fescue *Festuca ovina*–Common Bent *Agrostris capillaris*–Heath Bedstraw *Galium saxatile* grassland
U4a	Sheep's-fescue *Festuca ovina*–Common Bent *Agrostris capillaris*–Heath Bedstraw *Galium saxatile* grassland, typical sub-community
U4b	Sheep's-fescue *Festuca ovina*–Common Bent *Agrostris capillaris*–Heath Bedstraw *Galium saxatile* grassland, Yorkshire-fog *Holcus lanatus*–White Clover *Trifolium repens* sub-community (species-rich variant, including Lady's Bedstraw *Galium verum*, Harebell *Campanula rotundifolia* and Bitter-vetch *Lathyrus linifolius*)
U6	Heath Rush *Juncus squarrosus*–Sheep's-fescue *Festuca ovina* grassland
U10	Stiff Sedge *Carex bigelowii*–Woolly Fringe-moss *Racomitrium lanuginosum* moss-heath
U17	Great Wood-rush *Luzula sylvatica*–Water Avens *Geum rivale* tall-herb community
U21	Parsley Fern *Cryptogramma crispa*–Wavy Hair-grass *Deschampsia flexuosa* community
Swamps and tall-herb fens	
S27	Bottle Sedge *Carex rostrata*–Marsh Cinquefoil *Commarum palustre* tall-herb fen
Vegetation of open habitats	
OV37	Sheep's-fescue *Festuca ovina*–Spring Sandwort *Sabulina verna* community
OV40	Green Spleenwort *Asplenium viride*–Brittle Bladder-fern *Cystopteris fragilis* community

If Blue Moor-grass is omitted, this grassland community is widespread on calcareous soils in many northern districts. In Teesdale, some of the plant communities on the sugar-limestone (CG9) are difficult to classify, therefore some of the assigned sub-communities should be regarded as approximations.

Other familiar species are:

Ribwort Plantain	Limestone Bedstraw
Mouse-eared Hawkweed	Glaucous Sedge
Devil's-bit Scabious	Spring-sedge
Common Rock-rose	Heath-grass
Autumn Gentian	

The most constant mosses are Cypress-leaved Plait-moss, Comb-moss, Woolly Fringe-moss and Bendy Ditrichum.

On the sugar-limestone there are additional species of more or less local distribution. Some are widespread northern plants: Alpine Bistort, Mountain Everlasting, Alpine Cinquefoil, Hoary Whitlowgrass and Lesser Clubmoss. Of the true mountain plants, Hair Sedge occurs also in the Highlands where False Sedge has a few localities. Bird's-eye Primrose, Spring Sandwort and an endemic dandelion *Taraxacum pseudonordstedtii* are found in northern England; Teesdale Violet and Dwarf Milkwort are extreme rarities in the north of England and Spring Gentian is virtually confined to Upper Teesdale (CG9d). Two distinctive species at their extreme northern locations are the Rare Spring-sedge and the very rare Horseshoe Vetch; Small Scabious is also present (CG9a).

A few other species are Dark-red Helleborine, a subspecies of Kidney Vetch (ssp. *lapponica*) and Sea Plantain. Among the notable mosses Frizzled Crisp-moss var. *curta* is constant, but Wrinkle-leaved Feather-moss is very local. A number of 'meadow' species occur: Globeflower,

Calcareous grassland *MR*.

Goldenrod, Common Twayblade and, in vegetative form Great Burnet, Saw-wort and Lesser Meadow-rue, suggesting a herb-rich meadow-type ancestry (MG3), but without Wood Crane's-bill which characterizes this community elsewhere.

Many of these plants are inconspicuous and no one patch of grassland contains them all. On the summit, outcrops of sugar-limestone on Cronkley Fell, the turf contains two dwarf shrubs – prostrate patches of Mountain Avens and Hoary Rock-rose – as well as Common Rock-rose, Wild Thyme, Small Scabious, Dark-red Helleborine and Crowberry, ordinarily a plant of acidic soils.

Local damper patches within the Blue Moor-grass–Sheep's-fescue turf can be recognized by the increase of False Sedge and Bird's-eye Primrose and patches of Tawny Sedge now more obvious as a result of overgrazing by Rabbits. This dry sward is in some respects intermediate between the southern lowland and northern montane calcareous grasslands, but with a distinct northern bias. Some species are absent or rare in Scotland – Spring Gentian, Spring Sandwort, False Sedge, Rare Spring-sedge, Bird's-eye Primrose, Teesdale Violet and Dwarf Milkwort (CG9d). Although Spring Gentian, Mountain Avens and Blue Moor-grass grow together in western Ireland, the composition of that sward is not the same. No calcareous grassland elsewhere has quite the same combination of plants as found on Cronkley and Widdybank Fells.

Grassland on the unaltered limestone may contain several of these rare species, but with increasing distance from the sugar-limestone more of the distinctive species are absent. At higher altitudes (700–750 m) several 'Teesdale' species reappear: Alpine Forget-me-not, Spring Gentian, Spring Sandwort, Hoary Whitlowgrass, Alpine Bistort, Northern Bedstraw, Pyrenean Scurvygrass, Mountain Everlasting, Mossy Saxifrage, Mountain Pansy and Moonwort (CG9e).

TOP: Calcareous grassland (CG10); BOTTOM: Calcareous grassland species *both MR*.

Limestone heath

Where the sugar-limestone soil is mixed with a proportion of glacial drift and forms a brown calcareous soil, the Blue Moor-grass–Sheep's-fescue community has a sparse cover of short Heather and Crowberry. Amongst this many of the sugar-limestone plants, including Spring Gentian, Northern Bedstraw, Alpine Bistort, Mountain Everlasting, Alpine Meadow-rue, Harebell and the woodland relic Wood Anemone are frequent. A few flowers of Creeping Willow have been found, but no Wood Crane's-bill. This is a very rare type of vegetation that is only known from a few other places in northern England and Scotland.

Wet calcareous communities

A short sedge-marsh has developed where the sugar-limestone meets the blanket bog over the impervious Whin Sill rock and the mixture of granular sugar-limestone and redistributed peat is frequently flooded with calcareous water. In a ground layer of mosses and liverworts are False, Tawny, Carnation, Flea and Common Sedges and Long-stalked Yellow-sedge. Sheep's-fescue is also present, but generally grasses are scarce. Here Alpine

Blue Moor-grass – Heather heath in foreground *MEB*.

Meadow-rue is sometimes abundant and Bird's-eye Primrose and Scottish Asphodel occur (M10a).

Mossy spring-heads and gravelly flushes

These occur where lime-rich water drains out of the sugar-limestone above impervious layers of baked mudstone or the Whin Sill and below limestone strata on other parts of the Fells. The spring-heads may have a domed head of Curled Hook-moss, Fountain Apple-moss and Thick-nerved Apple-moss with Pyrenean Scurvygrass, Cuckooflower, Opposite-leaved Golden-saxifrage and Starry Saxifrage (M38). The more open gravelly areas are characterized by tight, dark green, cushions of two rare mosses, Hook-beaked Tufa-moss and the darker Golf-club Moss amongst a sparse cover of the other marsh mosses. In both habitats the mosses become encrusted with lime, precipitated out of the calcareous water and form the porous, fragile tufa rock that is easily broken by trampling (M10c).

These mini-hummocks are eventually colonized by many of the rare species: False Sedge, Bird's-eye Primrose, Hair Sedge, Alpine Meadow-rue, Scottish Asphodel and Spring and Teesdale Sandworts. Other species, usually in the open wet areas are: Yellow Saxifrage, Alpine Rush, Three-flowered Rush and Variegated Horsetail. Other more widespread flush and marsh plants include: Dioecious Sedge, Long-stalked Yellow-sedge, Carnation Sedge, Few-flowered Spike-rush, Common Butterwort, Knotted Pearlwort, Alpine Rush, Jointed Rush, Sea Plantain and very

Short sedge-marsh (M10a) *DM*.

Turfy calcareous, gravelly flush *GH*.

Hook-beaked Tufa-moss cushions (M10c) *JO'R*.

Spring head mound (potential tufa mound) *MEB*.

Centre of tufa mound with Alpine Bartsia *MR*.

Former tufa mound completely destroyed by trampling 2013 *MEB*.

occasionally Thrift (M10c and M37). These communities/sub-communities are found mainly on the upper parts of Widdybank and Cronkley Fells, and occasionally at higher levels. Less species-rich forms are also found in Cronkley Pasture below springs and in flushes.

Turfy marshes

On the dip slope of Widdybank Pasture, and to a lesser extent across the Tees in Cronkley Pasture, where the lime-rich glacial drift is deeper and has been formed into a series of drumlins and lateral moraines, combinations of very similar dwarf sedge communities are found on the wetter ground. These are subject to the grazing and trampling of cattle, as well as sheep. Poaching by the cattle has broken up the even 'swards', disturbing the drainage and, in places, creating vegetated mini-hummocks in a matrix of mud and gravel – the turfy marshes of Pigott (1956). The relatively dry tops support Blue Moor-grass, Spring Gentian, Hair and Glaucous Sedges, and are the particular habitat of the rare Alpine Bartsia. The wet ground carries an abundance of marsh sedges and rushes together with locally abundant Bird's-eye Primrose, Marsh Valerian, Grass-of-Parnassus, Frog Orchid, Marsh Fragrant-orchid, Early and Northern Marsh-orchids, Common Twayblade, Broad-leaved Cottongrass, Flat-sedge, Marsh Arrow-grass, Yellow Saxifrage, False Sedge, Scottish Asphodel, Alpine Rush, Marsh Horsetail and dispersed plants of Purple Moor-grass. Locally, where the grazing and poaching are absent, there is a damp Purple Moor-grass community with Globeflower and Wood Crane's-bill and Sneezewort. Communities of similar species occur on the moist, unstable, clayey sides below the spring-line of some moraines, and there is a fine example by the Tees where the river constantly erodes the base. More grass-dominated and slightly less species-rich communities are found in the upper part of the valley, on drift banks with solifluction terraces enhanced by trampling. Here may be Spring Gentian, Bird's-eye Primrose, Blue Moor-grass and Lesser Clubmoss (M10).

Also, at these lower levels are/were a few fine hook-moss spp.–apple-moss spp.-dominated tufa mounds over spring-heads. Too often, trampling has caused leaking from the sides and the lessening of the central artesian effect that enabled the deposition of tufa, with the consequential drying and invasion by herbaceous species such as Creeping Bent, Common Cottongrass, Selfheal and tall rushes *e.g.* Soft-rush, *etc.*

Meadows

In the first half of the 20th century the meadows in the valley bottom and up the south face of Teesdale and Harwood Dale, on the better brown earth and brown podsolic soils, consisted of a large number of higher plants. At the time, at almost 600 m, Grass Hill was the highest farm in England. In summer, this richness and colour, and their nutrient level was being maintained by light dressings of farmyard manure (FYM) and occasional applications of lime or basic slag. Unfortunately, only a few of these traditional upland hay meadows, with their spectacular botanical display, have survived the advent of selective weed-killers and the widespread applications of artificial Nitrogen–Phosphorus–Potassium (NPK) manures, the unavailability of basic slag, and reduced applications of lime. This century, following an awareness of the great decline of these species-rich meadows, much research, time and effort has been put into attempting to recreate the original flora, but it is essential to also restore the original quality of the soil. Does a diet of mixed herbs produce healthier livestock? If so, and there is evidence that it does, there would be an incentive to the farmers to value such pretty, but lower-yielding, meadows.

The flora of the original meadows showed a close similarity to that of the remaining upland deciduous woodlands, from which it is believed they were derived. Seasonal grazing favoured an increase in the grasses, and over time an equilibrium of broad-leaved species, grasses and sedges was reached, with none particularly dominant.

The usual grasses include: Sweet Vernal-grass, Red Fescue, Yorkshire-fog, Cock's-foot, Quaking-grass, Smooth and Rough Meadow-grasses, Crested Dog's-tail and some Perennial Rye-grass and Tufted

Wet Marsh-marigold meadow (MG8), Forest-in-Teesdale *DM*.

Hair-grass. The most conspicuous herbs are, or were, Globeflower, Wood Crane's-bill, and the occasional Melancholy Thistle, Meadowsweet, Great Burnet, dandelions, Pignut, Rough Hawkbit, Cat's-ear, Meadow and Bulbous Buttercups, Yellow-rattle, Oxeye Daisy, Heath Spotted-orchid, Heath Fragrant-orchid and Common Twayblade, the two common Lady's-mantles (Pale and Smooth) and Common Sorrel, producing a yellow–white–red/brown visual effect, instead of the yellow–white–mauve of earlier times. Other species include: Red and Zigzag Clover, Selfheal, Mountain Pansy, Lady's Bedstraw, Harebell and occasionally Field Gentian. Where the soil becomes leached the variety is much reduced and Wavy Hair-grass and even Mat-grass are found (MG3b). In damper areas Meadowsweet is more abundant, with Marsh Hawk's-beard, Ragged-Robin, Heath Spotted-orchid and Northern Marsh-orchid, Sneezewort, Marsh Valerian, Marsh Lousewort, Wild Angelica and more sedges and rushes: Carnation and Common Sedge, Common Cottongrass, Soft-rush, Sharp-flowered and Jointed Rushes. These meadows may only be mown in the drier years. The only rare species in the meadows include some eyebrights, occasional Northern Hawk's-beard and five species of lady's-mantle: Large-toothed, Velvet (Teesdale only), Starry (also in Weardale), Clustered and Rock – both rare in northern England (MG8).

Today, the finest meadow-type community lies between the south bank of the River Tees and the fenced-off meadows and pastures down the river below High Force. The Whin Sill and limestone rocks are exposed as small cliffs or flat slabs, or covered with alluvial soils to various depths, so a mosaic of basic and acidic substrates exists. When the river is high, the lower areas, even as far as the public footpath, are awash and flooded with debris. Scattered trees and bushes occur: the northern form of Downy Birch (ssp. *tortuosa*), Bird Cherry, Goat, Grey, Tea-leaved, Creeping and Eared Willows, Alder, Hazel, occasional Rock Whitebeam trees, Common Juniper and Stone Bramble. Under these, and in the wider open areas, are all the meadow species listed above, except for Velvet and Large-toothed Lady's-mantles, augmented with more frequent Globeflowers, Betony, Saw-wort, Common Knapweed, Field Scabious, Goldenrod, Northern Bedstraw, Wood and Field Horsetails, Burnet-saxifrage, Devil's-bit Scabious, Meadow and Downy Oat-grasses, Tall Fescue, Blue Moor-grass, Viviparous Sheep's-fescue, and several sedges: Glaucous and Flea Sedges, and Long-stalked Yellow-sedge. Rooted in the Whin Sill crevices are Common Rock-rose, Shrubby Cinquefoil, Mountain Everlasting, Goldenrod, Limestone Bedstraw, Lesser Clubmoss, Bird's-eye Primrose, Grass-of-Parnassus, Variegated Horsetail, Flat-sedge and Jointed Rush. The presence of Heather, Bell Heather, Mat-grass, Bilberry and Wood Sage indicate local, more acidic conditions (MG3b).

Woodland and scrub

Upper Teesdale, between Middleton and High Force, gives the impression of being wooded – apart from the conifer plantations and small deciduous woods, the roads, river and streams are lined with trees and shrubs and isolated trees dot the field boundaries. Above 300 m, just west of High Force, the wide valley floor is virtually bare of trees accentuating the 'wild' and barren appearance of this upland area.

Mixed deciduous woodland dominated by Ash and Wych Elm, with some Sessile Oak, once widespread in the area, is restricted to remnants as in Baldersdale and Brockers Gill. Most of the remaining woodland is of the northern form of the Downy Birch found above and below High Force and along some tributaries – Ettersgill and Mill Beck. Birch woodland on base-rich soils, which are often wet, may have Ash, Bird Cherry, Hazel, Alder and willows; the ground flora is varied and contains many tall herbs including: Meadowsweet, Common Valerian, Marsh Thistle, Ragged-Robin, Water Avens, Marsh-marigold, Wild Angelica and Globeflower, Wood

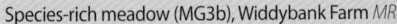

Tees bank species-rich meadow (MG4) *DM*.

Species-rich meadow (MG3b), Widdybank Farm *MR*.

Common Juniper with Wood-sorrel (W19) *DM*.

Crane's-bill and Melancholy Thistle; ferns and mosses are not prominent. More localised and rare species include Giant Bellflower, Northern Hawk's-beard, Herb-Paris, Mountain and Wood Melick grasses and Shady Horsetail (W9).

On acid soils over the Whin Sill the flora is poorer, composed of Bluebell, Wood-sorrel, Common Dog-violet, Creeping Bent, Creeping Soft-grass and the ferns: Broad Buckler-fern, Lemon-scented, Beech and Oak Ferns, Hard-fern and Bracken under Bird Cherry, Goat Willow and Hazel.

The most extensive wooded area is often of impenetrable stands of quite large junipers on the north-facing slopes west of Holwick and on and below Dine Holm Scar, on Whin Sill near Cronkley Farm (where the effects of one-time grazing by goats can be seen outside an existing exclosure fence) and scattered on other Scars and higher slopes, as on Cronkley Fell. Spreading and columnar junipers, with occasional Yews, shelter a sparse woodland flora with several ferns (including: Oak and Beech Ferns, Hard-fern and Bracken) and Wood-sorrel, but do not form a distinctive flora (W19). It is expected that formerly Common Juniper would have been the shrub layer in taller deciduous woodland. Evidence from 376 charcoal pits linked to iron-smelting hearths found between Holwick and Cronkley Scar suggest there must have been extensive medieval woodland in a large area that is now predominantly moorland or Common Juniper scrub. Three-quarters of the wood was birch, with smaller

Ash–Rowan–Dog's Mercury Woodland (W9) *DM*.

fractions of Alder, Hazel, cherry species, rose family (Rowan and Whitebeam) and willow or poplar unevenly distributed. If present, other trees such as oak, elm and Ash may have been reserved for other uses, significantly no Common Juniper or Yew was found – but this may be because conifers do not make good charcoal or had other uses, or were perhaps sacred. As this area was grazed by the commoners' cattle, regeneration by deciduous trees may have been prevented whilst the existing junipers increased in density.

Tees margins

The vegetation close to the river margins does not form a unique community, but in Teesdale it is characterized by shrubs of the Shrubby Cinquefoil from Falcon Clints to below Middleton. This deep-rooted plant can withstand submergence and the destructive force of the Tees in spate.

Shrubby Cinquefoil, which is submerged when the Tees is in flood (as below) *MR*.

Tees in spate submerging the Shrubby Cinquefoil shown in the image above *MR*.

Cliffs, screes, benches and the fell-top plateaux

The major cliffs in Teesdale are the impressive Whin Sill scars of Holwick Scar, Dine Holm Scar, Cronkley Scar, Raven Scar and Falcon Clints. At their bases are block and talus screes. The soils are mostly acidic and very free-draining (although the rocks are base-rich, but lacking calcium) and locally have lime-rich waters percolating from above. On these are, locally, impressive stands of Bell Heather, Bearberry and Parsley Fern with Heather, Bilberry and Crowberry. Where inaccessible ledges and block screes give protection from grazing are Great Wood-rush, native Rosebay Willowherb, Goldenrod, Holly-fern and others. Many ferns grow in the block and finer scree, the locally frequent Parsley Fern, and the widespread species: Broad Buckler-fern, Hard-fern, Male-fern, Golden-scaled and Mountain Male-ferns, and Fir Clubmoss. This community (U21) with Parsley Fern is a pioneer community, dependant on the accretion of fractured rock from above and a degree of grazing to maintain the unstable habitat. It is nationally rare, particularly so on the east side of the Pennines. A few trees survive on the cliffs, most notably Common Whitebeam, Yew, Aspen, Bird Cherry, Hawthorn and Common Juniper. Plants, grown from spores of Holly-fern and the long-extinct Oblong Woodsia, have been successfully reintroduced into the area of their original sites by the former English Nature (EN) and the Royal Botanic Garden, Edinburgh (RBGE).

Whin Sill block scree, Falcon Clints *GY*.

Talus and block scree below Holwick Scar *MR*.

In Teesdale there are no thick strata of limestone and sandstone as in the central and south Pennines. On the north side of Upper Teesdale the edge of the Great Limestone is prominent at High Hurth Edge, but other cliffs are small. Here are the calcicoles: Common Rock-rose, Wild Thyme, Blue Moor-grass, Hoary Whitlowgrass, Burnet-saxifrage, Rock Lady's-mantle, Meadow Saxifrage, Salad Burnet, Small Scabious and annuals such as Rue-leaved Saxifrage, Wall Speedwell and, on the talus, Spring Gentian. Benches of unaltered limestone, as at Cow Green and on the higher slopes south of Cronkley Fell, that have long been grazed by sheep and latterly by Rabbits, support a short bent–fescue turf of various degrees of species-richness, dominated by Sheep's-fescue and Common Bent. Other frequent species include: Sweet Vernal-grass, Crested Dog's-tail, Quaking-grass, Heath Bedstraw, Tormentil, White Clover, Yarrow, Smooth, Pale and Hairy Lady's-mantles, Spring-sedge, Ribwort Plantain, Field Wood-rush, Meadow Buttercup, Common Sorrel, Mountain Pansy, and Common Dog-violet and some of the following 'Teesdale' specials: Blue Moor-grass, Spring Gentian, Alpine Bistort, Northern and Limestone Bedstraws, Mountain Everlasting, Lesser Clubmoss and Hair Sedge (CG10/CG9b).

No deep limestone pavement, similar to that found in Yorkshire, exists today, although the irregular 'water-worn' slabs that cap some stone walls, as at Langdon Beck and in Middleton, suggest that it once did. The existing 'pavement' is shallow, with wide 'grykes' that allow grazing by Rabbits, if not sheep. The closest to the 'gryke' woodland-type community is to be found in some of the larger and deeper shake-holes/swallow-holes/mini-pot-holes. In these shaded, dank holes are woodland plants: Wood-sorrel, Wall Lettuce, Wild Angelica, Herb-Robert, Mossy Saxifrage, Opposite-leaved Golden-saxifrage and ferns, including Hart's-tongue and occasionally the rare Holly-fern. It was in such a hole with Common Nettle that Jacob's-ladder was first recorded.

At high levels (700–750 m) the close-grazed, species-rich limestone grassland on the talus may include: Alpine Forget-me-not, Spring Gentian, Spring Sandwort, Mossy Saxifrage, Pyrenean Scurvygrass, Mountain Everlasting, Hoary Whitlowgrass, Alpine Bistort, Northern Bedstraw, Mountain Pansy and, frequently, Moonwort. On ledges just over the watershed are Roseroot, Alpine Cinquefoil and the very scarce Alpine Cat's-tail (CG9e).

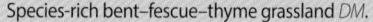

Species-rich bent–fescue–thyme grassland *DM*.

Fescue–bent–Heath Bedstraw (U4a) *DM*.

Cross Fell summit with (INSET) Woolly Fringe-moss and Stiff Sedge (U10) *both FJR*.

On the broad summit plateau of Cross Fell at 850–900 m, the soil hummocks amongst the stone polygons and stripes support Woolly Fringe-moss and lichens of the reindeer-moss type, including *Cladonia rangiferina*, whilst between these are fescues and bents, with Wavy Hair-grass and Stiff Sedge (U10).

Alpine Foxtail flush, Great Dun Fell *FJR*.

Vegetation below the summit plateaux and above the blanket bog

Above the blanket bog is a mosaic of plant communities on the leached and acidified soils where the influence of limestone has been lost or overridden, or over sandstone or shale. Fescue – bent – Heath Bedstraw (U4) grassland with Wavy Hair-grass occupies the steeper slopes, Mat-grass (U5) the moister, slightly gleyed podsols and Heath Rush swards (U6) the deeper, wetter gleys. Bracken is scarce and Alpine Lady's-mantle is absent (except where introduced in the NNR). So far, no rarities have been found in these communities. However, since the grazing pressure of sheep was reduced following the outbreak of Foot-and-mouth Disease in 2001, many species have grown to identifiable size. In the more base-rich fescue – bent grassland some herb-rich meadow plants have been found: Clustered Lady's-mantle, Globeflower, Water Avens, Pignut, Heath Spotted-orchid and, in short turf, Mountain Pansy, Wild Thyme, Spring Sandwort and Moonwort. The flushes, usually culminating in streams, often somewhat base-rich or mildly acidic, have added new northern species (Marsh Saxifrage, Water and Sheathed Sedges) to the known Alpine Foxtail, Three-flowered Rush, Dioecious Sedge, Marsh-marigold, Lesser Spearwort, Cuckooflower, Smooth Lady's-mantle, Common Cottongrass and Tufted Hair-grass.

Blanket bog

Extensive blanket bogs cover the gentle slopes of the Tees catchment, between approximately 460 m and 615 m, mostly co-dominated by Heather and Hare's-tail Cottongrass with varying amounts of bog mosses. Common Cottongrass is abundant, especially on bare and redistributed peat, and other typical species are Cross-leaved Heath, deergrass sp., Cowberry, Crowberry, Bog Asphodel and Round-leaved Sundew. Living Dwarf Birch was rediscovered in this community in 1965, previously also known in the Pennines as a sub-fossil in peat.

Very few areas of actively growing wet bog remain in the area due to burning and gripping (draining), but those that do remain have a high cover of bog-mosses – Papillose, Magellanic, Red and Feathery Bog-mosses, occasional hummocks of Austin's and Rusty Bog-mosses, and the locally rare Bog-sedge.

Heather–Hare's tail Cottongrass blanket bog (M19) *JO'R*.

Papillose Bog-moss and Magellanic Bog-moss, as found on Muckle Moss *JO'R*.

M2 Bog grading to M18a, Muckle Moss *JO'R*.

Eroding blanket bog, cages over original and transplanted Dwarf Birch *JO'R*.

Spring Sandwort, Cronkley Fell *GH*.

Heavy metal mine spoil

Upper Teesdale, situated in the North Pennine Orefield, was an important industrial area in the 18th and 19th centuries; relics of the lead-mining era are scattered over much of the uplands as 'hushes', open veins and spoil-heaps. These are sparsely colonized by several species of the unaltered limestone grassland that have evolved to tolerate the toxicity of the heavy metals that include lead, barium and zinc: Sheep's-fescue, Crested Hair-grass, Blue Moor-grass, Wild Thyme, Harebell, Common Dog-violet, Common Bird's-foot-trefoil, White Clover, Fairy Flax, Autumn Gentian, Mountain Pansy, Moonwort and, locally, Hair Sedge. Three northern species, characteristic of such habitats are: Alpine Penny-cress, Spring Sandwort, Pyrenean Scurvygrass and very occasionally Thrift (OV37).

Sheep's-fescue–Spring Sandwort Calaminarian vegetation (OV37), Widdybank Fell *MR*.

Geographical elements in the Teesdale Assemblage

Within Europe there are three main climatic factors that determine plant distribution – namely summer warmth, winter cold and summer drought. Preston and Hill built on work done by both H.C. Watson and J.R. Matthews to draw up a new classification of the distribution of British plants which was published in 1997. The paper's Appendix lists the species in each Floristic Element, as well as including an alphabetical list of UK plants. Species are classified by two criteria: occurrence in one or more of the four major terrestrial biomes, *i.e.* the Major Biome Category captured in the first number for Arctic-montane, Boreal-montane, Temperate or Southern; and then a criterion for the Eastern Limit Category represented by the second numeral, as included in the Key:

Key

Oceanic	Suboceanic	European	Eurosiberian	Eurasian	Circumpolar
Confined to Western Europe (Norway, W Denmark, Low Countries, Britain, Ireland, W France and the Atlantic fringe of Spain and Portugal).	Confined to Western and Central Europe (occurring west of a line from the Baltic to the Adriatic).	Widespread in Europe but with an eastern limit west of 60° E.	Widespread in Europe and western Asia, with an eastern limit between 60° E and 120° E.	Widespread in Europe and Asia, with an eastern limit east of 120°E.	Present in Europe, widespread in Asia and also present in North America.

1 ARCTIC-MONTANE

North of the tree line or (on mountains) above the tree-line, or both.

13 European

Alpine Bartsia *Bartsia alpina (p. 166)*
Dwarf Birch *Betula nana (p. 123)*
Chickweed Willowherb *Epilobium alsinifolium (p. 133)*
Spring Gentian *Gentiana verna (p. 156)*
Yellow Saxifrage *Saxifraga aizoides (p. 94)*

16 Circumpolar

Alpine Foxtail *Alopecurus magellanicus (p. 211)*
False Sedge *Carex simpliciuscula (p. 206)*
Alpine Clubmoss *Diphasiastrum alpinum (p. 70)*
Mountain Avens *Dryas octopetala (p. 104)*
Alpine Willowherb *Epilobium anagallidifolium (p. 132)*
Three-flowered Rush *Juncus triglumis (p. 185)*
Stag's-horn Clubmoss *Lycopodium clavatum (p. 72)*
Alpine Forget-me-not *Myosotis alpestris (p. 159)*
Alpine Meadow-grass *Poa alpina (p. 213)*
Teesdale Sandwort *Sabulina stricta (p. 145)*
Alpine Saxifrage *Micranthes nivalis (p. 96)*
Roseroot *Rhodiola rosea (p. 97)*
Alpine Meadow-rue *Thalictrum alpinum (p. 90)*
Scottish Asphodel *Tofieldia pusilla (p. 177)*

– CIRCUMPOLAR ARCTIC-ALPINE

Not in Preston and Hill (1997)

Northern Deergrass
Trichophorum cespitosum (p. 188)
'Hybrid' Deergrass *Trichophorum × foersteri (p. 190)*

2 BOREO-ARCTIC MONTANE

In both the Arctic and Boreal-montane zones.

23 European

Clustered Lady's-mantle *Alchemilla glomerulans (p. 118)*
Hoary Whitlowgrass *Draba incana (p. 138)*
Hairy Stonecrop *Sedum villosum (p. 98)*

24 Eurosiberian

Alpine Cinquefoil *Potentilla crantzii (p. 108)*

26 Circumpolar

Alpine Foxtail *Alopecurus magellanicus (p. 211)*
Dwarf Birch *Betula nana (p. 123)*
Alpine Bistort *Bistorta vivipara (p. 143)*
Water Sedge *Carex aquatilis (p. 204)*
Hair Sedge *Carex capillaris (p. 196)*
Sheathed Sedge *Carex vaginata (p. 198)*
Variegated Horsetail *Equisetum variegatum (p. 74)*
Fir Clubmoss *Huperzia selago (p. 68)*
Marsh Saxifrage *Saxifraga hirculus (p. 93)*
Oblong Woodsia *Woodsia ilvensis (p. 80)*

3 WIDE-BOREAL

In Arctic-montane, Boreal-montane and Temperate zones.

34 Eurosiberian

Sea Plantain *Plantago maritima (p. 160)*

36 Circumpolar

Thrift *Armeria maritima (p. 80)*

4 BOREAL-MONTANE

In the coniferous forest zone, either in the Boreal zonobiome or on mountains farther south, or both.

41 Oceanic

Pale Forget-me-not *Myosotis stolonifera* (p. 158)

42 Suboceanic

Mountain Male-fern *Dryopteris oreades* (p. 82)
Rock Whitebeam *Sorbus rupicola* (p. 106)

43 European

Rock Lady's-mantle *Alchemilla wichurae* (p. 120)
Parsley Fern *Cryptogramma crispa* (p. 76)
Small Cow-wheat *Melampyrum sylvaticum* (p. 129)
Alpine Penny-cress *Noccaea caerulescens* (p. 136)
Small-white Orchid *Pseudorchis albida* (p. 181)
Aspen *Populus tremula* (p. 128)
Globeflower *Trollius europaeus* (p. 88)

44 Eurosiberian

Wood Crane's-bill *Geranium sylvaticum* (p. 129)

45 Eurasian

Bird's-eye Primrose *Primula farinosa* (p. 149)
Teesdale Sandwort *Sabulina stricta* (p. 145)
Spring Sandwort *Sabulina verna* (p. 146)

46 Circumpolar

Bearberry *Arctostaphylos uva-ursi* (p. 151)
Rustyback *Asplenium ceterach* (p. 79)
Slender Sedge *Carex lasiocarpa* (p. 194)
Tall Bog-sedge *Carex magellanica* (p. 203)
Shrubby Cinquefoil *Dasiphora fruticosa* (p. 110)
Northern Buckler-fern *Dryopteris expansa* (p. 83)
Shady Horsetail *Equisetum pratense* (p. 73)
Bog Orchid *Hammarbya paludosa* (p. 180)
Alpine Rush *Juncus alpinoarticulatus* (p. 183)
Holly-fern *Polystichum lonchitis* (p. 81)

5 BOREO-TEMPERATE

In both Boreal-montane and Temperate zones.

53 European

Starry Lady's-mantle *Alchemilla acutiloba* (p. 113)
Shining Lady's-mantle *Alchemilla micans* (p. 121)
Velvet Lady's-mantle *Alchemilla monticola* (p. 116)
Large-toothed L'.-mantle *Alchemilla subcrenata* (p. 117)
Mountain Everlasting *Antennaria dioica* (p. 173)
Lily-of-the-valley *Convallaria majalis* (p. 182)
Few-flowered Spike-rush *Eleocharis quinqueflora* (p. 192)
Broad-leaved Cottongrass *Eriophorum latifolium* (p. 186)
Montane Eyebright
　Euphrasia officinalis ssp. *monticola* (p. 163)
Field Gentian *Gentianella campestris* (p. 154)
Dwarf Milkwort *Polygala amarella* (p. 103)
Yellow-rattle *Rhinanthus minor* ssp. *minor* (p. 167)
Blue Moor-grass *Sesleria caerulea* (p. 210)

54 Eurosiberian

Rare Spring-sedge *Carex ericetorum* (p. 200)
Dark-red Helleborine *Epipactis atrorubens* (p. 178)
Jacob's-ladder *Polemonium caeruleum* (p. 147)
Alpine Meadow-rue *Thalictrum alpinum* (p. 90)

55 Eurasian

Mountain Everlasting *Antennaria dioica* (p. 173)

56 Circumpolar

Rosebay Willowherb
　Chamaenerion angustifolium (p. 130)
Northern Bedstraw *Galium boreale* (p. 152)
Common Juniper *Juniperus communis* (p. 85)

6 WIDE-TEMPERATE

In Boreal-montane, Temperate and Southern-temperate zones.

7 TEMPERATE

In the cool-temperate, broad-leaved deciduous forest zone.

73 European

Flat-sedge *Blysmus compressus* (p. 193)
Northern Hawk's-beard *Crepis mollis* (p. 171)
Horseshoe Vetch *Hippocrepis comosa* (p. 101)
Downy Currant *Ribes spicatum* (p. 92)
Small Scabious *Scabiosa columbaria* (p. 175)

75 Eurasian

Orpine *Hylotelephium telephium* (p. 100)
Small Scabious *Scabiosa columbaria* (p. 175)
Saw-wort *Serratula tinctoria* (p. 169)
Teesdale Violet *Viola rupestris* (p. 124)
'Hybrid' Violet (Teesdale Violet × Common Dog-violet) *Viola × burnatii* (p. 126)

8 SOUTHERN

In the warm-temperate zone south of the broad-leaved deciduous forest zone, which in Europe is represented by the Mediterranean zone.

9 MEDITERRANEAN

92 Submediterranean-Subatlantic

Species with a broader distribution than those fairly strictly confined to the Mediterranean and Atlantic fringe of Europe; often extending into the south-western parts of Central Europe.

Rustyback *Asplenium ceterach* (p. 79)

93 Mediterranean-montane

Montane in the Southern biome but found in considerably warmer conditions than typical Boreal-montane fauna.

Hoary Rock-rose
　Helianthemum oelandicum ssp. *levigatum* (p. 79)

International Union of Nature Conservation (IUCN) Red List (see *p. 218*)

Under the IUCN Red List criteria, each species is assigned to one of the following categories based on an assessment of threats, reflecting the likely degree of extinction risk:

CR Critically Endangered   **VU** Vulnerable   **LC** Least Concern
EN Endangered   **NT** Near Threatened

Plants that are extant in other parts of Great Britain and Ireland but are extinct in England are categorized as **RE** Regionally Extinct; plants for which there is inadequate information to make an assessment of its risk of extinction based on its distribution and/or population status are categorized as **DD** Data Deficient; the species coded **WL** Waiting List is under consideration.

The categories **CR**, **EN** and **VU** indicate an appreciable risk of extinction in the near future, and are collectively described as 'Threatened': **CR** indicates the highest level of extinction risk in the wild, and **EN** and **VU** indicate progressively lower levels of risk. **Near Threatened** (**NT**) indicates that the species is close to qualifying as **Threatened**, or is likely to qualify as such in the near future.

IUCN Red List categorization and flowering periods of Teesdale's special flora

The table below lists all the species of the Teesdale Assemblage (in alphabetical order of scientific name). For each species, the IUCN Red List category is shown (following *A Vascular Plant Red List for England* (Stroh, 2014)) and a summary is provided of their flowering period (dark green cells indicate the main flowering period (or in the case of ferns and their relatives the 'spore-producing' period, and in the case of Viviparous Sheep's-fescue when plantlets are produced); pale green cells indicate months during which flowers may persist). Species of Principal Importance in England under the Natural Environment and Rural Communities (NERC) Act (2006) (see *page 216*) are highlighted in pink.

Cat.	Common name	Scientific name	Page	J	F	M	A	M	J	J	A	S	O	N	D
VU	Starry Lady's-mantle	*Alchemilla acutiloba*	113						▓	▓	▓				
LC	Clustered Lady's-mantle	*Alchemilla glomerulans*	118						▓	▓	▓				
VU	Shining Lady's-mantle	*Alchemilla micans*	121						▓	▓	▓				
EN	Velvet Lady's-mantle	*Alchemilla monticola*	116						▓	▓	▓				
EN	Large-toothed Lady's-mantle	*Alchemilla subcrenata*	117						▓	▓	▓				
LC	Lady's-mantle agg.	*Alchemilla vulgaris* agg.	112						▓	▓	▓				
VU	Rock Lady's-mantle	*Alchemilla wichurae*	120						▓	▓	▓				
NT	Alpine Foxtail	*Alopecurus magellanicus*	211						▓	▓					
VU	Mountain Everlasting	*Antennaria dioica*	173						▓	▓					
NT	Bearberry	*Arctostaphylos uva-ursi*	151				▓	▓	▓						
LC	Thrift	*Armeria maritima*	141				▓	▓	▓	▓	▓				
LC	Rustyback	*Asplenium ceterach*	79				▓	▓	▓	▓	▓	▓	▓		
LC	Green Spleenwort	*Asplenium viride*	78						▓	▓	▓	▓			
VU	Alpine Bartsia	*Bartsia alpina*	166						▓	▓					
CR	Dwarf Birch	*Betula nana*	123					▓							
LC	Alpine Bistort	*Bistorta vivipara*	143						▓	▓	▓				

	Common name	Scientific name	Page	J	F	M	A	M	J	J	A	S	O	N	D
VU	Flat-sedge	*Blysmus compressus*	193						█						
LC	Water Sedge	*Carex aquatilis*	204						█						
LC	Hair Sedge	*Carex capillaris*	196						█	█					
VU	Rare Spring-sedge	*Carex ericetorum*	200						█						
VU	Slender Sedge	*Carex lasiocarpa*	194						█						
EN	Bog Sedge	*Carex limosa*	202						█						
NT	Tall Bog-sedge	*Carex magellanica*	203						█	█					
LC	False Sedge	*Carex simpliciuscula*	206						█						
LC	Sheathed Sedge	*Carex vaginata*	198						█						
LC	Rosebay Willowherb	*Chamaenerion angustifolium*	130							█	█				
LC	Pyrenean Scurvygrass	*Cochlearia pyrenaica*	140						█						
LC	Lily-of-the-valley	*Convallaria majalis*	182					█	█						
VU	Northern Hawk's-beard	*Crepis mollis*	171						█	█					
VU	Parsley Fern	*Cryptogramma crispa*	76							█	█				
NT	Shrubby Cinquefoil	*Dasiphora fruticosa*	110						█	█					
LC	Alpine Clubmoss	*Diphasiastrum alpinum*	70							█	█				
LC	Hoary Whitlowgrass	*Draba incana*	138						█	█					
VU	Mountain Avens	*Dryas octopetala*	104						█	█					
LC	Northern Buckler-fern	*Dryopteris expansa*	83							█	█				
LC	Mountain Male-fern	*Dryopteris oreades*	82							█	█				
LC	Few-flowered Spike-rush	*Eleocharis quinqueflora*	192						█	█					
LC	Chickweed Willowherb	*Epilobium alsinifolium*	133							█					
VU	Alpine Willowherb	*Epilobium anagallidifolium*	132							█					
LC	Dark-red Helleborine	*Epipactis atrorubens*	178							█					
NT	Shady Horsetail	*Equisetum pratense*	73				█								
LC	Variegated Horsetail	*Equisetum variegatum*	74						█	█					
LC	Broad-leaved Cottongrass	*Eriophorum latifolium*	186					█	█						
DD	Montane Eyebright	*Euphrasia officinalis* ssp. *monticola*	163							█	█				
LC	Viviparous Sheep's-fescue	*Festuca vivipara*	209						█	█					
LC	Northern Bedstraw	*Galium boreale*	152						█	█					
VU	Spring Gentian	*Gentiana verna*	156					█	█						
NT	Field Gentian	*Gentianella campestris*	154							█	█	█			
NT	Wood Crane's-bill	*Geranium sylvaticum*	129						█	█					
VU	Bog Orchid	*Hammarbya paludosa*	180							█	█				
LC	Hoary Rock-rose	*Helianthemum oelandicum* ssp. *levigatum*	134						█	█					
LC	Horseshoe Vetch	*Hippocrepis comosa*	101						█						
LC	Fir Clubmoss	*Huperzia selago*	68							█	█				
LC	Orpine	*Hylotelephium telephium*	100							█	█				

	Common name	Scientific name	Page	J	F	M	A	M	J	J	A	S	O	N	D
LC	Alpine Rush	*Juncus alpinoarticulatus*	183							■	■				
LC	Three-flowered Rush	*Juncus triglumis*	185						■	■					
LC	Common Juniper	*Juniperus communis*	85					■							
VU	Stag's-horn Clubmoss	*Lycopodium clavatum*	72							■	■				
RE	Small Cow-wheat	*Melampyrum sylvaticum*	162						■	■	■				
VU	Alpine Forget-me-not	*Myosotis alpestris*	159						■	■	■				
LC	Pale Forget-me-not	*Myosotis stolonifera*	158						■	■	■				
LC	Alpine Penny-cress	*Noccaea caerulescens*	136				■	■	■						
LC	Sea Plantain	*Plantago maritima*	160						■	■	■				
VU	Alpine Meadow-grass	*Poa alpina*	213						■	■	■				
LC	Jacob's-ladder	*Polemonium caeruleum*	147						■	■					
EN	Dwarf Milkwort	*Polygala amarella*	103						■	■					
EN	Holly-fern	*Polystichum lonchitis*	81							■	■	■			
LC	Aspen	*Populus tremula*	128		■	■									
LC	Alpine Cinquefoil	*Potentilla crantzii*	108						■	■					
NT	Bird's-eye Primrose	*Primula farinosa*	149						■						
VU	Small-white Orchid	*Pseudorchis albida*	181						■	■					
WL	Yellow-rattle	*Rhinanthus minor* ssp. *minor*	167					■	■	■	■				
LC	Roseroot	*Rhodiola rosea*	97					■	■	■					
LC	Downy Currant	*Ribes spicatum*	92				■	■							
EN	Teesdale Sandwort	*Sabulina stricta*	145					■	■						
LC	Spring Sandwort	*Sabulina verna*	146					■	■	■	■				
LC	Yellow Saxifrage	*Saxifraga aizoides*	94							■	■	■			
LC	Marsh Saxifrage	*Saxifraga hirculus*	93								■	■			
CR	Alpine Saxifrage	*Micranthes nivalis*	96						■	■					
LC	Small Scabious	*Scabiosa columbaria*	175							■	■				
VU	Hairy Stonecrop	*Sedum villosum*	98						■	■					
LC	Saw-wort	*Serratula tinctoria*	169							■	■	■			
LC	Blue Moor-grass	*Sesleria caerulea*	210				■	■							
LC	Rock Whitebeam	*Sorbus rupicola*	106					■	■						
LC	Teesdale Dandelion	*Taraxacum pseudonordstedtii*	170					■	■						
LC	Alpine Meadow-rue	*Thalictrum alpinum*	90						■	■					
LC	Scottish Asphodel	*Tofieldia pusilla*	177						■	■	■				
DD	Northern Deergrass	*Trichophorum cespitosum*	188					■	■						
	'Hybrid' Deergrass	*Trichophorum* ×*foersteri*	190					■	■						
LC	Globeflower	*Trollius europaeus*	88						■	■					
	'Hybrid' Violet (Teesdale Violet × **Common Dog-violet**) *Viola* ×*burnatii*		126				■	■							
LC	Teesdale Violet	*Viola rupestris*	124				■	■							
CR	Oblong Woodsia	*Woodsia ilvensis*	80							■	■				

Flowering/spore-producing period

A guide to the species accounts

Conservation status (see *below*)

Names follow Stace, C. 2019. *New Flora of the British Isles* (Fourth Edition)

Legal protection (see *below*)

NB English names are used throughout the text and a list of the English and *scientific* names of all species mentioned in the book is on *page 278*.

English name
Schedule 8

Scientific name Naming authority

FIRST RECORD IN TEESDALE

Notes on the first reference to include the species.

General introduction and broad description of the plant.

Distribution: Summary of distribution of the plant in Great Britain and Ireland, with supplementary information covering the areas of Teesdale in which recorded.

ALTITUDE

The altitudinal range (metres above sea level) within which the plant can be found in Teesdale.

Habitat: Information on the plant's favoured habitat within the Teesdale area, including NVC community codes. See *page 43* for an explanation of these codes.

LIFE-CYCLE

Growth type; flowering and fruiting periods; seed and reproduction/germination details (where relevant).

Status and conservation: Overview of the recent and present status of the plant in Teesdale and of the conservation measures in place, plus, where appropriate, suggestions for future measures that may be beneficial.

Further information: Link(s) to relevant resources (some hyperlinks use former scientific names).

The plates
Photographs show the plant in its context with close-ups where appropriate. All are credited with the photographer's initials – see *page 283* for full details of contributors.

Legal protection (see *page 216*)
Species afforded legal protection are indicated as follows:

Schedule 8 – Protected under Schedule 8 of the Wildlife and Countryside Act (1981)

NERC – Species of Principal Importance, included in Section 41 of the Natural Environment and Rural Communities Act (2006)

Conservation status
(see *pages 64 and 218*)
The status box indicates the conservation (or Red List) status of the species in England from *A Vascular Plant Red List for England* (Stroh, 2014).

RE Regionally Extinct	DD Data Deficient
CR Critically Endangered	WL Waiting List
EN Endangered	
VU Vulnerable	
NT Near Threatened	
LC Least Concern	

Order of species The plant profiles are presented in the same order as in Stace (2019), although in a few cases species within a genus have been reordered to allow for better comparison of species.

LC Fir Clubmoss
Huperzia selago L.

FIRST RECORD IN TEESDALE
1794, Robson

ALTITUDE
450–675 m

LIFE-CYCLE
Perennial; SPORES are produced June–August; also reproduces vegetatively by gemmae.

Shoots usually in erect, light green clusters. Unlike most other clubmosses, the fertile sporangia of Fir Clubmoss are not clustered into cones but borne in leaf axils within the fertile zones that alternate with sterile zones up the stem. It also reproduces vegetatively from bud-like gemmae that are shed from the axils of the leaves. In some years after reproducing, whole clumps of shoots die off, before being replaced by new plants growing from the gemmae.

Distribution: Widespread, mainly upland and western, but from sea-level to 1,310 m; lost from many lowland sites. In Teesdale it is quite frequent in block scree at Falcon Clints, Cronkley, Dine Holm and Holwick Scars, Long Crag and Dodgen Pot; rare and sparse on wet rock, for example at Red Sike, Widdybank Fell and in old quarries; also rare in the drier blanket bogs. In the 19th century it was additionally recorded as frequent in the hills around Mickle Fell.

Fir Clubmoss: **1** growing at Walltown Crags *DM*; **2** with gemmae *MEB*.

Habitat: In block scree Fir Clubmoss is associated with several ferns (Parsley Fern – very local on the east side of the Pennines, Hard-fern and several species of male-fern, Herb-Robert, Wood-sorrel, Rosebay Willowherb and Woolly Fringe-moss. Also on drier blanket bogs/heaths of H10b Heather–Bell Heather sub-community with Crowberry, Bell Heather, Mat-grass and Hare's-tail Cottongrass. Very occasionally found as small, possibly relatively young plants, developed from gemmae, in gravelly flushes within moist/wet base-rich habitats such as the short sedge-marsh of the M10b Dioecious Sedge–Common Butterwort sub-community and on more or less bare rock flushed with drainage from the metamorphosed limestone over the Whin Sill rocks on Widdybank Fell, including the M10c Hook-beaked Tufa-moss sub-community with Spring Sandwort, Knotted Pearlwort and Sea Plantain.

Status and conservation: Although largely stable, it has been lost from former sites in the drier blanket bogs; the recent blocking of drains and rewetting may result in increases. Needs to be monitored for conservation purposes.

Further information: https://www.brc.ac.uk/plantatlas/plant/huperzia-selago
Merryweather, J. 2020. *Britain's Ferns.* Princeton WILD*Guides*

LC Alpine Clubmoss
Diphasiastrum alpinum L.

FIRST RECORD IN TEESDALE
1794, Robson

ALTITUDE
490–720 m

LIFE-CYCLE
Perennial; vegetative propagation is much more frequent than sexual reproduction.

Clubmosses are spore-bearing plants that separated from ferns and seed-bearing plants more than 360 million years ago. Alpine Clubmoss usually has a prostrate growth form, its shoots branched regularly into two, sometimes forming a fan shape. The stems are four-sided, with leaves folded longitudinally. Small yellow-green cones are formed on upright stems, but only immature cones have been seen in Teesdale.

Distribution: Alpine Clubmoss is found in the mountains and uplands from Wales, Derbyshire and the Lake District to central and north-west Scotland, although rather infrequent, and decreasing, in the northern Pennines and Southern Uplands. In Teesdale it is rare and sparse, found on Widdybank Fell, in the vicinity of Moor House (Nether Hearth and Dodgen Pot), Harthope Ganister quarry (with Stag's-horn and Fir Clubmosses), and a railway cutting near Barnard Castle. In the 19th century it was reported as frequent on the hills rising to the peak of Mickle Fell and abundant on Cronkley Fell: it has not been seen recently in these locations.

Habitat: Found mostly on shallow soil on lead-mining waste (and sometimes sandstone quarry waste) in the OV37 Sheep's-fescue–Spring Sandwort community. On Widdybank Fell small groups of shoots occur in the species-rich CG9d Blue Moor-grass–Limestone Bedstraw grassland community over sugar-limestone, with slightly larger groups in the CG10 Sheep's-fescue–Common Bent–Wild Thyme community on unaltered limestone. Associated plants include Mountain Pansy, Harebell, Glaucous Sedge, Wild Thyme, Spring Sandwort, Lesser Clubmoss and several lichens.

Status and conservation: On Widdybank Fell it is very scarce and thinly scattered in apparently ungrazed grassland; individual plants have been recorded as surviving here for more than 50 years. Plants from Helvellyn were introduced into exclosures in high-altitude grassland on Knock and Little Dun Fells and Hard Hill in the Moor House NNR in the mid-1950s, but did not survive, probably in part due to the dense growth of other species in the absence of grazing.

The small colonies must continue to be monitored, especially in view of the dangers of undergrazing now that Rabbit numbers have been reduced. Searches for the known 1970s sites in the Blue Moor-grass community on Widdybank Fell should be undertaken, along with searches of its former sites around Cronkley Fell and Mickle Fell.

Further information: https://www.brc.ac.uk/plantatlas/plant/diphasiastrum-alpinum
Merryweather, J. 2020. *Britain's Ferns*. Princeton WILD*Guides*

Alpine Clubmoss: **1**, **2** growing at Widdybank Fell *both MEB*.

VU Stag's-horn Clubmoss
Lycopodium clavatum L.

FIRST RECORD IN TEESDALE
1794, Robson

ALTITUDE
446–615 m

LIFE-CYCLE
Perennial, spreading by rooting shoots; SPORES produced June–August.

Often inconspicuous beneath stands of Heather, the stems of Stag's-horn Clubmoss are densely packed with hair-tipped, narrow leaves, and creep along the ground, rooting at intervals. Pairs of yellow-green fruiting cones terminate erect stems and produce bright yellow spores when mature. Plants on Widdybank Fell produce cones in some years, but no ripe spores have been seen. Bears a resemblance to Little Shaggy-moss, a turf-moss sometimes found in similar locations.

Distribution: Generally widespread on heaths, moors and mountains, although it was lost from many lowland locations during the 20th century. In Teesdale it is now unrecorded from the higher areas, despite being reported as frequent on Mickle Fell during the 19th century. Elsewhere it is rare and sparse: less frequent than Fir Clubmoss in block scree at Falcon Clints, Dufton Moss and High Force Quarries, the banks of upland streams on Widdybank Fell and quarry and mining spoil on Harthope Summit.

Habitat: Amongst Whin Sill boulder scree and in the drier M19 Heather–Hare's-tail Cottongrass community with Mat-grass, Crowberry, Common Deergrass, Red Fescue, Brown Bent and some mosses, especially *Hypnum* (plait-mosses), *Rhytidiadelphus* (turf-mosses) and *Polytrichum* (haircaps).

Status and conservation: The long, spreading and prostrate shoots are easily pulled out by sheep, although not eaten. It has been lost from some sites, probably due to burning, from which it should be protected. Since 2022, burning has been almost completely replaced by mowing on Widdybank Fell.

Further information: https://www.brc.ac.uk/plantatlas/plant/lycopodium-clavatum
Merryweather, J. 2020. *Britain's Ferns*. Princeton WILD*Guides*

Stag's-horn Clubmoss: **1**, **2** growing at Widdybank Fell *both MEB*.

JT Shady Horsetail
Equisetum pratense Ehrh.

FIRST RECORD IN TEESDALE
1844, J. Backhouse Jr

ALTITUDE
280–416 m

LIFE–CYCLE
Perennial, spreading vegetatively by rhizomes and producing SPORES in April.

A delicate horsetail with sterile stems up to 50 cm tall, Shady Horsetail spreads by rhizomes and can form dense patches. Its stem sheaths are toothed, with the same number of teeth as deep grooves down the rough main stem. Its stems generally have whorls of drooping branches, and fertile stems with cones seem to be rather rare. Wood Horsetail is quite similar but is an even more delicate plant, its branches always themselves forked and even more drooping, and the sheath teeth united into broad lobes.

Distribution: Found mainly in central Scotland, with scattered occurrences to the north and south, in north-west Ireland, and in England in the North Pennines and one site in Northumberland. In Teesdale, on the south bank of the Tees from Wynch Bridge to Holwick Head Bridge, by Harwood Beck from Haugh Hill to Saur Bridge, Marshes Gill and below the bridge at Langdon Beck.

Habitat: By the Tees and Harwood Beck, and occasionally in meadows, Shady Horsetail is found in the MG3 Sweet Vernal-grass–Wood Crane's-bill community with Wood, Field and Marsh Horsetails, Northern Bedstraw, Blue Moor-grass, Flat-sedge, Wood Crane's-bill, Globeflower, Grass-of-Parnassus, Silver Birch, Bird Cherry, Devil's-bit Scabious, Great Burnet and Water Avens.

Status and conservation: Although it has increased in density on the Tees bank since the 1950s, the population is generally considered to be stable. Monitoring of all locations should be continued, including between Wynch and Holwick Head Bridges, last counted in 2011.

Further information: https://bsbi.org/wp-content/uploads/dlm_uploads/Equisetum_pratense_species_account.pdf
Merryweather, J. 2020. *Britain's Ferns*. Princeton WILD*Guides*

Shady Horsetail, growing at Holwick *MEB*.

LC Variegated Horsetail
Equisetum variegatum Schleich, E.B.

FIRST RECORD IN TEESDALE
1829, Trevelyan

ALTITUDE
280–680 m

LIFE-CYCLE
Winter-green, long-lived **perennial**, with SPORES produced July–August.

An evergreen, more or less prostrate plant of both open and closed, unshaded communities, Variegated Horsetail usually grows where flushed with calcareous water, although it can be found on apparently 'dry' sugar-limestone, probably moist at depth. Its brittle stems are usually less than 20 cm long with rough angles and often branched at the base; the stem sheaths have a black band at the base and broad, white-edged teeth. Spore-bearing cones are bluntly pointed, but not numerous. It could be mistaken for a small Marsh Horsetail, although that species has unbranched, smooth, usually upright stems.

Distribution: Although scattered around the coast on sand dunes and similar habitats, as an inland plant it is found mainly in calcareous areas in the North Pennines, central Highlands and north-west Scotland. In Teesdale it occurs on Cronkley and Widdybank Fells, Widdybank Pasture and associated sikes by the Tees, below Falcon Clints and Cronkley Bridge. It is very rare at higher levels, on High Cup Nick Plain and Great Dun Fell. It used to grow by the Tees below High Force to Wynch Bridge, but it has not been seen there in recent years since the habitat has become closed.

Habitat: Variegated Horsetail occurs in a wide range of communities on the metamorphosed limestone on Widdybank and Cronkley Fells in both open and closed vegetation of the CG9d Blue Moor-grass–Limestone Bedstraw grassland sub-community with Sheep's-fescue, Crested Hair-grass, Quaking-grass, Wild Thyme, Harebell, Hoary Rock-rose, Alpine Meadow-rue, Spring Gentian, Northern Bedstraw, Hair Sedge, False Sedge, and Lesser Clubmoss. It is also found in limestone grass heath over metamorphosed limestone (again CG9d) with Heather, Red Fescue, Crowberry, Spring Gentian, Alpine Bistort, Northern Bedstraw, Harebell, Alpine Meadow-rue and Wood Anemone, and in the gravelly flushes of the M10 Dioecious Sedge–Common Butterwort community with Sheep's-fescue, False Sedge, Bird's-eye Primrose, Common Butterwort, Scottish Asphodel, Dioecious, Glaucous, Tawny and Flea Sedges and Three-flowered Rush. On these same fells and in Widdybank Pasture and Cetry Bank it is also known from the M11 Common Yellow-sedge–Yellow Saxifrage mire and in more or less closed species-rich vegetation on the flood-plains and banks of some sikes in the CG9d Hair Sedge–False Sedge sub-community. By the Tees it was found in gravel on Whin Sill at one site above Wynch Bridge in 2003.

Status and conservation: Although frequent on the sugar-limestone and calcareous flushes on both Widdybank and Cronkley Fells, its occurrence in Cronkley Pasture has been more sporadic. In Widdybank Pasture there was a considerable reduction between the surveys of 1976 and 2000, possibly due to the destruction of the structure of the gravelly flushes by cattle poaching. On Cetry Bank an observed increase between 1977 and 2012 may have been an artefact of different recorders. Below Holwick Head Bridge only a small number of plants were recorded on rocks at the water's edge in 2011, the previously larger population having been shaded out by taller vegetation that developed after grazing was removed and the river flow regulated. At higher levels, on High Cup Nick Plain (592 m), 30 shoots were found in 2009, and it has also been recorded from flushes at 680 m on Great Dun Fell, albeit not recently.

Monitoring is desirable in the locations where this species has seemingly declined (Cronkley and Widdybank Pastures and the Tees bank below High Force) due to changes in the type, and reduction in intensity, of cattle grazing. However, the exclusion of cattle from the unstable Cetry Bank should be continued.

Further information: https://www.brc.ac.uk/plantatlas/plant/equisetum-variegatum
Merryweather, J. 2020. *Britain's Ferns*. Princeton WILD*Guides*

Variegated Horsetail: 1 vegetative shoots; **2** immature strobili *both DM*.

VU Parsley Fern
Cryptogramma crispa (L.) R.Br. ex Hook

FIRST RECORD IN TEESDALE
1796, Oliver and Harriman

ALTITUDE
300–446 m

LIFE-CYCLE
Perennial, sometimes partially evergreen; SPORES produced July–August.

Forming dense tufts, especially on open screes, the outer, sterile fronds of Parsley Fern are deeply divided into flat lobes, bearing a resemblance to flat-leaved Parsley. Rising from the centre of the tufts are longer, fertile, spore-bearing fronds that are even more divided into linear segments with rolled margins under which the spores are produced.

Distribution: Occurs in the Welsh mountains and from the Lake District northwards through much of Scotland in the right habitat. In Teesdale it is rare, albeit locally frequent, on well-drained, base-poor rocks and scree, at Holwick, Dine Holm and Cronkley Scars, and Falcon Clints on Whin Sill, and on sandstone scree farther west.

Habitat: It occurs on screes (which may be grassed over), clefts and ledges mainly of Whin Sill and sandstone, in the nationally rare U21 Parsley Fern–Wavy Hair-grass community. This appears to be a pioneer community that may be superseded by the U4 Sheep's-fescue–Common Bent–Heath Bedstraw community. The soil tends towards acidic; associated species include Heather, Bell Heather, Bilberry and Cowberry, Great Wood-rush, Broad Buckler-fern, Hard-fern and various forms of male-fern, Fir Clubmoss and sometimes Woolly Hair-moss.

Status and conservation: Locally frequent, especially on Whin Sill scree, but not widespread. Open scree must be maintained free of shade in order to maintain the scree and scarce plant community U21 and its component species.

Further information: https://www.brc.ac.uk/plantatlas/plant/cryptogramma-crispa
Merryweather, J. 2020. *Britain's Ferns*. Princeton WILD*Guides*

Parsley Fern: **1** growing at Holwick Scar *MR*; **2** vegetative and fertile fronds, growing in Cumbria *SH*.

Parsley Fern, growing at Holwick Scar *MR*.

LC Green Spleenwort
Asplenium viride Huds.

FIRST RECORD IN TEESDALE
1794, Robson

ALTITUDE
up to 523 m

LIFE-CYCLE
Perennial; SPORES produced June–September.

Easily distinguished from similar small, tufted wall ferns by the green midrib of its frond, Green Spleenwort is found on calcareous substrates and old metal mine workings throughout the uplands of Britain and, to a lesser extent, Ireland. It requires cool, humid conditions in summer.

Distribution: Rather local in western and northern Britain, as far south as South Wales and Derbyshire. In Scotland it is found in the Southern Uplands and more frequently north of the Caledonian Canal. In Teesdale it is not rare in suitable habitats, mainly on limestone and dolerite rocks.

Habitat: On the faces and in crevices of limestone rocks, including the cracks of metamorphosed limestone such as on a north face on Cronkley Fell, and sometimes on lime mortar in walls. It grows with Wall-rue, Brittle Bladder-fern and Maidenhair Spleenwort to form the OV40 Green Spleenwort–Brittle Bladder-fern community.

Status and conservation: Not rare in suitable habitats, on limestone and dolerite and lime mortar in Upper Teesdale, and no special conservation action is necessary.

Further information: https://www.brc.ac.uk/plantatlas/plant/asplenium-viride
Merryweather, J. 2020. *Britain's Ferns*. Princeton WILD*Guides*

Green Spleenwort: **1** growing at Cronkley Fell *MEB*; **2** showing green rachis *FJR*.

Ⓒ Rustyback
Asplenium ceterach L.

Typical of lowland rocks and walls in western regions, Rustyback is a small fern with rather leathery, pinnate fronds. The underside of the frond is densely clothed in scales, at first white and then turning reddish-brown as the spores are released, hence its name. As a calcicole, it favours limestone rocks and the mortar of old walls where it can withstand considerable desiccation, appearing almost wholly shrivelled in dry conditions.

FIRST RECORD IN TEESDALE
1843, Spruce

ALTITUDE
300–470 m

LIFE-CYCLE
Perennial; SPORES produced April–October, germinate in spring.

Distribution: Common throughout Ireland, Wales and the western half of England, just extending north to south-west Scotland. Very rare on the east side of the Pennines in the upper Tees catchment. In Teesdale recorded only from Harwood-in-Teesdale, a roadside wall near High Force, and a wall in Arn Gill. It has now been lost from at least the first two of these localities.

Habitat: Crevices in limestone rocks, dry-stone walls and mortared walls.

Status and conservation: Now no known locations, having been destroyed by road alterations.

Further information: https://www.brc.ac.uk/plantatlas/plant/ceterach-officinarum
Merryweather, J. 2020. *Britain's Ferns*. Princeton WILD*Guides*

Rustyback: **1** growing near High Force Hotel *MEB*; **2** underside of frond showing brown scales *DM*.

CR Oblong Woodsia
Woodsia ilvensis (L.) R. Br.

Schedule 8   NERC

FIRST RECORD IN TEESDALE
1821, J. Backhouse Sr.

ALTITUDE
about 430 m

LIFE-CYCLE
Perennial, dying back in winter; reproduces by SPORES in summer.

A very rare and delicate fern, much reduced in the 19th century by 'pteridomaniacs', Oblong Woodsia was first found in Teesdale in 1821 at the Cauldron Snout end of Falcon Clints, from which site it was last recorded in 1950. It is a small, tufted fern, its pinnate fronds densely clothed beneath with long, pale-brown scales and wavy hairs, resembling an immature male-fern (*p. 82*).

Distribution: Extremely rare, occurring only in North Wales, the Lake District, Dumfries, the Central Highlands of Scotland and formerly in Teesdale. Here it was known from Falcon Clints and Cronkley Scar.

Habitat: Rock ledges and boulder scree.

Status and conservation: Following its apparent extinction in 1950, a reintroduction was attempted in the vicinity of its former sites in 1999 and 2000 by Royal Botanic Gardens, Edinburgh, who have found it easy to propagate from spores in cultivation. Ten years later only a quarter of the original plants introduced onto Falcon Clints survived, although a second establishment site across the river still held three-quarters of its plants after a decade. Plants at both sites have produced fertile fronds, but no young plants have ever been located. Continued monitoring is crucial, as is research to establish the cause of its failure to reproduce.

Further information: https://www.brc.ac.uk/plantatlas/plant/woodsia-ilvensis
Merryweather, J. 2020. *Britain's Ferns*. Princeton WILD*Guides*

Oblong Woodsia, reintroduced plant growing at Falcon Clints *FJR*.

Holly-fern

Polystichum lonchitis (L.) Roth

NERC

FIRST RECORD IN TEESDALE
1798, Oliver

ALTITUDE
430–750 m

LIFE-CYCLE
Long-lived **Perennial**; SPORES produced July–August.

As a favourite target for the fern-collecting mania of the 19th century, Holly-fern numbers in Teesdale and elsewhere were reduced substantially at that time. It is a long-lived species which increases only very slowly, but its fronds, with uniquely spine-tipped pinnae, are rather leathery and can persist for a considerable time.

Distribution: Occurs on base-rich rocks in the uplands of Snowdonia, northern England, Moffat Hills, Central Highlands and north-west Scotland, with a scatter of records on the western seaboard of Ireland. In Teesdale it is extremely rare, with just one plant on Cronkley Fell, two (plus introduced plants) on Falcon Clints, and similarly small numbers in some sink-holes in the limestone at higher altitudes in the Moor House NNR, Knock Fell and Meldon Hill.

Habitat: Found on limestone rock ledges, scree and in sink-holes, sometimes with other ferns, *e.g.* Brittle Bladder-fern.

Status and conservation: The tiny native population has been supplemented with plants grown from spores (origin unknown) and planted in crevices on Falcon Clints in the area of the two original plants. Also introduced to Rough Sike, Moor House in 1956 and still present in the exclosure until at least 2012. Monitoring should continue at all known sites.

Further information: https://www.brc.ac.uk/plantatlas/plant/polystichum-lonchitis
Merryweather, J. 2020. *Britain's Ferns*. Princeton WILD*Guides*

Holly-fern, growing at Cronkley Fell *JO'R*.

LC Mountain Male-fern
Dryopteris oreades Fomin

FIRST RECORD IN TEESDALE
1868, Baker & Tate

ALTITUDE
250–450 m

LIFE-CYCLE
Perennial, deciduous; SPORES produced July–September.

A fern that grows most luxuriantly on ledges and screes that are inaccessible to grazing animals, Mountain Male-fern is also believed to be frost-sensitive, perhaps surprising given that it can be found in our area up to 450 m altitude, and perhaps even higher close by in the upper parts of Moor House NNR. It is very similar to other male-ferns and indeed grows with Golden-scaled Male-fern and Male-fern; Mountain Male-fern tends to have concave, not flat, pinnae and in autumn the fronds turn a characteristic russet-brown before they are shed.

Distribution: Found in mountains from Wales, through the Lake District and North Pennines and into much of central and west Scotland. In Teesdale it occurs frequently on scree at Falcon Clints and Cronkley, Dine Holm and Holwick Scars, as well as on quarry faces and stone walls, and in a wood near High Force waterfall.

Habitat: Found mainly on Whin Sill rocks, in boulder scree and rock faces; occasionally under trees such as in High Force Gorge, where plants can be very large.

Status and conservation: Several thousand plants are known in Teesdale; given the species' susceptibility to frost and grazing, monitoring should be continued.

Further information: https://www.brc.ac.uk/plantatlas/plant/dryopteris-oreades
Merryweather, J. 2020. *Britain's Ferns*. Princeton WILD*Guides*

Mountain Male-fern, growing at Holwick Road *MR*.

C Northern Buckler-fern
Dryopteris expansa (C. Presl) Fraser-Jenkins & Jermy

FIRST RECORD IN TEESDALE
1860, Mitchinson

ALTITUDE
410–800 m

LIFE-CYCLE
Perennial: SPORES produced July–August; also spreads vegetatively by division of the rhizome.

A fern of open, wet woodland and around rock outcrops at low altitudes, and in damp, sheltered hollows of upland boulder scree, Northern Buckler-fern often grows (and hybridizes) with the very similar Broad Buckler-fern. The flat pinnules of Northern Buckler-fern contrast with those of Broad Buckler-fern which are slightly curled at the edge (giving a 'spikier' appearance); furthermore, the basal pinnule on the lowest pinna of Northern Buckler-fern is noticeably longer than the one adjacent, whereas on the commoner species they are more or less equal. The hybrid can be reliably confirmed only by microscopic examination of its abortive spores.

Northern Buckler-fern growing at Great Dun Fell *FJR*.

Northern Buckler-fern: 1 growing at Great Dun Fell *FJR*; **2** paler 'winged' spores (from Mickle Fell), compared with **3** darker spores of Broad Buckler-fern *both TLo.*

Distribution: Rare in Wales, the Lake District, the North Pennines and Southern Uplands; frequent farther north in Scotland. In Teesdale it is very rare, in the Falcon Clints area amongst Whin Sill boulders, on the south-east flank of Cross Fell and the north-east slope of Little Dun Fell.

Habitat: Found in open woodland and boulder fields, often in partial shade, with Lady-fern, Fir Clubmoss and Stag's-horn Clubmoss. The boulders give some protection from grazing and cast shade which favours shade-tolerant species such as ferns.

Status and conservation: The Falcon Clints site usually has 10–20 plants, with a slight increase in number in recent years; a smaller group of four or five plants lies about 100 metres to the west. There are also around 50 plants on Cross Fell and 10–15 on Little Dun Fell, but these are recent discoveries and thus no trends are yet discernible. Monitoring should be continued in all localities and further searches undertaken.

Further information: https://www.brc.ac.uk/plantatlas/plant/dryopteris-expansa
Merryweather, J. 2020. *Britain's Ferns*. Princeton WILD*Guides*.

Common Juniper

Juniperus communis L.

NERC

FIRST RECORD IN TEESDALE
1562, W. Turner

ALTITUDE
246–540 m

LIFE-CYCLE
Woody shrub; FLOWERS May–June; FRUITS ripen September–October, germinate in spring.

Common Juniper is not a Teesdale rarity, but it does have a continuous record in the dale from late-glacial times to the present day. However, its detailed history is far from clear. It is strange that Baker (1868) mentions it only near High Force in his descriptive account, with plant lists from the ridge of Mickle Fell via White Force, Cronkley Fell, Cronkley Scar and the Tees to High Force. Much earlier, no Common Juniper was found in the charcoal from the small medieval bloomery pits south of the river between High Force and White Force, but Alder, Hazel, birch, willows, poplars and woody Rosaceae, including Common Whitebeam, certainly were. It may be that the extensive, dense, almost single-species stand of Common Juniper developed since the 12th century following the removal of other trees, or, perhaps more likely, it was present but deliberately avoided by charcoal burners.

It is a woody, evergreen shrub or small tree which is very variable in growth form, some plants being columnar and at the other end of the scale others spreading widely but low to the ground.

Common Juniper showing two growth forms, opposite High Force *MEB*.

Common Juniper: **1** male cones *MR*; **2** female cones *MR*.

Male plants have cylindrical pollen-bearing cones about 6 mm long; those on female plants are a third of the size and then go on to produce berries which ripen after two or three years to a blue-black colour, and which when crushed give off the aroma used to scent gin. The berries are eaten and dispersed by birds.

Junipers are long-lived: the oldest in the main Teesdale population is believed to be 225 years old. They are thought to be descendants of the plants that covered Britain shortly after the end of the last glacial period, as evidenced by the continuous record of Common Juniper pollen in local deposits. Growth is very slow: on Cronkley Fell, seedlings from the late 1900s were only about 40 cm tall by 2012.

The only similar spiny shrub that could possibly be confused with Common Juniper is Gorse, when the latter is not in flower (which is rather infrequent). The spines of Gorse are pointed woody branches as opposed to the leaves of Common Juniper.

Distribution: Common Juniper is found on chalk in the south-east of England (but generally not regenerating), in north Wales, northern England through most of Scotland, and in western Ireland. In Teesdale the largest Common Juniper forest in England (approximately 100 hectares) occupies the south side of the Tees opposite High Force; occasional bushes grow by the river down to below Wynch Bridge and on a mid-stream island below Cauldron Snout. There are also dense stands by the Tees below Dine Holm Scar plus several near Falcon Clints and on Raven Scar; other habitats include metamorphosed limestone on Cronkley Fell and on a Whin Sill outcrop close to Black Ark, where there are a few plants.

Habitat: Especially on north-facing slopes with a variety of soils, Common Juniper trees dominate with a few specimens of Yew and Sycamore. This is the W19 Common Juniper–Wood-sorrel woodland community with Common Bent, Brown Bent, Sweet Vernal-grass, Red Fescue, Male-fern, Broad Buckler-fern, Oak Fern and occasional Beech and Lemon-scented Ferns. On Cronkley Fell, it grows on the sugar-limestone in the CG9d Hair Sedge–False Sedge sub-community of the CG9 Blue Moor-grass–Limestone Bedstraw grassland community, with Common and Hoary Rock-roses, Blue Moor-grass, Wild Thyme, Alpine Meadow-rue, Sheep's-fescue, Quaking-grass, Crested Hair-grass, and on Whin Sill rocks in the W19a Cowberry–Wavy Hair-grass sub-community of W19 Common Juniper–Wood-sorrel woodland with Heather, Bell Heather and Cross-leaved Heath.

Status and conservation: A high proportion of mature and older trees can be expected in a long-lived species such as Common Juniper, but in Teesdale there are few young plants, giving rise to concerns for the long-term health of the population. Since 1999, over 10,000 young trees grown from local seed or cuttings have been planted in the area, with a 60–70% survival rate; some of these are now bearing fruit.

Large parts of the main population are now fenced against sheep and several smaller areas have also been rabbit-proofed: Rabbits graze Common Juniper up to 60 cm from the ground, and sheep do so to a much greater height, as well as damaging the bark and small branches by rubbing. It is essential that the sheep and Rabbit fencing is maintained, and the population monitored for evidence of regeneration. However, such fencing is no defence against voles, which eat large quantities of seed and graze seedlings.

There is some evidence from the Lake District of the appearance of abundant seedlings following burning (unintentional or otherwise); it may therefore be prudent to consider a controlled burn of a small area within a stock/Rabbit-excluded area to see if this encourages the germination of new plants.

For some years the trees have been infected by fungi and many are slowly dying. More recently, in 2011, following an increase in die-back, a more virulent, often fatal, pathogen was discovered: *Phytophthora austrocedrae*, the spores of which can spread in wet soil and moving water. Evidence of infection is seen just under the bark in the lowermost parts of the stems. To contain the spread, all affected and adjacent trees are being cut out and burnt and sanitary procedures established. Alas, the fungus is still spreading and in 2018 the trees in approximately 20% of the area had to be destroyed. So far, there have been no outbreaks in the newly planted areas, but it would clearly be desirable to contain, and if possible eliminate, the pathogen.

Further information: http://sppaccounts.bsbi.org/content/juniperus-communis-1.html

LC Globeflower
Trollius europaeus L.

FIRST RECORD IN TEESDALE
1794, Oliver

ALTITUDE
260–520 m

LIFE-CYCLE
Perennial; FLOWERS June–August; SEED produced in July–August; germinates in spring, but over a period of years.

An erect, clump-forming herb with deeply palmate, 3–5 lobed, hairless leaves, Globeflower is very distinctive in summer (in the absence of grazing), with solitary, terminal, more or less globose yellow flowers, up to 3 cm in diameter. The colour is provided by approximately ten sepaloid petals, each strongly concave, incurved and overlapping. Within the flower, there are 5–15 nectaries (derived from the petals) which are also yellow and the same length as the stamens. In bloom, Globeflower is unmistakable but its leaves are somewhat similar to those of Wood Crane's-bill, with which it often grows. However, the leaves of the latter are more deeply divided, hairy rather than shiny, and have leaf-like stipules usually tinged pink at the base of the leaf-stalks.

Distribution: Widespread from south Wales, the Peak District and North York Moors northwards through Scotland, with an outlier in north-western Ireland, Globeflower is very much associated with our upland areas, although descending to sea level in the Inner Hebrides. In Teesdale it is found in herb-rich meadows and by the river and stream-sides, and occasionally on road verges. The leaves of small plants persist in limestone-grassland at 500 m on Widdybank Fell and about 700 m on Little Dun Fell, suggesting that both areas had some form of woodland in the past.

Globeflower: **1** growing in Harwood Meadow *MEB*; **2** flowers *DM*; **3** flower *MR*.

Habitat: Globeflower is characteristic especially of hay meadows and the tall-herb vegetation of stream-sides, damp roadside verges and moist open woodlands, generally on more or less neutral, loamy soils. Typically, it is found in the MG3 Sweet Vernal-grass–Wood Crane's-bill grassland community and the U4b Yorkshire-fog–White Clover species-rich sub-community of the U4 Sheep's-fescue–Common Bent–Heath Bedstraw grassland community; associated species include Lady's Bedstraw, Harebell, Bitter Vetch, Devil's-bit Scabious, Betony and Great Burnet. In the U17 Great Wood-rush–Water Avens tall-herb community and W9b Marsh Hawk's-beard sub-community of W9 Ash–Rowan–Dog's Mercury woodland it is found with Water Avens, Marsh Hawk's-beard, Tufted Hair-grass and Wood Crane's-bill.

An additional community in which it is found on Widdybank Fell is the CG9d Hair Sedge–False Sedge sub-community of the CG9 Blue Moor-grass–Limestone Bedstraw grassland community, with Wild Thyme, Common Rock-rose, Common Bird's-foot-trefoil, Sheep's-fescue, Quaking-grass, Glaucous Sedge, Rare Spring-sedge, occasional vegetative plants of Great Burnet, Lesser Meadow-rue and Water Avens and many rare Teesdale species.

Status and conservation: The distribution and quantity of Globeflower has reduced considerably in the last 50 years. The author undertook a re-survey in 2003–04 of 139 meadows in the Newbiggin/Holwick and Forest-in-Teesdale areas that were first surveyed in 1967: of the 62 meadows that held the species originally, only 52% still had it when re-surveyed (Bradshaw, 2009). Undoubtedly such declines are because of changes in farming practice: moving from hand-mown hay making to mechanization, the introduction of artificial fertilizers, and changing from loose hay to bales and then to large-bag silage and haylage. Management agreements and agri-environment schemes should seek to maintain the herb-rich meadows and banks containing Globeflower, and to encourage its spread by the application of green hay from species-rich fields into those that have become depauperate.

Unmown banks and awkward places have precious remnants of meadow vegetation that may have Globeflower and other rarities such as Clustered Lady's-mantle. It may be that the almost stalkless flower-buds are eaten in the now heavily winter- to spring-grazed meadows. The flower-buds are very nutritious, and although they contain the same toxic substance as buttercups, no cases of poisoning have been reported. Farmers should be encouraged to cut the vegetation in such places, rather than relying on grazing at times when the new season's growth is starting: a body such as Natural England could make such equipment available over the whole area. In the somewhat anomalous population on Widdybank Fell, while leaves have long been known as a feature, flowers have been seen only since the erection of an exclosure fence, which gives further justification to grazing limitation as a management technique.

Further information: https://bsbi.org/wp-content/uploads/dlm_uploads/Trollius_europaeus_species_account.pdf

LC Alpine Meadow-rue
Thalictrum alpinum L.

FIRST RECORD IN TEESDALE
Before 1795, Oliver

ALTITUDE
500–725 m

LIFE-CYCLE
Perennial, with stolons; FLOWERS June–July; FRUITS July–August.

With insubstantial, 'frothy' flower spikes, the smaller meadow-rue species are perhaps most noticeable by virtue of their leaves, each divided twice into three more or less equal portions. The ultimate leaflets are small, with usually three lobes and a wedge-shaped base. The small, well-spaced pale violet flowers lack petals, but have relatively conspicuous dangling yellow stamens. Alpine Meadow-rue has an unbranched flower spike, rarely more than 15 cm tall; the only confusion species could be a dwarfed Lesser Meadow-rue, a more widespread species that can grow in similar habitats, but is usually larger and has a branched inflorescence.

Being stoloniferous, it can form dense colonies in damp habitats especially. Plants rescued before Cow Green Reservoir was flooded were taken to Durham University, and soon filled their containers. On the fells, plants flower freely in most years, except in very tightly grazed vegetation, but few fruits are found. It is not known if this represents genuinely low productivity, whether they are picked off by birds, or whether the hooked beak of the fruits means they are dispersed on the fur or feathers of animals.

Distribution: Alpine Meadow-rue is widespread in northern and central Scotland, with disjunct locations in the Southern Uplands, northern Pennines, Lake District, Snowdonia and western Ireland. In Teesdale it is confined to the upper parts of Widdybank and Cronkley Fells, frequent in calcareous flushes on Meldon Hill and the head of Trout Beck, and rare on limestone rocks, such as Rough and Netherhearth Sikes and near the top of Knock Ore Gill.

Habitat: On Widdybank and Cronkley Fells, this is an inconspicuous member of all the base-rich plant communities except the very driest and most open sugar-limestone and metalliferous soils. It is also found, but rare, on wet rock ledges and calcareous flushes at higher altitudes.

It can be abundant in swards of the M10a Common Yellow-sedge–Bulbous Rush and M10b Quaking-grass–Bird's-eye Primrose sub-communities of the M10 Dioecious Sedge–Common Butterwort short sedge-marsh community, with Common, Tawny, Flea, Glaucous and False Sedges, Long-stalked Yellow-sedge, Sheep's-fescue, Quaking-grass, Selfheal and Autumn Hawkbit in a moss matrix; and in the gravelly flushes around hummocks with Sheep's-fescue, False Sedge, Bird's-eye Primrose, Common Butterwort, Scottish Asphodel, Dioecious, Glaucous, Tawny and Flea Sedges and Alpine Bistort.

In calcareous grass- and sedge-rich swards of the CG9 Blue Moor-grass–Limestone Bedstraw grassland community, it is found with Sheep's-fescue, Crested Hair-grass, Quaking-grass, Wild Thyme, Harebell, Spring Gentian, Northern Bedstraw, Hair and False Sedges and Lesser Clubmoss. On Cronkley Fell, it is associated with Hoary Rock-rose, Blue Moor-grass, Sheep's-fescue, Wild Thyme and Fairy Flax on a sugar-limestone-derived soil, while in a limestone grass-heath variant of the latter over sugar-limestone on Widdybank Fell it occurs with Heather, Red Fescue, Crowberry, Spring Gentian, Northern Bedstraw, Alpine Bistort, Harebell and Wood Anemone.

Status and conservation: Populations of Alpine Meadow-rue appear to be stable in most of its localities; although ripe fruits have been seen only infrequently, it does have a vigorous vegetative reproduction system of stolons. While overgrazing of the sugar-limestone grassland could be a threat, the prostrate habit of the leaves protects the plant from all but the closest grazing, but it severely reduces the production of flowers and fruits.

Undergrazing is a more serious risk. The increased height of the associated vegetation reduces the vigour of this light-demanding species, and a balance in the grazing level must be sought. Since 1995 when the sheep flock was greatly reduced, the need to maintain sufficient stock grazing has become increasingly clear, along with the need for continued Rabbit control. A few small areas of grassland and the short sedge-marsh have been mown and the toppings removed; the effects of this management, especially on flower production, are being monitored.

The small number of plants on rock-ledges at the highest altitudes are, of course, vulnerable to natural events. These, and ideally all, populations of Alpine Meadow-rue should be monitored to inform conservation management in the future.

Further information: https://www.brc.ac.uk/plantatlas/plant/thalictrum-alpinum

Alpine Meadow-rue: **1** flowers *DM*; **2** flowers and leaf *MEB*.

LC Downy Currant
Ribes spicatum E. Robson

FIRST RECORD IN TEESDALE
1793, Robson

ALTITUDE
210–270 m

LIFE-CYCLE
Perennial shrub; FLOWERS July; FRUITS ripen in August.

First recorded in 1793, Downy Currant could well have been misidentified for the commoner Red Currant, a species for which the presumed native distribution is clouded by escapes from cultivation, but which is found at its maximum altitude in Upper Teesdale. The two are very similar deciduous shrubs, up to 2 m tall, with green flowers in loose tassels; Downy Currant is usually hairier and has the two lobes of its anthers contiguous, rather than clearly separated. Both species can have edible red fruits, although Downy Currant, especially in deep shade, often fails to flower, and rarely produces ripe fruits. The other potential confusion species when not in fruit is Black Currant, generally clearly a relict or escape from cultivation, but having a strong scent when crushed, often likened to tangy cat urine.

Distribution: As a native species, Downy Currant is found mainly in the northern Pennines, the eastern Scottish Highlands and on Islay and Skye. In Upper Teesdale over the last two hundred years it has been found only on Cronkley Cliffs in the 19th century, near Low Houses, Newbiggin in 1950 and near Eggleston Bridge in the 1960s. Farther downstream it is still known from Deepdale Wood, just upstream from Barnard Castle, and at Brignall Banks by the River Greta, the catchment to the south of our area.

Habitat: Downy Currant has been found on steep banks of the Tees (and its tributaries downstream of Upper Teesdale) where base-rich soils support W9 Ash–Rowan–Dog's Mercury woodland, with some Wych Elm, Downy Birch, Hazel, Bird Cherry, Ramsons, Dog's Mercury, Marsh Hawk's-beard, Wood Avens and several species of fern.

Status and conservation: Not recorded within our area for some decades, the species should be sought in remnants of woodland, especially on steep banks, by the Tees and its side valleys.

Further information: https://bsbi.org/wp-content/uploads/dlm_uploads/Ribes_spicatum_species_account.pdf

Downy Currant: **1** growing at Orton *FJR*; **2** flowers *FJR*.

Marsh Saxifrage

Schedule 8   NERC

Saxifraga hirculus L.

FIRST RECORD IN TEESDALE
1801, Binks

ALTITUDE
600–730 m

LIFE-CYCLE
Perennial herb; FLOWERS July–August; FRUITS August.

Like Yellow Saxifrage (*p. 94*), which it resembles in many ways, Marsh Saxifrage inhabits upland wetland habitats, although at a higher altitude than the upper limit of the former. In addition, Marsh Saxifrage flowers individually are more showy, as their petals (viewed from above) mask the sepals; however, as there is usually only one, sometimes up to three, flowers per shoot and the shoots are dispersed through the habitat by stolons (not forming mats), the visual displays in flower are generally not as dramatic as with Yellow Saxifrage.

The bright yellow petals often have orange spots towards their base, and the sepals are clothed in long, reddish hairs. Close examination of the flowers also reveals another point of distinction from Yellow Saxifrage: in Marsh Saxifrage, the five petals radiate from the base of the ovary (the ovary is said to be 'superior'), but the ovary of Yellow Saxifrage is embedded within the petal bases – it is 'semi-inferior'.

Given that Marsh Saxifrage does not always flower well, vegetative identification is particularly important. Its untoothed, lanceolate leaves differ from those of Yellow Saxifrage which have toothed margins. In leaf only, it may also resemble other plants of similar upland wet habitats: Marsh Willowherb has darker green leaves with a prominent centre vein, whereas those of Marsh Saxifrage are mid-yellow-green with an obscure midrib, and the basal leaves of Lesser Spearwort are always hairless, while those of the saxifrage usually have some hairs on the leaf-stalk at least.

The species' habit of spreading by largely vegetative stolons is perhaps an adaptation to living in a habitat that is easily poached by the hooves of grazing animals. Shoots are easily pulled out and severed by grazers, although some stem damage has been attributed to the action of slugs.

Marsh Saxifrage: **1** growing at Widdybank Fell *MEB*; **2** flowers *LR*.

93

Distribution: With its distribution centred in the North Pennines, in particular the Upper Eden, Tees, South Tyne and Wear catchments, Marsh Saxifrage also occurs in both Scotland and Ireland, where it is scarce. In Teesdale there are between 15 and 20 sites (some with hundreds of clusters of shoots) between Little Fell and Cross Fell, on Yad Moss and formerly a site in Baldersdale. Three sites in the Sallygrain Head area are in the River Wear catchment.

Habitat: Marsh Saxifrage is found mostly around high-altitude spring-heads, and in flushes below these and limestone rocks. In the M38 Curled Hook-moss–Common Sedge spring community, it grows amongst mosses, with Marsh Willowherb, Lesser Spearwort, Mossy and Starry Saxifrages, Knotted Pearlwort, Marsh Valerian, Marsh Violet, and sometimes Hairy Stonecrop, Pyrenean Scurvygrass and Alpine and Chickweed Willowherbs. It also occurs in flushes with tall rushes, Smooth Lady's-mantle, Water Avens, Meadow Buttercup, Tufted Hair-grass, Marsh Hawk's-beard, Wild Angelica, Meadow Buttercup, Bogbean and Bottle Sedge, examples of or close to the M37 Curled Hook-moss–Red Fescue spring community.

Status and conservation: Moor House-Upper Teesdale NNR is the most important site for this species in the UK; it is a primary reason for the designation of the site as an SAC. Over recent years the removal of, or reduction in, the numbers of sheep on the higher fells has allowed plants to flower more freely, and this has led to the discovery of many new populations. However, some declines have occurred, especially where grazing has been excluded: a low level of grazing seems to be essential, highlighting the need for balanced, responsive management. Continued searches for new populations and monitoring of known ones is desirable, along with monitoring (and responding to) the activity of motorcycles, mountain bikes and quad bikes that can disturb the habitats and affect water flows.

Further information: https://bsbi.org/wp-content/uploads/dlm_uploads/Saxifraga_hirculus_species_account.pdf

LC Yellow Saxifrage
Saxifraga aizoides L.

FIRST RECORD IN TEESDALE
1798, Oliver

ALTITUDE
380–520 m

LIFE–CYCLE
Herbaceous perennial; **FLOWERS** June–September; **FRUITS** ripe from August.

A characteristic and often showy species of flushes and stream margins, the performance of Yellow Saxifrage is directly related to the quantity of water in its habitats: in a dry summer, plants are compact, often purple-red and with few flowers, whilst in wetter seasons plants are greener, with longer, loose growth and numerous flowers and seeding heads.

Numerous non-flowering decumbent stems contrast with erect flowering shoots with up to ten flowers. The leaf margins are often slightly toothed, and the yellow petals usually have small red spots. Marsh Saxifrage has similar flowers, although usually only up to three per shoot, while its leaves are untoothed and it is found in wet places at higher levels above the altitudinal range of Yellow Saxifrage.

Distribution: Widespread in the mountains of central and northern Scotland and at sea level in the west and north; while also frequent in the Lake District, it is rare in the northern Pennines and north-western Ireland. In Teesdale it is known around Widdybank and Cronkley Fells and Pastures, where it frequently occurs along stream sides, although it is scarce at higher altitudes.

Habitat: By steep, fast-flowing streams, Yellow Saxifrage often forms a border and is the only species present. It can also be found scattered in open, stony calcareous flushes which support the M11 Common Yellow-sedge–Yellow Saxifrage community that merges into the M10 Dioecious Sedge–Common Butterwort mire community, associated with Long-stalked Yellow-sedge, Tawny, Carnation and Flea Sedges, Few-flowered Spike-rush, Bird's-eye Primrose, Alpine Bistort, Alpine Meadow-rue, Variegated Horsetail, Knotted Pearlwort, Three-flowered Rush, Blue Moor-grass and Quaking-grass.

Status and conservation: Populations on the two Fells appear to be stable, within the parameters of climatically induced fluctuations, although a number of plants that grew on gravel over the Whin Sill rock were lost when the track to Cauldron Snout was surfaced and the flow of water reduced. Otherwise, in Widdybank Pasture, records show there has been a reduction of 10% of the area containing the species between 1976–81 and 2000, mainly due to poaching by the heavy, continental-type cattle. To protect the site and its flora, these have now been replaced by lighter native breeds. In Cronkley Pasture, it is locally frequent in the western part, and surveys of Cetry Bank in 1977 and 2012 showed a slight reduction. Cattle must be excluded from the unstable parts of the Bank; they can still access the river for drinking where the moraine tails off at its eastern end. Similarly, elsewhere around the lower streams, plants have been destroyed by livestock breaking the banks, and such areas also need protection by exclusion. Monitoring of populations in all habitats is desirable, especially on the sides of moraines and in the pastures.

Further information: https://www.brc.ac.uk/plantatlas/plant/saxifraga-aizoides

Yellow Saxifrage: **1** growing at Widdybank Fell *MEB*; **2** flowers *GH*.

CR Alpine Saxifrage
Micranthes nivalis L.

FIRST RECORD IN TEESDALE
1842, the Backhouses Sr. and Jr.

ALTITUDE
550 m

LIFE-CYCLE
Perennial, rhizomatous herb; FLOWERS August.

Often treated as part of the Teesdale Assemblage of rare and characteristic plants, Alpine Saxifrage has never actually been found in the catchment of the Tees: its only known locality in the area is just outside this catchment, and indeed it may now be extinct there. A denizen of high mountain rocks and cliffs, it forms basal rosettes of spoon-shaped leaves with gently toothed margins, which are green above and purple below. The pink-tinged, white flowers lack coloured spots on the petals, which (unlike many close relatives) are in tight heads of up to 12; all other saxifrages in the area have looser inflorescences.

Distribution: Found mainly in the Central Highlands and on the more mountainous larger islands of Scotland, Alpine Saxifrage is also known very locally on the mountains of the North Pennines, the Lake District, Snowdonia and north-western Ireland. In the immediate vicinity of Teesdale it is known from only one locality, on High Cup Nick.

Habitat: On High Cup Nick, Alpine Saxifrage has been found in a deep 'chockstone' gully; very typically, this is an area of damp, shady, base-rich rocks where potentially competing vegetation does not overtop it.

Status and conservation: When first discovered in the 19th century, there were two populations on High Cup Nick and it was described as 'tolerably abundant' and in 'little danger of extermination'. In 1984, just five rosettes were counted, which had reduced to two by 1992, followed by a slight recovery to four plants in 1995. Despite several targeted surveys, no plants have been found at this location since then, although given the remote nature and difficult terrain, searches should be continued.

Further information: https://www.brc.ac.uk/plantatlas/plant/saxifraga-nivalis

Alpine Saxifrage, growing in Scotland *SHW*.

Roseroot
Rhodiola rosea L.

FIRST RECORD IN TEESDALE
Before 1798, Oliver

ALTITUDE
580 m

LIFE-CYCLE
Perennial, long-lived; FLOWERS July–August; FRUITS ripen from August, germinate in spring.

Roseroot is a perennial with a thick, fleshy branched rootstock, which forms a winter food store and is marked by the scars of previous years' erect stems. It is hairless, with a waxy-blue appearance; the stems are clustered and grow to a height of about 30 cm. A dioecious plant, the small, yellow-green flowers are borne in compact terminal heads; male flowers are about 6 mm in diameter, while females are smaller.

Individual plants have been known in Maize Beck Gorge for over 200 years, and no seedlings or young plants have been observed near to established plants on the Pennine escarpment for decades. Studies of a small number of samples from different parts of its range have shown a reproductive capacity of around 30 flowers per plant stem at altitudes up to 538 m, but only 17 at 846 m altitude. Similarly, the proportion of seed germination varied with altitude: 65% of seed collected at sea level germinated successfully: whereas only 18% of seed collected at 534 m and 30% of that from 846 m.

The only similar species is Orpine (*p. 100*), which has a similar fleshy texture but is taller, often tinged red, with reddish-purple flowers and grows at a lower altitude. Unlike Orpine, the growth of Roseroot is not limited by low temperatures at higher altitudes; its normal height is about the same as adjacent plants. At lower altitudes, however, it cannot survive in the shade of taller plants.

Distribution: Roseroot is found in the uplands of Britain, from southern Wales northwards, and in western Ireland. In those areas it can also be found down to sea level on rocky cliffs and limestone pavement, and occasionally elsewhere as a garden escape. Whilst it is frequent and conspicuous in the Lake District it is very scarce in the northern Pennines: in Teesdale there is just one site: in Maize Beck Gorge at 580 m. In addition, there are nearby locations just over the watershed at Green Castle and on dolerite in High Cup Nick.

Roseroot: **1** male flowers; **2** female flowers *both AS*.

Habitat: In crevices and on ledges on the Carboniferous limestone, associated species with Roseroot include Alpine Cinquefoil, Wild Thyme, Harebell, Green Spleenwort and Slender Lady's-mantle, in the OV40 Green Spleenwort–Brittle Bladder-fern community.

Status and conservation: Roseroot is very rare in the Tees catchment with only a few plants in the Maize Beck Gorge; it is likewise scarce on the south-west-facing limestone and Whin Sill cliffs of the adjacent Eden Valley escarpment. Both areas are protected as SSSI and SAC; the plant is additionally protected by its restriction to ledges and crevices inaccessible to grazing animals, a state that must be maintained. The causes of the apparent absence of seedlings and young plants needs to be investigated. It is not known whether both male and female plants are present and, if so, whether viable seed is produced and successful germination can occur; assuming that good seed is produced, steps should be taken to raise plants in cultivation and use them to boost wild populations.

Roseroot in fruit, growing at Green Castle *MEB*.

Further information: https://www.brc.ac.uk/plantatlas/plant/sedum-rosea

VU Hairy Stonecrop
Sedum villosum L.

FIRST RECORD IN TEESDALE
1796, Oliver

ALTITUDE
370–750 m

LIFE-CYCLE
Perennial, sometimes annual/biennial; FLOWERS June–August; FRUITS ripen July–September.

Usually regarded as a perennial, Hairy Stonecrop is sometimes very short-lived; while it flowers freely in Teesdale, nothing is known about its fertility, seed production or germination. The succulent leaves are often reddish and covered in short, glandular hairs, flattened on their upper surface, and the few-flowered shoots bear pink, five-petalled flowers in summer. Although its flowers are similar to those of other stonecrops, the leaves of Hairy Stonecrop are longer and less swollen, and there are no other species likely to be found in damp, upland areas.

Distribution: Hairy Stonecrop is almost restricted to the northern Pennines and southern and central Scotland; it is very scarce in the Lake District and absent from the north-west of the Central Highlands. In Teesdale it occurs frequently in flushes at higher altitudes, but is now scarce lower down. Between 370–500 m altitude it has been found in recent years only on a seepage patch on a dolerite slab above Maize Beck (east of Birkdale) and by the old road near Dubby Sike mine.

Habitat: Most frequently found in the M38 Curled Hook-moss–Common Sedge spring community, associated with Alpine and Chickweed Willowherbs, Blinks, Cuckooflower, Autumn Hawkbit, White Clover, Alpine Bistort, Red Fescue, Brown Bent, Common Yellow-sedge and Carnation Sedge.

It is also found in vegetation that has some similarity with the U17 Great Wood-rush–Water Avens tall-herb community with Alpine Foxtail, Marsh Hawk's-beard, Marsh Cinquefoil, Lesser Celandine, Globeflower and Marsh Valerian, and Smooth Lady's-mantle, Marsh Foxtail, Wood Anemone, Marsh-marigold, Cuckooflower, Glaucous, Common and Flea Sedges, Common Mouse-ear, Alternate-leaved and Opposite-leaved Golden-saxifrages, Pyrenean Scurvygrass, Water Avens, Soft-rush, Meadow Buttercup, Mossy and Starry Saxifrages, White Clover and Marsh Violet. Several of these species are characteristic components of the herb-rich meadow flora of the MG3 Sweet Vernal-grass–Wood Crane's-bill community, which may represent an additional community featuring Hairy Stonecrop.

It also occurs in wet, open, stony, silty, base-rich habitats of the M10 Dioecious Sedge–Common Butterwort short sedge-marsh community, such as on Widdybank Fell and was formerly known in hollows in a Whin Sill slab in Forest-in-Teesdale and in limestone grassland at the base of a wall near Birkdale.

Status and conservation: At the lower altitudes there needs to be monitoring of known sites to see if plants reappear, so that active steps can be taken to conserve them. At higher levels, Hairy Stonecrop probably benefits from the lower level of grazing, but here too, survey and mapping needs to be undertaken, especially of the flush areas. There also needs to be better awareness of the potential damage that can be caused by off-road vehicles, quad bikes, mountain bikes and walkers, followed by appropriate action if damage does occur.

Further information: https://bsbi.org/wp-content/uploads/dlm_uploads/Sedum_villosum_species_account.pdf

Hairy Stonecrop: **1** growing at Red Sike *MEB*; **2** flowers *DM*.

LC Orpine
Hylotelephium telephium L.

FIRST RECORD IN TEESDALE
1794, Robson

ALTITUDE
410 m; formerly to 480 m at High Hag Wood

LIFE-CYCLE
Perennial, probably long-lived; FLOWERS July–September.

Orpine is a familiar garden plant, with broad, blue-green leaves and a terminal flat-topped inflorescence up to 10 cm across of small reddish-purple flowers. Two subspecies are often recognized, based upon differences in leaf shape and the presence of grooves on the fruits: native plants are probably all of the subspecies *fabaria*, whereas garden escapes, often close to settlements, are more of a mixture.

Its presence in Teesdale seems always to have been tenuous. It was first recorded here in 1798, and then sporadically throughout the ensuing centuries, but is now restricted to a well-known colony on Falcon Clints. This is close to the altitudinal limit of this primarily lowland plant, and experimental work has shown the size of plants, flower production and germination to be significantly restricted by the lower temperatures of higher altitudes. For example, compared with sea level, flower production is around two-thirds at 423 m and just a half at 553 m. Nevertheless, in 2007 all of the 45 stems on Falcon Clints at 455 m had flowering heads; whether viable seeds were produced is not known, but small plants with 2–3 leaves were found on nearby lower ledges five years later. Given that the current site is close to the extremes of its range, it is unlikely to have frequently reproduced by seed, and the present plants may be of a considerable age.

A related species, Roseroot (*p. 97*), is rather similar but has greenish-yellow flower-heads and grows in a more compact form: it is usually found on rock ledges at even higher altitudes, and restricted not by low temperatures but by the shading of tall herbs growing in the vicinity.

Orpine: **1** growing at Falcon Clints; **2** flowers *both GY*.

Distribution: Although its natural distribution is much obscured by garden escapes, Orpine is a widespread, usually lowland, species but absent from north-western Scotland and scarce in much of eastern England and Ireland. In Teesdale the only native site is on Falcon Clints at about 410 m, around its current upper altitudinal limit in Britain. In about 1980 it was seen near White Force at 480 m altitude, but it was lost from this site following rock-falls. Other historical sites that no longer survive include Hag Crag Wood, Cronkley Scar and High Force.

Habitat: It grows on a damp, south-facing, rock ledge on Falcon Clints at about 410 m with Rosebay Willowherb, Foxglove, Slender St John's-wort, Herb-Robert, Wood Sage, Goldenrod, Devil's-bit Scabious, Heather, Bell Heather, Bilberry, Red Fescue, Wild Thyme and Wild Strawberry, an assemblage probably of the U17 Great Wood-rush–Water Avens tall-herb community. In the 1960s the author also knew it on grassy, Whin Sill rocks under Scots Pine in High Hag plantation, near High Force Hotel (probably the Hag Crag Wood of older records).

Status and conservation: The plants at the only known site on Falcon Clints may be threatened by an increase of tall Rosebay Willowherb, leading to over-shading and instability or collapse of the vegetation on the rock ledge. In 2012 the site was evaluated with this in mind and considered to be satisfactory. However, monitoring of the site should be continued and action taken immediately when deemed necessary.

Further information: https://plantatlas.brc.ac.uk/plant/sedum-telephium

Horseshoe Vetch
Hippocrepis comosa L.

FIRST RECORD IN TEESDALE
1811, Backhouse Sr. and Binks

ALTITUDE
530 m

LIFE-CYCLE
Perennial; FLOWERS May–August.

At the northern edge of its natural British distribution, the Horseshoe Vetch on Cronkley Fell has in recorded times always been scarce; indeed until its rediscovery in 1972 it had been considered extinct. It may well have been that small plants had survived, undetected, for many years. The known plants nowadays may in fact all arise from one branched rootstock; no seedlings have ever been observed, despite the occasional production of seed pods.

The yellow, pea-like flowers could be mistaken for those of other similarly coloured legumes, but Horseshoe Vetch has a whorl of lemon-yellow flowers in a flat head on a long stalk, pods up to 30 mm long with horseshoe-shaped segments, and pinnate leaves, bearing 3–6 pairs of leaflets. Kidney Vetch leaves usually have a larger terminal leaflet and round, hairy flower heads, while Common Bird's-foot-trefoil flowers are larger and deeper yellow, often with red streaks.

Distribution: Found throughout the chalk and limestone areas of England and Wales as far north as Cumbria. In Teesdale it is known only from the eastern exposure of sugar-limestone on Cronkley Fell.

Habitat: Horseshoe Vetch is found within the CG9d Hair Sedge–False Sedge sub-community of the CG9 Blue Moor-grass–Limestone Bedstraw grassland community, with Sheep's-fescue, Quaking-grass, Blue Moor-grass, Limestone Bedstraw, Crested Hair-grass, Wild Thyme and Harebell, and Hoary Rock-rose, Rare Spring-sedge and Alpine Meadow-rue nearby. Although on very open sugar-limestone with skeletal soils that can become very dry in summer, the high rainfall (average 1,523 mm/year) probably ensures that the deeper rock into which the roots penetrate is constantly moist.

Status and conservation: The avidity of botanists in the 19th and early 20th century was such that much more dried material in herbaria remains than live plants on the fell today. The original extent of the population of the Horseshoe Vetch is unknown, but for a while, until its rediscovery in 1972, it was thought to be extinct. Since then the area covered by the species has varied in size inversely to the grazing pressure, from a mat 35 × 15 cm in 1979 down to just two small plants in 2018. Although now surrounded by a rabbit-proof fence the survival of the species in Teesdale is precarious. Overgrazing and the consequential fragmentation of the sward is just one of a suite of threats that also includes erosion of the sugar-limestone soil and rock by the action of rain, frost and wind, and shading as a result of undergrazing.

Such is the scarcity of Horseshoe Vetch on Cronkley Fell that one measure of monitoring is the number of leaves produced by the few plants. Since sheep grazing has been limited to the autumn and winter, and when Rabbit densities are low, the plants can develop more and larger leaves; these plants sometimes produce a few flowers. Life at the extremes of a geographical range is tenuous and this is a key species at this time of climatic change which should be monitored by Natural England, continuing the work of the author.

Further information: https://www.brc.ac.uk/plantatlas/plant/hippocrepis-comosa

Horseshoe Vetch: 1 Rabbit-grazed plant *MEB*; 2 growing at Cronkley Fell *MEB*; 3 flowers *MR*.

Dwarf Milkwort
Polygala amarella Crantz

FIRST RECORD IN TEESDALE
1852, the Backhouses Sr. and Jr.

ALTITUDE
500–530 m

LIFE-CYCLE
Perennial, short-lived; FLOWERS May until autumn, finishing earlier in dry summers; FRUITS from July.

A short-lived perennial, Dwarf Milkwort has bright blue or pink flowers: those on Widdybank Fell are all blue, while the population on Cronkley Fell has both pink- and blue-flowered plants. The species has a condensed, basal rosette of oval leaves, their margins often slightly upturned; the leaves are evergreen but may turn purple if stressed by extreme temperatures or drought. Approximately a third of the mature plants in a population die each year. Most plants come into flower at 3–4 years old and continue for several years. Population survival is dependent upon regular seed production; the seeds have an aril which suggests they may be dispersed by the ants, present in abundance.

Similar in flower, Heath Milkwort lacks the basal leaf rosette of Dwarf Milkwort. The rosette can be mistaken for those of Spring Gentian (*p. 156*) and Autumn Gentian, but these species have opposite pairs of somewhat pointed leaves unlike the spiral arrangement of blunt-ended leaves on the stems of Dwarf Milkwort.

Distribution: With a remarkably disjunct distribution in the North Downs and the northern Pennines, Dwarf Milkwort is found only in grassland on calcareous rocks. In Kent (and formerly Surrey), it is in chalk grassland, while in the Pennines it is on the Craven (Yorkshire) and Orton (Cumbria, not Pennines) limestones and the Teesdale sugar-limestone. Within Teesdale it is entirely restricted to Cronkley and Widdybank Fells.

Habitat: In the CG9 Blue Moor-grass–Limestone Bedstraw grassland community, including the variant with Heather and Crowberry, Dwarf Milkwort is found in closed and semi-open vegetation on rendzinas and calcareous brown earths, but not the driest, eroding sites or where

Dwarf Milkwort: **1** growing at Widdybank Fell *MR*; **2** close-up of plant growing at Widdybank Fell *AS*.

the sward is more than 70 mm tall. Closely associated plants include Blue Moor-grass, Quaking-grass, Sheep's-fescue, Common Rock-rose, Wild Thyme, Crested Hair-grass and Spring Gentian.

Status and conservation: The population size has varied over the years and it is clear that occasional 'good seed' years are necessary to maintain viable populations. The numbers of plants on the monitored plots on Widdybank Fell were 355 in 1970, 11 in 2002, 29 in 2012 and eight in 2014. The corresponding numbers on Cronkley Fell, where grazing has mostly been excluded, were 253, 35, 18 and 56.

The reasons for these fluctuations are mainly periods of severe undergrazing and overgrazing that make it difficult to maintain the optimum sward height (5–6 cm) for Dwarf Milkwort. Flexible, responsive management is needed to try and avoid those extremes, involving a combination of exclusion of grazers with fencing, controlling the number of Rabbits, supplementing the number of grazing sheep and mowing, all supported with monitoring to ensure management changes can be implement in the face of population declines of the milkwort.

Other causes of adverse population change are not so amenable to management, in particular cold springs and prolonged summer droughts. On Widdybank Fell in 2018, the long, cold winter followed by prolonged drought and high temperatures severely affected the species. Plants were small and the few short inflorescences dropped their fruit early; by July, many plants were flaccid or dead; following rain in August the remaining live plants produced more flowers but it is unlikely that fertile seed resulted. Interestingly, on Cronkley Fell plants were not so adversely affected, but the reason for this is unknown.

At present, lower numbers than in the middle of the 20th century are of concern. Formerly, Dwarf Milkwort was slightly more widespread across the areas of exposed limestone; these adjacent areas should be monitored for its possible reappearance.

Further information: https://bsbi.org/wp-content/uploads/dlm_uploads/Polygala_amarella_species_account.pdf

VU **Mountain Avens**
Dryas octopetala L.

FIRST RECORD IN TEESDALE
1796, Oliver

ALTITUDE
537 m

LIFE–CYCLE
Woody perennial; FLOWERS July; FRUITS July–August.

A prostrate, branched, dwarf shrub, some of the specimens of Mountain Avens growing in Teesdale may be true glacial relicts. They are certainly long-lived, some showing more than 50 annual growth rings, but despite flowering and fruiting when protected from grazing no seedlings have ever been found in the wild.

When in flower, Mountain Avens is unmistakable, its flowers up to 3 cm across, bearing usually eight white petals. Equally, in fruit, its long, feathery, persistent styles are unlike those of any other species present in this area. And even if the flowers and fruits are grazed off, or are out of season, at least the semi-evergreen, dark green leaves to 2·5 cm long, with deeply crenate margins, often curled under, are still unique.

Distribution: With a distribution concentrated in the Scottish Highlands and islands and the Burren in Ireland, small populations of this glacial relict species remain in Snowdonia, the Pennines, the Lake District and north-western Ireland, ranging from sea-level to mountain top.

In Teesdale it is known only on part of the sugar-limestone on Cronkley Fell, inside and outside of the White Well Exclosure.

Habitat: Plants are mostly deep-rooted on sugar-limestone, in turf of the CG9d Hair Sedge–False Sedge sub-community of the CG9 Blue Moor-grass–Limestone Bedstraw grassland community, with Sheep's-fescue, Blue Moor-grass, Crested Hair-grass, Rare Spring-sedge, Common and Hoary Rock-roses; the presence of Small Scabious and Horseshoe Vetch could be indicators also of the CG9a Hoary Rock-rose–Squinancywort sub-community. The skeletal soil is almost pure sugar-limestone, a rendzina or calcareous brown earth; the exposed edges suffer wind erosion which leaves roots exposed and, together with seasonal droughts, causes the woody subterranean stems and shoots to dry-out and die. Another small colony is in closed vegetation on damper calcareous brown earth with Sheep's-fescue, Common Bent, Spring-sedge and False Sedge.

Mountain Avens: **1** flower *GH*; **2** leaves, with Spring-sedge (BOTTOM) and Small Scabious (RIGHT) *MEB*; **3** in fruit *MEB*.

Status and conservation: Cronkley Fell has been grazed by sheep and Rabbits for several centuries. In the past the Rabbit population was controlled by regular severe winters with deep snow. However, latterly, milder winters and the control of most predators triggered a massive increase in the Rabbit population and in 1971–2, an exclosure was erected around the main patch of Mountain Avens. Inevitably, the Rabbits penetrated the fence, grazed the turf very closely and exposed the woody underground parts of Mountain Avens and Hoary Rock-rose, causing soil erosion and die-back of both species. The security of the fence has now been restored and the Rabbits subjected to some control but from time to time numbers have risen again. Continued vigilance is essential: plants weakened by defoliation produce new leaves a mere 0·5 cm long, only a fifth of the size of leaves produced at times of good growth conditions, as for example in 2017.

The lower population, in the White Well Exclosure, needs to continue to be protected from grazing, mapped and subsequently monitored; the upper population, nearer the top gate into the exclosure, is in closed, grassy vegetation and should be enclosed, mown, and winter grazed.

The sub-population outside the exclosure should be mapped and monitored. It is close to a public right of way and the route of the sheep flocks as they are moved to and from the higher parts of the fell.

Further information: https://bsbi.org/wp-content/uploads/dlm_uploads/Dryas_octopetala_species_account.pdf

LC Rock Whitebeam
Sorbus rupicola (Syme) Hedl.

FIRST RECORD IN TEESDALE
1810, J. Backhouse Sr.

ALTITUDE
254–410 m

LIFE-CYCLE
Perennial small tree; FLOWERS May–June; FRUITS fruits ripen in August–September, germination in spring.

The only native whitebeam in Teesdale, Rock Whitebeam grows as a shrub or small tree up to a height of about 6 m. It has narrowly obovate leaves, which are more or less entire in the lower half, but with sharp teeth in the terminal sections, the teeth slightly curved towards the apex. The leaves are dark green above and densely white-downy below. The larger trees in Teesdale flower and fruit successfully: the ripe fruits are a deep red colour, 12–15 mm in diameter, and often slightly broader than long. The skin of the berries is covered with numerous, evenly spaced pores (lenticels) that allow gas circulation.

Distribution: Always found on limestone and other basic rocks, this species is known patchily from south Devon to the far north of Scotland, and west to the Atlantic coast of Ireland: it is the most widespread of the apomictic whitebeams in Britain and Ireland. In Teesdale it grows on rocks and cliffs in several locations, the largest populations being downstream of Wynch Bridge and at High Force. Although the habitat seems suitable, Rock Whitebeam has never been found on Cronkley Scar, Falcon Clints or Maize Scar.

Habitat: Rock Whitebeam is restricted to cliffs of limestone and Whin Sill, where associated plants include Yew, Hazel, Bird Cherry, Common Juniper, Bearberry, Heather and Bell Heather.

Status and conservation: Almost all the ten or so trees and perhaps 70 shrubs known are within the Upper Teesdale SSSI and those on the cliffs are not easily accessible. The most vulnerable cliff site is Holwick Scar, but this is currently out-of-bounds to climbers following an agreement between Natural England and the British Mountaineering Council. Regular monitoring is needed to confirm the agreement is being respected.

However, those growing on rocks near the River Tees are vulnerable to browsing damage by Rabbits, particularly during periods of deep snow cover, and by the large number of visitors. The trees appear to be sufficiently well anchored to withstand river floods. Again, monitoring is required, leading to remedial action if necessary.

Further information: https://www.brc.ac.uk/plantatlas/plant/sorbus-rupicola

Rock Whitebeam: **1** growing at Holwick Scar *MR*; **2** leaves *MR*; **3** growing along Tees bank *MR*.

LC Alpine Cinquefoil
Potentilla crantzii (Crantz) Beck

FIRST RECORD IN TEESDALE
1798, Binks and Oliver

ALTITUDE
260–580 m

LIFE-CYCLE
Perennial; FLOWERS June–July; FRUITS July–August.

Alpine Cinquefoil is a perennial herb, up to 25 cm in height. When in bloom (which in grazed situations especially is not always the case) the bright yellow flowers 15–25 mm across, often with an orange spot at the base of each petal, are distinctive. However, without flowers, care needs to be taken to separate the species from other members of its genus, some of which have similar palmate leaves with five leaflets. One feature of Alpine Cinquefoil that helps identification is the presence of shaggy hairs on its leaf petiole and especially the margins of the leaflets.

Tormentil occurs in grazed grassland, although more usually base-poor; in flower it has just four petals, and its basal leaves have only three leaflets. However, on the stems the leaves with three leaflets and two stipules resemble the five-parted leaves of Alpine Cinquefoil, albeit totally hairless. Spring Cinquefoil is found on calcareous grassland and rocky slopes; it forms mats and has flowers less than 15 mm in diameter, whereas Alpine Cinquefoil does not spread by rooting runners and generally has larger flowers. But beware, the latter two species are known to hybridize and form apomictic microspecies of intermediate appearance.

Distribution: Alpine Cinquefoil is known in Britain mainly from the Central Highlands, northern Pennines and Lake District, with outliers in Snowdonia, the Peak District and elsewhere in Scotland. In Teesdale it is found thinly scattered in grassland on Widdybank Fell, and on rock faces in Harwood Dale, Maize Beck, Dufton Fell, Wynch Bridge and White Force.

Alpine Cinquefoil: **1** growing at High Cup Nick *JP*; **2** flowers *MEB*; **3** leaves *MEB*.

Habitat: This plant grows mainly on dry, base-rich faces, cliffs and ledges of limestone and Whin Sill. It is also found very sparsely in close-grazed calcareous grassland in the CG9d Hair Sedge–False Sedge sub-community of CG9 Blue Moor-grass–Limestone Bedstraw grassland community on the sugar-limestone of Widdybank Fell (although not on Cronkley Fell). Associated plants include Blue Moor-grass, Quaking-grass, Sheep's-fescue, Common Rock-rose, Wild Thyme, Crested Hair-grass, Spring Gentian, Teesdale Violet, Mountain Everlasting, Alpine Bistort and Lesser Clubmoss.

Status and conservation: Apparently scarce in all its Teesdale localities, Alpine Cinquefoil may be overlooked, and continued searching for new or 'lost' sites would be of value. In the Widdybank Fell grassland site it is very thinly scattered, and flowering is infrequent: for 30 years from 1980 only a single flower was recorded there. The number of shoots is also of concern: in the last two decades, this has fallen by a half. This decline is believed to be a result of undergrazing leading to the overshading by other plants: the average sward height now exceeds 18 cm.

Monitoring of this and other rare species in the grassland will help to determine the level of grazing required to benefit the majority of the rare and characteristic species. The need to control the Rabbit population will be ongoing and the sheep numbers that currently are being increased can be adjusted as necessary. As with some other perennial species (*e.g.* Teesdale Violet and Horseshoe Vetch) in this community, it is likely that the plants can continue to survive for very many years when stressed, even producing new shoots on old rootstocks after appearing to be 'dead', a welcome justification for maintaining conservation efforts even if all hope seems to be lost. Similarly, Alpine Cinquefoil is known to produce a persistent seed bank, so the introduction of ground disturbance, either planned (by management) or unplanned (by allowing Rabbit activity) may help to recover seemingly lost populations.

On cliffs there is the danger of loss due to rock-falls, and in the gill sites this species must be considered when planting shrubs and small trees to benefit birds, especially Black Grouse.

Further information: https://bsbi.org/wp-content/uploads/dlm_uploads/Potentilla_crantzii_species_account.pdf

NT Shrubby Cinquefoil
Dasiphora fruticosa L.

FIRST RECORD IN TEESDALE
1677, Ray; found by Willisel and Johnson

ALTITUDE
120–380 m

LIFE-CYCLE
Perennial deciduous shrub; FLOWERS May–September; FRUITS August–October; SEEDS viable for more than a year, germinate in spring.

One of the more iconic species of the River Tees, if not Teesdale as a whole, Shrubby Cinquefoil is also one of the most recognizable of the rare plants. While its flowers with five yellow petals surrounded by sepals and epicalyx segments are rather similar to those of other cinquefoils, its shrubby growth form, up to 2 m tall, makes it unmistakable. The leaves are similarly distinctive, with 5–7 pairs of leaflets, dark green above and paler below, and both surfaces softly hairy. It is a deep-rooted shrub, providing anchorage when the river is in spate, and can withstand being submerged when water levels are high. It appears to be unaffected by frost, drought and high temperatures. As well as spreading by seed into bare germination sites created by the river, it can also spread vegetatively by layering, any bent or broken stems rooting where they touch the ground. The flowers of Shrubby Cinquefoil open over the course of the whole summer, with an early flush in May and a second, more productive, one in August.

Distribution: Often grown in gardens and sometimes establishing in the wild, Shrubby Cinquefoil as a native plant has a very disjunct distribution. In the Burren in Ireland it is a lowland species of open scrub habitats, especially around temporary pools; in the Lake District it colonizes montane rock ledges and screes; and in Teesdale it is strongly associated with the river banks and gravels westward from Abbey Bridge (east of Barnard Castle) to below Raven Scar, and particularly west of Middleton-in-Teesdale.

Shrubby Cinquefoil: **1** growing by the River Tees *JP*; **2** female flowers *MEB*; **3** male flowers *MEB*.

Habitat: Shrubby Cinquefoil is intolerant of shade and by the Tees occupies habitats that are kept open by variation in the river flow. Plants, mostly as single shrubs, are rooted in the cracks in Whin Sill and limestone rocks and in riverside shingle, frequently covered by fast-flowing water. Associated species may include Sea Plantain, Northern Bedstraw, Wild Thyme and Tea-leaved and Grey Willows. Opposite Widdybank Farm, plants extend for some metres up the stabilized scree near grassy, base-rich flushes in the M10b Quaking-grass–Bird's-eye Primrose sub-community of the M10 Dioecious Sedge–Common Butterwort mire community.

Until recently there was a large remnant population beside a former course of the river, some 200 m away from the Tees at the base of a now stable, eroded drumlin. The vegetation here comprised the MG3b Quaking-grass sub-community of the MG3 Sweet Vernal-grass–Wood Crane's-bill grassland community, with Wood Crane's-bill, Meadow Buttercup and Devil's-bit Scabious. A closed sward and changes to the soil chemistry, being acidic as it was derived from glacial drift and river shingle, eventually eliminated Shrubby Cinquefoil, possibly aided by grazing pressure despite the relative unpalatability of the species.

Status and conservation: The last full survey, in 1979, on both banks of the Tees from Raven Scar almost to Middleton located hundreds of plants. Some of these have subsequently been lost as a result of rock-falls and trampling by sightseers, picnickers and kayakers around the popular Low Force–Wynch Bridge area. The effects of such pressures must be monitored and remedial action taken if the effects become too great.

Of perhaps greater concern is the wider picture following the regulation of the river flow since the filling of the Cow Green Reservoir in 1971. The reduction in high flow events is likely to have reduced the creation of open germination sites as well as allowed the development of more dense, shading swards. The demise of the isolated population below Cronkley Scar is instructive: cut off from the main river, by 1980 the shrubs did not look healthy, being stunted, covered with lichens and with few flowers. They gradually succumbed and by 2004 no trace of the plants could be found. After 50 years of regulated river flows, a comprehensive re-survey is overdue, in order to devise management strategies if identified as necessary.

Further information: https://bsbi.org/wp-content/uploads/dlm_uploads/Potentilla_fruticosa_species_account.pdf

Lady's-mantle agg.:
Starry, Velvet and Large-toothed Lady's-mantles
Alchemilla vulgaris L. agg: *A. acutiloba, A. monticola* and *A. subcrenata*

See individual profiles for detailed species information.

LIFE-CYCLE

Perennial, long-lived; FLOWERS from May–October, especially in May–June and August–September.

These three species in the aggregate have a British distribution that is almost restricted to Co. Durham. They are found principally in traditional hay meadows, on road verges and very occasionally in pastures, all communities created by the management actions of humans. As on the Continent, these species could have been a component of the prehistoric herb-rich northern woodland flora that became the original meadows. Otherwise, as they have been (and still are) valuable medicinal herbs, they could have been introduced by any of the early farmers or later herbalists, or even accidentally imported in seeds, hay or packing material. The true status of these lady's-mantles is therefore somewhat uncertain.

Lady's-mantle flowers give off an 'apricot' scent and are visited by small flies for nectar, but the pollen aborts into a solid black mass; seed is produced without the need of pollination or fertilization, a phenomenon known as apomixis. Thus the genus comprises a large number of relatively minor variants (morphologically and genetically) which are classed as species (often as 'microspecies') because they 'breed' true, without variation resulting from sexual reproduction. Large numbers of fruits are produced, and after a necessary period of cold temperatures, germination of ripe seed is good, at least in cultivation. The seed is probably long-lived in the soil; similarly, individual plants also have considerable longevity, certainly persisting in the wild for more than 50 years.

Habitat: In the mid-20th century several species of lady's-mantle were frequent in the herb-rich upland meadows and verges of the MG3 Sweet Vernal-grass–Wood Crane's-bill community. Associated species include Red Fescue, Rough Meadow-grass, Quaking-grass, Crested Dog's-tail,

Lady's-mantles, growing on road verge near Leadgate, Nr Alston, Cumbria *JO'R.*

Pignut and Common Knapweed. Also found in the rather damper MG4 Meadow Foxtail–Great Burnet community with Red Fescue, Crested Dog's-tail, Perennial Rye-grass, Meadowsweet, Red Clover, Meadow Buttercup, Common Sorrel, Devil's-bit Scabious and Rough Hawkbit, and occasionally in pasture of the MG6b Sweet Vernal-grass sub-community of the MG6 Perennial Rye-grass–Crested Dog's-tail grassland community, with Common Bent, Red Fescue, White Clover, Meadow Buttercup, Yarrow, Daisy, Common Ragwort and Creeping Thistle.

Status and conservation: A return survey in 2000 of the sites of all three species recorded in the early 1950s revealed decreases of 47%, 86% and 53% respectively, losses being noted in both meadows and road verges. In the former, losses were attributed to changes in farming practices including the greater application of artificial fertilizer and decrease in basic slag and liming, as well as the change to making large bale silage and haylage instead of hay. On the verges, declines occurred due to the use of herbicides, flail mowers that form a thick mulch that favours robust plants, from extra spray from vehicles and salt, fertilizer run-off from adjacent fields and various road schemes.

Some meadows have been in SSSI, ESA or Countryside Stewardship Scheme management agreements for several years and still the species have declined. Attempts have been made to target sites with agri-environment schemes, to replace at least some artificial fertilizer with farmyard manure, a shift from silage to hay or haylage production, and autumn grazing with native cattle breeds. On the verges, surveys were undertaken in 2002–03 to identify herb-rich examples, but plans for a meadow-type management regime by the County Council have progressed only very slowly.

Lady's-mantles are a critical group in which the occurrence of rare species can be masked by several common ones. Better identification and awareness of the rarities is required by botanists and field workers, and landowners and tenants need to be informed of the presence and significance of these species, especially those included in national and local Biodiversity Action Plans.

Starry Lady's-mantle
[PHOTO **1**, *p. 114*] **NERC**

Alchemilla acutiloba Opiz

FIRST RECORD IN TEESDALE
1933, Chapple

ALTITUDE
153–480 m

LIFE-CYCLE
As for the Lady's-mantle agg. (*p. 112*).

Although first collected in 1933, it is a measure of the difficulty this genus creates that its identity was not ascertained until 1946. A robust, tall-growing plant, Starry Lady's-mantle is a colonizer of open sites where it is very vigorous and can form dense patches one or two metres in diameter, as for example on road verges and railway embankments. In meadows it is more scattered and is scarce in Teesdale, but was formerly very frequent in some meadows in Weardale. Like Velvet Lady's-mantle, it has not been found in pastures, seemingly intolerant of frequent grazing.

The leaves of Starry Lady's-mantle have characteristic long, triangular, pointed lobes. The teeth in the middle of each side of the lobes are much larger than those at the top or the bottom, while the apical tooth is much smaller than those either side. The stems and leaf stalks are clothed in dense, spreading hairs, as are early season leaves, whereas later leaves are variably hairy, sometimes even hairless, on the upper side.

Smooth Lady's-mantle may have a similar leaf shape with long, triangular lobes and similar larger teeth on the sides of the lobes, but hairs on the leaf surface, petioles and stems are closely adpressed.

Distribution: Occasional records from Cheshire, Northumberland, Scotland and east Durham probably do not represent native occurrences. The main population is in Weardale and Teesdale; all known sites lie to the north of the River Tees apart from single plants on the southern side west of Wynch Bridge and near Holwick Head Bridge.

Habitat: Occurs most frequently in hay meadows and on road verges, occasionally on railway embankments as above, but it is not known from pastures.

Status and conservation: Starry Lady's-mantle was abundant in some hay meadows and verges in Weardale in the 1950s but there had been almost a 60% reduction by 2000. In Teesdale it was never plentiful in meadows but was very frequent on verges; the loss here has been just 20%. Not only has the number of sites declined but so has the density of plants within some sites, despite their inclusion in agri-environment schemes. It has been found in a few additional sites since 2000 including the first record in North Yorkshire in 2003; targeted survey of the herb-rich meadows by knowledgeable field workers may well reveal new sites.

Further information: https://bsbi.org/wp-content/uploads/dlm_uploads/Alchemilla_acutiloba_species_account.pdf

1 Starry Lady's-mantle, growing in Weardale; **2** Velvet Lady's-mantle, growing at Hayberries Quarry; **3** Large-toothed Lady's-mantle *all MEB.*

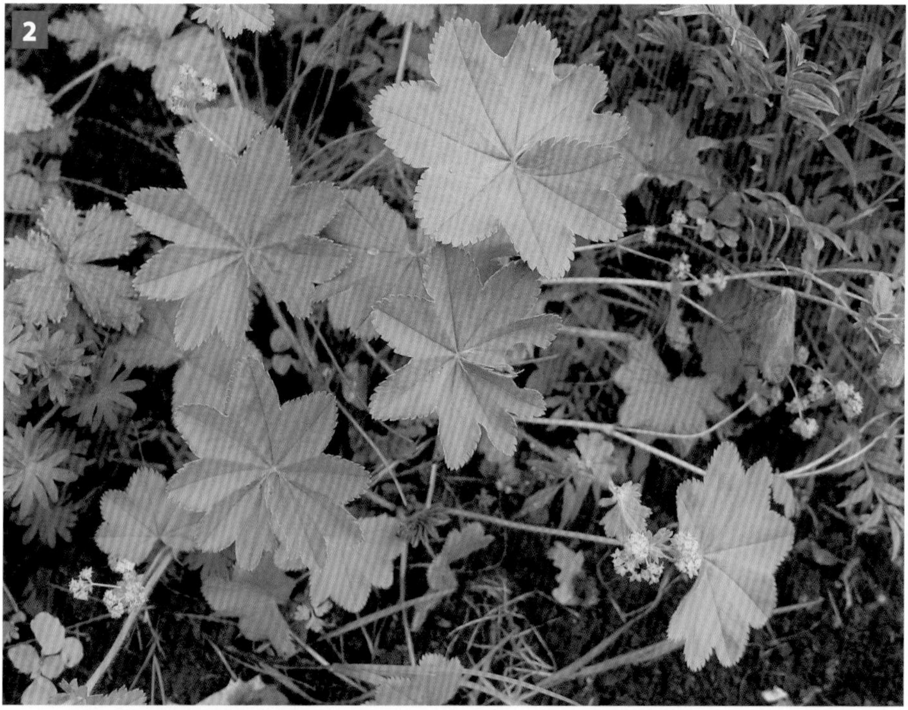
2

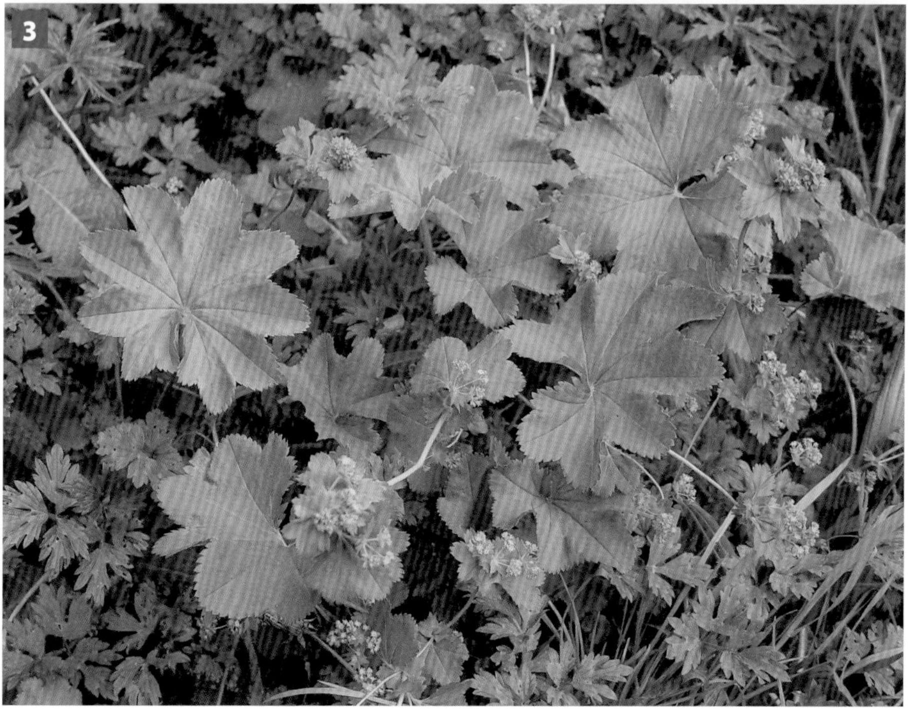
3

EN Velvet Lady's-mantle
Alchemilla monticola Opiz.

[PHOTO **2**, *p. 115*] **NERC**

FIRST RECORD IN TEESDALE
1903, Wilmott

ALTITUDE
107–500 m

LIFE-CYCLE
As for the Lady's-mantle agg. (*p. 112*).

Often growing with Starry Lady's-mantle (*p. 113*), this is another species that was identified retrospectively, in this case almost two decades after its discovery. Its basal leaves are kidney-shaped to circular, palmately lobed with 9–11 rounded lobes that have even teeth. They are densely velvety-hairy and a slightly bluish-green colour.

Hairy Lady's-mantle in the same habitats is smaller, has kidney-shaped leaves, usually with seven lobes, is less densely hairy and usually has a wine-red base. Garden Lady's-mantle (a garden escape) has yellow-green, fuller, rounded, wavy leaves, and is covered in long, spreading hairs, while the silvery, circular-leaved Silky Lady's-mantle is not known in Teesdale. As a plant primarily of the central Pennines, it would not however be unreasonable to search for the last of these species in our area.

Distribution: Almost wholly confined to Upper Teesdale westward from Barnard Castle almost to the Co. Durham boundary, and one site in Weardale. There are a few outlier sites, some of the more distant ones of which (Surrey, Buckinghamshire and Lanarkshire) are certainly naturalized aliens.

Habitat: Occurs in meadows, on road verges and open, lightly shaded woodland, especially in the MG3 Sweet Vernal-grass–Wood Crane's-bill community but only very rarely in pastures. The species is not found in more acidic CG10 Sheep's-fescue–Common Bent–Wild Thyme pastures, nor in the wetter meadows, such as the MG8 Crested Dog's-tail–Marsh-marigold community. It can however be a primary colonizer of ruderal sites, such as sand quarries, if there is a source of seed nearby.

Status and conservation: Between the 1950s and 2000 there was a reduction of 47% in the number of recorded sites: Velvet Lady's-mantle appears not to survive frequent grazing, such as when a meadow becomes a pasture, nor frequent mowing, as on road verges. More recently, further losses occurred when some meadows were ploughed and re-seeded. The loss of sites is especially concerning given the apparent longevity of some individual plants, in some cases known to have persisted for more than 50 years. Fortunately, between 2007 and 2010 a few new sites were reported during meadow surveys: a comprehensive re-survey would benefit efforts to conserve this species.

Further information: https://bsbi.org/wp-content/uploads/dlm_uploads/Alchemilla_monticola_species_account.pdf

Large-toothed Lady's-mantle

Alchemilla subcrenata Buser

NERC

[PHOTO **3**, *p. 115*]

FIRST RECORD IN TEESDALE
1951, Walters and Bradshaw

ALTITUDE
± 260 m

LIFE-CYCLE
As for the Lady's-mantle agg. (*p. 112*).

This is the most difficult of our lady's-mantle species to recognize in the field. It has circular, pleated leaves with 9–11 broad lobes, the lowest two of which are upturned. It is only sparsely hairy, and the hairs are spreading and deflexed. Small plants in grazed pasture are very difficult to identify, but the upturned basal lobes and characteristic hair cover can still be seen.

There are two particular confusion species, both common and widespread. Smooth Lady's-mantle is somewhat similar in terms of leaf shape but lacks the upturned basal lobes and its hairs are closely adpressed. In Pale Lady's-mantle the stems and petioles are densely clothed with spreading hairs, while the leaf is generally hairless on the upper side.

Distribution: Confined to Upper Teesdale (Newbiggin/Holwick area), three meadows near Allendale, and in Weardale, where it was recently re-found in a small meadow near to a former site. In Teesdale, surveys between 2008 and 2012 revealed plants in several meadows close to the original site; however the number of plants is now much fewer than when first located.

Habitat: Most frequent in hay meadows with the MG3 Sweet Vernal-grass–Wood Crane's-bill community, although it has always been very scarce on road verges. A few plants are known in one permanent pasture of the U4a Sheep's-fescue–Common Bent–Heath Bedstraw typical sub-community; some very small plants are also surviving in a pasture that was a meadow, now a MG6a Perennial Rye-grass–Crested Dog's-tail community. Grazing was subsequently restricted and these plants developed to full meadow size.

Status and conservation: This was and still is the scarcest of the meadow lady's-mantles in Teesdale and Weardale. Between the 1950s and 2000, there was a 53% reduction in the number of extant locations, but this century, thanks to a greater recognition of the microspecies by field workers and an emphasis on the value of herb-rich meadows, more plants have been found within the original area in Teesdale and in a new location around Allendale in Northumberland.

Unlike the other two rare meadow species, Large-toothed Lady's-mantle tolerates grazing and survives as very small plants and probably as buried seed. In one field it has responded vigorously to artificial fertilizer (unlike associated rare lady's-mantle species) and in another it has survived being sprayed with herbicide to kill Broad-leaved Dock. However, such use of herbicides is not a recommended management technique.

Management of the meadows for hay is essential, ideally formalized under an agri-environment scheme: the site of the original discovery of Large-toothed Lady's-mantle is outside such schemes and its management is clearly not ideal, as between 2000 and 2012 the plants became fewer and less vigorous. Conversely, pastures in which grazing has been excluded or restricted have shown increases. Control of grazing, including by Rabbits, is essential, along with monitoring of the effects of management changes. And the whole area is overdue for a complete resurvey of this and other rare lady's-mantles, the most recent having been in 2000.

Further information: https://bsbi.org/wp-content/uploads/dlm_uploads/Alchemilla_subcrenata_species_account.pdf

Lady's-mantle agg.:
Clustered Lady's-mantle and Rock Lady's-mantle
Alchemilla vulgaris L. agg. : *A. glomerulans* and *A. wichurae*

These two species are distributed in the uplands and mountains of northern England and Scotland. Their locations in the north of England form a disjunct fringe to their centres of distribution in the Scottish Highlands. The **Rock Lady's-mantle** is slightly more frequent than the **Clustered Lady's-mantle**, especially in England where both are found as small plants in hill pastures. In meadows and verges Clustered Lady's-mantle is a larger, more robust plant whilst the other, more slender, Rock Lady's-mantle was only occasionally found in meadows and is now mostly confined to hill pasture, track sides, wet and dry rock ledges and the banks of small streams.

LC Clustered Lady's-mantle
Alchemilla glomerulans Buser

FIRST RECORD IN TEESDALE
1947, Walters

ALTITUDE
250–720 m

LIFE-CYCLE
As for the Lady's-mantle agg. (*p. 112*).

A robust, medium-sized plant, densely clothed with silky, adpressed hairs that give the yellowish-green plant a silvery sheen, Clustered Lady's-mantle is named for the dense inflorescences with flowers clustered into small balls, or glomerules. Its leaves are full and wavy with overlapping basal lobes, the lobes rounded and broad, and teeth broad but subacute. No other lady's-mantle is so uniformly covered with adpressed, shining hairs; in the very rare Shining Lady's-mantle (*p. 121*) the abundant hairs are ascending, rather than adpressed, most clearly seen on the petioles and stems, and the leaf lobes are more triangular, with a distinct gap between the basal ones.

While this species is often robust in meadow-type communities, it can survive for many years as a very small plant in grazed sites; if grazing pressure is removed, these plants attain the stature of meadow plants, growing to several decimetres in diameter. Individual plants can be very long-lived, some having been recorded for more than 50 years.

Distribution: Found in many of the same places as Rock Lady's-mantle (*p. 120*), Clustered Lady's-mantle is the rarer of the two in the Pennines, the Central Highlands and north-west Scotland, and completely absent from the Lake District, although it was found on a road verge in Lancashire in 2019. Its main centre of distribution in England is in Upper Teesdale, along with one site near the top of the Pennine escarpment near Knock Fell in Cumbria and the South Tyne valley, although it is now probably lost from Weardale. In Teesdale it is found mostly between 250 and 480 m altitude, but a couple of higher records up to 720 m represent altitudes more typical of its Scottish range.

Habitat: In Teesdale it is found in primarily in meadows with the MG3 Sweet Vernal-grass–Wood Crane's-bill community on neutral brown earths; other localities include a herb-rich road verge, sike side and river margin, but it is absent from rock ledges. Where it occurs in grazed grassland it occupies the base-rich flushed CG10 Sheep's Fescue–Common Bent–Wild Thyme community, with Quaking-grass, Sweet Vernal-grass, Harebell, Common Dog-violet, Meadow Buttercup,

1 Clustered Lady's-mantle; **2** Rock Lady's-mantle *both MEB*.

Common Bird's-foot-trefoil and Ribwort Plantain. In high altitude (690 m) base-rich grassland its associates are Sweet Vernal-grass, Mat-grass, Sheep's-fescue, Marsh Willowherb, Marsh Saxifrage, Sheathed Sedge, Sneezewort, Water Avens, Smooth and Hairy Lady's-mantles, Lesser Clubmoss, and Common, Flea, Star and Glaucous Sedges.

Status and conservation: A re-survey in 2000 found that the plant had been lost from four-fifths of its sites known in Teesdale in the 1950s. Changes in farming practice were the reasons assumed to be responsible for most of these losses; those changes include ploughing, reseeding and overgrazing. More selective surveys since 2013 have managed to locate a few new plants and individuals previously considered to have been lost, partly a result of the improved awareness of lady's-mantle microspecies by fieldworkers. However, numbers of plants at most sites are critically low, a recipe for future extinctions and emphasizing the need for a comprehensive re-survey for all rare members of this genus. Known sites should be managed to maintain the existing hay meadows and, at higher levels, to manage down the intensity of grazing. As with all the rare lady's-mantles, it would be prudent to maintain a living collection off-site for use if future restocking becomes necessary.

Further information: https://bsbi.org/wp-content/uploads/dlm_uploads/Alchemilla_glomerulans_species_account.pdf

VU Rock Lady's-mantle

[PHOTO **2**, *p. 119*]

Alchemilla wichurae (Bus.) Stef.

FIRST RECORD IN TEESDALE
1947, Walters

ALTITUDE
277–720 m

LIFE-CYCLE
As for the Lady's-mantle agg. (*p. 112*).

A small to medium-sized lady's-mantle, the leaves of Rock Lady's-mantle are rounded to reniform and often saucer-shaped. The lobes are round or triangular with a clear 'V'-shaped incision between the lobes; the teeth are numerous, narrow and with acute tips curved towards the apex. Its inflorescence is slender and sparse, usually with adpressed hairs on the lower branches, petiole and the veins on the underside of the leaf. In comparison with the other rare species, most plants are smaller and more slender, often comprising a single shoot, but plants on wet rocks have full, undulate leaves and less regular, larger teeth; in cultivation they develop a leaf form reminiscent of Smooth Lady's-mantle. It is probably very long-lived, as a small plant in hill pastures near Scoberry Bridge alongside the Pennine Way is known to be over 50 years old.

Distribution: Rock Lady's-mantle has a disjunct distribution, occurring in Craven (Yorkshire), the Lake District, the Teesdale area, the Southern Uplands, Central Highlands and north-western Scotland. In Teesdale it is very thinly scattered in at least eight locations from the riverside near Holwick to the rim of High Cup Nick and in short turf over limestone near the summit of Knock Fell. There is also one plant on a waterfall in the South Tyne. In total approximately 60 plants are known, some very small with mature leaves only 20 mm across.

Habitat: All sites are neutral to base-rich, generally within short, open vegetation which casts little shade. It is found in a range of habitats: very occasionally in meadows with the MG3 Sweet Vernal-grass–Wood Crane's-bill community, upland pasture (usually in damp flushes and by the sides of small streams), on small limestone ledges with some well-drained soil in the CG8 Blue Moor-grass–Small Scabious community with Sheep's-fescue, Burnet-saxifrage, Meadow Saxifrage, Limestone Bedstraw, Rue-leaved Saxifrage and Wall Speedwell, and by waterfalls over wet Whin Sill rock.

Status and conservation: During a survey of 2000 only just over half of the records from the 1950s were re-found. Plants had been lost as a result of a change of management, overgrazing and at one site by the conversion of a barn area to a bunk-house and camp site. The largest population contains fewer than 20 plants, of which most are single plants and thus very vulnerable to destruction by grazing or by physical disturbance of the habitat from Rabbits or walkers.

Meadow sites with this species have been entered into agri-environment schemes to promote the use of farmyard manure and lower levels of artificial fertilizer, hay or haylage production rather than silage and grazing with native breeds of cattle in the autumn. In the hill grasslands overgrazing by Rabbits has been a problem, while reduced numbers of sheep may allow plants to grow taller, allowing the rare species to be recognized; it is important to achieve the correct balance between undergrazing and overgrazing. It may be possible to boost the populations with plants grown from seed, and continued monitoring is essential, including a full re-survey as the last one was more than 20 years ago.

Further information: https://www.brc.ac.uk/plantatlas/plant/alchemilla-wichurae

Shining Lady's-mantle

Alchemilla micans Buser

NERC	FIRST RECORD IN TEESDALE
	1924, Druce

ALTITUDE
400 m

LIFE–CYCLE
As for the Lady's-mantle agg. (*p. 112*).

Recognized as a British species only in 1976, Shining Lady's-mantle is currently known only from Northumberland. However, a single Teesdale record from 1924 was tentatively identified retrospectively; it is considered that this record may have referred to second growth leaves of Starry Lady's-mantle (*p. 113*). Nevertheless, as it occurs frequently with the other three meadow lady's-mantles in the uplands of central Europe, its occurrence here would not be entirely unexpected.

Its dark green basal leaves are kidney-shaped to rounded, with more or less triangular lobes bearing equal-sized teeth. The upper surface of the leaves, at least along the folds, the veins on the underside and the lower part of the stem are clothed in diagnostic semi-erect hairs standing at an angle of 45°, giving the plant a silky sheen. The late-summer leaves of Starry Lady's-mantle are somewhat similar, with ascending hairs, but earlier mature leaves have larger teeth in the middle of the lobes and the hairs on the petioles stand out at right-angles. Clustered Lady's-mantle (*p. 118*) has adpressed hairs and rounder lobes and leaf shape, while young plants in pasture are often a pale, golden-green.

Shining Lady's-mantle can survive as very small plants in grazed pastures, and its seeds remain viable in soil for many years, germinating when brought to the surface. Both of these factors give hope that it may reappear in Teesdale.

Distribution: Extant only in Northumberland in three pastures, on a river border and a lane verge; there are also two casual occurrences in Lanarkshire. In Teesdale the sole record (which may be a misidentification) came from Langdon Beck, possibly in the field to the south of the hotel.

Habitat: The original Northumberland record was in CG10 Sheep's–fescue–Common Bent–Wild Thyme pasture community; it is now known also in MG6 Perennial Rye-grass–Crested Dog's-tail pasture.

Status and conservation: Currently not known in Teesdale, but the possibility of its occurrence here should be considered in any future surveys.

Further information: https://www.brc.ac.uk/plantatlas/plant/alchemilla-micans

Shining Lady's-mantle: **1** growing at Coldwell Farm; **2** growing near Cockplay, the original site *both MEB*.

Dwarf Birch
Betula nana L.

FIRST RECORD IN TEESDALE
1722, Camden

ALTITUDE
460–500 m

LIFE-CYCLE
Deciduous shrub; leaves expand from April; FLOWERS in May; SEEDS ripen in September–October, wind-dispersed.

Although recorded in Teesdale as early as 1722, knowledge of the location of Dwarf Birch was lost until 1965 when it was re-found on Widdybank Fell. It is a slow-growing, deciduous dwarf shrub, no more than 1 m in height. Its leaves are rounded and small (only up to 15 mm long), deeply crenate and hairless; they turn a dull yellow colour before being shed in October. Presumably because this location is at the southern extremity of its natural range, flowers have not been observed in Teesdale. Elsewhere, the separate male and female catkins are produced in May; seeds with a crescent-shaped wing for wind dispersal are shed in early autumn.

Saplings of the larger birches can have a similar stature, but they generally have a single leading shoot, and have larger, pointed leaves than the rounded, fingernail-sized ones of Dwarf Birch.

Distribution: Widespread in central and northern Scotland, but present in only three sites in England: one in Northumberland, and the others in Teesdale on Widdybank and Cronkley Fells.

Habitat: In the M19 Heather–Hare's-tail Cottongrass blanket bog community, with Heather and Crowberry.

Status and conservation: Known only in two areas, Dwarf Birch is susceptible to grazing. It is protected from sheep in Widdybank Fell by wire cages, but this was no protection in 2007 when it was defoliated by the abundant caterpillars of Northern Eggar moth. Continued monitoring is required, of the native plants and those that Natural England has introduced from Northumberland.

Further information:
https://bsbi.org/wp-content/
uploads/dlm_uploads/
Betula_nana_species_
account.pdf

Dwarf Birch, growing at Widdybank Fell *MEB*.

LC Teesdale Violet
Viola rupestris F. W. Schmidt

FIRST RECORD IN TEESDALE

1862, the Backhouses Sr. and Jr.

ALTITUDE

490–515 m

LIFE–CYCLE

Perennial; FLOWERS in May; FRUITS ripen July–August, seeds germinate in spring.

Teesdale Violet is a widespread species across the north temperate zone of Eurasia, from Sakhalin to Britain, but restricted to uplands in the southern parts of its extensive range, which are glacial relict locations such as in northern England

Care must be taken to distinguish Teesdale Violet from small examples of other species and hybrids; if seed capsules are found, their downy covering of short hairs differentiates the species from all other dog-violets in Britain and Ireland. The leaves are scoop-shaped, with upturned sides, whereas those of other species are flatter, and its flowers are usually a rather pale mauve colour, without a dark zone on the lower petal. Flowers come in two forms: the normal, pansy-like, open-faced ones, and small closed flowers (termed cleistogamous) that self-pollinate inside the closed bud; such flowers are an insurance policy for living in extreme habitats when pollinators may not be available at the necessary time.

Teesdale Violet grows from a thick, woody rootstock clothed with dead leaf-bases; the stock generally forks, terminating in two rosettes, which are for monitoring purposes treated as individual reproductive units. As a light-demanding species, it responds negatively to the density and height of surrounding vegetation: the average lifespan of rosettes has been measured in closed vegetation as two-thirds of that in open sites. Similarly for flowering: in open sites up to one-third of rosettes flowered but in the more closed areas flower, fruit and seed production was lower and sometimes none. The production of ripe seed capsules is also affected by grazing: in particular the close grazing of Rabbits reduces seed production, especially from open flowers whose capsules are on longer stalks than those of closed flowers.

Dwarfed specimens of Common Dog-violet look similar to Teesdale Violet but have deeper violet-coloured flowers with a dark zone on the lower petal, and more pointed, deeply cordate leaves with sparse slender, bristly hairs on the upper surface. In addition, there are habitat differences, as Common Dog-violet usually grows on deeper soils, including in more acidic grassland. The hybrid Teesdale Violet × Common Dog-violet (*p. 126*), much rarer than the parents, often grows in dense patches. Its leaf-blade is more like that of Common Dog-violet in shape, but both leaf- and flower-stalks are usually pubescent like those of Teesdale Violet. The flowers are intermediate between those of the parents, but it is sterile so no seed capsules are produced.

Distribution: Known from only four sites in Britain, in addition to its eponymous location (Widdybank Fell, on sugar-limestone), Teesdale Violet is found on Carboniferous limestone at Long Fell in Cumbria, Arnside Knott in Westmorland, and on the south-eastern slopes of Ingleborough in the Yorkshire Dales.

Habitat: On the well-drained sugar-limestone of Widdybank Fell, Teesdale Violet is widespread but local, usually growing in close proximity to exposed rock. Soils range from dry immature rendzinas to deeper and damper brown calcareous soils and brown earths, all with high pH vales of 7·0–7·5 (exceptionally to 8·1). It grows in the CG9d Hair Sedge–False Sedge sub-community of CG9 Blue Moor-grass–Limestone Bedstraw grassland, especially in the almost bare exposures with Sheep's-fescue, Blue Moor-grass, Common Rock-rose, Spring Sandwort, Wild Thyme and

Fairy Flax, and several mosses and lichens. However, it is also found in more closed forms of the community with False and Hair Sedges, Quaking-grass, Wild Thyme, Limestone Bedstraw, Sea Plantain, Mountain Everlasting and Harebell.

Status and conservation: The Teesdale population is comparatively large, an estimated 2,000–2,500 plants. Like other late-glacial relict species, Teesdale Violet is a light-demander and cannot tolerate the shade and competition of more vigorous species, for example those that respond well during periods of undergrazing.

The need to regulate grazing pressure is highlighted by the fortunes of Teesdale Violet over the last 50 years. Monitoring in 1968–75 showed the violet population maintained itself under the sheep numbers at that time. Although the sheep flock had been reduced to less than half of its 1975 level, a rapid rise in the numbers of Rabbits in the early 2000s, resulted in severe overgrazing of the habitat and loss of violets because of the excessively tight grazing by Rabbits. In a series of marked plots, the number of plants fell to as low as 379 but increased after the Rabbit numbers were brought under control, to 449 by 2008. But then the prolonged snow cover in winter 2010–11 killed more Rabbits, such that the shading effects of undergrazing knocked violet numbers back to 247 in 2012 and 239 in 2018.

As an interim measure the grassland within the violet plots is now being mown and cleared of the cuttings. The plan is to start increasing sheep numbers once again; control of Rabbits will have to be maintained because their numbers (and effects) are not so easily regulated as sheep. Monitoring is thus essential to determine the optimum size of the sheep flock for the important, shade-intolerant plant populations.

Further information: https://bsbi.org/wp-content/uploads/dlm_uploads/Viola_rupestris_species_account.pdf

Teesdale Violet: 1 flower; **2** fruit *both MEB*.

'Hybrid' Violet
(Teesdale Violet × Common Dog-violet)

Viola × burnatii Gremli (*V. rupestris × V. riviniana*)

FIRST RECORD IN TEESDALE
1949(?), Valentine

ALTITUDE
505–508 m

LIFE-CYCLE

Perennial, spreading by runners; FLOWERS in May, on average, later than Teesdale Violet, but earlier than Common Dog-violet; flowers are sterile.

This hybrid violet is of both conservation interest and concern. The taxon is a natural hybrid that is rarer than either of its parents, which gives it conservation value and scientific interest. But on the other hand, at least in parts of its range there is the risk that genetic swamping may be taking place, with the complete replacement of the scarcer parent, Teesdale Violet (*p. 124*), by hybrids. Indeed, this seems to be the case in the Long Fell (Cumbria) population of Teesdale Violet where unhybridized specimens are difficult to find.

In Teesdale, hybrids are present on Widdybank Fell, but at a lower frequency, it is believed because the parent species occupy a slightly different plant community and have somewhat different, although overlapping, flowering periods. While they could be within the flight range of pollinators, the weather at altitudes of more than 500 m means that opportunities for successful pollination and hybrid seed productions are few. This may be the reason why there are only ten large clones (up to a few square metres each) and a few very small ones known on Widdybank Fell within the area of very much larger populations of both parents.

The hybrid has features of both its parents. For example, it can spread by runners and form dense patches as in Common Dog-violet, but its leaf stalks are usually densely pubescent as in Teesdale Violet. Both open and closed flowers are produced, but as the hybrid is sterile, no seed capsules are produced. The number of open flowers per rosette is similar to that of Common Dog-violet, but greater than that of Teesdale Violet; fewer closed flowers are produced than in either parent .

Distribution: Reported from many countries across the extensive Eurasian range of the two parent species, the hybrid is known from all four of the British localities of Teesdale Violet. In Teesdale, there are localized colonies on the metamorphosed limestone on Widdybank Fell.

Habitat: The hybrid violet grows in habitats intermediate between those typical of the two parents. It is never found on open sugar-limestone but usually in disturbed ground within more or less closed grassland of the CG9d Hair Sedge–False Sedge sub-community of the CG9 Blue Moor-grass–Limestone Bedstraw community, in which Blue Moor-grass and Sheep's-fescue are frequent, and Quaking-grass, Wild Thyme, Tormentil, Mountain Pansy, Alpine Bistort and Glaucous Sedge are also present. The soil is a calcareous brown earth, with a pH of 6–7, a little more acidic than is typical of Teesdale Violet. A few solitary rosettes have also been found in a grassy form of the M10 Dioecious Sedge–Common Butterwort short sedge-marsh community between the sugar-limestone escarpment and Red Sike Moss.

Status and conservation: It is thought that around one tenth of the Teesdale population of the hybrid violet was lost during the construction of Cow Green Reservoir, although some of these plants were rescued for research purposes in Durham University Botanic Garden where they thrived. Despite this loss, Teesdale has the largest population in Britain; numbers of rosettes have fluctuated, with some reductions due to the scratching activities of Rabbits and in other patches to an increase of Sheep's-fescue and the consequent decrease of Blue Moor-grass and other plants. In a broad-scale survey in 2018 most populations found in the 1970s survey were re-located, together with a few new plants.

Although the huge population of Rabbits of the early 2000s was virtually wiped out by control activities and the severe winter of 2010–11, some have returned. Pockets of bare ground in the vicinity of both parents are necessary for a new hybrid to become established; it is better that these are established in the limestone grassland by sheep grazing and not the less controllable, more unpredictable Rabbits. In an undergrazed sward, hand-mowing and the deliberate creation of bare patches is used as a technique to favour light-demanders such as the hybrid violet. This will need to be continued periodically, informed by the results of monitoring, until such time as a more sustainable solution can be found, presumably involving the continued suppression of Rabbit numbers but allowing an increase in sheep numbers up to the as-yet-unknown optimum density.

Teesdale Violet × Common Dog-violet: 1 flowers; **2** cleistogamous buds *both MEB.*

LC Aspen
Populus tremula L.

FIRST RECORD IN TEESDALE
1805, Winch

ALTITUDE
446 m

LIFE-CYCLE
Long-lived woody tree; FLOWERS March–April; perennation by suckers and perhaps seeds.

Aspen grows as solitary trees or single-sex clones and has orbicular, shallowly lobed leaves borne on petioles up to 6 cm long. The slender, laterally flattened leaf stalks cause the leaves to tremble in even light breezes, hence its specific name *tremula*. The trees at High Force and Wynch Bridge often flower profusely, but it is not known whether this is the case at higher altitude sites. At least the Wynch Bridge grove produces abundant seeds but, again, performance at other sites is unknown, as is the fertility of the seeds that are produced.

Distribution: Occurs throughout Britain as both a native and a planted tree, but more scattered in Ireland. In Teesdale there are well-known trees on Falcon Clints by the sugar-limestone cave, Dine Holm Scar and the cliffs of High Force Gorge, two trees at the head of Blackton Reservoir, a grove near Wynch Bridge and an eight-stemmed clone on the cliff by Hunder Beck. In the past it has also been noted on Cronkley and Holwick Scars, Punchard's Gill and Cauldron Snout.

Habitat: Found on cliffs of limestone or Whin Sill with Wych Elm, Downy Birch, Hazel, Common Juniper, and various willows and male-fern species; this vegetation is probably a degraded W9 Ash–Rowan–Dog's Mercury community.

Status and conservation: As Aspens are few in Teesdale, new sites should be sought and all plants or clones monitored. The isolated trees may be old and just surviving, but the clone at High Force is increasing since sheep grazing has been reduced.

Further information: https://www.brc.ac.uk/plantatlas/plant/populus-tremula

Aspen, growing at Park End Farm, Holwick (planted)
MEB.

Wood Crane's-bill
Geranium sylvaticum L.

FIRST RECORD IN TEESDALE
1794, Robson

ALTITUDE
240–430 m

LIFE-CYCLE
Perennial; FLOWERS June–Jul, occasionally August; FRUITS August–September, seeds germinate in spring.

Although widely dispersed in the hay meadows, Wood Crane's-bill merits inclusion in this book because of its association with this habitat. It flowers profusely, is visited by bumblebees, and generally produces plenty of viable seeds which are dispersed by the catapult action of the drying, twisting seed appendages. Explosive dispersal is important for species like this that can germinate only in open microsites. It can be confused with Meadow Crane's-bill, in which the flowers are a little larger (25–30 mm, rather than 22–26 mm), bluer rather than pinkish-purple and lacking an obvious whitish centre. The leaves of both species are rounded but deeply lobed: those of Meadow Crane's-bill have narrower lobes and are not so softly hairy.

Distribution: Widely distributed from North Yorkshire and Lancashire north to the Great Glen; elsewhere in our islands it is at best occasional, and sometimes no more than a colonist from gardens. It is not rare in Teesdale, found from Piercebridge westwards to upper Harwood Dale, in meadows, woodland, riversides and road verges, although less frequent than before the 1950s.

Habitat: Wood Crane's-bill occurs in hay meadows, moist woodlands and along stream sides and damp roadside verges, generally on more or less neutral, loamy soils. It is often part of the MG3 Sweet Vernal-grass–Wood Crane's-bill community and U4 Sheep's-fescue–Common Bent–Heath Bedstraw community, the latter in its U4b Yorkshire Fog–White Clover species-rich sub-community, which may include Lady's Bedstraw, Harebell, Bitter-vetch with frequent Devil's-bit

Wood Crane's-bill, growing on a road verge at Allendale *GC*; INSET flower *DM*.

Scabious, Betony and Great Burnet. It is also found in the U17 Great Wood-rush–Water Avens tall-herb community and W9b Marsh Hawk's-beard sub-community of the W9 Ash–Rowan–Dog's Mercury woodland community with Water Avens and Tufted Hair-grass.

Status and conservation: Over the last 60 years, this species has decreased due to changes in agricultural practice and, especially from the 1960s to the 1980s, the management of road verges, as herbicides and gang-mowers replaced lines-men. Verges, ideally those lengths with the species, should be mown early, with the mowings removed, and then not again until after fruiting. In meadows it may also be adversely affected by the overgrazing of emerging leaves in the early spring. The answer is to try to manage hay meadow sites with as near as possible traditional methods, including moderate applications of farmyard manure. Wood Crane's-bill has also proved to be one of the more successful introductions through the application of green hay from fields with the species to less species-rich meadows.

Further information: https://bsbi.org/wp-content/uploads/dlm_uploads/Geranium_sylvaticum_species_account.pdf

LC Rosebay Willowherb
Chamaenerion angustifolium (L.) Scop.

FIRST RECORD IN TEESDALE
1805, Winch, Thornhill and Waugh

ALTITUDE
530 m

LIFE-CYCLE
Rhizomatous perennial; FLOWERS June–September; FRUITS late July–August.

Rosebay Willowherb underwent a major change in status during the 20th century from being a rather local plant of higher ground to a widespread lowland plant, especially characteristic of urban brownfield sites and coppice plots in woodland. Although not currently considered a separate taxon, the 'native' form is believed to have shorter stolons, thick, very wavy-edged leaves, and on average longer seed pods; some of the plants on cliffs and screes in Teesdale may be of this form.

Distribution: Now ubiquitous throughout Britain and Ireland, except for a few parts of Ireland, its distribution especially in 19th century floras reflected its original subalpine, rocky habitat preferences. There are early records of it in Teesdale from Falcon Clints, Langdon Dale and Cronkley Scars; after the 20th century spread of the aggressive form, the few records of the species from remote, rocky, potentially native localities included Force Burn, Cronkley and Raven Scars, and Falcon Clints. It is clearly capable of persisting at certain sites, and is still at Falcon Clints, with an accompanying cast of montane specialities including Orpine.

Habitat: Rock ledges and gullies at high altitude.

Status and conservation: As the putative native form is no longer treated as a valid taxon, its distribution is obscured by that of the widespread aggressive form. It would be instructive to search for plants bearing the supposed wild-type morphological features growing in suitably remote rocky habitats, and to subject those to DNA analysis to elucidate their status. If sufficiently genetically distinctive, conservation of the remnant populations would become a priority.

Further information: https://www.brc.ac.uk/plantatlas/plant/chamerion-angustifolium

Rosebay Willowherb: **1** leaves *LR*; **2** flower *DM*; **3** growing at Dodd Fell *LR*.

VU Alpine Willowherb
Epilobium anagallidifolium Lam.

FIRST RECORD IN TEESDALE
1832, Trevelyan

ALTITUDE
430–780 m

LIFE-CYCLE
Perennial; FLOWERS July–August; SEEDS released August–September.

A montane perennial, Alpine Willowherb grows in similar habitats to and is often confused with Chickweed Willowherb (*opposite*). Its stems are usually a wine-red colour, and the leaves are yellowish-green and elliptical-lanceolate, tapered at both ends, unlike those of Chickweed Willowherb which are bluish-green and have a rounded base with a distinct stalk. Another potential confusion species is Marsh Willowherb, which can also occur in high-level springs; that species has paler pink flowers and rounded, usually downy stems, unlike Alpine Willowherb on the stems of which run two lines of hairs on faint ridges.

Distribution: A more northerly species than Chickweed Willowherb, Alpine Willowherb is found in the North Pennines, the Southern Uplands and central and north-west Scotland. In Teesdale it is found in the higher parts, but the quantity varies considerably from year-to-year.

Habitat: Found in high altitude flushes, springs and stream sides in the M32 Fountain Apple-moss–Starry Saxifrage spring community, in which bryophytes predominate along with Starry Saxifrage, and sometimes Marsh Saxifrage, Opposite-leaved Golden-saxifrage, Marsh Willowherb and sometimes Chickweed Willowherb. It is found in both non-alkaline and calcareous flushes, in the latter on the east side of the Pennine ridge with Three-flowered Rush and Alpine Foxtail.

Status and conservation: At higher levels its status is probably stable, although there is significant variation between years; consequently, monitoring and mapping of all its habitats, especially the flushes, needs to be undertaken. There needs to be better awareness of the potential damage by off-road vehicles, quad bikes, mountain bikes and walkers, and appropriate action taken immediately if damage occurs. There is considerably more uncertainty about its status at the lower end of its altitudinal range.

Further information: https://www.brc.ac.uk/plantatlas/plant/epilobium-anagallidifolium

Alpine Willowherb: **1**, **2**, Caenlochan, Scotland *both FJR*.

Chickweed Willowherb
Epilobium alsinifolium Vill.

FIRST RECORD IN TEESDALE
1810, Oliver and Binks

ALTITUDE
430–780m

LIFE-CYCLE
Perennial, with yellowish stolons; FLOWERS July–August.

A plant of the higher parts of the Fells, Chickweed Willowherb seems to be susceptible to sheep grazing: when Foot-and-mouth Disease struck in 2000 and grazing stock had to be removed, it responded spectacularly in some stream beds, forming highly floriferous patches up to a metre across. It grows up to 30 cm in height and is almost hairless apart from two rows of hairs on its slender stems. The shining, blue-green, opposite leaves are rather broad and distinctively heart-shaped, very different from the elliptic-oblong leaves of Alpine Willowherb (*opposite*) and the linear-lanceolate ones of Marsh Willowherb, two similar species sharing similar habitats. The flowers of all are rather similar, although those of Chickweed Willowherb are more wine-red than the pure pink of the other species.

Distribution: A montane species, known from Snowdonia, the Lake District, North Pennines, Cheviot Hills and Southern Uplands, with one site in north-western Ireland, and over a wide area of central and northern Scotland. In Teesdale it is found mainly at higher altitudes; it is more frequent and has a wider altitudinal range than the similar Alpine Willowherb.

Habitat: Occurs by streams, in flushes and on rock ledges, usually in the M32 Fountain Apple-moss–Starry Saxifrage spring community, in which bryophytes predominate along with Starry Saxifrage, and sometimes Marsh Saxifrage, Opposite-leaved Golden-saxifrage and Marsh Willowherb. It is found in both non-alkaline and calcareous flushes, in the latter on the east side of the Pennine ridge with Alpine Willowherb, Three-flowered Rush and Alpine Foxtail.

Chickweed Willowherb: **1**, **2** growing at Knock Ore Gill (with an eyebright) *both FJR*.

Status and conservation: Although more frequent in Teesdale than Alpine Chickweed, Chickweed Willowherb is generally rather sparsely distributed in suitable habitats. At higher levels its status is probably satisfactory, but monitoring and mapping of all the higher-level habitats, especially the flushes, needs to be undertaken. There needs to be better awareness of the potential damage by off-road vehicles, quad bikes, mountain bikes and walkers, and appropriate action taken immediately if damage occurs. There is considerably more uncertainty at lower levels, with some populations seemingly lost in recent years.

Further information: https://www.brc.ac.uk/plantatlas/plant/epilobium-alsinifolium

LC Hoary Rock-rose

NERC

Helianthemum oelandicum ssp. *levigatum* (M. Proctor) D.H. Kent

FIRST RECORD IN TEESDALE
1789, Oliver

ALTITUDE
537 m

LIFE-CYCLE
Perennial with a woody base, evergreen; **FLOWERS** June. **SEEDS** ripen in August.

There are three subspecies of Hoary Rock-rose in Britain and Ireland, differing in the hairiness of their leaves and the number of flowers per inflorescence. Each differs also in its geographical distribution; subspecies *levigatum*, which is found nowhere else in the world other than Cronkley Fell, is arguably the most distinctive, being hairless on the upper side of its leaves and having only up to three flowers on each flowering shoot. This local subspecies is low-creeping, rising no more than 6 cm from the ground, and its small yellow petals (2 shades) soon become reflexed, exposing a tuft of stamens. Common Rock-rose, which may grow with it, has deeper yellow, flat flowers, almost twice the size (up to 25 mm across).

Following pollination, probably mainly by bees and wind, the seed capsules often hold the seeds for several months, shedding them gradually and usually close to the parent. As the seeds have a hard coat, they do not all germinate quickly, but viability seems to remain high. At the seedling stage, above-ground growth can be slow as an adequate root system develops to tolerate drought conditions, but plants can flower in their first summer after germination. Established plants can be up to 30 cm across with a central rootstock from which older vegetative shoots die back and are replaced by new shoots from the centre of the plant.

Distribution: Different subspecies of this species are found on Carboniferous limestone in south and north Wales, Cumbria and the Burren in Ireland. In Teesdale, subspecies *levigatum* is the only form, and it is found only on Cronkley Fell, the most northern and highest of the five localities for the species in the British Isles.

Habitat: Subspecies *levigatum* is confined to three areas of sugar-limestone on Cronkley Fell in more or less open vegetation, often adjacent to bare rock, or in closed turf of the CG9d Hair Sedge–False Sedge sub-community of the CG9 Blue Moor-grass–Limestone Bedstraw grassland community, with Sheep's-fescue, Blue Moor-grass, Crested Hair-grass, Rare Spring-sedge, Common Rock-rose, Mountain Avens, Alpine Meadow-rue, Small Scabious and Horseshoe Vetch; these last two species also characterize the CG9a Hoary Rock-rose–Squinancywort sub-community in which it grows elsewhere. It is always on rendzina-like skeletal soils with a small amount of black humus or a calcareous brown earth with pH >7. In contrast to the other localities of the other subspecies, the rainfall is high (up to 1,420 mm/year), insolation is low and winter temperatures are often below zero. The exposed edges of sugar-limestone suffer wind erosion which leaves the roots exposed and, together with seasonal droughts, causes the woody subterranean stems and shoots to dry out (and eventually break) and the shoots to die.

Status and conservation: It is an idle pastime to speculate on how much Hoary Rock-rose clothed the limestone at the end of the 18th century. Suffice to say that today there is probably a larger quantity of dried material in herbaria than living plants on the fell. Natural causes – the harsh climate, frost and wind – have contributed to the erosion of the friable sugar-limestone rock and accretion of soil derived from it, aided by fragmentation of the ground cover by Moles (creating hills and sub-surface runs), overgrazing by Rabbits and sheep (and the rubbing of exposed edges by these animals). Exclosures have been erected around all of the sites on Cronkley Fell to exclude sheep and Rabbits, but the Moles and destructive winds and rain remain. At one time, fine netting was placed over the eroded areas and edges to aid stability and recolonization. Constant vigilance is needed to maintain the fences and control the Rabbits. To prevent declines caused by shading due to undergrazing, sheep are allowed into the exclosures in the autumn and winter. Consideration needs to be given to renewing the protection from wind erosion.

Further information: https://bsbi.org/wp-content/uploads/dlm_uploads/Helianthemum_oelandicum_subsp_oelandicum_species_account.pdf

Hoary Rock-rose subspecies *levigatum*: **1** flowers *MR*; **2** flowers *DM*; **3** growing at Cronkley Fell *MEB*.

LC Alpine Penny-cress
Noccaea caerulescens (J. & C. Presl) F.K. Mey.

FIRST RECORD IN TEESDALE
1796, Oliver

ALTITUDE
250–750 m

LIFE-CYCLE
Biennial/perennial; FLOWERS March–September; SEEDS June–October.

Almost confined in Britain to rocks or soils enriched with lead or zinc, Alpine Penny-cress is found especially upon spoil heaps and mine waste and on metalliferous river gravels. It is one of a characteristic group of species that can thrive in such places where the toxic nature of the soil suppresses the growth of competing plants.

It is a rosette-forming plant, with erect, leafy, hairless stems that bear white or pale lilac flowers. After flowering, the stem elongates as the fruits mature, the fruits eventually becoming a flattened oval shape, up to 1 cm long, with obvious membranous wings: the 'penny' of its name. Characteristically, the style at the tip of the fruit is as long or longer than the notch formed by the converging wings. There are no related plants that have similar seeds and are found in such localities.

Distribution: While there are outliers on suitable metalliferous and limestone soils in the Scottish Highlands, Isle of Rum, Lake District, Welsh mountains and the Mendips, the main distribution of Alpine Penny-cress lies along the Pennine chain, from the North Pennines to the Peak District.

In Teesdale it can be found at Ravelin, Dubby Sike Mine and Green Hurth Old Mine, and at several sites around Nether Hearth, Rough Sike and Dodgen Pot. It is also known on old mine-workings in the higher part of the catchment, around Green Castle rocks, Maize Beck Scar and High Cup Nick. It formerly occurred lower down on rocks below Wynch Bridge.

Alpine Penny-cress, growing with Sheep's Sorrel, an atypical association, at Ravelin *MEB.*

Habitat: Alpine Penny-cress is locally abundant on heavy-metal spoil-heaps and shallow soils over Carboniferous limestone in lead-mining areas. It is found on open stony ground with sparse vegetation of the OV 37 Sheep's-fescue–Spring Sandwort community, where associated species are rather few: Wild Thyme, Fairy Flax, Harebell, Autumn Gentian and sometimes Moonwort and Pyrenean Scurvy-grass.

In addition, at Ravelin it can be found on shallow, peaty soils with Sheep's Sorrel, and nearby in ungrazed, closed Red Fescue grassland, where fruiting stems can reach 25 cm in height, rising above the grass sward by 5 cm or so.

Status and conservation: Alpine Penny-cress is largely protected from natural competition and overshading from plants by the toxic nature of the soil in which it grows. Destruction by human trampling, quad-bikes, four-wheel-drive vehicles and mountain bikes could pose a threat as more people are encouraged into the upland areas. Access to the most important and vulnerable sites needs to be controlled and supplemented by a good education programme, especially aimed at geologists and mineral collectors, not to destroy the rare plants.

Further information: https://plantatlas.brc.ac.uk/plant/thlaspi-caerulescens

Alpine Penny-cress: **1** in flower, growing at Ravelin *CS*; **2** in seed, growing at Ravelin *MEB.*

LC Hoary Whitlowgrass
Draba incana L.

FIRST RECORD IN TEESDALE
1789, Oliver

ALTITUDE
280–750 m

LIFE-CYCLE
Biennial or **short-lived perennial**; FLOWERS from May onwards; FRUITS from July.

Over its large altitudinal range, from sea level to mountain tops, Hoary Whitlowgrass is a rather variable species, growing in loose tufts up to 40 cm on sand dunes, for example, but compact rosettes with flower stems up to only 3 cm on mountain ledges. The rosettes comprise grey-green leaves densely covered in star-shaped hairs. As with many crucifers, the white, four-petalled flowers are not especially distinctive, in contrast to the seed pods which, are a broadly oval with a distinct twist.

Montane plants, such as in Teesdale, are mostly short-lived perennials that die after flowering: the age at which flowering occurs varies with the growing conditions and can be as much as eight years. A comparative study of plants on Widdybank and Cronkley Fells, the latter protected from grazing by an exclosure, showed the ungrazed ones to be almost twice as likely to flower and producing 50% more seed pods. With up to 20 seeds per pod, seed production can be high, but the study showed that only one in a hundred seedlings survives to become a three-year-old plant, capable of flowering.

Somewhat similar, Wall Whitlowgrass has leaves only sparsely hairy, a pod without a twist, and it is primarily a rock and wall plant of lower altitudes. Common Whitlowgrass is altogether more insubstantial, always annual, with a small rosette and petals that are deeply divided into two segments.

Distribution: Primarily montane, Hoary Whitlowgrass shows a disjunct distribution, from Snowdonia through the Pennines, the Lake District and Central Highlands, to coastal areas of northern Scotland and north-western Ireland. In Teesdale (and also in upper Weardale) it is widespread but thinly scattered and never abundant. On Widdybank Fell on open sugar-limestone and mining spoil, it forms discrete small colonies, whereas on Cronkley Fell it is more frequent. Additional populations are found on limestone outcrops, in broken turf up to the Pennine summit ridge, including Mickle Fell, and on lead and barytes mining spoil.

Habitat: On almost bare exposed sugar-limestone on both Cronkley and Widdybank Fells, it is in the CG9d Hair Sedge–False Sedge sub-community of the CG9 Blue Moor-grass–Limestone Bedstraw grassland community, with Sheep's-fescue, Spring Sandwort, Teesdale Violet, Rare Spring-sedge and Fairy Flax. It is sometimes found in the small, open pockets created by Moles in closed turf. At higher altitudes (above 750 m), additional species include Alpine Forget-me-not, Spring Gentian and Mossy Saxifrage of the CG9e Mossy Saxifrage–Pyrenean Scurvygrass sub-community. Hoary Whitlowgrass is also characteristic of soils on lead and barytes veins and mine spoil, in the open OV37 Sheep's-fescue–Spring Sandwort community with Sea Plantain, Hair Sedge, Mountain Pansy, Moonwort, Quaking-grass and some Blue Moor-grass.

Status and conservation: Numbers of this species have fluctuated considerably over the past 50 years, in response to drought, wind erosion and the impacts of Rabbits. On Widdybank Fell, the number of plants in the monitored plots peaked at more than 300 in the 1970s, but fell to four by 2002, and zero four years later. By that time there were only 12 plants known on the whole sugar-limestone area of the fell. On the summit of Cronkley Fell, most of the plants are within an exclosure; here the population is greater, but again much reduced compared with 50 years ago. Rabbits invaded the exclosure in 2004/5; numbers have subsequently been controlled, both by culling and naturally, as a result of the prolonged snow of winter 2009/10, but it is essential the rabbit-proof status of the exclosures is maintained. Conversely, undergrazing will also reduce habitat suitability for Hoary Whitlowgrass, so the exclosures will need to have periods of controlled grazing by sheep.

Further information: https://www.brc.ac.uk/plantatlas/plant/draba-incana

Hoary Whitlowgrass: **1** flowers *GH*; **2** leaves *MEB*; **3** growing at Cronkley Fell *GH*.

LC Pyrenean Scurvygrass
Cochlearia pyrenaica DC.

FIRST RECORD IN TEESDALE
1805, Winch

ALTITUDE
150–600 m

LIFE-CYCLE
Biennial/perennial; FLOWERS June–July; FRUITS July–September.

One of a confusing complex of montane forms of a genus that is primarily associated with the salt-affected maritime zone (and increasingly, road verges), Pyrenean Scurvygrass varies according to its habitat. It can be lanky and free-flowering by streams, or very compact on mossy spring-heads in higher areas, where it flowers less reliably. All forms have glossy basal leaves, heart-shaped at their base, and strongly reticulate veins on the dried fruits; the white flowers are markedly smaller than the more familiar coastal species.

Distribution: The core distribution of Pyrenean Scurvygrass runs from the Pennines and Lake District to the Scottish Highlands, with outliers in Skye, western Ireland, Snowdonia and the Mendips. Within this range there lies some taxonomic complexity: the subspecies in northern England (including Teesdale) and on the Isle of Skye is an ancestral form that is also known from the mountains of continental Europe. In Teesdale it is known by the River Tees and its tributaries down to Barnard Castle, often on heavy metal-contaminated ground.

Habitat: On open, damp, mostly base-rich soils and on heavy metal spoil-heaps mostly in upland areas, the habitats of Pyrenean Scurvygrass include the OV37 Sheep's-fescue–Spring Sandwort community with Wild Thyme, Harebell, Common Sorrel, Fairy Flax, Yarrow, Common Bird's-foot-trefoil and the CG9e Mossy Saxifrage–Pyrenean Scurvygrass sub-community of CG9 Blue Moor-grass–Limestone Bedstraw grassland, with Red Fescue, Hoary Whitlowgrass,

Pyrenean Scurvygrass, growing near Langdon Beck *MEB*.

Alpine Forget-me-not and an extensive bryophyte layer. Riverside communities are usually very open and the associated flora very varied.

Status and conservation: Locally frequent in damp, base-rich habitats, often contaminated with heavy metals, including where these have been washed down to lower river levels. Some losses have taken place where banks of streams in pastures have been damaged by trampling and storm floods; the main conservation requirement is to monitor its distribution to inform future actions.

Further information: https://www.brc.ac.uk/plantatlas/plant/cochlearia-pyrenaica

Thrift
Armeria maritima (Mill.) Willd.

FIRST RECORD IN TEESDALE
1796, Oliver

ALTITUDE
470–480 m

LIFE-CYCLE
Perennial, hummock-forming; **FLOWERS** April–August; **FRUITS** not found in Teesdale.

Predominantly a coastal plant, Thrift is found on salt marshes and clifftops all around Britain and Ireland, and increasingly on salt-affected major road verges. However, in common with a few other primarily maritime species such as Sea Plantain, it is also characteristic of bare habitats at altitude.

The plant grows from a thick rootstock, its leaf rosettes mounded into a rounded cushion. From this sprout the flower heads (if they are not grazed off), up to 2 cm across, dense clusters of white to rose-pink flowers. Thrift is a very variable plant in growth form, leaf length and flower details, and the 'rescue' of plants threatened by the filling of Cow Green Reservoir to the Botanic Garden of Durham University provided a fascinating opportunity to study this variation. It seems that the majority of variation has a genetic base, as the different forms from the wild were maintained in cultivation.

Outside the flowering period, Thrift could be mistaken for Sea Plantain (*p. 160*). Both plants produce similar rosettes, but Thrift has flat leaves that radiate like the spokes of a wheel and one distinct vein groove on the upper surface while those of Sea Plantain are 'U'-shaped in section, curved like a scimitar, and with long, white hairs in the centre of the rosette.

Thrift: **1** growing at Widdybank Fell *MR*; **2** flowers *JO'R*.

Distribution: As a montane species, Thrift is found in Scotland, the Lake District and the Pennines, often around old mine workings where the soils are contaminated with heavy metals. In Teesdale it is now to be found only on Widdybank Fell by Slapestone and Sand Sikes.

Habitat: A considerable quantity of Thrift grew in a closed sward of the CG10 Sheep's-fescue–Common Bent–Wild Thyme community over outwash from Rod's Vein, sugar-limestone sand contaminated with heavy metals in the mine-workings higher up the slope of Widdybank Fell. It was probably an early colonizer of the bare substrate that established well and persisted when the rest of the vegetation invaded.

Although rather rare, it is also found in the M10c Hook-beaked Tufa-moss sub-community of the M10 Dioecious Sedge–Common Butterwort community on fine silty gravel over almost bare rock, and on silty mud substrates kept moist with base-rich drainage. Associated species are very few: in the hummocks of moss are Bird's-eye Primrose, Spring Sandwort, Knotted Pearlwort and Sea Plantain, and in the silty mud Few-flowered Spike-rush may also be frequent.

Status and conservation: Thrift was one species severely affected by the flooding of Cow Green Reservoir. All plants under threat of flooding were removed into the safety of the botanic gardens at Durham and Manchester Universities and elsewhere. Alas the stocks of plants at both universities have been destroyed. The existing hummocks produce some flowers; most of which are soon eaten. Individual plants are well-anchored into the substrate and the cushions increase by lateral rosettes; this aids their long-term survival, but ideally individual plants should be protected from grazing to allow flowering and seed production to occur.

Further information: https://www.brc.ac.uk/plantatlas/plant/armeria-maritima

Thrift, growing at Sand Sike *JO'R*.

Thrift, leaves (LEFT) with Sea Plantain leaves (RIGHT) *MEB*.

Alpine Bistort
Bistorta vivipara (L.) Delarbre

FIRST RECORD IN TEESDALE

1798, E. Robson

ALTITUDE

280–750 m

LIFE-CYCLE

Perennial; FLOWERS June–August; bulbils present July–August.

Alpine Bistort is a slender perennial, with a straight, stout rhizome that produces shoots with glossy, dark green, lanceolate leaves up to 7 cm long. Few of the shoots remain purely leafy, as most produce a terminal flower spike up to 8 cm long. The inflorescence has small white or pink flowers in the upper half, and purple bulbils in the lower section. The flowers are said not to be fertile, hence reproduction is vegetative: the bulbils are condensed shoots that may produce a few small leaves from July onwards before dropping off and developing roots in the soil.

Distribution: Frequent in central and northern Scotland, present in the Southern Uplands and widespread in the central and northern Pennines; elsewhere it is rare and local in the Lake District, North Wales and Ireland. In Teesdale it is now rare in meadows, but fairly common in upland lime-rich grasslands, basic flushes by the river and on damp rock ledges from Wynch Bridge to the watershed.

Habitat: Occurs in a wide range of habitats, from upland basic to neutral grassland, pasture and occasionally meadows to wet rock ledges, and so is a component of several plant communities.

In calcareous grass- and sedge-rich swards of the CG9d Hair Sedge–False Sedge sub-community of the CG9 Blue Moor-grass–Limestone Bedstraw grassland community, it grows with Sheep's-fescue, Crested Hair-grass, Quaking-grass, Wild Thyme, Harebell, Spring Gentian, Northern Bedstraw, Hair Sedge, False Sedge and Lesser Clubmoss, as well as in a limestone grass-heath variant of CG9 over metamorphosed limestone with the additional species of Heather, Red Fescue, Crowberry, Alpine Meadow-rue and Wood Anemone.

On lead-mining spoil in the OV37 Sheep's-fescue–Spring Sandwort community, Spring Sandwort, Sheep's-fescue, Crested Hair-grass, Wild Thyme and Autumn Gentian are associates, and on hummocks in gravelly flushes in the short sedge-marsh of the M10 Dioecious Sedge–Common Butterwort community with Sheep's-fescue, False Sedge, Bird's-eye Primrose, Common Butterwort, Scottish Asphodel, Dioecious, Glaucous, Tawny and Flea Sedges and Alpine Meadow-rue. In the associated M11 Common Yellow-sedge–Yellow Saxifrage community, it occurs with Dioecious, Tawny, Carnation and Flea Sedges, Long-stalked Yellow-sedge, Broad-leaved Cottongrass, Common Butterwort and various mosses and liverworts.

In some herb-rich meadows and similar habitats near the Tees, it is part of the MG3 Sweet Vernal-grass–Wood Crane's-bill community with Red Fescue, Rough Meadow-grass, Quaking-grass, Timothy, Yellow Oat-grass, Crested Dog's-tail, Globeflower, lady's-mantle spp., Pignut, Common Knapweed, Great Burnet, Northern Bedstraw and several orchids.

Status and conservation: The species is still widespread but has decreased slightly in the last 50 years. While it is fairly tolerant of trampling, such pressures will damage the plants and, if on a slope, the rootstocks will become exposed, then detached and die. Neither is it eaten by Rabbits apparently, but the plants are damaged by burrowing and scuffing; conversely it is also vulnerable to over-shading resulting from undergrazing. All of these activities can reduce the number of flower spikes, and thus the potential for increase from bulbils. It is therefore important to ensure that grasslands are neither overgrazed nor undergrazed, that herb-rich meadows and banks are managed appropriately, and that plants are protected from trampling when adjacent to footpaths.

Further information: https://www.brc.ac.uk/plantatlas/plant/persicaria-vivipara

Alpine Bistort: **1** growing at Garrigill, Cumbria *LR*; **2** flowers and bulbils *MEB*

N Teesdale Sandwort
Sabulina stricta (Sw.) Rchb.

Schedule 8

FIRST RECORD IN TEESDALE
1844, Gibson

ALTITUDE
490–510 m

LIFE-CYCLE
Perennial; FLOWERS June–July; FRUITS July–August.

Although perennial, Teesdale Sandwort in its eponymous location is generally short-lived, acting more like an annual, needing to set seed each year. Flowing water may be a dispersal mechanism for seeds, as small plants are sometimes found 'down-stream' from known sites. With five-petalled white flowers, the petals about the same length as the sepals, it looks very much like related species. Knotted Pearlwort, with which it frequently grows, is a more robust annual with conspicuous large white flowers that appear in late summer. Spring Sandwort, although larger and glandular flowers at the same time (1 cm across, rather than 5 mm, with petals longer than the sepals) and four or five (not three) styles. Spring Sandwort, grows in many of the same areas, but is larger and more cushion-forming, with larger flowers that have red anthers.

Distribution: Primarily a sub-Arctic plant with a circumpolar distribution, in Britain it is known only from Teesdale, and there only on Widdybank Fell. It is mainly scattered in base-rich flushes on the west- and east-facing slopes on the dolerite, and occasionally amongst the grass and dry-heath communities over the sugar-limestone.

Habitat: Teesdale Sandwort is found in open, gravelly and silty flushes, in a stream-bed over dolerite and baked marl in sugar-limestone, all with base-rich flushing. It is most frequent in closed short sedge-marsh vegetation of the M10 Dioecious Sedge–Common Butterwort community, especially the M10c sub-community characterized by Hook-beaked Tufa-moss.

Status and conservation: Six localities have been found for Teesdale Sandwort, all within the NNR. Sporadic counts from 1984, with full surveys in 1985 and 2018, have indicated an overall decline, with an average of 360 plants in the early part of that period, but now only around half that number. However, individual colonies do fluctuate widely, as might be expected with a short-lived perennial.

Plants are susceptible to trampling damage, and sadly one of the main causes of decline seems to be botanists looking for the plant, and especially photographers – please be careful with your feet, elbows and tripod legs! All sites should be monitored regularly, including for invasion by other species, such as Red Fescue and Cuckooflower, which may suppress small plants such as Teesdale Sandwort.

Further information: https://bsbi.org/wp-content/uploads/dlm_uploads/Minuartia_stricta_species_account.pdf

Teesdale Sandwort, growing at Widdybank Fell *DM*.

LC Spring Sandwort
Sabulina verna (L.) Rchb.

FIRST RECORD IN TEESDALE
1796, Oliver and Harriman

ALTITUDE
280–800 m

LIFE-CYCLE
Perennial, with rooting branches; FLOWERS May–September, finishing earlier in extreme weather conditions such as drought or frost; FRUITS from June onwards.

Spring Sandwort is one of the two plant species most tolerant of heavy metal contamination, the other being Alpine Penny-cress; the former is an accumulator of heavy metals, perhaps because of the absence of mycorrhiza in the roots, whereas the latter is not. It is a winter-green perennial that forms low cushions or mats by the rooting of prostrate shoots. The five-petalled, white flowers are up to 9 mm in diameter and have distinctive red anthers: this growth form and anther colour distinguishes it from related white-flowered species such as Knotted Pearlwort.

In windy and/or extremely cold seasons, the green leaves can be strongly flushed with red or purple. It has a long flowering season, unless summer conditions are very dry. The numerous flowers produce many seeds, most of which are thought to germinate in the autumn, although some form a persistent seed bank. It is most frequent on south-facing aspects, but shade-intolerant and absent from steep slopes.

Distribution: Spring Sandwort has a disjunct distribution from Cornwall to Shetland on Carboniferous limestone, metal-rich soil, dolerite, serpentine and base-rich volcanic rocks, largely in the uplands. It is especially frequent in the Pennines and the Lake District. In Teesdale it is widely scattered on both sides of the dale on mining spoil and associated heavy metal-contaminated soils, on limestone-derived soils as well as on river and stream gravel and adjacent rocks.

Spring Sandwort, growing on Cronkley Fell *MR*.

Habitat: A characteristic species of habitats that are contaminated with heavy metals, such as the spoil of lead mines and on stable river gravels below such workings, Spring Sandwort is most frequent in the OV37 Sheep's-fescue–Spring Sandwort community on metalliferous soils; associated species include Alpine Penny-cress (very rare in Teesdale), Wild Thyme, Common Bent, Limestone Bedstraw, Harebell, Fairy Flax and Moonwort. These habitats remain sparsely vegetated, largely due to the toxic nature of the soil to most plants.

It is also found in open, calcareous, rocky sites and adjacent grassland and on Whin Sill: its localities are typically mildly acidic to neutral, pH 5–8. It grows in the semi-closed CG9 Blue Moor-grass–Limestone Bedstraw community, with Yarrow, Red Fescue, eyebrights, Ribwort Plantain, White Clover and Common Sorrel and, more scattered, in open, stony calcareous flushes of the M11 Common Yellow-sedge–Yellow Saxifrage community that merges into the M10 Dioecious Sedge–Common Butterwort community. Associated plants of this mixed community include Long-stalked Yellow-sedge, Tawny, Carnation and Flea Sedges, Few-flowered Spike-rush, Bird's-eye Primrose, Alpine Bistort, Alpine Meadow-rue, Variegated Horsetail, Knotted Pearlwort, Three-flowered Rush, Blue Moor-grass and Quaking-grass..

Status and conservation: This species is largely protected from natural competition and shade by the toxic nature of the soil. Damage by human trampling, quad bikes, four-wheel-drive vehicles and mountain bikes could pose a threat as more people are encouraged to visit upland areas, including to study the geology or search for minerals or geological specimens. Access to vulnerable sites must be matched by education to create an awareness of the need to avoid damaging the flora or removing any geological material.

Further information: https://www.brc.ac.uk/plantatlas/plant/minuartia-verna

Jacob's-ladder
Polemonium caeruleum L.

FIRST RECORD IN TEESDALE
*c.*1700, Johnson

ALTITUDE
186–480 m

LIFE-CYCLE
Perennial; FLOWERS June–July; REPRODUCTION by seed.

Jacob's-ladder has a very long recorded history in Teesdale as it has been identified in the post-glacial pollen record from Cow Green. However, as a plant it has rarely been seen in recent centuries. It was first reported in Johnson's list around 1700, but then disappeared from subsequent lists until it was rediscovered by James Backhouse Sr. and Jr. in 1843 at an undisclosed location.

Its habitat requirements elsewhere suggest that it could still be present in Teesdale, although if so it must be at a very remote locality, given that it is a showy plant, up to a metre tall, with many large, blue (occasionally white) flowers, and readily recognizable even when not flowering by its long, pinnate leaves.

Distribution: Considered to be native in the Pennines, between Derbyshire and Northumberland, Jacob's-ladder is also frequently naturalized from gardens elsewhere, with the exception of Ireland and north-western Scotland. It is locally frequent in the Peak District (Dovedale, Manifold Valley and Monsal Dale), Yorkshire Dales (especially the Malham area) and at its northernmost native locality, Bishop Dale near Alwinton, Northumberland. In Teesdale extensive recent searches have failed to find the plant and it must be presumed extinct locally; knowledge of the past locations has been lost but a suggested place for potential survival unnoticed would be in shake-holes in limestone strata of the Yoredale Series.

Habitat: Extrapolation from extant populations in the Yorkshire Dales and Peak District suggests that in Teesdale Jacob's-ladder is likely to have been present on stabilized scree and limestone/dolerite cliffs that were never completely wooded. In such places it occurs in tall-herb communities with Globeflower and Melancholy Thistle, sometimes in open woodland of Ash, Wych Elm, Hazel and Bird Cherry.

Status and conservation: Searches for remnant populations of Jacob's-ladder should continue and, if re-found, appropriate steps taken to protect and manage the habitat.

Further information: https://www.brc.ac.uk/plantatlas/plant/polemonium-caeruleum

Jacob's-ladder: **1** growing at Bishopdale *TLa;* **2** flowers *MEB.*

T Bird's-eye Primrose
Primula farinosa L.

FIRST RECORD IN TEESDALE
1794, Oliver

ALTITUDE
280–554 m

LIFE-CYCLE
Perennial, short-lived; FLOWERS May–June, occasionally in the autumn; FRUITS July–August; SEED germinates in spring.

With rosettes of grey-green, crinkly edged leaves, covered especially underneath and on the stems with a pale yellow mealy coating – and hence its specific name from *farina* the Latin for flour – Bird's-eye Primrose is recognizable even when not in flower. But in bloom its loose heads of small, pink (occasionally white) flowers are simply unmistakable and one of the visual delights of early summer in damp grassland on limestone.

In the nearby Yorkshire Dales, most plants have their flower clusters raised on stems up to 15 cm long, usually a single flowering stem per rosette. This form does occur in Teesdale, but there is also a form that is stemless, the flowers nestled into the rosette of leaves. Studies have shown that this variety, *acaulis*, occupied 0·1% of the total Teesdale population at any time and is believed to have a genetic basis. Another axis of variation, like in other primrose species, is in the form of the flowers: in one study 86% of plants were thrum-eyed (having stamens longer than the stigma), the remainder being pin-eyed, their stigma protruding from the stamens.

On Widdybank Fell, until relatively recently at least, grazing pressure ensured that only between 5% and 15% of rosettes fruited successfully in any one summer; it is believed that the sweet scent of the flowers attracts the attentions of sheep. Some grazing is, however, necessary as Bird's-eye Primrose is a light-demander and is therefore eliminated by the tall vegetation that results from undergrazing; one sample population in short sedge-marsh declined by two-thirds when the sward grew to a height of just 15 cm.

Distribution: Widespread on Carboniferous and Magnesian limestones in North Yorkshire, Durham and Cumbria, with a few localities outside this core range. In Teesdale it is found by the Tees and on the sides of streams and becks in calcareous rough pastures, turfy marshes and grasslands and flushes associated with the metamorphosed limestone; also on High Hurth Edge, in Harwood Dale, by Ashgill Beck and in flushes by the Maize Beck near Birkdale.

Habitat: A plant of moist to wet base-rich habitats, Bird's-eye Primrose grows most frequently in the often cattle-poached, turfy, marshes with M10 Dioecious Sedge–Common Butterwort short sedge-marsh and the M11 Common Yellow-sedge–Yellow Saxifrage mire communities, as well as on the eroding sides of drumlins that are flushed with base-rich, calcareous water. Associated species include Dioecious, Tawny and Carnation Sedges, Small-fruited and Long-stalked Yellow-sedges, Broad-leaved Cottongrass, Common Butterwort, and various mosses and liverworts.

It is also present in CG9 Blue Moor-grass–Limestone Bedstraw grassland in the CG9c Flea Sedge–Carnation Sedge and CG9d Hair Sedge–False Sedge sub-communities, particularly on the moister areas of Widdybank and Cronkley Fells, and occasionally in the Heather–Crowberry variant. Constant species include Quaking-grass, Harebell, Glaucous Sedge, Sheep's-fescue, Fairy Flax, Blue Moor-grass and Wild Thyme.

Status and conservation: Almost all the locations of Bird's-eye Primrose in Teesdale have SSSI status. A twenty-year gap in monitoring after 1983 covered a period when most of the sampled populations fell to approximately a third of their pre-1983 levels. It would seem that much of this decline was due to suboptimal grazing pressures. In 1995, the number of sheep on Widdybank Fell was reduced by a half, leading to undergrazing of the less palatable plants which became taller and denser and shaded out many of the Bird's-eye Primroses. Then from 2002 the Rabbit population increased hugely, which led to overgrazing of the grassland and short sedge-marsh, as well as damage from burrowing and scraping.

Effective Rabbit control was eventually introduced in 2005 and the vegetation, including the populations of Bird's-eye Primrose on the fell-top, began to recover, but by 2012 the numbers had decreased again in closed communities due to undergrazing. Clearly, management of grazing intensity by both sheep and Rabbits is essential, and monitoring of the sward height is a key part of this.

Bird's-eye Primrose: 1 growing at Cronkley Fell *MR*; 2 flowers *MR*; 3 var. *acaulis MEB*; 3 white form *MR*.

If undergrazing persists, mowing and removal of the cuttings can be considered as an additional approach. In the lower rough pastures and on streamside flats, it was the spread of tall rushes into the short sedge-marsh communities that adversely affected the primrose. Where these rushes have been mown and removed biennially there has been some increase in flowering plants, but monitoring has been inadequate. A further management approach could be to reduce the dominance of tall rushes by re-opening some of the existing drains (grips) and lowering the water table; this may also provide new bare patches for seedlings to establish.

Further information: https://www.brc.ac.uk/plantatlas/plant/primula-farinosa

Bearberry
Arctostaphylos uva-ursi (L.) Spreng.

[PHOTOS: *p. 152*]

FIRST RECORD IN TEESDALE
1798, Binks and Oliver

ALTITUDE
385–430 m

LIFE-CYCLE
Perennial; FLOWERS May–July; FRUITS July–September.

A predominantly northern species, the outlying populations of Bearberry to the south of its main range are evidence of a former, more widespread distribution. It is a prostrate shrub with long, rooting branches which forms large mats of dark green foliage, the leaves leathery and obovate, 1–2 cm long, conspicuously reticulately veined and borne on a twisted leaf stalk. Its attractive flowers with 5–12 in a dense raceme are almost globose, and white with a pinkish tinge; the fruits are red and glossy, up to 8 mm in diameter. However, flowering and fruiting success is variable: on Dine Holm Scar, for example, in 2007 flowers were produced in profusion, but subsequent fruits barely ripened and were few in number.

The related Cowberry is similar, with leathery, evergreen leaves that have less strongly reticulate leaf veins, while in Bilberry the leaves are thinner, pointed and deciduous.

Distribution: Widespread in central and northern Scotland from sea level to 915 m, also in parts of western Ireland. South of its main range, it is rare and local in the Southern Uplands, the Lake District and the Pennines, from Northumberland to Derbyshire. Considerable losses have taken place through moor burning and rock falls leading to a very disjunct distribution. In Teesdale it is found on Whin Sill crags and block scree on Dine Holm Scar and the western face of Cronkley Scar, a large patch on Raven Scar and a small quantity on Falcon Clints. A population on rocks by Cauldron Snout now appears to have been lost.

Habitat: Found on Whin Sill crags and block scree, with Parsley Fern, Bell Heather, Common Juniper, Heather, Woolly Hair-moss and Fir Clubmoss. It also occurs by the Tees near Wynch Bridge on Whin Sill and limestone rocks.

Status and conservation: Very scarce in Teesdale, individual plants of Bearberry on cliffs have been known in their present sites for many years. While populations are stable, they are always at risk of rock collapse; the Dine Holm site is in the NNR and therefore should be safe from any application to extend the adjacent High Force Quarry.

Further information: https://www.brc.ac.uk/plantatlas/plant/arctostaphylos-uva-ursi

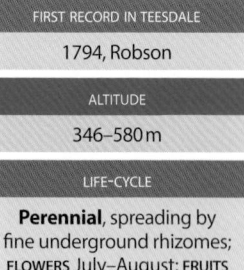

Bearberry: **1** growing on Dine Holm Scar *MEB*; **2** flowers *DM*; **3** fruit *MEB*.

LC Northern Bedstraw
Galium boreale L.

FIRST RECORD IN TEESDALE
1794, Robson

ALTITUDE
346–580 m

LIFE-CYCLE
Perennial, spreading by fine underground rhizomes; FLOWERS July–August; FRUITS August–September.

A perennial with creeping rootstock, Northern Bedstraw has erect, stiff, four-angled stems and whorls of four leaves, which are rough on the margin and midrib below. In the absence of grazing it produces branched stems up to 45 cm tall, with masses of white, star-like flowers and variable numbers of brown fruits, clothed in hooked bristles.

All bedstraws have a degree of similarity with whorled foliage, but the only patch-forming, white-flowered perennial relative, Woodruff, has leaves in whorls of 6–9 and is predominantly a woodland species.

Distribution: A largely montane species, Northern Bedstraw is found from the Brecon Beacons and Snowdonia, through the northern Pennines and Lake District to the Southern Uplands, central and north-western Scotland and northern and western Ireland. In Teesdale it occurs by the Tees from Cauldron Snout to below Middleton, and on Cronkley and Widdybank Fells, including

Cronkley Scar. It is very scarce in both Cronkley and Widdybank Pastures, and scattered on base-rich rocks and flushes up to the western watershed.

Habitat: Among boulders and riverside shingle by the Tees, in meadow-type vegetation of the MG3 Sweet Vernal-grass–Wood Crane's-bill community and particularly in CG9 Blue Moor-grass–Limestone Bedstraw grassland; associated species include Spring Gentian, Mountain Everlasting, Alpine Bistort, Wild Thyme, Common Rock-rose, Sheep's-fescue and Red Fescue, Quaking-grass, Hair and Glaucous Sedges and Spring-sedge. Alongside the river it is found with a variety of plants including Shrubby Cinquefoil, Spring Sandwort and willows, including Tea-leaved Willow.

Status and conservation: Most populations appear to be stable, although those in Cronkley and Widdybank Pastures have undergone declines as a result of overgrazing. In an exclosure established in 1970 at approximately 500 m on Widdybank Fell, Northern Bedstraw has formed dense, freely flowering patches 40–50 cm tall. As overgrazing has been addressed though lower stocking levels and Rabbit control, undergrazing has started to become a problem for species such as this, and mowing has been introduced, along with some increase in sheep numbers. In such a dynamic situation, monitoring must be continued, not only on the two fells and pastures, but also by the Tees where more stable communities are developing now that the river flow is regulated and grazing has been removed. Monitoring should also include fruit production and germination; stock transplanted to Durham and Manchester Universities did, after some years, produce viable seed and new seedlings, but these have never been recorded in the wild. These stocks no longer exist.

Further information: https://www.brc.ac.uk/plantatlas/plant/galium-boreale

Northern Bedstraw, growing on the Tees bank *GH*.

EN Field Gentian
Gentianella campestris (L.) Borner

NERC

FIRST RECORD IN TEESDALE
1805, Winch

ALTITUDE
260–385 m

LIFE-CYCLE
Biennial; FLOWERS July–October; FRUITS August–October.

The flowers of Field Gentian are divided into four parts, with two broad outer sepals almost concealing the two lanceolate inner ones. This distinguishes it from the more widespread Autumn Gentian, which has five petals and usually five lanceolate sepal lobes. Generally, Field Gentian can be recognized by its bluish-lilac, rather than purplish, flowers.

As a biennial that cannot spread vegetatively, it needs to reproduce by seed each year. As flower production and seed ripening are strongly affected by the weather, populations vary considerably in number between years. One population on the riverbank to the west of Wynch Bridge has been monitored closely: between 2006 and 2012 the number of flowering plants varied between zero and 77, smaller numbers being associated with very dry spring weather. However, drought has a beneficial effect in subsequent years as it helps to create the open patches that are essential germination niches for this plant. It would seem that the seed can remain dormant and viable in the soil for several years, as plants have been found in new locations following the creation of germination niches either by natural processes such as drought or by management intervention.

Distribution: Widespread but local throughout Scotland, northern England, coastal Wales and northern and western Ireland, Field Gentian has suffered a severe historical decline, and is now very rare south of the Lake District and the adjacent Pennines. In Teesdale it is found by the Tees between Wynch and Holwick Head Bridges, in open vegetation on the embankment at the former mouth of the Little Tees, on Haugh Hill in Harwood Dale, on Cetry Bank, above Crookburn Bridge on limestone slopes with Lesser Clubmoss and Mountain Everlasting, and on slopes above

Field Gentian, growing at Harwood *MR*.

Maize Beck near Birkdale. At some of these sites, numbers were very small and may no longer be extant; one known former locality is by Harwood Beck opposite Seavy Hill Barn.

Habitat: Plants have been found in hay meadow vegetation, with the essential open niches, of the MG3 Sweet Vernal-grass–Wood Crane's-bill community, as for example on the bank of the Tees west of Wynch Bridge and on Haugh Hill. Associated species include Downy Oat-grass, Quaking-grass, Crested Dog's-tail, Common Bent, Sheep's-fescue and Red Fescue, Glaucous Sedge, Lady's Bedstraw, Harebell, Sea and Ribwort Plantains, Fairy Flax, Great Burnet, Devil's-bit Scabious and Yarrow. It has also been found in broken, short sedge-marsh of the M10 Dioecious Sedge–Common Butterwort calcareous flush community, as on Cetry Bank and by the Maize Beck, and at Crook Burn over limestone strata in CG9 Blue Moor-grass–Limestone Bedstraw grassland with Lesser Clubmoss and Mountain Everlasting. It was formerly found on very open stream-side shingle with Wild Thyme and Spring Sandwort by the Harwood Beck and on a roadside bank in Harwood Dale.

Status and conservation: Plants with the life history of Field Gentian always provide conservation challenges, their populations responding strongly to both natural and human-related events. It is assumed that the status in many sites is more or less stable as their physical state is unlikely to change. However, by the river, the picture is very different. High flows and periodic flooding have always happened, and help to create bare patches that benefit the germination of this species; conversely, the deposition of gravel banks during flood events can cover and kill established plants. Furthermore, populations in riverbank areas are susceptible to trampling by visitors.

Since the construction of Cow Green Reservoir, the situation has changed. Downstream river flow is regulated by the reservoir with the result that extreme high flows are now less extreme, and the river-margin habitats are becoming overgrown. In the absence of grazing, the germination niches for Field Gentian are fewer, and grazing is impractical because of both the limited extent of grassland by the river and of the large number of people and dogs using the area. It may be that mowing, with removal of the cut vegetation, could maintain a suitably open sward for this species.

Further information: https://bsbi.org/wp-content/uploads/dlm_uploads/Gentianella_campestris_species_account.pdf

Field Gentian, flowers *MR*.

Spring Gentian
Gentiana verna L.

Schedule 8

FIRST RECORD IN TEESDALE
1796, Harriman

ALTITUDE
400–830 m

LIFE-CYCLE
Perennial, with long stolons; FLOWERS April–May (sometimes as early as March or as late as early June); FRUITS June–August.

Arguably the most iconic of the rare plants of Teesdale, if only for its unmistakable intensely blue flowers, Spring Gentian is a disjunctly distributed plant of the mountains of central and southern Europe, extending north into the Arctic. Across its range it has developed morphological differences: Teesdale plants have affinities with those from the Pyrenees and Alps, for example, while Irish plants may be closer to ones from Arctic Russia.

It has a compact basal rosette of opposite pairs of oval, pale green leaves, which are either solitary or grow together to form a dense tuft. Similar rosettes include those of Autumn Gentian (which are darker green and more pointed), Dwarf Milkwort (with leaves spirally arranged) and Daisy (dark green spoon-shaped leaves). Seedling cotyledons of Spring Gentian and those of Dwarf Milkwort (*p. 103*) and Teesdale Violet (*p. 124*) are all oblong and of similar size and need true leaves for separation.

Most flowers appear in May and they open when conditions are warm and bright. The flowering period is shorter when there are frequent hot, sunny days, but prolonged by intermittent periods of cool and dull weather. Flower stems grow to a height of about 50 mm, but in fruit these elongate up to 150 mm. Studies on Widdybank Fell have shown that individual rosettes live typically for three to five (maximum seven) years, with greatest mortality in the first year, giving an average annual death rate of around a third. Each rosette flowers just once, usually in its second or third year. Pollination appears to be by bumblebees, although these insects also steal nectar by biting through the base of the flower.

Distribution: Spring Gentian is limited to the limestones of Upper Teesdale and western Ireland, centred on the Burren and Galway Bay. Within Teesdale it was found in 48 one-kilometre squares in both 1963 and in 2002, from Forest- and Harwood-in-Teesdale to Long Crag, Mickle Fell, Little Fell and Crook Burn.

Habitat: Spring Gentian is widespread where limestone grassland grows on calcareous brown earths around pH 7, most frequently in the CG9d Hair Sedge–False Sedge sub-community of CG9 Blue Moor-grass–Limestone Bedstraw grassland; also in CG10 Sheep's-fescue–Common Bent–Wild Thyme grassland. Avoiding extremes of soil moisture, it is absent from the driest areas on or around eroding sugar-limestone edges, where the almost humus-free, shallow rendzina soils are subject to intense drought conditions. It is also usually absent from the gravelly flush areas such as the M10 Dioecious Sedge–Common Butterwort community, except on small hummocks of calcareous glacial drift within them, and steep, eroding banks by the Tees as at Cetry Bank and Haugh Hill. It can tolerate some competition from dwarf shrubs and the light shade they produce, and is found in an unnamed variant of the CG9d sub-community characterized by Heather and Crowberry.

Status and conservation: A recent survey (2017) showed a 54% reduction since the 1970s in the area occupied by Spring Gentians on Widdybank Fell, similar or greater reductions will have occurred in the rest of its range, except in the exclosures on Cronkley Fell.

Spring Gentian: 1 flower *DM*; 2 fruit *CG*; 3 growing at Cronkley Fell *MR*.

It has been lost from most meadows and calcareous rough pastures, a result of increased fertilizer use, a reduction in the application of basic slag and lime and a change from hay to silage/haylage production. On the higher grasslands, some losses have resulted from a rapid increase in the Rabbit population, partly because they are no longer controlled by severe winter weather with long periods of deep snow cover on a regular basis.

On the Moor House-Upper Teesdale NNR, exclosures have been erected on Mickle Fell to prevent grazing by sheep, and on Cronkley Fell to exclude sheep and Rabbits. The number of sheep on the fells has been reduced as a consequence of the outbreak of Foot-and-mouth Disease in 2001 and by management agreements with the landowners and tenant farmers. In addition, where the Rabbit population is being controlled, undergrazing is now of concern. On Cronkley Fell sheep have been allowed into the exclosures in autumn and winter, and numbers are being increased on Widdybank Fell to at least 400, from a previous ceiling of 250, although still fewer than the 600 pre-1995.

Monitoring of plants in marked plots on Widdybank Fell has illustrated the changes well. From 698 rosettes in the plots in 1969, numbers fell to 112 by 2002 as the effects of undergrazing intensified. Subsequently numbers continued to fall to a low point of just 17 in 2012, before rising again to 168 by 2018 as management levels were rationalized, involving additional grazing and occasional mowing.

There was continuous monitoring of sample plots on Widdybank Fell from 1968–80 and 2000 to the present day, while on Mickle Fell monitoring has been irregular and sometimes only of flowering plants. It is essential that monitoring of this iconic species should continue.

Further information: https://bsbi.org/wp-content/uploads/dlm_uploads/Gentiana_verna_species_account.pdf

LC Pale Forget-me-not
Myosotis stolonifera (DC.) J. Gay ex Leresche & Levier

FIRST RECORD IN TEESDALE
1927, Lousley

ALTITUDE
130–820 m

LIFE-CYCLE
Perennial, spreading by stolons; **FLOWERS** June–August; **FRUITS** July–August.

First recorded in Britain in 1919 from the northern Pennines, Pale Forget-me-not is a characteristic upland plant often spreading by stolons along mountain rills. Its flowers are small for a forget-me-not, only 5 mm in diameter, and often very pale blue, appearing white or grey. It is also distinguished from other wetland forget-me-nots by its relatively short leaves, rarely more than three times as long as wide.

Distribution: Found throughout the upland areas of northern England and southern Scotland, it is well known in the Lake District and on the west escarpment of the Tees catchment; its apparent scarcity on the east side of the Pennines may be due to under-recording, related to the belated recognition of its identification features. In Teesdale it is locally frequent in rills and high-level flushes in Moor House NNR, including Trout Beck Head, the flanks of Great Dun Fell, Maize Beck, Dufton and Meldon Fells, on the south-western side of Cow Green Reservoir and Swarth Beck Head. The first record, from 1927, was on Widdybank Fell.

Habitat: It is to be found usually lining the sides of high-altitude rills and in spring-head flushes with abundant Blinks and Marsh Saxifrage.

1 Pale Forget-me-not *JO'R*; **2** Alpine Forget-me-not *MEB*.

Status and conservation: Pale Forget-me-not is still probably under-recorded, so more searches are required, along with monitoring (and responding to) potential threats including off-road mountain bikes, motorcycles and quad bikes causing ruts and altering the hydrology.

Further information: https://www.brc.ac.uk/plantatlas/plant/myosotis-stolonifera

Alpine Forget-me-not
Myosotis alpestris F. W. Schmidt.

FIRST RECORD IN TEESDALE
1852, Backhouse Sr. and Jr.

ALTITUDE
≥720m

LIFE–CYCLE
Perennial, some basal leaves over-wintering; FLOWERS late-June–July; FRUITS late-July–August; GERMINATION spring.

Resembling many of the other forget-me-not species in having sky-blue flowers with a yellow centre, Alpine Forget-me-not is a true mountain species, a perennial herb rising to 20 cm when in flower, although often very much smaller in grazed turf rather than on ungrazed rock ledges. Although it can be common over small areas, it does not spread vegetatively and is never dominant; its basal leaves, clothed in spreading hairs, may survive through the winter and are frost- and apparently drought-tolerant. With 5–30 flowers per plant, each producing four shiny black nutlets, seed production is high, as is the germination rate (at least in cultivation experiments) of more than 70%. Plants grown from seed flowered in their second year.

The more abundant Wood Forget-me-not is often confused with this species, especially in its dwarfed montane form. The base of its calyx tube is rounded, its brown nutlets pointed and fruiting pedicels 1·5–2× longer than the calyx. In contrast, Alpine Forget-me-not has a narrowed base to its calyx tube, rounded, black nutlets and fruiting pedicels as long as the calyx. Furthermore, in Teesdale at least, Wood Forget-me-not is believed to occur only at altitudes below 520 m.

Distribution: In the UK, only in the Ben Lawers area of central Scotland and Teesdale. **Teesdale:** two populations near the summit of Mickle Fell; many plants on Little Fell; and a few on Great Dun Fell.

Habitat: Semi-open stabilized scree flushed with calcareous drainage, covered with turf of the CG9d Hair Sedge–False Sedge sub-community of the CG9 Blue Moor-grass–Limestone Bedstraw grassland community, with Spring Gentian, Spring Sandwort, Mountain Everlasting, Mossy

Saxifrage, Hoary Whitlowgrass, Wild Thyme, Quaking-grass, Crested Hair-grass, occasional Blue Moor-grass and several mosses and lichens.

Status and conservation: The three Teesdale locations have been subjected to heavy grazing by sheep and Rabbits. The population on Great Dun Fell declined to around 40 plants in 2003, but since the decrease in sheep numbers from 2001, the number of plants count rose to >3,000 in 2009. On Little Fell around 100,000 were estimated in 1987 and on Mickle Fell >12,000 in 2010. The latter population is now protected from sheep and Rabbit grazing by an exclosure. Furthermore, sheep numbers on Little Fell and Great Dun Fell have been greatly reduced, and the Rabbit population was depleted during the severe winter of 2010–11. Consequently, undergrazing is now a threat to the Alpine Forget-me-not in all its locations. Monitoring needs to be continued and grazing in the exclosures adjusted as necessary. In future, the survival of the species may be affected by a decrease in the snow cover and wetter, warmer winters leading to rotting and death. Other more unexpected factors may also be of concern: the Little Fell population flowered extremely profusely in 2006 but the following year they were being devoured by caterpillars.

Further information: https://bsbi.org/wp-content/uploads/dlm_uploads/Myosotis_alpestris_species_account.pdf

LC Sea Plantain
Plantago maritima L.

FIRST RECORD IN TEESDALE
1805, Winch

ALTITUDE
<150–877 m

LIFE–CYCLE
Perennial; FLOWERS June–August; **FRUITS** (with two seeds) July–September.

A typical plantain, with rosettes of linear leaves and spikes of brownish-green flowers bearing showy yellow anthers, Sea Plantain is familiar all around the coastlines of Britain and Ireland, and increasingly on salted road verges. As a montane plant it is a colonizer of bare ground, including trampled path sides, around Rabbit workings and areas of heavy-metal contamination. It flowers and fruits well in all but the most heavily trampled sites.

Outside the flowering period, Sea Plantain could be mistaken for Thrift (*p. 141*), with which it may grow. Both plants produce similar rosettes, but Thrift has flat leaves that radiate like the spokes of a wheel, while those of Sea Plantain are 'V'-shaped in section, curved like a scimitar, and with long white hairs in the centre of the rosette.

Distribution: As an upland plant this species is found especially in the base-rich areas of the Central Highlands to north-western Scotland, with just a few localities in the northern Pennines and Lake District. In Teesdale it is frequent in the Cronkley and Widdybank Fells area and by the Tees downstream to Barnard Castle.

Habitat: Sea Plantain is found in a wide range of upland basic grassland, base-rich stony flushes and unstable slopes, river and sike margins, and occasionally in meadows. It occurs in calcareous grass and sedge-rich swards of the CG9d Hair Sedge–False Sedge sub-community of the CG9 Blue Moor-grass–Limestone Bedstraw grassland community with Sheep's-fescue, Crested Hair-grass, Quaking-grass, Wild Thyme, Harebell, Spring Gentian, Northern Bedstraw, Hair Sedge, False Sedge and Lesser Clubmoss. It is also found on lead-mining spoil in the open OV37 Sheep's-fescue–Spring Sandwort community with Spring Sandwort, Sheep's-fescue, Crested Hair-grass, Wild Thyme, Hair Sedge and Autumn Gentian.

In gravelly flushes it grows together with Sheep's-fescue, False Sedge, Bird's-eye Primrose, Common Butterwort, Scottish Asphodel, Dioecious, Glaucous, Tawny and Flea Sedges and Alpine Meadow-rue as part of the M10 Dioecious Sedge–Common Butterwort community. Occasionally, it is found in some herb-rich meadows and similar vegetation near the Tees in the MG3 Sweet Vernal-grass–Wood Crane's-bill community with Red Fescue, Rough Meadow-grass, Quaking-grass, Yellow Oat-grass, Crested Dog's-tail, Pignut, Northern Bedstraw and various orchids.

Status and conservation: Still widespread in Teesdale, but very scarce in Cronkley Pasture and reduced in Widdybank Pasture between 1976–81 and 2000 by almost 20%, largely from the spread of tall rushes (particularly Soft-rush) and by heavy cattle trampling the gravelly flushes. These cattle have been replaced by lighter, hard-mouthed breeds which may also graze the tall rushes. Where the rushes have been mown and removed it is not known if the rarer species – Sea Plantain and Bird's-eye Primrose – have increased, as no monitoring has been undertaken. On the fells, in the calcareous grasslands and flushes, the plant should be safeguarded by protecting the habitat from overgrazing and managing the effects of undergrazing.

No recent survey has been made on Cetry Bank, which was badly trampled by cattle, so its status there is not known. It is essential that cattle should continue to be excluded from the unstable part of this site.

Sea Plantain: **1** flowers *AS*; **2** trampled leaves at Widdybank Fell track *MEB*. (See also *p. 143*.)

Sea Plantain was recorded in all sections of the riverside vegetation between Holwick Head and Wynch Bridge in 2003–04, although plants are being damaged on the bank of the Tees at Low Force, near Wynch Bridge, by kayakers entering and leaving the water.

Overgrazing of the small flood plains and damage to the banks of smaller streams need to be prevented, and destruction of the vegetation through trampling needs to be reduced, perhaps by restricting open access to parts of the bank.

Further information: https://www.brc.ac.uk/plantatlas/plant/plantago-maritima

RE Small Cow-wheat
Melampyrum sylvaticum L.

FIRST RECORD IN TEESDALE
1798, Binks and Oliver

ALTITUDE
280 m

LIFE-CYCLE
Hemiparasitic annual; FLOWERS June–August.

Teesdale used to be one of the few disjunct localities for Small Cow-wheat away from the core of its UK distribution in the mountains of Scotland. Care needs to be taken to distinguish it from Common Cow-wheat which also occurs here. Size and flower colour do not provide reliable separation as has sometimes been claimed: the best distinction is the lower lip of the flower of Small Cow-wheat which is reflexed, such that the mouth of its tubular corolla appears wide open. The lower lip of Common Cow-wheat is straight and the mouth consequently more closed.

As a hemiparasite it requires attachment to the roots of suitable host species to reach flowering size. However, its host range and preferences are poorly known; suggestions include trees such as birch, Hazel and Rowan, woody shrubs such as Heather and Bilberry, and/or grasses.

Distribution: A plant of the mountains of Scotland and Northern Ireland, Small Cow-wheat is now probably extinct in its former localities in northern England and Wales. From herbarium material, it used to be widespread in Teesdale near the Tees from above High Force to Middleton, and possibly Eggleston and even Barnard Castle and the ancient woodland of Park End Wood. The last recorded sighting in this area was in 1976.

Habitat: Small Cow-wheat used to be found in humid, lightly shaded situations on damp, usually somewhat enriched, acidic soils, in wooded ravines, in woodlands and on cliff ledges. Associated species included Downy Birch, Hazel, Rowan, Wood Anemone,

Small Cow-wheat, growing in Finland *FJR*.

Ramsons, Bluebell, Slender St. John's-wort, Bitter Vetch, Great Wood-rush, Dog's Mercury, Wood Sage, Brown Bent, False Brome, Quaking-grass, Wavy Hair-grass, Red Fescue, Viviparous Sheep's-fescue and Creeping Soft-grass.

Status and conservation: Having seemingly been widespread in Teesdale, its local extirpation seems likely to have been as a result of several factors. Some of the decline is indeed likely to have been from over-collecting, as many herbarium sheets through which we know of its past range contain numerous specimens. Other factors seem likely to include changes in forestry management and more recently the grazing and burrowing activities of Rabbits. Although its seeds are not believed to be long-lived, a watching brief for the species should be maintained in the event of its reappearance or rediscovery.

Further information: http://sppaccounts.bsbi.org/content/melampyrum-sylvaticum-0.html

Montane Eyebright [PHOTOS **1** & **2**, *p. 165*] NERC
Euphrasia officinalis ssp. *monticola* Silverside

FIRST RECORD IN TEESDALE
1933, T. J. Foggitt

ALTITUDE
280–460 m

LIFE-CYCLE
Hemiparasitic annual; FLOWERS June–July.

Montane Eyebright is an annual plant that shows marked variation in numbers from year-to-year depending on germination and survival. As a genus, the eyebrights are readily recognizable by their two-lipped, white flowers, often with a pink or purple flush, but identification of individual species (and subspecies and hybrids) is altogether much more difficult. At up to 12 mm across, the flowers of Montane Eyebright are larger than those of any other British species, and the lowest flowers are found at nodes 2–6 up the stem. Rostkov's Eyebright, subspecies *pratensis* of *Euphrasia officinalis*, has its lowest flowers at node six or higher, and shorter internodes, less than three times the length of the leaf; it has not been recorded in Teesdale, but would not be unexpected.

Distribution: The distribution of all eyebrights is imperfectly known because of identification difficulties: this species is always in the uplands. It has been recorded from Wales, the Lake District and the Pennines north of Craven, with outliers in the North York Moors and Kerry in Ireland. In Teesdale it is known from a number of sites, including five in Harwood Dale.

Habitat: In Upper Teesdale, Montane Eyebright is found on steep, species-rich banks and in upland hay meadows. In Harwood Dale it has been recorded in the M26 Purple Moor-grass–Marsh Hawk's-beard mire community and MG3b Quaking-grass sub-community of the MG3 Wood Crane's-bill–Sweet Vernal-grass meadow community.

Status and conservation: Between the 1950s and 2000 there was a reduction of almost a half in the number of recorded sites. More recently, although not comprehensively resurveyed, there are known to have been further losses as a result of agricultural intensification, although it was also found at a few more sites during herb-rich meadow surveys in 2007, 2008 and 2010. More searching for new sites and monitoring of known ones would be valuable.

Further information: https://www.brc.ac.uk/plantatlas/plant/euphrasia-rostkoviana-subsp-montana

Additional notes on eyebrights and their habitats

The identification of eyebrights is so tricky that a brief overview would be useful. In an exception to the rest of the plants covered in this book, the scientific names are also given in the text here, reflecting the always uncertain, often changing, taxonomic status of these entities.

The two most widespread species of eyebright from meadows in Teesdale are **Montane Eyebright** *Euphrasia officinalis* ssp. *monticola* and **Arctic Eyebright** *E. arctica* Lange ex Rostrup although the hybrid between Arctic and Common Eyebrights is typical of some meadows.

Arctic Eyebright has until recently been treated as two subspecies, although these are not currently differentiated. However, for completeness, and recognizing that taxonomic views may change, var. *robusta* is the least frequent in Teesdale, while var. *arctica* has been found in at least a quarter of all meadows surveyed.

Slender Eyebright *E. micrantha* Rchb. is a species of dry moorland, usually with Heather. It is slender, the leaves and stems commonly flushed purple, and has small flowers, usually purple (but may be violet, lilac or whitish) and the lower lip is longer than the upper.

Scottish Eyebright *E. scottica* Wettst. is closely related to, and sometimes hybridizes with, Slender Eyebright. It is a species of wet moorland flushes: very slender with small leaves, which are green above but strongly purple below. Flowers are small and white and the lower lip is a little longer than the upper.

NERC **Ostenfeld's Eyebright** *E. ostenfeldii* (Pugsley) Yeo has been recorded, although doubts have been expressed about at least some of the records. It is, however, fairly distinctive, by being densely hairy and small-flowered.

And finally, there are several other forms that might be expected to occur in Teesdale, given their national distributions and habitat preferences: Common Eyebright *E. nemorosa* (Pers.) Wallr., Confused Eyebright *E. confusa* Pugsley, and Rostkov's Eyebright *E. officinalis* ssp. *pratensis* (Fr.) Schübl. & G. Martens. The extensive meadow surveys of Teesdale have never recorded these, but their presence here should certainly be considered a possibility by future surveyors.

Eyebrights, growing in typical habitat at Long Crag *JO'R.*

Eyebrights: **1**, **2** Montane Eyebright *both JO'R*; **3** Arctic Eyebright *JO'R*; **4** Ostenfeld's Eyebright *FJR*.

VU Alpine Bartsia
Bartsia alpina L.

FIRST RECORD IN TEESDALE
1796, Oliver

ALTITUDE
370–400 m

LIFE-CYCLE
Hemiparasitic perennial; FLOWERS June–September; pollinated by bumblebees.

A sometimes densely tufted perennial, Alpine Bartsia is hemiparasitic on the roots of a range of host species: proven hosts include a range of sedges and willows, Alpine Bistort and Scottish Asphodel. Its tubular, purple corolla and often purplish, hairy, toothed bracts make it almost unmistakable when in flower within its habitat: the related Marsh Lousewort has hairless leaves and pinker flowers. When not in bloom it could be confused with Germander Speedwell, distinguished by its two opposite rows of long hairs down the stem, and Yellow-rattle, which is hairless and has longer, more sharply toothed leaves.

Distribution: Has a disjunct distribution, restricted to the Central Highlands of Scotland and scattered locations in the Yorkshire Dales and North Pennines. In Teesdale it is found on the lower slopes of Widdybank Fell, the pasture and meadow near Widdybank Farm, and Cetry Bank and adjacent pastures. Formerly, it grew on or below Cronkley Scar but was not found there in extensive searches in 1973 and 2004.

Habitat: Alpine Bartsia is a plant of moist, open habitats, on moderately calcareous (pH 6·4–7·2) soil on the eroding sides of moraines, turfy marshes with hummocks on poached clay, and unstable river and stream sides. At all sites the vegetation is short sedge-marsh of the M10 Dioecious Sedge–Common Butterwort community. Associated species include many of the moisture-loving Teesdale rarities: Bird's-eye Primrose, Common Butterwort, Dioecious, Hair and Tawny Sedges,

Alpine Bartsia, growing at Widdybank Pasture *MR*.

Scottish Asphodel, Grass-of-Parnassus, Sea Plantain, Spring Gentian, False Sedge, Alpine Rush, Quaking-grass and Blue Moor-grass.

Status and conservation: Alpine Bartsia requires open sites maintained by natural water flow and erosion, or by light grazing and trampling by native, hard-mouthed cattle and sheep to keep the vegetation fairly short. Repeat surveys of Widdybank Pasture in 1976–81 and 2000 showed a decline of around two-thirds, which was attributed to the invasion of tall rushes (encouraged by the higher water table created by choked drains) and heavy cattle trampling; elsewhere, declines have resulted from overgrazing.

Management of grazing is crucial to ensure the required balance between undergrazing and overgrazing. Lighter native cattle breeds are beneficial in that they damage the turf to a lesser extent, but on the eroding, unstable Cetry Bank, cattle should be excluded. Mowing may be used to try and keep tall rushes in check, while occasional sheep-grazing can be useful to maintain the necessary open habitat character. However, the flowers are palatable to both stock and wild grazers: flowering, and hence reproduction by seed, has benefitted (in the short-term at least) from the creation of grazing exclosures.

Further information: https://bsbi.org/wp-content/uploads/dlm_uploads/Bartsia_alpina_species_account.pdf

Yellow-rattle

[PHOTOS: *p. 168*]

Rhinanthus minor ssp. *minor* L.

FIRST RECORD IN TEESDALE
1968, Bradshaw

ALTITUDE
500 m

LIFE-CYCLE
Hemiparasitic annual; FLOWERS late July–early August; SEEDS ripen August–September, germinate in spring.

A familiar, albeit declining, grassland species, Yellow-rattle is conventionally divided into a number of subspecies, although these are perhaps better considered as ecotypes and seasonal variants. Subspecies *monticola* and *stenophyllus* are the characteristic forms of northern uplands and wetlands respectively, but the author discovered plants differing from these forms on Widdybank Fell in 1968. While not wholly conclusive, perhaps as a result of the tenuous nature of subspecies definition, expert examination of these plants has concluded they can be assigned to ssp. *minor*, the form that seems to be most associated with lowland and southerly regions.

As a species, Yellow-rattle is easily identified by its yellow, two-lipped flowers with two short but broad, violet (occasionally white) teeth at the tip of the upper lip. Subspecies *monticola* generally has brownish-yellow flowers, while the flowers of subspecies *minor* and *stenopyllus* are usually bright yellow; otherwise, distinctions are based largely on branching pattern and the number of leaf-pairs between the topmost branch and lowest flower. However, the Widdybank Fell plants are rather depauperate which makes precise identification difficult: the plants here are only up to 11 cm tall, contrasting with heights up to 40 cm in more favourable conditions. This taxon requires further research.

As an annual plant, numbers vary year-on-year and, given that it forms little or no seed-bank, the species depends on setting seed each year. No studies have been undertaken to determine which host species are preferred at this site; the 'quality' of different hosts also affects plant stature and form.

Distribution: The species as a whole, of which subspecies *minor* is the most frequent form, is found almost throughout Britain and Ireland, but especially in the lowlands. In Teesdale this subspecies is known only from Widdybank Fell.

Habitat: Subspecies *minor* is found in open, species-rich, short sedge-marsh and gravelly flush habitats in the M10b Quaking-grass–Bird's-eye Primrose sub-community of the M10 Dioecious Sedge–Common Butterwort mire community, with Sheep's-fescue, Purple Moor-grass, Quaking-grass, False, Hair, Carnation and Flea Sedges, Common Yellow-sedge, Yellow Saxifrage, Scottish Asphodel, Lesser Clubmoss, Wild Thyme, Alpine Meadow-rue, Alpine Rush, Bird's-eye Primrose, Fairy Flax and Knotted Pearlwort.

Status and conservation: The number of plants has varied, as would be expected with an annual species, between four and 68, dependent probably upon climatic variations. In the uneven tussocky habitat, the plants which are mostly small do not appear to be grazed. The location in which it grows is very open and fragile, contains several rare flowering plants and is easily damaged by trampling. The whole area should be protected from trampling and disturbance by people, and monitoring should be continued.

Further information: https://www.brc.ac.uk/plantatlas/plant/rhinanthus-minor-subsp-minor

Yellow-rattle ssp. *minor*: **1** habitat on Widdybank Fell *MEB*; **2** flowers *MEB*.

Saw-wort
Serratula tinctoria L.

FIRST RECORD IN TEESDALE
1805, Winch

ALTITUDE
262 m

LIFE-CYCLE
Herbaceous perennial; FLOWERS July–September; FRUITS September–October.

Saw-wort is found in two contrasting habitats in Teesdale: by the river, it is a tall herbaceous perennial that flowers regularly and produces fertile seed; while on the fell only small leaves have been found. The latter plants must be of great age, as no evidence of flowers has been seen.

The English name of Saw-wort alludes to its most distinctive feature when not in flower, the lanceolate, hairless leaves with saw-tooth bristle-tipped margins. Male and female flowers are found on separate plants. Female flower-heads are ovoid, with white, abortive anthers, while male heads are more slender and cylindrical, with dark blue anthers. In both sexes, the florets are reddish-purple (occasionally white), surrounded by sharply pointed, adpressed bracts which are usually coloured purple. In seed, the pappus is a yellowish colour. In winter it is equally distinctive: the stems remain upright and the bracts around the flower-heads expose their beautiful, golden inner surface.

Superficially resembling a thistle, Saw-wort is distinguished by its absence of prickles, and the generally neater growth form helps to separate it from Common Knapweed.

Distribution: A species with a southerly distribution in Britain, Saw-wort is found primarily in Wales and the western half of England, together with a small part of south-western Scotland. In Teesdale it grows on the south bank of Tees near Wynch Bridge and in the limestone grassland on Widdybank Fell. In the latter locality it is found mainly as small leaves, stunted by grazing, along with those of other meadow plants, such as Great Burnet, Lesser Meadow-rue, Globeflower and Goldenrod. Several of these species have managed to flower in areas from which grazing stock were excluded during the summer.

Saw-wort: 1 fruit *MEB;* **2** flowers *DM.*

Habitat: On the fell, Saw-wort is found in the CG9d Hair Sedge–False Sedge sub-community of the CG9 Blue Moor-grass–Limestone Bedstraw grassland community on the deeper calcareous brown earth soil, with Blue Moor-grass, Sheep's-fescue, Quaking-grass, Mountain Everlasting, Alpine Bistort, Lesser Clubmoss and occasionally leaves of Globeflower, Great Burnet, Goldenrod and Lesser Meadow-rue. By the river, it occurs with with Grey and Tea-leaved Willows, Globeflower, Melancholy Thistle, Meadowsweet and Common Knapweed.

Status and conservation: By the Tees, Saw-wort has been monitored since 2003 and the population appears to be stable. On the fell, it was first found in the short calcareous grassland in the early 1970s, and while it has been noted subsequently, there has been no further detailed recording. Continued monitoring is required in both locations, especially to observe any effect of the currently undergrazed state of the grassland.

Further information: https://www.brc.ac.uk/plantatlas/plant/serratula-tinctoria

LC Teesdale Dandelion
Taraxacum pseudonordstedtii A. J. Richards

FIRST RECORD IN TEESDALE
1972, Richards

ALTITUDE
350–500 m

LIFE-CYCLE
Perennial, reproducing by seed only; FLOWERS May–June; SEEDS ripen in June–July.

Some 240 microspecies of dandelion are now known from Britain and Ireland. In 2005, the national authority on *Taraxacum*, A. J. Richards, provided the author with notes on some of the members of this very difficult genus in Teesdale. The special upland grassland habitats are characterized by *T. faeroense* (wet) and *T. unguilobum* (drier), with *T. nordstedtii* and *T. pseudonordstedtii* in the streamsides and flushes. On Whin Sill cliffs, *T. maculosum* is typical, along with commoner species such as *T. hamatum*, while the tall-herb meadows commonly have a rich, high-quality range of species with Scandinavian affinities (*T. naevosum*,

Teesdale Dandelion: **1** flower; **2** in seed, growing at Widdybank Fell *both MEB.*

T. naevosiforme and *T. stictophyllum*), some widespread endemics (*e.g. T. pseudolarssonii*) and a selection of interesting plants from the *Celtica* and *Hamata* groups.

Of these, one species clearly justifies the English name Teesdale Dandelion, as adopted here: *Taraxacum pseudonordstedtii* is probably found nowhere else in the world than Teesdale, where it characterizes one of the unique habitats locally, sugar-limestone grassland. Because the majority of dandelions reproduce apomictically, the consensus of experts is that it would be unwise to try and claim any species as 'glacial relics', but this has as good a claim as any to be considered part of the Teesdale Assemblage.

The differences between dandelion microspecies are always relatively slight, but any growing on sugar-limestone or in the high-altitude flushes and showing strong purple suffusion on the leaves (especially the midrib), bracts and flower-stalks, and triangular leaf lobes incised to the midrib is likely to be this species.

Distribution: Considered to be a near-endemic to Upper Teesdale, found there and in few other places in the world, Teesdale Dandelion is known for certainty elsewhere only in other parts of the North Pennines. Records claimed from west Cumberland and north Lancashire need verification. In Teesdale it has been identified on Widdybank Fell, and in pastures within the triangle more or less bounded by the River Tees and Harwood Beck westward to Peghorn Farm.

Habitat: This dandelion is a plant of moist or wet habitats, such as in the M10 Dioecious Sedge–Common Butterwort short sedge-marsh. On Widdybank Fell, it occurs in calcareous flushes on the lower slopes and wet sugar-limestone sand in the CG9 Blue Moor-grass–Limestone Bedstraw community with Sheep's-fescue, Wild Thyme and Spring Sandwort.

Status and conservation: The species was described and named as recently as 1972 and, given the challenges posed by dandelion identification, its range in Teesdale and elsewhere should be regarded as provisional. On the sugar-limestone it appears to be adversely affected by drought in the spring, but otherwise, provided the important plant communities are managed and maintained, its future should be secured. The only known anthropogenic change occurred when some plants at the Langdon Beck Hotel were lost when the car park was resurfaced.

Northern Hawk's-beard

NERC

Crepis mollis (Jacq.) Asch.

FIRST RECORD IN TEESDALE
1842, J. Backhouse Jr.

ALTITUDE
280–370 m

LIFE-CYCLE
Perennial, evergreen; **FLOWERS** July–August; **FRUITS** August–September.

A winter-green perennial, characteristic of herb-rich hay meadows and other grassland, Northern Hawk's-beard is probably long-lived and able to tolerate intermittent close grazing. In some years it flowers strongly, its yellow flower-heads 2–3 cm in diameter, held aloft the grassland sward up to a metre off the ground. Unable to spread vegetatively, it presumably propagates by seed although this has not been demonstrated in the wild; seeds from plants in cultivation have been shown to be highly fertile, with most successful establishment coming from spring-germinating seeds.

There are several species whose similar-shaped leaves may be confused with the variably pubescent ones of Northern Hawk's-beard: those of Devil's-bit Scabious have a hairless midrib, while the basal leaves of Common Knapweed are roughly hairy, especially on the lower surface.

Marsh Hawk's-beard has a fruiting head that is blunt when closed, brownish seeds and a grey-brown pappus, in contrast with the conical fruiting head, yellow seeds and pure white pappus of Northern Hawk's-beard.

Distribution: Northern Hawk's-beard is primarily a plant of the North Pennines to the Scottish Borders, with outliers as far south as north Wales and north into the Scottish Highlands. In Teesdale it is found in a few sites near the Tees below High Force, on Haugh Hill near Cronkley Bridge and east of Wynch Bridge, both south of the Tees and in the wood on the north side. Nearby it is also found in upper Weardale and at the head of the Derwent valley.

Habitat: Grows in meadows, on grassy banks, verges and upland woodlands, mostly in the MG3 Sweet Vernal-grass–Wood Crane's-bill herb-rich hay meadow community, with Red Fescue, Rough Meadow-grass, Great Burnet, Pignut, lady's-mantle species, Globeflower, Ribwort Plantain, Meadow and Bulbous Buttercups, Common Sorrel and dandelion species. It is found in all three sub-communities, typified respectively by Soft-brome, Quaking-grass and False Oat-grass, but especially the latter, MG3c. Also in the MG5 Crested Dog's-tail–Common Knapweed community with Red Fescue, Yorkshire-fog, Perennial Rye-grass, Quaking-grass, Common Bird's-foot-trefoil, White and Red Clovers, Yarrow, Selfheal, Yellow-rattle and Oxeye Daisy, along with several of the common species of MG3. In addition, it can be found in the related MG6 Perennial Rye-grass–Crested Dog's-tail community with most of the grasses of MG5, plus Smooth and Rough Meadow-grasses, Common Sorrel, Cat's-ear, Field Wood-rush, Rough Hawkbit, and Common Knapweed.

Northern Hawk's-beard: **1** growing at Ayle Burn *FJR*; **2** flowers *MP*.

Habitat: For at least 150 years, Northern Hawk's-beard has been a feature of riverside hay meadows at Wynch Bridge and below Holwick. Ten further plants were located in 2007 on Haugh Bank above Cronkley Bridge. It remains a scarce plant, but increased interest in the species, together with a search of herb-rich banks in improved meadows and former woodland locations may produce more records. Further searches are recommended, along with monitoring of known sites and steps taken to avoid the intensification of management of the hay meadows.

Further information: https://bsbi.org/wp-content/uploads/dlm_uploads/Crepis_mollis_species_account.pdf

Mountain Everlasting
Antennaria dioica (L.) Gaertn.

FIRST RECORD IN TEESDALE
1794, Oliver

ALTITUDE
280–570 m

LIFE-CYCLE
Dioecious perennial, spreading by stolons; FLOWERS May–July; FRUITS July–August.

A perennial herb, spreading vegetatively by stolons that root at the nodes, often forming patches of one sex. The flowers are white and/or pink and in terminal heads, on woolly stems up to 20 cm tall, but often much less, especially where grazed. The flower-heads on male plants are about 12 mm in diameter, those on female plants about 6 mm in diameter. The leaves are in rosettes of pointed half-open leaves, dark green above and white-woolly beneath. Basal leaves of Mouse-eared Hawkweed are somewhat similar, but with sparse stiff hairs on the upper surface, and that plant has lemon-yellow flowers.

It flowers well in grassland or among Heather where grazing levels are light, but it is not known if fertile seed is produced or if germination occurs in the wild. However, in cultivation at lower altitudes, plants that were rescued from the Cow Green Reservoir basin did produce viable seeds.

Mountain Everlasting, male flowers *CJP*.

Distribution: Although now rare in the lowlands of England and Wales, Mountain Everlasting is widespread in the uplands, from the Brecon Beacons and the Peak District northwards, especially through north-western Scotland, and in western and central Ireland. In Teesdale it is scattered in grassland on limestone and Whin Sill.

Habitat: Mountain Everlasting in Teesdale is found in a number of different grassland and heathland plant communities. On the sugar-limestone on Widdybank and Cronkley Fells, it is found in the CG9d Hair Sedge–False Sedge sub-community of the CG9 Blue Moor-grass–Limestone Bedstraw grassland with Spring Gentian, Alpine Bistort, Lesser Clubmoss, Common Rock-rose, Sheep's-fescue, Quaking-grass and False, Hair and Glaucous Sedges and Spring-sedge. It is also found in the sub-community of CG9 with Heather, Crowberry, Northern Bedstraw, Spring Gentian, Alpine Bistort and Wood Anemone, and in the CG10 Sheep's-fescue–Common Bent–Wild Thyme community. It occurs on rendzinas, calcareous brown soils and brown earths all over metamorphosed limestone. The U4 Sheep's-fescue–Common Bent–Heath Bedstraw community is associated with Common Milkwort, Tormentil, Common Dog-violet, Red Fescue, Heath-grass and Heather. Additionally, it is rooted in crevices in Whin Sill rocks by the Tees and at higher altitudes on limestone outcrops, sometimes with Hoary Whitlowgrass and Blue Moor-grass.

Status and conservation: There is only a very small number of plants between Wynch Bridge and High Force, mostly growing on the Whin Sill near the Tees. These are very susceptible to all kinds of recreational disturbance and damage, ranging from 'paddlers' scrambling up the cliff outside of the permitted marked route, often dragging equipment, to walkers and picnickers on top of the rocks. Monitoring of these activities and their effects on the number of rosettes and flower stems must be continued, and action taken when necessary.

On the upper parts of Widdybank Fell threats include excessively close grazing and the scuffing and burrowing activities of Rabbits. But, highlighting the need to balance grazing levels, there is a risk that the plant may be lost as a result of vegetation changes following undergrazing, although in such situations plants have been shown to survive, without flowering, for up to five years.

The results of an extensive re-survey of sites for this species undertaken in 2018 will, when available, help to inform future management priorities.

Further information: https://bsbi.org/wp-content/uploads/dlm_uploads/Antennaria_dioica_species_account.pdf

Mountain Everlasting: **1** fruits *MEB*; **2** female flowers *DM*.

Small Scabious
Scabiosa columbaria L.

FIRST RECORD IN TEESDALE
1805, Winch

ALTITUDE
525–640 m

LIFE-CYCLE
Perennial; FLOWERS July–September; FRUITS ripen August–October.

A widespread southern species in Britain, Small Scabious is included here because of its occurrence alongside the arctic-alpine Mountain Avens, Alpine Meadow-rue and Alpine Bistort, the northern subspecies *lapponica* of Kidney Vetch and southerly species such as Hoary Rock-rose, Rare Spring-sedge and Horseshoe Vetch. All these species grow together in the same plant community on the sugar-limestone on the same fell, a unique combination of plants that makes the Teesdale Assemblage so special.

It is a perennial with a deep tap-root and produces flowering stems up to 30 cm tall bearing pale mauve to pinkish flower-heads, and sepals with five long, blackish bristles clearly visible among the flowers, but most obvious on the ovoid fruiting heads. The individual flowers in the head have five corolla-lobes, which distinguishes this species from Field Scabious, a similar but usually taller plant of similar habitats, which has just four corolla-lobes. In both species, the outer flowers are longer than the inner ones, which in turn distinguishes both from Devil's-bit Scabious, in which the flowers are all the same size. Devil's-bit Scabious has four-lobed corollas, but the calyx has four or five bristle-tipped teeth, rather bluer flowers, and is usually found in damper habitats.

Small Scabious is highly attractive to pollinators, especially bumblebees and butterflies. However, despite the production of seed-heads, no seedlings have been found in Teesdale, although on Cronkley Fell at least it appears, in the absence of detailed monitoring, to be increasing at the present time.

Small Scabious, growing on Cronkley Fell *MR*.

175

Distribution: Found mainly on calcareous and well-drained soils in England and Wales, scarce in south-eastern Scotland and almost absent from Ireland, Small Scabious is generally a lowland species, but reaches 640 m on Cross Fell. In Teesdale it is found sparingly by the Tees, particularly above High Force, and is locally frequent on sugar-limestone grassland in the Thistle Green and White Well areas of Cronkley Fell. In the past it occurred on a limestone outcrop in Forest-in-Teesdale and there is some suggestion it may be present on High Hurth Edge, but thus far it has not been recorded on Widdybank Fell.

Habitat: On three areas of sugar-limestone on Cronkley Fell Small Scabious is found in more or less closed turf of the CG9d Hair Sedge–False Sedge sub-community of the CG9 Blue Moor-grass–Limestone Bedstraw grassland community, with Sheep's-fescue, Blue Moor-grass, Crested Hair-grass, Rare Spring-sedge, Common Rock-rose, Mountain Avens, Alpine Meadow-rue and Horseshoe Vetch. In these areas, it is on rendzina-like skeletal soils with a small amount of black humus or a deeper calcareous brown earth, with pH >7. On riverside shingle above High Force it is found with a variety of plants including Shrubby Cinquefoil, Blue Moor-grass and Northern Bedstraw, and it was formerly found on exposed Carboniferous limestone rock behind the Youth Hostel with Rock Lady's-mantle and Meadow Saxifrage.

Status and conservation: Although not demonstrated by detailed monitoring, Small Scabious is believed to be increasing, especially on Cronkley Fell. Here, the plants are located within the grazing exclosures; as with the associated species that are intolerant of grazing, it is important that the rabbit-proof fencing is maintained and that any Rabbits that do enter the exclosures are controlled. All these plant species should be monitored regularly, and the height and density of the vegetation adjusted by allowing sheep into the exclosures in the autumn and winter.

Further information: https://www.brc.ac.uk/plantatlas/plant/scabiosa-columbaria

Small Scabious: **1** flower; **2** fruit *both MR*.

Scottish Asphodel
Tofieldia pusilla (Michx.) Pers.

FIRST RECORD IN TEESDALE
1722, Camden

ALTITUDE
370–630 m

LIFE-CYCLE
Perennial; FLOWERS July; FRUITS ripe from August.

A diminutive plant of upland wet habitats, Scottish Asphodel has cream flowers, with six perianth segments, each about 2 mm long in a dense flowering spike 5–15 mm long. Its leaves are linear and arranged 3–5 in a fan; the leaves look like a small iris plant and are all the same length. In Teesdale, being a relict population at the southern edge of its range, it is perhaps not surprising that there is normally only one fan per plant; occasionally here, and more frequently in Scotland, it can form a tuft of several parallel fans.

Although winter-green and frost-hardy, young inflorescences and flowers can be damaged by late frosts in July. Weather conditions are also likely to explain much of the variation in flowering success: studies of marked areas demonstrated a three-fold difference between years in the number of flowering spikes produced, and a similar variation in the number of flowers per inflorescence.

The only similar plant to have fans of leaves like this, Bog Asphodel, has yellow flowers, leaves of different lengths which turn salmon-pink in autumn. This is mainly an inhabitant of acid bogs, but on Widdybank Fell both species can be found growing very close together.

Distribution: Scottish Asphodel occurs frequently in the Central Highlands of Scotland, and more sparsely to the north including at sea level. The only extant location outside Scotland is in Upper Teesdale, on Widdybank and Cronkley Fells and Pastures and Cetry Bank.

Habitat: Scottish Asphodel is a plant of moist to wet habitats, most frequently in the short sedge-marsh M10 Dioecious Sedge–Common Butterwort community (including the open M10c Hook-beaked Tufa-moss sub-community) and M11 Common Yellow-sedge–Yellow Saxifrage mires,

Scottish Asphodel: **1** growing at Red Sike *MR*; **2** flowers *AS*.

turfy marshes and the eroding sides of drumlins that are flushed with base-rich, calcareous water. Associated species include False, Dioecious, Tawny, Hair, Carnation and Flea Sedges, Long-stalked and Common Yellow-sedges, Alpine Meadow-rue, Three-flowered Rush, Variegated Horsetail, Common Butterwort and various mosses and liverworts. It tends to be found on hummocks in the gravelly flushes within these communities and those areas receiving drainage from the metamorphosed limestone over the Whin Sill rocks on Widdybank Fell.

In more or less closed, species-rich vegetation on the flood plains of some sikes, it is also found in the CG9d Hair Sedge–False Sedge sub-community of the CG9 Blue Moor-grass–Limestone Bedstraw community.

Status and conservation: Scottish Asphodel ranges from occasional to frequent in the above communities but is showing signs of decline. In Widdybank Pasture, it showed a 10% decrease between 1976–81 and 2000, and a further reduction by 2018. A similar trend was observed on both Cetry Bank and Cronkley Fell over comparable timescales.

Some of the declines are attributable to the effects of grazing animals. Plants are sometimes pulled up by sheep eating the fruiting heads and those growing on the edges of stream banks (*e.g.* Sand Sike) may be destroyed by cattle trampling. It is essential that cattle should be excluded from the unstable part of Cetry Bank and similar vulnerable habitats. Undergrazing may however also be of concern, as Scottish Asphodel is probably intolerant of the shade from insufficiently grazed vegetation. Monitoring is essential, and if the effects of undergrazing are detected, mowing and removal of the clippings should be considered.

Further information: https://www.brc.ac.uk/plantatlas/plant/tofieldia-pusilla

LC Dark-red Helleborine
Epipactis atrorubens (Hoffm.) Besser

FIRST RECORD IN TEESDALE	1952, Park
ALTITUDE	520 m
LIFE-CYCLE	**Perennial**; FLOWERS July–August; FRUITS August–September.

A true limestone specialist, the preferred habitat of Dark-red Helleborine is the scree-filled cracks in limestone pavement, the absence of which probably explains its scarcity in Teesdale. Another reason why it is not well known here may be that it is an erratic flowerer and indeed in some years fails to produce aerial shoots. But when in full flower it is unmistakable, with spikes of up to 15 drooping, wine-red flowers that have yellow centres. When not flowering, the relatively broad, softly hairy leaves in two rows down the stem resemble those of Broad-leaved Helleborine, but they are usually distinguished by having a deep red or purple tinge, especially at the tip and base.

Distribution: Dark-red Helleborine has a very disjunct distribution in northern and western limestone areas, from north Wales and the Peak District through to northern Scotland and the Burren in Ireland. In Teesdale it is known only from Cronkley Fell, on the White Well and East Knoll sugar-limestone areas. Although the habitat would appear suitable, it has not been found on Widdybank Fell despite intensive rare plant surveys in the early 1970s which did locate Early-purple and Frog Orchids and Heath Fragrant-orchid.

Habitat: In closed and semi-open grassland on sugar-limestone in the CG9d Hair Sedge–False Sedge sub-community of the CG9 Blue Moor-grass–Limestone Bedstraw grassland community, with Sheep's-fescue, Red Fescue, Wild Thyme, Common and Hoary Rock-roses, Mountain Avens, Glaucous Sedge and Rare Spring-sedge, and locally Devil's-bit Scabious, Water Avens and Meadow Buttercup.

Status and conservation: When first shown to the author in 1952 there were just three plants. In 2007, there were 17 flowering and more than ten non-flowering shoots in that location. There are also some plants in the eastern outcrop of sugar-limestone but there is no record of the number there. All are in grazing exclosures in the NNR, although Rabbit control has been difficult to achieve; it may become necessary to introduce controlled grazing or mowing to produce the right conditions for the plant to thrive.

Further information: https://bsbi.org/wp-content/uploads/dlm_uploads/Epipactis_atrorubens_species_account.pdf

Dark-red Helleborine: **1** growing at Cronkley Fell; **2** flowers; **3** in bud *all MR*.

VU Bog Orchid
Hammarbya paludosa (L.) Kuntze

FIRST RECORD IN TEESDALE
1796–97, Oliver and Harriman

ALTITUDE
360–380 m

LIFE-CYCLE
Perennial; FLOWERS July–September.

Among the most inconspicuous of orchids, Bog Orchid is small and yellow-green, up to 12 cm tall with a pair of small green leaves, growing in moss of the same colour, and not in flower until mid-summer. The flower spike comprises up to 15 flowers, each 3 mm long, having a lip with light and dark green stripes and lateral petals folded back around the base of the flower; they have a faint smell of cucumber.

Distribution: Occurs in the New Forest, Wales, the Lake District, North Pennines and western Scotland, but it is declining, especially in lowland sites, and frequently overlooked as a result of its inconspicuous nature. In Teesdale it has always been scarce; the last reports are from Blea Beck in the 1960s and in 1985 near Skyer Beck, Noon Hill.

Habitat: Found in acidic bogs with some lateral movement of water, especially by small upland streams through the M21 Bog Asphodel–Papillose Bog-moss mire community with other bog-moss species, Common Cottongrass, Purple Moor-grass, Cross-leaved Heath and Heather.

Status and conservation: This very inconspicuous plant may well be overlooked but its last confirmed sighting was in 1985. Future surveys need to be focused upon the Skyer Beck area and the potential Blea Beck site; whether or not it is relocated, the habitat should be protected from burning and drainage.

Further information: https://bsbi.org/wp-content/uploads/dlm_uploads/Hammarbya_paludosa_species_account.pdf

Bog Orchid: **1** growing at Blea Moss; **2** fallen flower; **3** flowers *all FJR*.

Small-white Orchid

NERC

Pseudorchis albida (L.) Á.& D. Löve

FIRST RECORD IN TEESDALE
1810, J. Backhouse Sr.

ALTITUDE
280–400 m

LIFE-CYCLE
Perennial, with underground tubers; **FLOWERS** June–July; **SEEDS** ripen July–August.

Flowering irregularly and being of short stature, often as little as 10 cm when in bloom, Small-white Orchid is easily overlooked by casual surveyors. The greenish-white flowers, only up to 2·5 mm long, have a short, thick, downcurved spur and form a spike up to 5 cm in length; smelling faintly of vanilla, they attract day-flying insects to the nectar within the spur. A short flowering season adds to the hard-to-find nature of this species.

Usually found as single plants, Small-white Orchid can tolerate the shade of other plants in old meadows, and can even survive in Heather moorland that is subject to a regular burning regime. Very occasionally it forms hybrids with Heath Fragrant-orchid, but this has not to date been confirmed in Teesdale

Distribution: Historically, Small-white Orchid was found throughout the upland areas of Wales, northern England, Scotland and Ireland but is now much reduced south of the Central Highlands, and indeed extinct in some outlying localities such as the South Downs and Peak District. In Teesdale it seems to be very rare and sporadic, although the irregular flowering habit must contribute to its apparent rarity. In the 19th century it was recorded between Cronkley Scar and the Tees; more recently, in the 1970s, Harwood Dale (Bowes Close), Heathery Hill, Widdybank Pasture, near Cetry Bank, High Force and Cronkley Bridge were known localities, but since 2008 it has been found only near Scorberry Bridge.

Small-white Orchid: **1** growing at Scoberry Bridge *MEB*; **2** flowers *GH*.

Habitat: Most locations are in meadows of the MG3c False Oat-grass sub-community of the MG3 Sweet Vernal-grass–Wood Crane's-bill herb-rich hay meadow community with Red Fescue, Rough Meadow-grass, Great Burnet, Pignut, Globeflower, Ribwort Plantain, Field and Bulbous Buttercups, Common Sorrel and various lady's-mantle and dandelion species. Small-white Orchid has also been found in the MG5 Crested Dog's-tail–Common Knapweed grassland community with Red Fescue, Yorkshire-fog, Perennial Rye-grass, Quaking-grass, Common Bird's-foot-trefoil, White and Red Clovers, Common Sorrel, Rough Hawkbit, Yellow-rattle and Oxeye Daisy, and in the U4 Sheep's-fescue–Common Bent–Heath Bedstraw pasture community with Sweet Vernal-grass, Ribwort Plantain, Yarrow, White Clover, Field Wood-rush and Selfheal.

Status and conservation: Given the small size and sporadic flowering habits of Small-white Orchid, there is a suspicion that it may be overlooked. However, it does seem to be less frequent in Teesdale than as recently as the 1970s, and to be currently a very rare plant. Searches should continue for the species and where it is found monitoring should commence, and the sites protected through agri-environment schemes.

Further information: https://bsbi.org/wp-content/uploads/dlm_uploads/Pseudorchis_albida_species_account.pdf

LC Lily-of-the-valley
Convallaria majalis L.

A patch-forming perennial plant that spreads by short rhizomes. Its familiar sweet fragrance arises from globular to bell-shaped, white flowers in nodding, one-sided spikes. Each flower can give rise to a large berry containing three seeds, which ripen from green to red, before shrivelling to rusty-brown. Throughout the summer,

FIRST RECORD IN TEESDALE
1798, Harriman and Oliver

ALTITUDE
260 m

LIFE-CYCLE
Perennial, rhizomatous; **FLOWERS** May–June.

Lily-of-the-valley, growing in Finland *FJR*.

the paired obovate-lanceolate leaves are obvious, and can be mistaken (in the absence of flowers) for the more shiny, floppier, garlic-scented leaves of Ramsons.

Distribution: Most frequent as a native in woods on limestone in western and northern Britain, the natural distribution of Lily-of-the-valley is now obscured by frequent garden escapes. In Teesdale, the only site is in woodland on the left side of the Tees about 400 m east of Wynch Bridge, on a steep slope between the path and river above a basalt cliff.

Habitat: Found towards the margin of a planted conifer woodland of Larch and Scots Pine in a remnant of more natural woodland, probably of the W11 Sessile Oak–Downy Birch community, with Silver Birch, Pedunculate Oak, Rowan, Hazel, Bracken, Wood Sage, Wood Anemone, Common Dog-violet, Betony, Great Woodrush, Red Fescue, Creeping Soft-grass, Sweet Vernal-grass and False Brome. The presence of Lily-of-the-valley indicates an ancient origin for this remnant of woodland close to the river Tees.

Status and conservation: In 1979, two patches of Lily-of-the-valley were present, linked by scattered shoots, amounting to some 400–500 plants. It was recorded as still present in 2012, but not seen in 2018. However, it may well still be present, although the habitat and its rare species (also including Shrubby Cinquefoil, Alpine Cinquefoil, Mountain Melick and Rock Whitebeam) are threatened by kayakers exiting the river and consequential – and/or natural – rock-falls. The site would benefit from statutory designation.

Further information: https://www.brc.ac.uk/plantatlas/plant/convallaria-majalis

Alpine Rush
Juncus alpinoarticulatus Chaix

FIRST RECORD IN TEESDALE
1903, Druce

An erect perennial, Alpine Rush resembles a small to medium-sized and slender form of Jointed Rush, from which it is best separated by mature fruits. The stem has purplish scale-leaves and 2–3 almost cylindrical leaves with cross walls (septae), while the inflorescence has few branches, arising from two points about 4 cm apart. In Teesdale plants these branches often curve inwards. It occurs in the same habitats as Jointed Rush, and the two species hybridize, producing plants that are intermediate in morphology with reduced fertility.

ALTITUDE
280–510 m

LIFE-CYCLE
Perennial, with short rhizomes; FLOWERS late July–September; FRUITS August–September.

Regeneration from seed in the field is not known, but transplanted Teesdale plants in cultivation flowered freely, forming fruits with good viability; however, seedlings did not persist long after the very dry summer of 1976.

Distribution: Found in disjunct areas in the Craven district, the North Pennines, the Southern Uplands, and the Central Highlands of Scotland. In Teesdale it has been recorded from Widdybank Fell and Pasture, Birkdale and Maize Beck flushes, Cetry Bank and the lower Sand Sike, Cronkley Pasture and on rocks by River Tees near Wynch Bridge.

Habitat: Alpine Rush is a plant of moist/wet base-rich habitats, most frequently in the short sedge-marsh M10b Quaking-grass–Bird's-eye Primrose sub-community of the M10 Dioecious

Sedge–Common Butterwort mire community, turfy marshes, sike sides and the eroding edges of drumlins that are flushed with base-rich, calcareous water. Associated species are Dioecious, Tawny, Carnation and Flea Sedges, Long-stalked and Common Yellow-sedges, Broad-leaved Cottongrass and many rare species, including False Sedge, Scottish Asphodel, Alpine Meadow-rue, Alpine Bartsia, Lesser Clubmoss, Sea Plantain, Hair Sedge, Spring Sandwort and Knotted Pearlwort in a matrix of mosses and liverworts. On Widdybank Fell, in areas receiving drainage from metamorphosed limestone over the Whin Sill rocks, it is also found in gravelly flushes within the M10c Hook-beaked Tufa-moss sub-community of the M10 community. In such locations hummocks of Hook-beaked Tufa-moss and Golf-club Moss are prominent, along with Sea Plantain, Knotted Pearlwort and Spring Sandwort.

Status and conservation: Still widespread in suitable habitats on and near Widdybank Fell, Alpine Rush is probably under-recorded as mature fruits are required to confirm identification. In Widdybank Pasture numbers have been reduced by the spread of tall rushes, particularly Soft-rush, and trampling of the gravelly flushes. It is very scarce in Cronkley Pasture with only 33 plants across four sites in 2012. Cetry Bank was re-surveyed in 2012 and showed the rush to be slightly more widespread than in 1977 but it was not recorded at its former site by the River Tees, west from Wynch to Holwick Head Bridge, in a survey from 2003.

In Widdybank Pasture, the heavy cattle that destroyed the flush habitats have been replaced by lighter, hard-mouthed breeds which will hopefully graze the tall rushes that invade the flushes. Opening of existing drains could lower the water table and may also reduce the spread of taller rushes and sedges that shade out Alpine Rush. It is essential that cattle, but not sheep, are excluded from the unstable part of Cetry Bank. Similarly, overgrazing of the small flood-plains and damage to the banks of lower Sand Sike needs to be monitored and controlled.

Further information: https://www.brc.ac.uk/plantatlas/plant/juncus-alpinoarticulatus

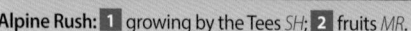
Alpine Rush: **1** growing by the Tees *SH;* **2** fruits *MR.*

Three-flowered Rush
Juncus triglumis L.

FIRST RECORD IN TEESDALE
1796–97, Binks

ALTITUDE
490–855 m

LIFE-CYCLE
Perennial, forming small tufts; FLOWERS June–July; FRUITS July–August.

Grows in open rocky, gravelly and silty sites, forming small tufts up to 20cm tall except in damp flushes where the tufted structure is not so pronounced. Leaves three-sided, one side with fine groove. At the end of stiffly erect stems is a terminal inflorescence of three (occasionally just one) flowers, which are cream when fresh and mature to a red-brown colour. In Scotland, it can grow together with Two-flowered Rush, which is similar but smaller, with on average fewer flowers in the inflorescence, a relatively longer lowest bract and smaller seed capsules: past records of this rarer species in Teesdale have never been confirmed, but it could possibly occur.

Distribution: The plant occurs frequently in mountains of the Central Highlands and north-west Scotland and is also found in disjunct areas of the North Pennines, Lake District and Snowdonia. In Teesdale it occurs on Widdybank and Cronkley Fells and is frequent at higher levels in flushes on both sides of the Tees watershed, from Knock Fell to the Great Dun Fell/Cross Fell col, Meldon Hill and the north-east side of Little Fell.

Habitat: Three-flowered Rush appears to require either running water or a high water table. It occurs in calcareous flushes and shallow hollows on almost bare, irrigated Whin Sill rocks, in a very open M10 Dioecious Sedge–Common Butterwort short sedge-marsh community. At higher altitudes it is found in basic or neutral flushes and streams where Alpine Meadow-grass, Chickweed Willowherb, Alpine Bistort, Marsh Saxifrage and several rare mosses are suggestive of the M38 Curled Hook-moss–Common Sedge community. Additional species include Brown Bent, Red Fescue, Cuckooflower, Yellow and Glaucous Sedges, Autumn Hawkbit and Marsh-marigold.

Three-flowered Rush: **1** in fruit at Widdybank Fell *MEB*; **2** fruit *DM*.

Status and conservation: Overall, the species appears to be stable, but the higher flush sites are vulnerable to damage by motorcyclists and four-wheel-drive vehicles, including quad bikes. On Widdybank and Cronkley Fells the water-flow in some sites is very variable, leading to fluctuations in population size, flowering and fruiting. Records in a dry spring show there are only about a third of the number of inflorescences as in a wet spring; the many decapitated stalks suggest that the flowers may be eaten, probably by grouse.

For the present time, continued monitoring is required at the fells sites as persistent low numbers could be an indication of climate change. At higher altitudes, monitoring is also needed in order to observe the effects of the reduction of sheep grazing and the impact of the activities of motorized vehicles and mountain cyclists.

Further information: https://www.brc.ac.uk/plantatlas/plant/juncus-triglumis

LC Broad-leaved Cottongrass
Eriophorum latifolium Hoppe

FIRST RECORD IN TEESDALE
1799, J. Dickson

ALTITUDE
254–508 m

LIFE-CYCLE
Perennial; FLOWERS May–June; FRUITS July–August.

Usually forming tufts 20–60 cm in height, with sharply triangular stems in cross-section, the olive-green leaves of Broad-leaved Cottongrass are 3–8 mm wide, and flat with a short triangular end. The cottony bristles of its inflorescence are a brilliant white, in contrast to the dull white of Common Cottongrass, a feature which is noticeable at a distance. The tufted growth form is characteristic of more open communities, but where the vegetation is denser, such as in Widdybank Pasture, it grows throughout the sward, producing many single-flowering shoots.

Distribution: Widespread in Britain and Ireland, especially in upland areas from the North Pennines and Southern Uplands northwards. Lowland populations have declined considerably in the 20th century as a result of drainage, agricultural intensification and afforestation. In Teesdale it is very localized, limited to base-rich flushes and damp, base-rich meadows at Widdybank Pasture and Fell, one site below Cronkley Scar, near Wynch Bridge, Cetry Bank, Middleton-in-Teesdale Quarry and the moors beyond Cauldron Snout, bordering Maize Beck.

Broad-leaved Cottongrass, with Bottle Sedge, in base-rich stream *MEB*.

Habitat: Calcareous flushes include many rare species in Widdybank Pasture and on Widdybank Fell. In all sites, the vegetation comprises short sedge-marsh of the M10 Dioecious Sedge–Common Butterwort community. Associated species include many of the moisture-loving Teesdale rarities: Bird's-eye Primrose, Common Butterwort, Dioecious, Hair and Tawny Sedges, Bog Asphodel, Grass-of-Parnassus, Sea Plantain, Spring Gentian, False Sedge, Alpine Rush, Quaking-grass and Blue Moor-grass. In the Quarry, there are strong tussocks of Broad-leaved Cottongrass in a very open calcareous silty/mud habitat with isolated tussocks of Long-stalked Yellow-sedge.

Status and conservation: Stable on Widdybank Fell, but in the Pasture there was a 10% decrease in frequency between 1976 and 2000; some colonies are being invaded by tall rush species, in part because open drainage ditches have become filled with vegetation. On Cetry Bank there was a small increase between 1977 and 2012, and the Quarry population may be stable. Monitoring should continue, and in Widdybank Pasture the spread of the tall Soft-rush and Sharp-flowered Rush needs to be checked by frequent mowing and grazing, and improvement to the flow of water in the open ditches.

Further information: https://www.brc.ac.uk/plantatlas/plant/eriophorum-latifolium

Broad-leaved Cottongrass: **1** flowers with stigmas; **2** growing at Widdybank Meadow *both MEB.*

DD **Northern Deergrass**
Trichophorum cespitosum (L.) Hartm.

FIRST RECORD IN TEESDALE
2008, Roberts

ALTITUDE
380–550 m

LIFE-CYCLE
Perennial; FLOWERS June–July.

The two deergrasses and their hybrid are all superficially similar, forming dense, spiky tufts, each stem tipped with a spikelet that drops after midsummer, after which the stem elongates. Northern Deergrass differs from Common Deergrass by its smaller and more open tufts, a more distinctly ridged stem, and its sheath opening is circular rather than oval. It seems that Common Deergrass can be found in a broad range of peaty, mire habitats, whereas Northern Deergrass prefers those areas influenced by base-rich waters.

When not in flower there is the potential for confusion with spike-rushes and Hare's-tail Cottongrass in similar habitats, but these species lack the short leaf-blade arising from the top of the upper sheath in deergrasses.

Northern Deergrass, growing a Glen Fender Meadows SSSI, Perthshire *FJR*.

Northern Deergrass: **1** fruits; **2** cross-section of stem *both FJR*.

Distribution: Recognized in Britain as recently as 1988, Northern Deergrass is considered to be rare and under-recorded. It is known rarely from Somerset and the Welsh Borders, and scattered from the Lake District northwards through Scotland and in central Ireland. In Teesdale it has been identified only on Widdybank Pasture and Fell, Valley Bog and Moor House.

Habitat: In Widdybank Pasture, Northern Deergrass grows in the base-rich gravelly flushes and hummock and runnel habitat of the M10b Quaking-grass–Bird's-eye Primrose short sedge-marsh sub-community of M10 Dioecious Sedge–Common Butterwort. This supports many other characteristic species including Bird's-eye Primrose, Common Butterwort, Scottish Asphodel, Alpine Bartsia and Alpine Rush. Also associated are False, Dioecious, Glaucous, Tawny and Flea Sedges and Blue Moor-grass, Quaking-grass and Sheep's-fescue. Purple Moor-grass is occasionally found as single shoots, while in the silty runnels Few-flowered Spike-rush is characteristic. The few tufts on Widdybank Fell are in the same plant community, M10b. On Valley Bog, it and 'Hybrid' Deergrass (*p. 190*) are in the M17 deergrass sp.–Hare's-tail Cottongrass blanket mire community, with Feathery, Flat-topped and other Bog-moss species, Heather, Common Deergrass, Cranberry, Round-leaved Sundew, Bog Asphodel and Cross-leaved Heath.

Status and conservation: In part because of the only recent separation of Northern Deergrass as a full species from Common Deergrass, the distribution of the rarer species is probably imperfectly known. Targeted surveys need to be undertaken in, for example, flush habitats on Cronkley Fell and communities with Tall Bog-sedge in which it is likely to occur.

As for the associated rare species, it is essential that the habitats be maintained in good condition and protected from trampling by cattle and people, and from burning.

Further information: https://www.brc.ac.uk/plantatlas/plant/trichophorum-cespitosum-subsp-cespitosum

'Hybrid' Deergrass

Trichophorum × foersteri (G. A. Swan) D. A. Simpson

FIRST RECORD IN TEESDALE
1905, T. J. Foggitt

ALTITUDE
410–615 m

LIFE-CYCLE
Perennial; FLOWERS July–September; sterile, reproduces by plantlets from proliferous shoots.

Herbarium specimens confirm that this hybrid was present in Teesdale for more than a century before its recognition. Most of its morphological characters are intermediate between those of its parents, including for example the large, dense tufts of Common Deergrass as compared with the looser, depauperate ones of Northern Deergrass. The hybrid is sterile, but its flowers are sometimes proliferous, producing plantlets from the floret, which are shed and spread vegetatively.

Distribution: Occurs from Wales to Scotland and Northern Ireland, with a particular concentration in Northumberland through to Sutherland and Shetland. Its known range is being expanded all the time, most recently into north-west Yorkshire. In Teesdale it has been found at Widdybank Pasture and Fell, Cronkley Fell, Guy's Moss, Valley Bog, Hard Hill and Moor House.

Habitat: In Widdybank Pasture, 'Hybrid' Deergrass grows in the base-rich, gravelly flushes and hummock and runnel habitat of the short sedge-marsh of the M10b Quaking-grass–Bird's-eye Primrose sub-community of the M10 Dioecious Sedge–Common Butterwort mire community. This supports many characteristic species, including Bird's-eye Primrose, Common Butterwort, Scottish Asphodel, Alpine Bartsia, Alpine Rush, Northern Deergrass, False, Dioecious, Glaucous, Tawny and Flea Sedges, Few-flowered Spike-rush, and Blue Moor-grass, Quaking-grass and Sheep's-fescue with occasional single shoots of Purple Moor-grass. On Valley Bog, it is in the M17 deergrass sp.–Hare's-tail Cottongrass community, with a range of bog-mosses, Heather, Cranberry, Round-leaved Sundew, Bog Asphodel and Cross-leaved Heath, and in the M16d Heath Rush–Broom Fork-moss sub-community of M16 Cross-leaved Heath–Compact Bog-moss blanket bog.

'Hybrid' Deergrass: **1** proliferous form *MEB*; **2** dead heads from Butterburn Flow *FJR*.

'Hybrid' Deergrass: **3** growing at Butterburn Flow, Northumberland *FJR*; **4** cross-section of stem *FJR*.

Status and conservation: Re-identified in 2008 from material collected in Teesdale in 1905, the distribution of this hybrid is still being discovered. It is now known in six areas, as summarized previously, but it is too early to know if any changes are taking place. The current wider distribution of the hybrid than that of Northern Deergrass, one of its parents, suggests that at least parts of its present habitat may have been less acid in the past. In order to understand and conserve the hybrid and its rarer parent, all areas with deergrasses should be critically examined to check for the presence of the hybrid.

Further information: https://bsbi.org/wp-content/uploads/dlm_uploads/Deergrass-Id.pdf

'Hybrid' Deergrass, growing at Butterburn Flow, Northumberland, where it is the dominant plant *FJR*.

LC Few-flowered Spike-rush

Eleocharis quinqueflora (Hartmann) O. Schwarz

FIRST RECORD IN TEESDALE
1805, D. Turner and Dillwyn

ALTITUDE
262–284 m

LIFE-CYCLE
Perennial, shortly creeping; **FLOWERS** July–August.

A somewhat tufted, glabrous perennial with stems up to 20 cm in Teesdale, the leaves reduced to a papery, sometimes reddish, sheath. Has fine stems and leaves. Few-flowered Spike-rush can be distinguished from other spike-rushes by its lowest glume being more than half as long as the 3–7-flowered spikelet and the stem being rounded, lacking ridges. Small shoots of Northern Deergrass (*p. 188*) are rather similar, but these have a leaf extending from the uppermost sheath.

Distribution: Widespread in western and northern Britain and Ireland, but sparse and declining elsewhere as a result of drainage and a lack of grazing. Rare in Teesdale, it is known from Widdybank Fell and Pasture, Cetry Bank, Sand Sike and Whey Sike; now very rare between Wynch and Holwick Head Bridges and in Cronkley Pasture.

Habitat: Most frequent in silty or muddy/gravelly calcareous flushes in very open short sedge-marsh and also occasionally in more closed vegetation of the M10b Quaking-grass–Bird's-eye Primrose sub-community of the M10 Dioecious Sedge–Common Butterwort mire community, with Dioecious Sedge, Alpine and Three-flowered Rushes, Bird's-eye Primrose, Variegated Horsetail, False and Carnation Sedges and Long-stalked Yellow-sedge.

Status and conservation: Stable; sites should be managed to maintain open, silty flush habitats while avoiding excessive poaching and invasion by rushes.

Further information: https://www.brc.ac.uk/plantatlas/plant/eleocharis-quinqueflora

Few-flowered Spike-rush, growing at Creag An Lochain, Perth and Kinross, Scotland *FJR*.

Flat-sedge
Blysmus compressus (L.) Panz. ex L.ink

NERC

FIRST RECORD IN TEESDALE
1868, Baker and Tate

ALTITUDE
262–475 m

LIFE-CYCLE
Perennial, spreading by rhizomes; **FLOWERS** June–July; **FRUITS** ripen in August.

With a far-creeping rhizome, Flat-sedge appears as single shoots dispersed in a community or spreading along the margin of a stream or river, only occasionally forming a dense population. A high proportion of the shoots produce inflorescences which are very distinctive: a flattened spike of up to 25 reddish-brown spikelets, and the whole head shows a spiral twist. It has a superficial resemblance to other sedges, especially False Sedge (*p. 206*), although that species lacks a twist in its inflorescence, and has chestnut-brown basal leaf-sheaths.

Distribution: Widespread but localized throughout England and southern Scotland and very rare in Wales, the distribution of Flat-sedge has declined considerably since the 1930s, and it is now found predominantly in the Carboniferous limestone area of northern England. In Teesdale it is found on the lower slopes of Widdybank Fell by streams (sikes) and on the banks of Harwood Beck and the Tees to Barnard Castle and beyond.

Flat-sedge, growing on the bank of the Tees AS.

Habitat: In short, sedge-rich, damp grassland on freely drained calcareous soils, in ground that is periodically flooded by the sikes draining Widdybank Fell in the CG9a Hair Sedge–False Sedge sub-community of CG9 Blue Moor-grass–Limestone Bedstraw, with Variegated Horsetail, Grass-of-Parnassus, Sea Plantain, Bird's-eye Primrose, Yellow Saxifrage, Lesser Clubmoss, Knotted Pearlwort, Dioecious and Flea Sedges and Alpine Rush. In disturbed, turfy marshes in Widdybank Pasture and on Cetry Bank it occurs in the M11 Common Yellow-sedge–Yellow Saxifrage mire community, in which it has many of the same associates, plus Spring Gentian, Northern Bedstraw, Alpine Bistort, Blue Moor-grass, Scottish Asphodel, Marsh Valerian, Tawny Sedge and Broad-leaved Cottongrass. On the banks of the Tees at lower levels it occurs as 18 small populations on the south bank, from opposite the entry of Ettersgill to Wynch Bridge; in these the associated species are very varied.

Status and conservation: Although still fairly frequent, it was lost from more than 70% of its recorded areas in Widdybank Pasture between 1976 and 2018, mostly on turfy marshes that had been subject to trampling by heavy cattle: this has now been addressed by a change to lighter traditional breeds. On Cetry Bank, surveys in 1977 and 2012 showed little change; here it is important to keep cattle off to reduce poaching and land slips. By the Tees, west from Cronkley Bridge and in the Low Force area, it has been and continues to be reduced by human trampling. It would be desirable to restrict access to the river by kayakers and other visitors. At all sites monitoring is needed to identify any signs of overgrazing or trampling.

Further information: https://bsbi.org/wp-content/uploads/dlm_uploads/Blysmus_compressus_species_account.pdf

VU Slender Sedge
Carex lasiocarpa Ehrh.

FIRST RECORD IN TEESDALE
2014, Sarker

ALTITUDE
525 m

LIFE-CYCLE
Perennial; reproduces vegetatively by far-reaching rhizomes and by seed; FLOWERS June–July; FRUITS July–September.

Little is known about the Teesdale population of Slender Sedge as it was first found as recently as August 2014, the first record from Co. Durham. With a far-creeping rhizome producing large stands of loosely tufted shoots, its narrow leaves, up to 100 cm long with drawn-out, stiff, whip-like points, it looks en-masse like a slender, shortened form of Water Sedge (*p. 204*). In the dry season of 2018, inflorescences were present in the Cronkley Fell population, but it is not known if any mature fruits were produced.

Distribution: Widespread north of the Caledonian Canal from low levels to a maximum of 650 m. Also present in south-west Scotland, the Southern Uplands and the Lake District, scarce in Northumberland and scattered in Ireland, Wales and parts of eastern and southern England. It has declined especially in East Anglia and eastern Ireland due to land drainage. In Teesdale, known only from Cronkley Fell.

Habitat: Slender Sedge is an indicator species of mesotrophic to eutrophic mires. In Black Ark Pool on Cronkley Fell, it is found as a fringe species with Bottle Sedge in a base-rich, peaty watershed mire where the water table is known to fluctuate greatly from year-to-year. Associated species include Shoreweed and Water-purslane.

Status and conservation: The distribution of Slender Sedge within Teesdale is suspected to be incompletely known, so its current status cannot be ascertained. At the known location, it should be monitored and the current habitat conditions maintained, while searches for more populations should be undertaken.

Further information: https://www.brc.ac.uk/plantatlas/plant/carex-lasiocarpa

Slender Sedge: **1** flowers *MR*; **2** fruits *MR*; **3** large patch growing at Black Ark, Cronkley Fell *MEB*.

LC Hair Sedge
Carex capillaris L.

FIRST RECORD IN TEESDALE
1800, Winch and Harriman

ALTITUDE
280–710 m

LIFE-CYCLE
Perennial, deciduous; FLOWERS May–June; FRUITS July–September.

This bright green, tufted perennial is completely deciduous, and its tufts of chocolate-brown dead leaves can be very obvious in short grassland in the autumn. Otherwise, it is most easily noticed when in fruit, its stalked, drooping female spikes bearing relatively few, large, dark brown nuts. In some years large numbers of fruits are produced, both in the wild and in cultivation. Small tufts of yellow-green leaves with browning tips, about 5 cm long. When not in flower Hair Sedge can be mistaken for other small, tufted sedges, especially Pill Sedge (which occurs on more acid ground) and False Sedge (*p. 206*), the leaves of which are channelled rather than flat.

Distribution: Has a disjunct distribution, mainly in the Central Highlands, north-west Scotland and the North Pennines; very rare in Snowdonia and the Moffat Hills. In Teesdale it is very rare by the Tees east of High Force, but frequent above 300 m by the Tees and Harwood Beck and their tributaries, in Widdybank and Cronkley Pastures, Black Hill, Cronkley Scar and on Widdybank and Cronkley Fells. It also occurs higher up in suitable habitats around Moor House, Mattergill Sike, Green Burn Spoil, on Mickle Fell north to Birkdale and Maize Beck and Meldon Hill, rising to 710 m on Dufton Fell.

Habitat: Found on base-rich soils and areas flushed with base-rich water in calcareous grassland (pH 6·0–7·5) of the CG9 Blue Moor-grass–Limestone Bedstraw community and especially in the CG9d Hair Sedge–False Sedge sub-community on the moister parts of the sugar-limestone. Here it occurs alongside several northern montane, alpine and sub-alpine species such as Blue Moor-grass, Sheep's-fescue, Spring Gentian, Lesser Clubmoss, Mountain Everlasting, Alpine Bistort,

Hair Sedge: **1** young fruits; **2** mature fruits *both MEB*.

Common Rock-rose, Fairy Flax and Wild Thyme, plus Red Fescue, Quaking-grass, Crested Hair-grass, Glaucous Sedge and Spring-sedge.

Hair Sedge is also found in the damper, sedge-rich, grassy swards of CG10c Yellow Saxifrage–Bendy Ditrichum sub-community of Sheep's-fescue–Common Bent–Wild Thyme grassland with a number of arctic-alpine species, and on lead-mining spoil in a very open OV37 Sheep's-fescue–Spring Sandwort community with Wild Thyme, Fairy Flax, Harebell and Limestone Bedstraw.

In damper base-rich habitats, such as the short sedge-marsh of the M10 Dioecious Sedge–Common Butterwort community and M11 Common Yellow-sedge–Yellow Saxifrage mires, and in broken, turfy marshes and the eroding sides of drumlins that are flushed with base-rich, calcareous water, associated species are Long-stalked Yellow-sedge, Dioecious, Tawny, Carnation and Flea Sedges, Broad-leaved Cottongrass, Common Butterwort, mosses and liverworts. It is present on hummocks in the gravelly flushes within these communities and those receiving drainage from the metamorphosed limestone over the Whin Sill rocks on Widdybank Fell, the M10c Hook-beaked Tufa-moss sub-community.

Status and conservation: Locally abundant in Teesdale, Hair Sedge may indeed be expanding in the species-rich limestone grasslands where it appears not to be grazed by Rabbits. But plants have been lost from peripheral localities – only one plant was found by the Tees near Wynch Bridge in 2003 and, although recorded in 1863 between Cronkley Scar and the Tees, only one record was made in a widespread search of the flushes and grassland in Cronkley Pasture in 1973 and again in 2012. Cronkley Pasture has been overgrazed by cattle, sheep and Rabbits for several years, but recently new management agreements have been made to reduce the numbers of cattle and sheep and remove them completely in the winter. However, the Rabbits remain, many living in the boulder scree below the Scar, and are therefore difficult to control. Continued monitoring is required.

Further information: https://www.brc.ac.uk/plantatlas/plant/carex-capillaris

Hair Sedge, typical habitat on Cronkley Fell *MEB*.

LC Sheathed Sedge

Carex vaginata Tausch.

FIRST RECORD IN TEESDALE
2002, Corner, Roberts and Robinson

ALTITUDE
700–800 m

LIFE-CYCLE
Herbaceous **perennial**; FLOWERS in June.

A recent discovery in the Pennines, Sheathed Sedge is a shy flowerer and may often be overlooked. Forming loose patches of shoots with yellowish, keeled, winter-green leaves, its male glumes are longer and lighter red-brown than in the closely related (and more common) Carnation Sedge, which also has fewer, less inflated fruits and more blue-green leaves. The similar Stiff Sedge has darker green leaves that die back completely in winter.

Sheathed Sedge is clearly capable of surviving long periods of heavy grazing, in common with several of the 'meadow-type' species. Flowering is erratic: in the same year, some patches appear sterile whilst others have an abundance of inflorescences. Patches contain plants of differing genetic types, suggesting that its spread has been by sexual reproduction and seed dispersal; the large size of the clonal mats indicate considerable age.

Distribution: Widespread in the mountains of Scotland, Wales and the Lake District. In Teesdale it has been found on the southern and western slopes of Dufton Fell, on the west flank of Meldon Hill, Little Dun Fell and Mickle Fell, in the last of these within the grazing exclosure. Patches are well-defined and localized, on sites with base-rich drainage, often below limestone outcrops.

Sheathed Sedge, in limestone turf at Long Fell *FJR*.

Habitat: Sheathed Sedge has been found in species-rich grassland, somewhat similar to the MG8 Crested Dog's-tail–Marsh-marigold grassland community and in MG3 Sweet Vernal-grass–Wood Crane's-bill meadows. Associated plants on Dufton Fell include Sweet Vernal-grass, Cuckooflower, Sheep's-fescue, Meadow Buttercup, White Clover, Marsh Violet, Wood Anemone, Marsh-marigold, Carnation Sedge, Water Avens, Alpine Bistort, Lesser Spearwort, Mossy and Starry Saxifrages, Hairy Stonecrop, Marsh Valerian, Pyrenean Scurvygrass, Marsh Hawk's-beard, Wood Horsetail, Sneezewort, Meadowsweet, Ragged-Robin, Marsh Cinquefoil, Lesser Clubmoss and Globeflower. It is also found in the U17 Great Wood-rush–Water Avens tall-herb community.

Status and conservation: As a relatively recent discovery, its local distribution is still unclear, and the population trend is unknown. The search for high-altitude populations should be continued and their performance monitored so that the grazing pressure can be adjusted if necessary. Locations of the populations of this and other rare species should be mapped so they can be avoided when access off the rights of way is implemented. Unauthorized access by motorized wheeled vehicles in the NNR and higher Fells should be prevented, and the impacts of walkers and mountain cyclists need to be monitored, leading to appropriate action when necessary.

Further information: https://www.brc.ac.uk/plantatlas/plant/carex-vaginata

Sheathed Sedge: **1** fruits *FJR*; **2** leaf tips showing blunt tips *FJR*.

Rare Spring-sedge
Carex ericetorum Pollich

NERC

FIRST RECORD IN TEESDALE
1949, Tutin

ALTITUDE
495–550 m

LIFE-CYCLE
Perennial; FLOWERS in early May; FRUITS June–July.

A glabrous, tufted or open mat-forming sedge, dense tufts of which may become dead in the centre, forming a ring. In Teesdale the leaves are rather stiff and dark green, which helps to separate them from those of the similar Spring-sedge, the leaves of which are usually thin and yellow-green. In the former, veins are not obvious and margins have very fine teeth. Rare Spring-sedge has a single club-shaped male spike, with 1–3 female spikes crowded below the male; the glumes of both sexes are purplish-brown, whereas in Spring-sedge the male glumes are yellow-brown and female glumes red-brown with a projecting green midrib.

When the leaves of Rare Spring-sedge are shortened by severe winter weather, only weak inflorescences are produced, often with just a male spike; reproduction is primarily vegetative. From 1969–77, the population increased as the mean annual increase of ramets was 36%, exceeding the death rate of 26%. The size of female flowers, and hence the number of seeds, has varied through the years, being lower after dry winters and on grazed sites. Seedlings have not been found in the field, but transplants to Durham University Botanic Garden from the reservoir area before it was flooded did flower, set fruit and produce seedlings.

Distribution: Occurs very locally on calcareous soil from west Suffolk to Derbyshire, Yorkshire, Durham and Westmorland. In Teesdale it is known only on the sugar-limestone of Cronkley and Widdybank Fells.

Habitat: On areas of sugar-limestone it is found in closed or more open vegetation and on almost bare rock; the soils are skeletal and rendzina-like with a small amount of black humus, or slightly deeper and humus-rich. The highly porous nature of the soil compensates for the high rainfall (1,420 mm/yr), compared with other British localities such as in Breckland, and winter

Rare Spring-sedge, growing at Cronkley Fell *MEB*.

temperatures are often below zero. Associated species are those of the species-rich calcareous grassland of the CG9 Blue Moor-grass–Limestone Bedstraw community and especially the CG9d Hair Sedge–False Sedge sub-community with Blue Moor-grass, Sheep's-fescue, Red Fescue, Quaking-grass, Crested Hair-grass, Glaucous Sedge, Spring-sedge, Spring Gentian, Lesser Clubmoss, Mountain Everlasting, Alpine Bistort, Rock-rose, Fairy Flax and Wild Thyme. On Cronkley Fell it is found with the characteristic species of the CG9a Hoary Rock-rose–Squinancywort sub-community and Horseshoe-vetch and Small Scabious.

Status and conservation: The present status of Rare Spring-sedge varies in relation to the habitat and grazing pressure. In three marked plots, counts of ramets over the last 50 years varied twenty-fold, with a tendency to be lower in recent years. Particularly low counts have been associated both with high levels of Rabbit grazing (and associated scuffing) and also with the development of dense, tussocky Blue Moor-grass following Rabbit control. Where the Rabbit population, including within the Cronkley Fell exclosure, was extremely high in 2003–04, most species (including Mountain Avens) were very closely grazed. The flowers, but not the leaves, of Rare Spring-sedge were eaten, nor were the leaves of Blue Moor-grass, which spread and outcompeted the sedge.

Autumn mowing has been introduced in some areas, the cuttings being left to then be dispersed by strong winds. This practice has led to some signs of recovery of Rare Spring-sedge due to the reduction of shading and competition which arose from previous undergrazing. Active Rabbit control commenced in 2005 and has been continued, with a few interruptions, such that numbers are now very low, aided by several weeks of hard frost and prolonged snow in the winter of 2009–10 and a long, cold winter 2017–18 with deep snow drifts as late as April. Sheep are now grazing these areas and, as their numbers are increased, it is hoped they will keep the turf short for the light-demanding rare plants. Monitoring is undertaken by Natural England and the author to ascertain the effectiveness of these management interventions.

Further information: https://bsbi.org/wp-content/uploads/dlm_uploads/Carex_ericetorum_species_account.pdf

Rare Spring-sedge: **1** flowers *MEB*; **2** fruit *DM*.

EN Bog-sedge
Carex limosa L.

FIRST RECORD IN TEESDALE
1885, W. Foggitt

ALTITUDE
460 m

LIFE-CYCLE
Perennial, far creeping; **FLOWERS** May–June; **FRUITS** June–July.

A northern species now rather rare outside Scotland, Bog-sedge has far-reaching rhizomes that produce loosely tufted shoots. Its leaves are very slender and a pale bluish-green colour, distinguishing it from Tall Bog-sedge, which forms more solid clumps and has wider leaves of a clearer green. The female spikes, up to three per inflorescence, are nodding and the glumes are broad, covering the silvery-glaucous utricles when mature, unlike Tall Bog-sedge in which the narrower glumes expose more of the apple-green utricles.

Distribution: Found throughout the north-western parts of Scotland and Ireland, in north Wales, the Lake District, North Pennines and Southern Uplands, and more locally in the bogs of the New Forest; usually found below 450 m but ascending to 830 m in Scotland. In Teesdale, known only from the Black Hill area, opposite Cauldron Snout.

Habitat: Grows in very wet blanket bogs and valleys, in and around pools with Feathery Bog-moss, Common Cottongrass, Bogbean, and bladderworts (the M1 Cow-horn Bog-moss bog pool community); with Bottle Sedge, Slender Sedge and other sedges in the M9 Bottle Sedge–Pointed Spear-moss/Giant Spear-moss mire community; and in more mesotrophic mires with Bottle Sedge and Flat-topped Bog-moss, the M4 Bottle Sedge–Flat-topped Bog-moss mire community.

Status and conservation: At its only known location at Black Hill, the habitat must be conserved, including giving it protection from burning.

Further information: https://www.brc.ac.uk/plantatlas/plant/carex-limosa

Bog-sedge: **1** growing at Eycott Hill *FJR*; **2** fruits *MP*.

⊤ Tall Bog-sedge
Carex magellanica Lam.

FIRST RECORD IN TEESDALE
1883, Marshall

ALTITUDE
460–554 m

LIFE-CYCLE
Perennial, shortly creeping; FLOWERS June–July; FRUITS June–July.

An erect, tufted sedge of bogs, Tall Bog-sedge can be mistaken for Bog-sedge in similar habitats. It has wider, more blue-green leaves, and the drooping female spikes have narrower, red-purple glumes that expose more of the apple-green utricle.

Distribution: Very local in north Wales and Northern Ireland, and scattered from the Lake District through western Scotland. In Teesdale it was formerly frequent on Near Foolmere, north-west of the Cow Green Reservoir dam, where some plants remain. Also found on Valley Bog, between Force Burn and Mattergill Sike, and Black Hill, opposite Cauldron Snout. Populations on Yad Moss and Burnhope Seat have probably been lost due to drainage.

Habitat: A plant of bog-moss lawns with Feathery and Flat-topped Bog-mosses and at least gently flowing water (the M2 Feathery Bog-moss/Flat-topped Bog-moss bog pool community) and the M17 deergrass sp.–Hare's-tail Cottongrass community, with a range of bog-mosses, Heather, deergrass sp., Cranberry, Round-leaved Sundew, Bog Asphodel and Cross-leaved Heath.

Status and conservation: A proportion of the population near the Cow Green Reservoir dam was lost around 1969, although some plants remain outside the Moor House-Upper Teesdale NNR but within the Appleby Fells SSSI. Valley Bog is in the original Moor House NNR; its current status there and in the pasture near Moor House is currently unknown. The habitats in which it grows should be conserved and protected from burning.

Further information: https://www.brc.ac.uk/plantatlas/plant/carex-magellanica

Tall Bog-sedge, growing at Tarn Moss *FJR*.

LC Water Sedge
Carex aquatilis Wahlenb.

FIRST RECORD IN TEESDALE
1968, Proctor

ALTITUDE
285–840 m

LIFE-CYCLE
Perennial, with far-creeping rhizomes; FLOWERS June–July; FRUITS not known.

Water Sedge was first discovered in Teesdale as recently as 1968, in an old channel of the Tees some distance above Cauldron Snout, now submerged by the Cow Green Reservoir. At lower levels it grows with, and may be mistaken for, the much commoner Lesser Pond-sedge, although this species has keeled leaves 7–10 mm wide, as opposed to the 3–5 mm wide, flat or 'U'-shaped leaves of Water Sedge.

A rhizomatous plant, apparently able to survive close grazing for decades, large patches have now been found at higher altitudes. These were recognized only after 2001 when sheep were removed from the fells. Grazed, non-flowering plants may have been overlooked as Common Cottongrass as both have channelled leaves, although the latter has a long, solid, three-sided point at its leaf-tip.

Distribution: Widespread in Scotland at both lower and higher altitudes and scattered throughout Ireland, it has outlier populations in Wales and northern England, especially in river and lake swamps. In Teesdale there are several patches (60–340 m²) above 800 m on the north flanks of the Great and Little Dun Fells, while at lower levels it is known from the Tees below Falcon Clints, the Little Tees near Cronkley Bridge, near Whey Sike Farm and Holwick Head Bridge. In addition to the site of its original discovery, populations around Mickleton and Middleton may now have been lost, and some of its apparent records have been misidentifications of Lesser Pond-sedge.

Water Sedge: 1 the largest patch, at Great Dun Fell *FJR*; **2** inflorescence *FJR*; **3** growing at Tees bank *MEB*.

Habitat: At higher sites on the northern flanks of Great and Little Dun Fells the sedge is in peaty soils irrigated by nutrient-poor and base-poor waters, characteristically in hollows and drainage channels, which may be where snow has lain long. Associated species include Alpine Foxtail, Velvet Bent, Marsh-marigold, White Sedge, Common Sedge, Tufted Hair-grass, Marsh Violet, Starry Saxifrage with Stiff Sedge nearby. These are typical species of the M7b Water Sedge–Flat-topped Bog-moss sub-community of the M7 White Sedge–Russow's Bog-moss mire.

In the Little Tees, it grows between Bottle Sedge in deeper water and Common Sedge in the shallows, with Soft-rush and Jointed Rush, Meadowsweet, Marsh-marigold, Sneezewort, Marsh Lousewort, Wild Angelica, occasionally Wood Crane's-bill and formerly Globeflower in the S27 Bottle Sedge–Marsh Cinquefoil tall-herb fen community.

At the lowest site (200 m) it grew in a former river-bed of the Tees, in an Alder wood with Bay Willow and Hybrid Crack-willow on a constantly wet, deep peaty-silt with local, more nutrient-rich irrigation below a boulder clay bank. Associated species include Lesser Pond-sedge, Fibrous Tussock-sedge, Yellow Iris, Marsh Bedstraw, Cleavers, Common Nettle and Marsh Thistle, perhaps representing the W3 Bay Willow–Bottle Sedge community.

Status and conservation: Water Sedge was found at the fells only after sheep had been almost removed and the vegetation had recovered from the previous intense grazing pressure. Since that time however, much damage has been done by motorcycles and quad bikes, creating deep ruts in the soft vegetation containing Water Sedge and Alpine Foxtail, and by a tractor and trailer which disturbed the important drainage systems. In the Moor House NNR, most of the grazing rights in the Tees catchment have been bought by Natural England, so sheep grazing can now be controlled, but action needs to be taken to prevent unauthorized access by motorized wheeled vehicles in the NNR and on the higher levels of the fells. In addition, the effects of walkers and mountain bike riders should be monitored and appropriate action taken when necessary.

More recently four sites have been added to its distribution at lower levels, including the Little Tees near Cronkley Bridge and a larger pure stand at Whey Sike Farm, but conversely some former sites have been lost, perhaps a result of the spread of trees and undergrowth, possibly linked to eutrophic drainage from the meadows above the bank. The Whey Sike population has shrunk, the feeder spring being choked with freshwater vegetation and Soft-rush, Meadowsweet and Creeping Thistle invading the margins. Also, during the long, dry summer of 2014, cattle damaged the sedge bed by extensive trampling and leaving dung. Habitat management work and other conservation measures are in progress here to try and address these issues, and all new and former sites should continue to be monitored.

Further information: https://www.brc.ac.uk/plantatlas/plant/carex-aquatilis

LC **False Sedge**
Carex simpliciuscula (Wahlenb.) Mackenzie

FIRST RECORD IN TEESDALE
1799, Dickson

ALTITUDE
370–530 m

LIFE-CYCLE
Herbaceous perennial, FLOWERS May–June.

False Sedge, as its name suggests, was until recently classified in its own genus *Kobresia*, differentiated from 'true' sedges by flower details: the spikelets have only one floret, and the female florets are enfolded by an extra, inner glume. The leaves are narrow, stiff and channelled. In autumn, the leaf sheaths turn a distinctive chestnut-brown colour which reveals its presence, especially in short grassland on sugar-limestone. It is superficially similar to several other sedges: Flea Sedge, especially in an immature state, is the most likely confusion species although this has only a single spike, and Flat-sedge has its flowers flattened into one, twisted plane.

Distribution: Elsewhere in Britain it is known only from the Central Highlands of Scotland, where there are several very small colonies. In Teesdale it is found on Widdybank and Cronkley Fells and Pastures, and by streams that run off these two fells; also by the Tees at Cetry Bank and near Birkdale. The latter site was discovered as recently as 2010.

Habitat: A tufted or dispersed perennial, False Sedge grows in three situations. It forms tufts in short sedge-marsh, dense patches in grassland and open networks of single shoots in the silty mud over impervious rocks that receives calcareous drainage, as on Widdybank Fell.

It is found most frequently in open, short sedge-marsh of the M10 Dioecious Sedge–Common Butterwort community and M11 Long-stalked Yellow-sedge–Yellow Saxifrage mires, often cattle-poached, turfy marshes and on the eroding sides of drumlins that are free-draining and flushed with base-rich water. Constant species include several sedges (Dioecious, Tawny, Carnation and Flea Sedges and Long-stalked Yellow-sedge), Broad-leaved Cottongrass and Common Butterwort; other associates include Bird's-eye Primrose, Alpine Bistort, Alpine Meadow-rue, Variegated Horsetail, Knotted Pearlwort, Three-flowered Rush, Few-flowered Spike-rush, Alpine Rush, Blue Moor-grass and Quaking-grass.

Found also in the CG9 Blue Moor-grass–Limestone Bedstraw grassland of the CG9d Hair Sedge–False Sedge sub-community, particularly on Widdybank and Cronkley Fells in the moister areas. Here it is frequently dominant over small areas, the only rare arctic-alpine to achieve dominant status. Associated species include Quaking-grass, Harebell, Glaucous Sedge, Sheep's-fescue, Fairy Flax, Blue Moor-grass and Wild Thyme.

False Sedge, in flower at Widdybank Fell *MR*.

False Sedge: **1** chestnut-brown sheath bases *MEB*; **2** in fruit *MR*.

Status and conservation: On and around the metamorphosed limestone, False Sedge populations are fairly stable, the stiff stems being largely unpalatable to sheep, Rabbits, hares and voles. In Widdybank Pasture the upper sites decreased by 15% between the surveys of 1976–81 and 2000 largely due to the spread of tall rushes, while there was only a small decrease in the lower pasture. On Cetry Bank, surveys of 1977 and 2011 showed little change, although cattle have created wide tracks diagonally across the unstable slope. In Cronkley Pasture, where the banks of small streams are being broken by cattle and the flood plains overgrazed, it was scarce in 1973, more so in 2005, but locally frequent and widespread in 2012.

False Sedge is intolerant of shade and so is vulnerable to the undergrazing of rough pastures and marshes, which leads to the spread of tall rushes and other sedges. The re-opening of existing drains (grips) lowers the water table and may help to check the spread of overshading species. Conversely, overgrazing, especially on Cetry Bank, can lead to habitat damage: getting the grazing level correct is therefore crucial. Especially in fenced exclosures, repeat surveys are needed to detect adverse changes, and to guide the introduction of hard-mouthed traditional breeds of cattle that are able to graze the coarser species, or mowing (with removal of the toppings) where the terrain permits.

Experimental work has demonstrated the species' requirement for low-nutrient sites, especially low in phosphorus. Transplants have met with variable success in terms of seed production; given that this is high in most years at the native sites, understanding variability in transplant success would be an important part of any conservation strategy.

Further information: htt https://bsbi.org/wp-content/uploads/dlm_uploads/Kobresia_simpliciuscula_species_account.pdf

Viviparous Sheep's-fescue
Festuca vivipara (L.) Sm.

FIRST RECORD IN TEESDALE
Unknown

ALTITUDE
262–1,900m

LIFE-CYCLE
Perennial; reproduces by plantlets in June–July.

A densely tufted grass with slender, wiry, sometimes glaucous leaves, Viviparous Sheep's-fescue is very distinctive in flower. Most of its florets, and occasionally all of them, are proliferous, reproducing vegetatively by means of small plantlets bearing two or three leaves. True seeds seem to be produced only rarely. The plantlets have much greater carbohydrate and mineral nutrient content than the seeds of Sheep's-fescue, which aids their establishment in the summer and autumn. The proliferous lifestyle is generally regarded as an adaptation to a short growing season and extremes of cold and/or rainfall. Alpine Meadow-grass (*p. 213*), which overlaps in habitat, usually has some viviparous flowers, but its leaves are much wider and not wiry. Without flowers, Viviparous Sheep's-fescue is difficult, or perhaps impossible, to tell apart from Sheep's-fescue.

Distribution: Common on mountains and extending down to sea level, in northern and western Scotland, the Lake District, northern England, Snowdonia and the Brecon Beacons, and Ireland, especially the west. In Teesdale it can be found on the bank of the Tees at Wynch Bridge, by Cauldron Snout, in Maize Beck Gorge and on the higher Fells.

Habitat: Found predominantly in upland hill pastures, heathlands, rock ledges, and mountain slopes and plateaux at high altitude; also in open woodland, on the banks of streams and in bogs. It seems to live in both basic and acidic conditions, and can grow on immature and thin soils.

Status and conservation: Its full distribution within Teesdale is poorly known, and no population trends can be ascertained. It is important therefore to monitor known locations, search for more and maintain the current habitat conditions.

Further information: https://www.brc.ac.uk/plantatlas/plant/festuca-vivipara

Viviparous Sheep's-fescue: **1**, **2**, growing at Tees bank *both MEB*.

LC Blue Moor-grass
Sesleria caerulea (L.) Ard.

FIRST RECORD IN TEESDALE
1800, Winch (or Binks)

ALTITUDE
200–800 m

LIFE-CYCLE
Perennial; FLOWERS April–June; SEEDS July.

The unmistakable indigo-purple flower spikes with shining membranous bracts of Blue Moor-grass are a feature of many of the limestone grasslands of Teesdale from the end of April. The colour fades as the seeds ripen and fall; they germinate immediately, with apparently very high viability of up to 90%. Despite this, there is no evidence that it can establish in closed habitats: in dense grassland, it is considered to be a relict feature of the original pioneer stage of colonization. At the end of the season, the leaves turn a characteristic salmon-fawn colour.

On deep soils Blue Moor-grass cannot compete with taller grasses, but on shallower soils on limestone a balance with associated species is maintained. When grazing is reduced, established Blue Moor-grass can become tussocky and crowd out other plants, including such specialities as Rare Spring-sedge on Cronkley Fell. It appears to be tolerant of considerable frost, while prolonged summer drought causes die-back of the leaves. However, the roots are undamaged and new shoots soon develop with the return of moisture. Plants do occur in permanently moist situations, even with roots in running water, but not where standing water reaches the base of its shoot system.

In a vegetative state it could be misidentified for some meadow-grass species and Heath-grass; from these it can be distinguished by the rough margin to its leaves, and in autumn by the salmon colour of its dying foliage.

Distribution: Blue Moor-grass has a clearly defined association with limestones in northern England, from the Lake District eastwards through the Pennines to east Durham, and western Ireland, with just a few isolated occurrences elsewhere, including on micaceous schists and metamorphosed limestone in the Central Highlands of Scotland. In Teesdale it is widespread

Blue Moor-grass: **1** flowering at Widdybank Fell; **2** in seed, Cronkley Fell *both MEB.*

and frequent on limestone and base-rich soils, hummocks in gravelly flushes, Whin Sill and river shingle.

Habitat: Blue Moor-grass grows in many habitats, all on calcareous rock: rock ledges, stabilized scree, calcareous grassland, grass heath and open woodland. The main community is CG9 Blue Moor-grass–Limestone Bedstraw grassland with Sheep's-fescue, Wild Thyme, Spring Gentian, Lesser Clubmoss, Alpine Bistort, Limestone and Northern Bedstraws, Common Rock-rose and Fairy Flax. On hummocks in the M10b Quaking-grass–Bird's-eye Primrose sub-community of M10 Dioecious Sedge–Common Butterwort short sedge-marsh it is found with, for example, Hair and False Sedges, Alpine Bartsia, Spring Sandwort and Variegated Horsetail. On very open, heavy metal mine-spoil it is in the OV37 Sheep's-fescue–Spring Sandwort community with Hair Sedge, Sheep's-fescue, Wild Thyme, Hoary Whitlowgrass, Spring Sandwort and Alpine Penny-cress, while by the Tees below High Force it is found in hay meadow-type vegetation.

Status and conservation: As a species that characterizes much of the grassland on limestone, changes in frequency are rarely recorded and it would appear to be fairly stable in most of its habitats. It is possible that it has decreased in the communities by the Tees below High Force since the reduction in the number of spates and the exclusion of grazing stock from the banks, which has allowed the grassland to grow taller and denser.

To identify any changes in the future, the collection of a set of baseline records for a few sample sites in each of the plant communities with Blue Moor-grass should be established. Where grazing levels have been reduced the effect of the unpalatable Blue Moor-grass and Glaucous Sedge on the associated species should be monitored.

Further information: https://www.brc.ac.uk/plantatlas/plant/sesleria-caerulea

Alpine Foxtail
Alopecurus magellanicus Lam.

FIRST RECORD IN TEESDALE
1959, Ratcliffe and Eddy

ALTITUDE
659–820 m

LIFE-CYCLE
Perennial; FLOWERS June–August; SEEDS August.

The relatively recent discovery in Teesdale of Alpine Foxtail, a low, patch-forming grass with distinctive ovoid to cylindrical flower spikes, is due to the fact that when subject to heavy grazing, few flowers survive, and it remains very inconspicuous. Following years with low grazing pressure, however, flowering can be very profuse, with for example in 2002, more than 400 spikes counted in a 3 × 3 m patch: the pink or rusty anthers make the plants very conspicuous.

Alpine Cat's-tail, a grass of similar stature and appearance, can be found in the same habitats as Alpine Foxtail, although it is rare in the high Pennines and has not yet been found in the Tees catchment. It has awnless glumes and red-purple flower heads, rather than what has been described as 'the colour of a thunder-cloud'.

Distribution: A few sites are known for this species in the Cheviot, Moffat and Tweedsmuir Hills, Ochil Hills and the Scottish Highlands. In Teesdale it can be found from Little Fell to Cross Fell as well as over the Pennine Ridge to the west and in the upper South Tyne catchment. Well defined and localized patches are known from Dufton Fell, Meldon Hill, Little Dun Fell and Mickle Fell, usually below limestone outcrops and receiving base-rich drainage.

Habitat: A plant of spring-heads, cold and bryophyte-rich, slightly sloping, very wet, sometimes stony areas. It forms part of the M38 Curled Hook-moss–Common Sedge community with associated species such as Sheathed Sedge, Hairy Stonecrop, Alpine and Chickweed Willowherbs and Blinks. Also found in flushed, wet grass and along stream banks and in stream beds, often with Water Sedge, Tufted Hair-grass, Common Sedge and Soft-rush.

Some sites have a rich flora suggestive of the U17 Great Wood-rush–Water Avens community, with Marsh Hawk's-beard, Marsh Cinquefoil, Lesser Celandine, Globeflower, Marsh Valerian. Smooth Lady's-mantle, Marsh Foxtail, Wood Anemone, Marsh-marigold, Cuckooflower, Glaucous, Common and Flea Sedges, Common Mouse-ear, Alternate-leaved and Opposite-leaved Golden-saxifrages, Pyrenean Scurvygrass, Water Avens, Soft-rush, Meadow Buttercup, Mossy and Starry Saxifrage, dandelions, White Clover and Marsh Violet. Such an array of species also perhaps points towards a herb-rich meadow flora of the MG3 Sweet Vernal-grass–Wood Crane's-bill community.

Status and conservation: Alpine Foxtail seems to be very palatable to sheep. Following its almost complete absence from the higher Fells since 2001, many new patches of the plant have been found in addition to the original two sites from 1959. At least eight sites are known in the watershed of the Tees, six in that of the Eden and two in the South Tyne. Although these sites are above 650 m, their very remoteness attracts walkers, mountain bike riders and those with motorcycles, quad bikes and other four-wheel-drive vehicles. Since 2000, motorized activities have caused much damage, creating deep ruts in the soft vegetation containing Alpine Foxtail and Water Sedge. This can have broad-scale impacts by disrupting the important drainage systems, as shown by a channel that cut off the nutrient-rich water supply to the lower part of a flush which soon turned into impoverished acid heath.

A number of conservation actions are therefore imperative. Unauthorized access by motorized wheeled vehicles in the NNR and on the higher Fells should be prohibited and prevented, while the erosion caused by walkers and mountain cyclists should be monitored and appropriate action taken. Adjustments to the grazing pressure may be needed: the necessity of introducing more grazing or mowing should not be ruled out. All the while, the search for new high-level populations should be continued, and all populations fully mapped to inform future access provisions and restrictions.

Alpine Foxtail, growing at Great Dun Fell *FJR*.

Further information: https://bsbi.org/wp-content/uploads/dlm_uploads/Alopecurus_magellanicus_species_account.pdf

Alpine Meadow-grass
Poa alpina L.

FIRST RECORD IN TEESDALE
1962, Lloyd

ALTITUDE
580 m

LIFE-CYCLE
Perennial; FLOWERS June–August; SEEDS August.

Probably as an adaptation to inclement summer weather, Alpine Meadow-grass usually produces some viviparous spikelets, but unlike Viviparous Sheep's-fescue (*p. 209*) it also produces seed-bearing spikelets. A short, tufted perennial, its leaves are usually glaucous and up to 4 mm wide; the rootstock is clothed with persistent, fibrous remains of basal leaves and sheaths. Chromosome counts have shown plants from the Maize Beck site at least to be genetically distinct from the nearest population outwith Teesdale, at Ingleborough in north-west Yorkshire.

Glaucous Meadow-grass is an equally rare grass of mountains; although not known from the Pennines, its similarity to, and shared habitat with, Alpine Meadow-grass could mean it has been overlooked. Its leaves are usually intensely glaucous (although less so in the shade-loving variety once known as Balfour's Meadow-grass), and its flowers are always seed-bearing, not proliferating.

Distribution: Most widespread in Scotland, from the Central Highlands northwards, Alpine Meadow-grass has small outlying populations in the Lake District, the Pennines, Snowdonia and the west coast of Ireland. In Teesdale it is known only from cliffs on the west side of Maize Beck and two sites, found in 1999 and 2005, on High Cup Nick.

Habitat: Found on limestone cliffs, sometimes among tufts of Blue Moor-grass, alongside Alpine Cinquefoil, Wild Thyme, Roseroot, Hoary Rock-rose, Green Spleenwort, Mossy Saxifrage and Sheep's-fescue.

Status and conservation: The last survey at Maize Beck cliffs in 2009 revealed just seven fruiting and 17 vegetative shoots, although more may have been present in the Blue Moor-grass dominated areas. One of the two High Cup Nick populations has not been found recently. Monitoring must be continued at all locations, ideally more frequently than at present when the most recent results are more than a decade old.

Further information: https://www.brc.ac.uk/plantatlas/plant/poa-alpina

Alpine Meadow-grass: **1 2** growing at High Cup Nick *both JO'R*.

Notes on seven very local aquatics in Teesdale

There are seven aquatic macrophytes that occur or have occurred in Teesdale, mainly in Tarn Dub below Cronkley Scar and the former Weel, a natural waterbody that is now subsumed by Cow Green Reservoir. All are widespread in the UK but rare in Co. Durham; several have a long post-Ice Age record but are not considered to qualify as part of the Teesdale Assemblage on account of their wider distribution pattern, which is not shared with terrestrial members of the rarer Teesdale flora (Godwin, 1975).

Lesser Marshwort *Apium inundatum* (L.) W.D.J. Koch – found in Tarn Dub. Scattered throughout Britain and Ireland, it reaches its maximum altitude in Teesdale *FJR*.

Shoreweed *Littorella uniflora* (L.) Asch. – present in Tarn Dub and around a peaty pool on Cronkley Fell. Frequent in the north-western half of Britain and Ireland, especially in mud along the edge of standing waters *MEB*.

Tarn Dub, between Cronkley Scar and a long moraine, is an A22 Shoreweed–Water Lobelia community *DM*.

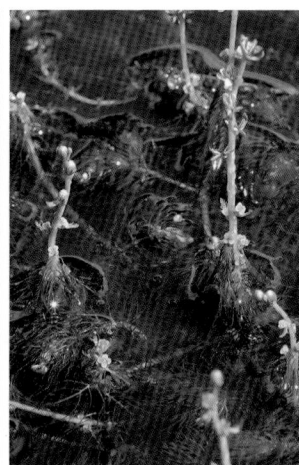

Water-purslane
Lythrum portula (L.)
D.A. Webb – occurs in Tarn
Dub. Occupies the margins
of mildly acidic waters,
especially in the south-
western half of Britain and
Ireland *PS*.

Alternate Water-milfoil
*Myriophyllum
alterniflorum* DC. – present
in Tarn Dub and formerly
in the Weel. With a westerly
and northerly distribution,
found in still and flowing
waters *FJR*.

Unbranched Bur-reed
Sparganium emersum
Rehmann – several records
by the Tees in the west or
Upper Teesdale, although
none in recent decades.
Widespread in Britain and
Ireland, although much less
frequent from the Scottish
Highlands northwards *RLan*.

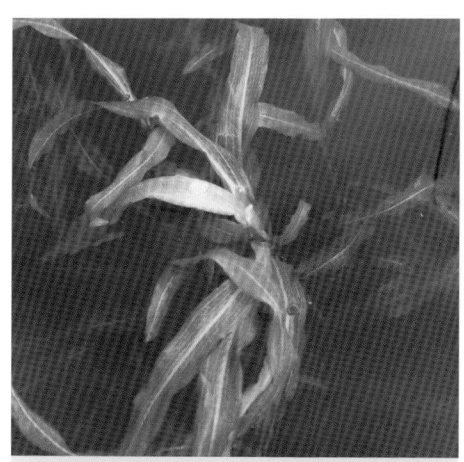

Red Pondweed *Potomageton alpinus*
Balb. – formerly recorded in the Weel.
Mainly west of the Pennines, in Scotland
and the northern half of Ireland, often in
mildly acidic water *RLan*.

Floating Club-rush *Eleogiton fluitans*
(L.) Link – previously known from Tarn Dub,
but not recorded since 20th century. Found
in peaty pools throughout Britain and
Ireland, especially in the north and west *FJR*.

Plants and Protection

There are a variety of means by which organizations, including governments, can design and implement policy which aims to protect wildlife. Options include:

- **Regulation** – such as legislation or recommendations.
- **Economic** – incentives or disincentives.
- **Suasive** – knowledge, including the scientific evidence underlying policy and/or the information disseminated to a wider community in the form of reports, leaflets or posters to clarify/explain the situation.

Once it became possible to collect and collate large amounts of data and the declines were obvious in all forms of wildlife, including plants, the move to introduce laws began. In May 2019, the IPBES[1] declared a Biodiversity Emergency to highlight the enormous losses of species and habitats taking place worldwide.

National UK legislation

The first plant to be controlled by law was one of those found in arable fields, the Corncockle, which had to be removed from corn before it was ground into flour for making bread on account of the bitter taste that resulted. That was back in the 13th century. Six centuries later, concerns began to form around the demise of certain species. One of these was the Lady's-slipper. Having occupied a wide range in northern England, collection of the plant decimated its wild populations, leaving just one specimen.

Wildlife and Countryside Act 1981 (W&C Act)

The Lady's-slipper was just one example of a species threatened with extinction that led the UK Government to introduce the Wildlife and Countryside Act in 1981. The Act includes **Schedule 8**, which names particular species that are afforded special protection. All wild plants in the UK now have some form of protection. Uprooting plants for commercial purposes was made illegal by the earlier Theft Act in 1968. The W&C Act made it illegal to uproot any wild plant without the landowner's permission. In this case, the word 'plant' is interpreted widely and covers algae, bryophytes, mosses and liverworts, fungi and lichens, as well as vascular flowering plants.

Countryside and Rights of Way Act 2000 (CROW Act)

This Act focuses on access, public rights of way and wildlife conservation, adding to the important designations the issue of limestone pavement protection orders. It gives a public right of access to land mapped as 'open country' (mountain, moor, heath and down) or registered common land. This is known as the 'right to roam'.

Natural Environment and Rural Communities Act 2006 (NERC Act)

Given the devolution of parts of the UK with their own administrations, the Natural Environment and Rural Communities Act 2006 was introduced, but shaped by different administrations in Scotland and Wales. This law includes **Section 41**, which requires the Secretary of State to publish a list of habitats and species which are of principal importance for the conservation of biodiversity in England. In addition, it imposes a **duty** on Local Authorities and public bodies to conserve biodiversity.

---

[1] IPBES, International Science-Policy Platform for Biodiversity and Ecosystem Services.

Habitats of Principal Importance

There are 56 Habitats of Principal Importance listed in Section 41 of the NERC Act. These are the habitats in England that are identified in the UK Biodiversity Action Plan (UK BAP), which continued to be priorities in the new UK Post-2010 Biodiversity Framework. The list includes terrestrial habitats (*e.g.* upland hay meadows and lowland mixed deciduous woodland) and freshwater (*e.g.* ponds and marine habitats such as sub-tidal sands and gravels). Some of these are broad, others very specific.

Species of Principal Importance

There are 943 Species of Principal Importance listed in Section 41 of the NERC Act, again deriving from the UK BAP, which continued to be priorities after the 2010 biodiversity review. Of these, 403 are plant species, comprising six algae, 77 bryophytes, 61 fungi, 98 lichens, nine stoneworts and 152 vascular plants.

Protected plant species

Wildlife and Countryside Act 1981 (W&C Act), Schedule 8

The Schedule 8 species (apart from Bluebell) that occur in Teesdale are:

Oblong Woodsia *	*Woodsia ilvensis* (*p. 80*)
Marsh Saxifrage	*Saxifraga hirculus* (*p. 93*)
Teesdale Sandwort	*Sabulina stricta* (*p. 145*)
Spring Gentian	*Gentiana verna* (*p. 156*)

(* The only population remaining in Teesdale was planted.)

Natural Environment and Rural Communities Act 2006 (NERC Act), Section 41

There are 18 Species of Principal Importance found in Teesdale (listed below). The majority of these are considered to be part of the Teesdale Assemblage; those that are the subject of a species account are cross-referenced to the relevant page:

Oblong Woodsia	*Woodsia ilvensis* (*p. 80*)
Holly-fern	*Polystichum lonchitis* (*p. 81*)
Common Juniper	*Juniperus communis* (*p. 85*)
Marsh Saxifrage	*Saxifraga hirculus* (*p. 93*)
Starry Lady's-mantle	*Alchemilla acutiloba* (*p. 113*)
Velvet Lady's-mantle	*Alchemilla monticola* (*p. 116*)
Large-toothed Lady's-mantle	*Alchemilla subcrenata* (*p. 117*)
Shining Lady's-mantle	*Alchemilla micans* (*p. 121*)
Hoary Rock-rose	*Helianthemum oelandicum* ssp. *levigatum* (*p. 134*)
Field Gentian	*Gentianella campestris* (*p. 154*)
Montane Eyebright	*Euphrasia officinalis* ssp. *monticola* (*p. 163*)
Ostenfeld's Eyebright	*Euphrasia ostenfeldii* (*p. 164*)
Northern Hawk's-beard	*Crepis mollis* (*p. 171*)
Lesser Butterfly-orchid	*Platanthera bifolia*
Small-white Orchid	*Pseudorchis albida* (*p. 181*)
Frog Orchid	*Coeloglossum viride*
Flat-sedge	*Blysmus compressus* (*p. 193*)
Rare Spring-sedge	*Carex ericetorum* (*p. 200*)

Evidence and evaluation

Red List

In 1964, the International Union for Conservation of Nature (IUCN) produced a first assessment of plants and their status, taking into account the threats they faced. Since then there have been three editions of the Red Data Book for vascular plants in Great Britain (Perring & Farrell, 1977, 1983; Wigginton, 1999). These were all based on the distribution data provided in the first plant atlas, with additional information from targeted surveys looking at rare and scarce taxa. With the publication of the *New Atlas for the Millennium* (Preston *et al.*, 2002) more data became available.

Following publication of *The Vascular Plant Red Data List for Great Britain* (Cheffings & Farrell, 2005) an assessment of threat using the same methodology was applied to the Welsh flora, published by Plantlife as *A Vascular Plant Red Data List for Wales* (Dines, 2008).

In 2014, the Plant Working Conservation Group, made up of representatives from the key statutory organizations and botanical NGOs, carried out a rigorous assessment of English plant species using the IUCN criteria: *A Vascular Plant Red List for England* (Stroh *et al.*, 2014).

Species are classified under the IUCN Red List into one of nine categories, based on criteria such as rate of decline, population size, area of geographic distribution, and degree of population and distribution fragmentation. For a detailed explanation of the Red List categories, refer to the following document: http://www.iucnredlist.org/technical-documents/categories-and-criteria.

IUCN RED LIST CATEGORIES (based on IUCN, 2022)

EX **Extinct** – No known individuals remaining globally; **RE** **Regionally Extinct**.

EW **Extinct in the wild** – Known only to survive in captivity or cultivation, or as a naturalized population outside its historic range.

CR **Critically Endangered** – Extremely high risk of extinction in the wild.

EN **Endangered** – High risk of extinction in the wild.

VU **Vulnerable** – High risk of endangerment in the wild.

NT **Near Threatened** – Likely to become Threatened (coloured categories above) in the near future.

LC **Least Concern** – Lowest risk (does not qualify for a more at-risk category; widespread and abundant taxa are included in this category).

DD **Data Deficient** – Insufficient data to make an assessment of its risk of extinction.

NE **Not Evaluated** – Has not yet been evaluated against the criteria.

WL **Waiting List** – A pragmatic categorization to cover contentious taxa until agreement is reached on taxonomy.

International legal protection

1971 Ramsar Convention

A framework for the conservation and wise use of wetlands and their resources, which was drawn up in Ramsar, Iran.

1973 CITES (the Convention on International Trade in Endangered Species of Wild Fauna and Flora)

An international agreement between governments. Its aim is to ensure that international trade in specimens of wild animals and plants does not threaten their survival. In the UK, orchids are the only plants to which this applies.

1992 Habitats Directive (Council Directive 92/43/EEC)

In order to ensure the survival of Europe's most endangered and vulnerable species, EU governments adopted the Habitats Directive in 1992 (Council Directive 92/43/EEC of 21 May 1992, on the conservation of natural habitats and of wild fauna and flora). In the UK this applies to eight species of flowering plant (none of which occur in Teesdale). See Post-Brexit section (*below*), which explains how the legislation was able to continue.

Sites and places

Nationally protected sites include:
- Site of Special Scientific Interest (SSSI).
- Marine Conservation Zone (MCZ).
- A locally protected site: could include Local Wildlife Site, nature reserve or geological site.

Protected areas include:
- National Park (NP).
- Area of Outstanding Natural Beauty (AONB).
- Heritage Coast.

Post-Brexit: places and habitats

The UK left the European Union (EU) on 31 January 2020. This was followed by a transition period until the end of that year. In England, amendments to the Habitats Regulations were largely limited to 'operability changes' to ensure the Regulations continued to have the same working effect. The Regulations should be quoted as the 'Conservation of Habitats and Species Regulations, 2017 (as amended)'. The Offshore Marine Regulations are treated in a similar manner.

Following the UK EU Exit and transition period, the level of protection afforded to habitats and species in the wider countryside and in the designated European sites remains unchanged. Special Protection Areas (SPAs) and Special Areas of Conservation (SACs) became part of the UK national site network.

EU Directives concerning wildlife protection (the Birds, Habitats, Water Framework, Environmental Impact Assessment and Environmental Liabilities Directives) have been transposed into UK Regulations. It is the case that these Regulations could fall away if the European Communities Act was simply repealed; however, it is more likely that they would be kept in place until they could be deliberated by Parliament. A report by the UK Law Commission recommended strengthening the legislation and the Joint Nature Conservation Committee (JNCC) reviews species legislation on a five-yearly basis.

The Conservation of Habitats and Species (Amendment) (EU Exit) Regulations 2019 established a single-stage designation process and created a new national site network on land and at sea. This network includes the existing Special Areas of Conservation (SACs) and Special Protection Areas (SPAs), which no longer form part of the EU's Natura 2000 Ecological network. European Protected Species (EPS) continue to be protected; this relates to a range of mammals, reptiles and amphibians.

The UK Environment Act, became law in 2021, providing the UK's new framework for environmental protection. Once the UK had left the EU, rules on nature protection, water quality, clean air and other environmental protections that originated in Brussels needed to be replaced. This Act is intended to fill the gap. The Act has established the Office for Environmental Protection (OEP) as a new environmental watchdog covering England and Northern Ireland. This body is tasked with holding the Government and other public bodies to account, ensuring that environmental laws are complied with. It also includes a commitment to increase biodiversity by requiring planning applications to include Biodiversity Net Gain (BNG), amounting to a minimum of 10% gain in habitats, as set out in a metric drawn up by NE. This becomes mandatory in Sept 2023.

International agreements

There are some international treaties that commit the UK to working towards halting the loss of biodiversity. These operate separately from the EU, notably:

- The Ramsar Convention on Wetlands of International Importance (1971): a treaty for the conservation and sustainable use of wetlands. It is named after the city of Ramsar, Iran, where the convention was signed in 1971. (Information at https://www.ramsar.org.)
- The Convention on Biodiversity (1992), with three main goals: the conservation of biological diversity; the sustainable use of its components; and the fair and equitable sharing of benefits arising from genetic resources.
- The Aarhuus Convention (1998): establishes rights of access to information, public participation in decision-taking and access to justice in environmental matters. (Information at https://unece.org/environment-policy/public-participation/aarhus-convention/text.)

Policy commitments

The United Nations issued 17 Sustainable Development Goals, some of which apply to the natural environment. While many are interlinked, numbers 13 (climate action); 14 (life below water); and 15 (life on land), plus 17 (partnership for the goals), are particularly relevant for biodiversity.

Global Strategy for Plant Conservation (GSPC)

In 2002 the parties to the Convention on Biological Diversity (CBD) approved the Global Strategy for Plant Conservation (GSPC), which aims to slow the current and continuing loss of plant biodiversity. Target 1 involves documenting plant diversity, recognizing the fundamental importance of having a working list of known plant species.

Important Plant Areas (IPA)

Target 5 of the GSPC stipulates that 75% of the most important areas for plants should be protected. These Important Plant Areas (IPAs) are based on exceptional botanical richness, and/or support an outstanding assemblage of rare, threatened and/or endemic plant species and/or vegetation of high botanical value. The Moorhouse to Upper Teesdale IPA was designated principally for its range of internationally important habitats noted for their vascular plant assemblage. It supports an exceptional diversity of vascular plants growing in dry limestone grassland, as well as some of the UK's most important populations of Marsh Saxifrage and Hoary Rock-rose. Some of the top 5% of the following habitats in the UK occur here: alpine and boreal heaths, montane wet seepage areas, montane limestone screes, limestone rocks with vegetated fissures, blanket bogs, grassy metal-rich mine sites, Common Juniper scrub, nutrient-poor lakes and ponds with stone-wort algae, alkaline fens, ungrazed upland lime-rich cliffs, Purple Moor-grass meadows, mountain hay meadows, hard-water springs, flower-rich limestone grasslands with scrub, acidic alpine grassland, acid rocks with vegetated fissures and acidic montane scree.

Postscript: Changes to these arrangements will arise from further discussion of the Environment Bill, the regular five-yearly review of protected species by the JNCC, and the implementation of the changes to agricultural policy. See https://www.gov.uk/browse/environment-countryside.

UK conservation organizations

STATUTORY ORGANIZATIONS:

Joint Nature Conservation Committee (JNCC) www.jncc.gov.uk/
The public body that advises the UK Government and devolved administrations on UK-wide and international nature conservation.

Natural England www.gov.uk/government/organisations/natural-england.
Email: enquiries@naturalengland.org.uk
Statutory adviser on wildlife in England (see *page 284*).

NatureScot www.nature.scot/
Formerly known as Scottish Natural Heritage, NatureScot is an executive non-departmental public body of the Scottish Government responsible for the country's natural heritage, especially its natural, genetic and scenic diversity. Email: enquiries@nature.scot

NON-GOVERNMENTAL ORGANIZATIONS:

Botanical Society of Britain and Ireland https://bsbi.org

Plantlife www.plantlife.org.uk/uk

Wildlife Trusts: Each county in the UK has a group taking care of its local area. In Teesdale this involves Co. Durham and Northumberland – see *page 222* for Wildlife Trust information.

World Wildlife Fund www.wwf.org.uk

International conservation organizations

European Environment Agency, an Agency of the EU
www.eea.europa.eu/policy-documents#c0=10&c5=all&b_start=0
The European Environment Agency provides sound, independent information on the environment for those involved in developing, adopting, implementing and evaluating environmental policy, covering issues such as air and climate; biodiversity and ecosystems; sustainability and wellbeing; and economic sectors.

European policy document listing
The European Commission has adopted the new EU Biodiversity Strategy for 2030 and an associated Action Plan. See https://www.eea.europa.eu/policy-documents/eu-biodiversity-strategy-for-2030-1.

INTERNATIONAL POLICY:

Global Plant Strategy
2002: the parties to the Convention on Biological Diversity approved the Global Strategy for Plant Conservation (GSPC), which aims to slow the current and continuing loss of plant biodiversity. *Target 1* involves documenting plant diversity, recognizing the fundamental importance of having a working list of known plant species.

Ex situ conservation and recovery
2000: the UK conservation agencies, in partnership with the Royal Botanic Gardens Kew (RBGK) established a Millennium seedbank that aims to conserve 25% of the world's plant species by 2020. As it states on the Wakehurst Place website, collecting seeds and preserving them *ex situ* (away from their natural habitat) offers an economical and effective way to save seeds and keep them for posterity. In the future, if required, they can be germinated and reintroduced to the wild, or used in scientific research.

Teesdale: groups working for conservation

Bowes Museum, Barnard Castle
The Bowes Museum, Barnard Castle,
Co. Durham DL12 8NP
Tel: +44 (0) 1833 696060;
Email: info@thebowesmuseum.org.uk

Bowlees Visitor Centre
Bowlees, Newbiggin, Barnard Castle,
Co. Durham DL12 0XE
Tel: +44 (0) 1833 622145;
Email: visitbowlees@northpenninesaonb.
org.uk

Darlington and Teesdale Naturalists' Field Club
Membership Secretary, Fleur Miles
Tel: +44 (0) 1325 243323; Membership £10·00,
Website: www.dtnfc.org

Durham County Council, County Hall,
Aykley Heads, Durham DH1 5UZ
Tel: +44 (0) 3000 260000
Website: www.durham.gov.uk

Durham Wildlife Trust,
Chilton Moor, Houghton-le-Spring,
Tyne and Wear DH4 6PU
Tel: +44 (0) 191 584 3112
Website: www.durhamwt.com

Environmental Records Information Centre for the NE (ERIC NE)
Website: www.ericnortheast.org.uk

Northumberland Biodiversity Action Plan
Website: www.nwt.org.uk/northumberland-BAP

Northumberland Wildlife Trust
Garden House, St Nicholas Park, Jubilee Road,
Gosforth, Newcastle upon Tyne, NE3 3XT
Tel: +44 (0) 191 2846884
Email: mail@northwt.org.uk
Website: www.nwt.org.uk/

Cronkley Scar, Mickle Fell and Widdybank Fell after snow fall in April *RLai*.

North East England Nature Partnership
c/o Capability North East, Ouseburn Farm, Ouseburn Road, Newcastle upon Tyne, NE1 2PA
Tel: +44 (0) 191 5623262
Website: www.neenp.org.uk/

North Pennines Area of Outstanding Natural Beauty (NPAONB)
Weardale Business Centre, The Old Co-op Building, 1 Martin Street, Stanhope, Co. Durham DL13 2UY
Tel: +44 (0) 1388 528801
Email: info@northpenninesaonb.org.uk
Website: www.northpennines.org.uk

Teesdale Conservation Volunteers
Conservation Centre, Deepdale Woods, Barnard Castle, Co. Durham DL12 9TB
Tel: +44 (0) 1833 690022
Website: www.rotters.org

Stargazing
Website: www.northpennines.org.uk/visit-explore/stargazing

UNESCO Global Geopark
For contact information, see North Pennines Area of Outstanding Natural Beauty (NPAONB) (*left*)

Weardale Wildlife Group
Website: www.weardalewildlifegroup.co.uk

Wear Rivers Trust
Website: www.wear-rivers-trust.org.uk

Teesdale – Walks leaflets
Website: www.facebook.com/Dr-ME-Bradshaws-Teesdale-Special-Flora-Research-Conservation-Trust-10502387757600/

Teesdale Special Flora Research and Conservation Trust
Website: www.teesdalespecialflora.uk

The construction of Cow Green Reservoir

In 1964 I first heard of the proposal to build a reservoir in the Tees valley. The expanding industries at Tees mouth (principally ICI) required more water, and so another dam in Teesdale was proposed.

The dam was named 'Cow Green' after the area of limestone grassland (*Fig. i*), which was not far from the present car park and 1·6 km from where the dam was built near Cauldron Snout, at the south-east end of the Weel (*Fig. ii*). Here, for almost 3 km the Tees behaved like a mature, slow-flowing, lowland river rather than a young mountain tearaway from its source on Cross Fell, which then cascaded down Cauldron Snout.

This proposal to put a reservoir in an area encompassing the Teesdale area of rare plants outraged British and international botanists (*Figs. iii & iv*). Consequently, the proposal was strongly opposed by the BSBI, Northumberland and Durham Naturalists' Trust, the Ramblers Association, CPRE and others.

As some of the ground to be flooded was Common Land, the reservoir proposal was presented as a Private Member's Bill and examined by Select Committees in both Houses of Parliament.

I recall the Parliamentary process:

"The morning walk through four London Parks to Westminster Bridge, entering Westminster Hall and gazing in awe at its size and thinking this is where our Parliament and the Law of the Land began, I felt privileged on each of the many times that I crossed that Great Hall. Of the detailed proceedings of the Select Committee examinations in both Houses I wish to recall little, except the final question to me by the Chairman of that Committee."

"Dr Bradshaw, if, in a few years, ICI find they do not require the water from the [Cow Green] reservoir and the water was drained away – will the plants still be there?"

"The Lords Select Committee members visited the site on a dull, cold day in December when the area fulfilled the opinion of the Chairman of the Tees Valley and Cleveland Water Board (TV&CWB) that it was just a wilderness. When the notables had departed, one of the Board members shared their flask of coffee with me. The only bright bit of the day for me when I went up to London, was to sit in the House of Commons Gallery, with a handful of other botanists including Ted Lousley, President of BSBI and Chairman of the Teesdale Defence Committee to hear the final Reading of the TV&CWB. When it was over the others went home and left me to fill in time till the overnight train back to Durham. I was sad and desolate."

Fig. i Cow Green crossed by a road to the car park *MEB*.

Fig. ii The Weel (just out of picture are the dam (*left*) and Cow Green (*right*)) *MEB*.

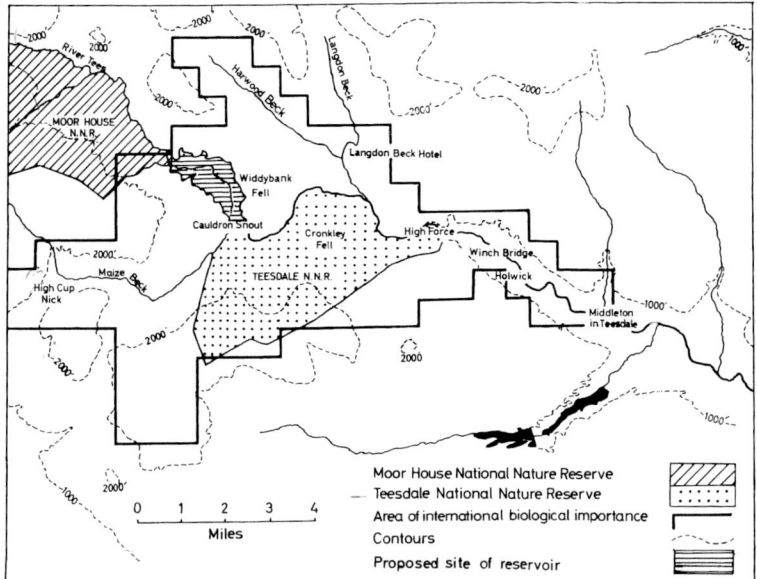

Fig. iii Map in N&DNT Appeal Brochure 1965.

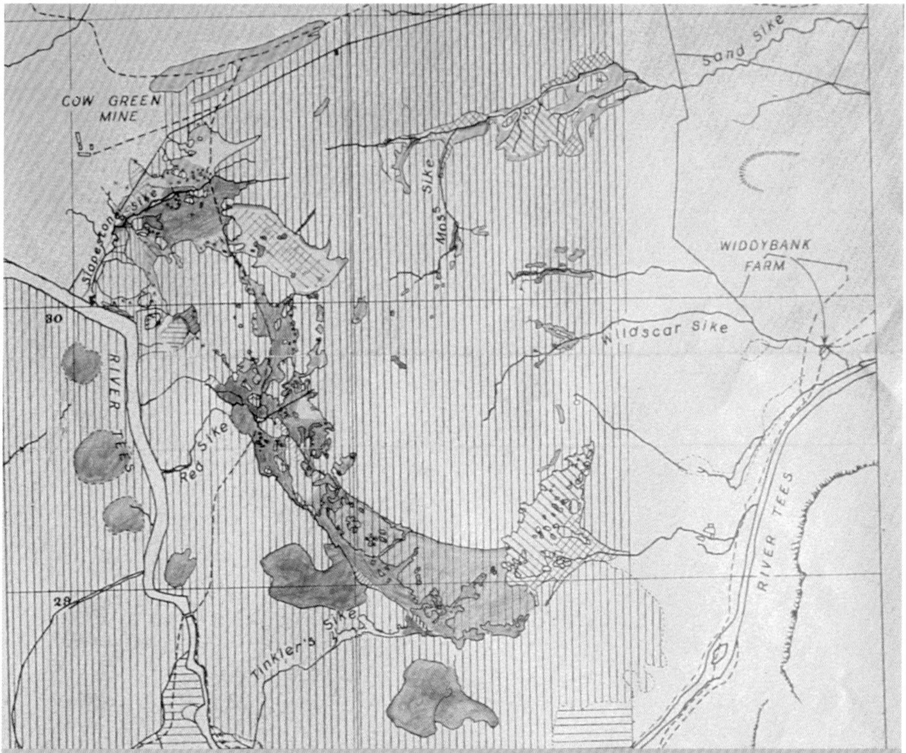

Fig. iv Botanical interest Widdybank Fell Exhibit MB1 Select Committee hearings.

Fig. v Creating the access road to the dam site *MEB*.

Fig. vi The site offices *MEB*.

Fig. vii A bridge to carry derricks *MEB*.

Fig. viii The dam site over the buried River Tees and glacial till *MEB*.

Fig. ix Into Whin Sill *MEB*.

Fig. x Three seals twix sections *MEB*.

Fig. xi Early days of dam construction I *MEB*.

Fig. xii Early days of dam construction II *MEB*.

Fig.xiii The Appeal brochure.

Fig.xiv N&DNT Cow Green Reservoir 2nd Appeal.

Eventually, on March 22, 1967, the TV&CWB's Cow Green Reservoir Bill received Royal Assent.[1]

The construction of the Cow Green Reservoir was the most major damaging change in the dale in my lifetime. Stages in the building of the dam 1967–70 are shown in the *Figs. v–xii opposite*.

Whilst the Upper Teesdale Defence Committee, on which I represented the Northumberland and Durham Naturalists' Trust, organized the opposition to the TV&CWB Bill in Parliament, it was obvious that money would have to be raised. In Durham, I, together with volunteers, stuffed envelopes and posted out several hundred copies of the appeal brochure (*Fig. xiii*). Similar activities were taking place in Newcastle-upon-Tyne, London, the south and elsewhere; a second appeal was made (*Fig. xiv*) and later a third. Botanists, ramblers and other groups responded magnificently and a total of £23,000 was raised (equating to £100,000 today) between 1965 and 1967 to mount the case against the reservoir.

Even though many professional and amateur botanists knew Teesdale and its flora at that time, there was no account of its distribution on Widdybank Fell or in the dale. The proposers were only interested in which rare species would be destroyed by the creation of the reservoir, *i.e.* below top-water-line (TWL) at 488·5 m. To make their case, the objectors realized that it was the proportions of each rare species of each population below TWL on the SW side of Widdybank

---

[1] See Gregory (1971) and Whitby & Willis (1978) for an overview of the controversy prior to the construction of the Cow Green Reservoir; a very brief background to the 'Cow Green Episode' is in *Upper Teesdale* (Clapham (ed), 1978); additional information is in the Case Study in Chapter 8.3 of *Planning and Ecology*, 1984, by Bines, Doody, Findlay & Hudson (eds Roberts, R.D, and Roberts, T.M.).

Fell that was important. The major species under threat were: Teesdale Violet, Rare Spring-sedge, Spring Gentian, Hoary Whitlowgrass, hybrid violet (Teesdale Violet × Common Dog-violet), False Sedge, Thrift, Alpine Rush and Broad-leaved Cottongrass. People searched for these species in the Slapestone Sike – Rod's Vein area, initially below TWL (it had been marked with pegs (*Fig. xv*)). The wide variety of plant communities is shown in the map by A. V. Jones, 1976 (*Fig. xvii*). Subsequently, I walked much of the sugar-limestone grassland and flushes (seen as a strip from NW to SE in *Fig. xvii*) searching for these species. The subsequent maps by Jones showed that my quick survey had been very accurate, using a 1965 map from the then Nature Conservancy of the area of sugar-limestone grassland flushes and calcareous flushes on Widdybank Fell (*Fig. iv* was based on that map) as a basis. Calculations showed the losses due to the flooding would be:

- 10% of the rare-plant communities (21 hectares)
- 10% of the Teesdale Violet population
- 40% of the Rare Spring-sedge population
- 95% of the Thrift plants
- Quantities of: False Sedge, Scottish Asphodel, the hybrid Teesdale Violet × Common Dog-violet, gentians, Hoary Whitlowgrass, Alpine Rush, Blue Moor-grass and others.

Plant rescue

Members of The Teesdale Trust must have considered transplantation within the Upper Teesdale area or elsewhere – as indeed did I. However, there was no bare sugar-limestone, nor sites flushed with water that had seeped through sugar-limestone, that was not already filled to their presumed ecological carrying capacity. An attempt to create a new area of bare sugar-limestone was made by removing the vegetation, top-soil and glacial till from an area of acid vegetation, but this did not go far enough to expose the underlying sugar-limestone.

Fifty years later this area is still 80% bare and, surprisingly, in July 2020 the first Teesdale Assemblage species was recorded by John O'Reilly: a cluster of eleven small Hoary Whitlowgrass plants. In retrospect, a much better idea would have been to create an area of bare sugar-limestone adjacent to species-rich Blue Moor-grass and a semi-open site from which species such as Teesdale Violet, whose seed can dehisce 2–3 m, could then have spread. This could still be done.

On-site research

The area of Slapestone Sike seen in *Figs. xv & xvi* was particularly rich in rare species and their habitats (this mosaic is well displayed in *Fig. xvi*). As all of this is below TWL, and was about to be destroyed by flooding, this presented a unique opportunity for the removal of rare plants to be used to grow and make into herbarium specimens or for habitat-altering investigations. In the small exclosure above the bare limestone, two rectangular shapes show the effect of fertilizer treatment on Blue Moor-grass vegetation, rich with False Sedge (the results are displayed graphically in *Fig. xviii, p. 230)* – for more details see Jefferies, 1971). Investigations in the two fenced areas to the left (*Fig. xv*) were supervised by David Bellamy. A small group from Cambridge Botany School with Peter Sell (*Fig. xix*) collected rare and common species for distribution to the major herbaria in the country.

Gene banks were established at the Universities of Manchester and Durham – twelve species and up to 50 specimens of each were removed from below TWL by myself and Tom Buffey using a bulb-planter (*Fig. xx*) and then stacked in trays ready for collection. Thrift had colonized the out-wash fan of debris from the Rod's Vein adit; these plants were removed and sent to those Universities. Plants were also sent to other universities and botanic gardens that requested them.

Fig. xv Research areas; Bellamy & Pigott *MEB*.

Fig. xvi Species-rich Slapestone Sike communities – all eventually submerged-drowned *MEB*.

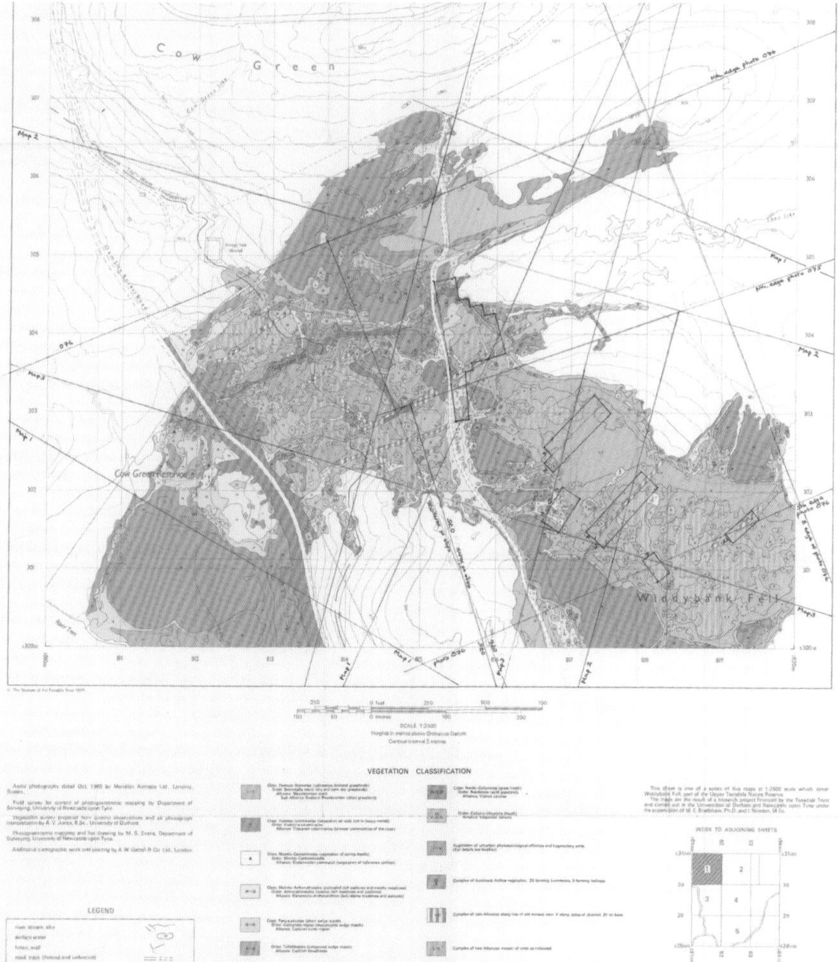

Fig. xvii Slapestone Sike vegetation map.

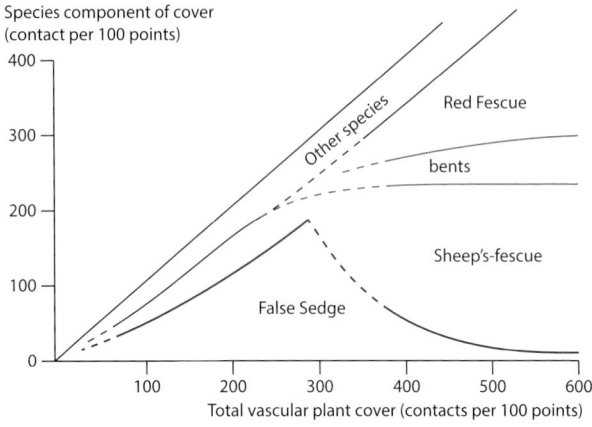

Fig. xviii. The effect of fertilizer treatment on Blue Moor-grass vegetation (Jeffrey, 1971).

The twelve species placed in gene-banks were: Thrift, False Sedge, Spring Gentian, Teesdale Violet, the hybrid Teesdale Violet × Common Dog-violet, Bird's-eye Primrose, Yellow Saxifrage, Sea Plantain, Blue Moor-grass, Alpine Meadow-rue, Scottish Asphodel and Spring Sandwort.

Quantities of sugar-limestone rock and soil were transported to both locations. At Durham upturned concrete sewage pipe-sections were half-filled with rubble and topped with the Teesdale soil and lumps of rock (*Fig. xxi*); each tub had a central rotating water sprinkler (*Fig. xxii*). The plants were supplied in cores of vegetation, which undoubtedly helped them to establish, but subsequently created a troublesome 'weed' problem (*Fig. xxiii*). There were some unexpected results: the hybrid hybrid Teesdale Violet × Common Dog-violet (*Viola ×burnatii*) 'took-off', producing masses of flowers that were sterile; Mountain Everlasting male capitula were pink as well as the usual white, some had compact heads with a dark red centre; Thrift showed the most variation – tall, long scapes and leaves and loose growth habit; others were compact with short leaves and scapes; colours ranged from deep-pink to white. Records of the flowering, fruit and seed production were made of most of these plants at Manchester and Durham Universities (Cranston & Valentine, 1983). In addition to the cores, turfs were removed (*Fig. xxiv*) to form samples of vegetation in raised beds at the two universities and at Widdybank Fell outside the present NNR near the Site Liaison Officer's Hut). Additionally, a quantity was reserved for display at the new Interpretive Centre in the redundant Chapel at Bowlees, near Newbiggin.

Fig. xix Collecting plants to press and distribute *MEB.*

Fig. xx Cores of individual species *MEB.*

Fig. xxi Tubs at Durham Botanical Gardens with plants from Cow Green Reservoir basin *MEB*.

Fig. xxii Water sprinkler – Spring Gentian first year after transplanting *MEB*.

Fig. xxiii Established plants: hybrid violet (TOP); Bird's-eye Primrose (MIDDLE); Rare Spring-sedge (BOTTOM) *MEB*.

Fig. xxiv Removing turf from the future reservoir basin (TOP); turfs awaiting collection (BOTTOM) *MEB*.

The gene banks were intended to provide stocks of plant material available for research of many kinds: DNA, isoenzyme comparisons, genetics, physiology, *etc*. Alas, no one was interested. Accounts of the performance of these plants at Manchester and Durham Universities can be found in Sayers & Gaman (1972) and Cranstan & Valentine (1983).

Losses

Both gene banks have been destroyed – one by the expansion of the Jodrell Bank Discovery Centre and secondly at Durham by the creation of the Botanic Garden Visitor Centre, which opened in 1988. Some may regret that at Durham a place was not found for the famous Teesdale Assemblage of Rare Plant Species rescued from the Cow Green Reservoir basin. Are any of those rescued plants of the Teesdale rarities still alive somewhere – Manchester University, Liverpool Botanic Garden at Ness, Edinburgh, Cambridge, Newcastle upon Tyne or Salford – today?

Stimulated by the need to know the size and locations of the rare flora of Upper Teesdale and drawing on a small amount of the ICI £100,000 Research Fund, I organized groups of volunteers each July to search for and map some 24 rare species, at first in the reservoir basin and then along the whole of the grassland and heath over the sugar-limestone exposure. It took five years: three weeks each year, around 15 volunteers each week; the youngest was just 13, the oldest I did not ask. Several volunteers came repeatedly; many were university students (*Fig. xxv*). *Fig. xxvi* shows the distributions of Bird's-eye Primrose and the much scarcer Hoary Whitlowgrass that were recorded. We began to record the vegetation types in the reservoir basin and on Widdybank Fell, eventually produced as vegetation maps at two scales (*e.g. fig.* 14.1 in Bradshaw & Jones, 1976). A third project was the beginning of the study of population dynamics of several rare species that continues

Fig. xxv Volunteers mapping the distribution of 24 rare species *MEB*.

Fig. xxvi. Distribution of Bird's-eye Primrose (TOP) and Hoary Whitlowgrass (BOTTOM).

Fig. xxix Dumper truck caught in heavy rain *MEB*.

Fig. xxvii The dam nearing completion; Tees flow stopped *MEB*.

Fig. xxviii The first trickle of the restored River Tees *MEB*.

Fig. xxx The dam nearing completion *MEB*.

today. Meanwhile, the dam was nearing completion (*Fig. xxvii*), with just the last section to do. The flow of the Tees had to be stopped and then diverted through the dam (*Fig. xxviii*) and this photo shows the first trickle of the restored Tees, prior to the final section being completed. In the following weeks heavier rain than expected began to fill the reservoir and *Fig. xxix* shows a dumper-truck, (rear tyres approx. 2m in diameter), crossing the 'Slapestone Sike 'bridge' on the access road to the dam; the road had to be shored-up and only just survived the dam's completion. *Fig. xxx* shows two views of the dam. Winter storms on a full reservoir created some impressive waves (*Fig. xxxi*), greater than those the objectors had calculated. These ate into the soft sugar-limestone shore around the mouth of Slapestone Sike and destroyed species-rich turf. ICI's answer was to clothe the margin with plastic webbing (*Fig. xxxii*) – but the next storms ripped it apart. Lengths of webbing continued to be picked-up for years. The final solution was a rip-rap of

Fig. xxxi Winter storms produce big waves *MEB*.

large boulders of Whin Sill (*Fig. xxxiii*), the same as had been placed on the water side of the earth embankment part of the dam.

Apart from the loss of plants caused by flooding and wave action, did the creation of a large body of water in the Tees cause changes and loss of more rare plant species? Certainly, there was an effect in the atmospheric temperature in that this body of water was slow to warm in the spring, but when warmed in the summer it retained the heat later in the autumn that might delay resumption of growth of plants in the spring, but prolong plant-growth in the autumn. Changes in the numbers of plants (in the long-term population dynamic studies begun in 1968) resulting from temperature amelioration have been dwarfed by the effect of big changes in the intensity of grazing.

Fig. xxxii Plastic webbing proved ineffective in protecting the shoreline *MEB*.

Fig. xxxiii A rip-rap of Whin Sill boulders provided the best protection solution *MEB*.

Fig. xxxiv Waves of water pouring down the dam face from a full reservoir *MEB*.

Fig. xxxv An unusually calm reservoir with mirror image of the skyline seen from Slapestone Bay *MEB*.

Case studies

So, what have we learned about what the constituent parts of the Teesdale Assemblage require? At one time, the greatest threat to many of the Teesdale rarities was overgrazing. The universal answer to this in the designated sites, the NNR and SSSIs, is to put up a fence around the habitat or plant to be protected. This is not an easy option, as well-erected, rabbit-proof fencing is expensive and frequent 'walking the bounds' is necessary to check that the artful diggers have not forced an entry. In snowy winters (*e.g.* 2009–10) snow piled up against the fence and the Rabbits walked over the top and, here and there, the weight of the snow broke down the wire or the posts. When intact, not only may the desired plants prosper, but so does everything else, for a period at least, thus creating a different problem – undergrazing. This can be controlled in the exclosures by allowing sheep to graze there in winter. On Widdybank Fell where fencing is not possible, the only solution is to increase the size of the sheep flock (this was reduced in 1995 to 250 ewes – less than half the previous number) by retaining more female lambs and buying in suitable hill sheep when available.

Histories

Environmental conditions can change and a reserve manager needs to be alert to insidious variations to the *status quo*. Following the reduction of the number of Rabbits on both Widdybank Fell and in the exclosures on Cronkley Fell, the resulting increase in height of the ungrazed vegetation led to several rare species producing fewer shoots and flowers. These 'light-demander' species were being denied this essential light by the tall, coarse, silica-filled mature leaves and stems of Blue Moor-grass, Red Fescue and Glaucous Sedge, herbage that neither sheep nor Rabbits would eat, as both prefer a short turf. These are the same rare species that have endured severe overgrazing by Rabbits and are now being smothered by this tall associated vegetation because of undergrazing. As an experiment, areas including a few of the long-term plots were mown to lawn height and the toppings removed to encourage the sheep to graze there and the rare species to increase and flower.

Case Study 1: Marsh Saxifrage

This is a W&C Act Schedule 8 species, which is declining in Europe. In July 1955, I recorded the close-grazed vegetation of a slightly acidic flush in the (then) Moor House NNR, known as Johnny's Flush (NY 744315). Cover value was about 75% on a matrix of moss and peat with a pH 5·88. The species composition was recorded using Domin scale values 1–10; all plants were very small and rated: Domin 6 = Common Sedge; Domin 3–4 = Sheep's-fescue; Domin 3 = horsetail species, Bulbous Rush (ssp. *kochii*), Smooth and Hairy Lady's-mantles, Autumn Hawkbit, Cuckooflower, Fen Bedstraw, Mat-grass and Creeping Bent; Domin 1 = White Clover, Common Dog's-violet, Marsh Thistle, Lesser Spearwort, Meadow Buttercup, Alpine Willowherb, Marsh and Starry Saxifrages, Hairy Stonecrop, Yarrow, Common Mouse-ear, Selfheal, Meadowsweet and Common Yellow-sedge.

In the late 1950s, a 100 m² exclosure was erected around Johnny's Flush, fencing in the Marsh Saxifrage, but without an option of occasional grazing. By 2008, this contained a tall community dominated by Meadowsweet, Water Avens, Marsh Valerian, Smooth Lady's-mantle, Marsh-marigold and others, none of which are montane species. Outside the exclosure there were a few scattered shoots of Marsh Saxifrage amongst the dominant Bottle Sedge, whereas within the exclosure the saxifrage had been ousted by the tall herbs. A rather similar situation is developing in another exclosure on the west side of the escarpment and again in Weardale and NW Yorkshire, where sheep were removed to allow the Heather moor to develop.

Case Study 2: Mountain Avens
In 2019, as part of a Climate Change Project initiated by myself, a baseline has been fixed ± parallel to the edge of the Mountain Avens plants, above the lower and major cliff face of the sugar-limestone in the White Well Exclosure. Measurements have been taken from this line to the edge of the Mountain Avens plants, and this will be repeated in subsequent years to record the increase or decrease in its extent the spread of the Mountain Avens.

Case Study 3: Rare Spring-sedge
Rare Spring-sedge cannot compete with ungrazed Blue Moor-grass that has developed into tussocks as on Cronkley Fell, nor in communities dominated by Blue Moor-grass, Red Fescue and Glaucous Sedge as on Widdybank Fell. In the latter community, the number of sedge tillers reached its highest number (254 in 2003 in the plot) when the Rabbit density was at its highest in 2003–04, the vegetation was very (too) short and high light-intensity had reached the sedge plants. In 2009, when the Rabbit numbers had been reduced to virtually nil, the number of tillers declined to 131, and further to 28 by 2014. At this time the plants were failing to survive in the 12·5–18 cm-tall vegetation. Following clipping of the plot the number of tillers rose to 82. Overall, flower and fruit production has been low for some time, initially because of grazing of the flowering spikelets and latterly due to the smothering effect resulting from the undergrazing.

The following observations are from a population dynamics study of five rare species in calcareous habitats on Widdybank and Cronkley Fells in 1970–83 and 2002–09.

Case Study 4: Spring Gentian
Spring Gentian was recorded in four plots in closed vegetation, on calcareous brown earth soil over sugar-limestone and open to grazing. Counts of rosettes of Spring Gentian were as follows:

1969–76	1970	1980	2002–07	2014	2015	2018	2019
632 ± 32·32 (mean annual total)	549	1,385	98 (mean annual total)	49	112	168	217

It is easy for an observer to believe that all is well when many gentian flowers can still be seen over a large part of the fell on a bright day following dull weather in the spring, but this is a delusion. The show of blue is not an accurate indicator of the number of plant rosettes. The four recording sites are widely spaced in the calcareous grassland. In 1970, when the Blue Moor-grass grassland was sky-blue with flowers, the percentage of flowering rosettes was the lowest record made in the previous three years. Monitoring showed a puzzling large decline between the 1980s and 2002. Was there a connection with the large reduction (almost two-thirds) of the sheep flock in 1995, at a time when the Rabbit population was low, but which gradually increased and expanded to reach the top of the fell and exploded to a maximum in 2003–04 causing severe overgrazing? The Rabbits were brought under control to virtually none by 2009 and the gentian population rose to 183 in 2006, so why had there been a further drop to 17 by 2012? By now, the vegetation was undergrazed and taller; neither sheep nor Rabbits eat the silica-loaded summer leaves of Blue Moor-grass, nor its co-dominant Glaucous Sedge, causing the light-demanding gentians to produce fewer, weaker shoots and fewer flowers, while in 2014, the total was 49. To simulate grazing, two of the plots were mown in the autumn of 2013. These plots showed a slight increase in the following year; a favourable growing season may have boosted all numbers over the fell. Mowing continued, irregularly at first, and the sheep flock has been increased to 400 and the count of the gentians stood at 217 in 2019.

Rabbit-grazed species-rich grassland *MEB*.

Undergrazed grassland *MEB*.

Case Study 5: Hoary Whitlowgrass

A monocarpic biennial/perennial species the population of which at the two well-spaced recorded sites on Widdybank Fell dropped dramatically between the 1970s and the 21st century, from the total in four plots of 535 in 1971 and 520 in 1972 to three in 2005–18.

n/r = not recorded	1971	1972	1974	1976	1977	2002	2005
Total plants in four plots	535	520	409	n/r	n/r	0	0
Total plants in two plots	286	323	178	49	29	4	3

These declines were mirrored on the wider area of this fell, and to a lesser extent in the exclosures on Cronkley Fell. Speculation on the possible causes of this decline correlates the decrease with the very dry summer of June to August 1976 when the plants finished flowering early because of drought in the very shallow soils where this species grows; as this species is dependent upon good seed production, and germination the following spring, only a low number of plants appeared able to produce seed in the following year. No records were made between 1978 and 2002, which is unfortunate. The sheep flock was reduced to less than half in 1995 at the time the Rabbit population was expanding rapidly; when Rabbits remove the flowering and fruiting inflorescences seed production ceases and the population crashes. There are few colonies of Hoary Whitlowgrass on either fell now. Unfortunately, the ability of the species to spread is very limited.

Case Study 6: Lady's-mantle agg.

Records are available for another group of Teesdale rarities: the five rare lady's-mantle species. Three occur mainly in meadows and on road verges, whereas the two scarcer species occur occasionally in meadows and also in a wider variety of habitats in the upland pastures (see the species accounts). In the 1950s, some 40% of the typical dales meadows were searched for Starry, Velvet, Large-toothed, Clustered and Rock Lady's-mantles. A sixth species, the Shining Lady's-mantle, was once found near Langdon Beck, and was looked for but so far has not been found. I marked the locations of these species as dots onto 1:25,000 scale maps of Teesdale and Weardale. Most of these sites were re-visited in 2000 and the survey was completed by 2007. Each species had become less frequent; the magnitude of the decline at these sites is set out below. This is most easily observed in the verges of the main roads through the dale where the Starry and Velvet Lady's-mantle plants were very frequent in the 1950s, but are scarce and only sporadic today. Some plants of Velvet, Clustered and Rock Lady's-mantles were destroyed when several small meadows were ploughed

Table 7 | Survey of five rare lady's-mantle species in Teesdale west of Cotherstone made in the 1950s and repeated in 2000–07 (adapted from Bradshaw, 2009)

A 'dot' represents one or more plants at a 'site'.	Nos. of sites visited	Number of dots found		Lost
		in 1950s	in 2007	
Starry Lady's-mantle	20	27	16	41%
Velvet Lady's-mantle	380*	498*	56	89%
Large-toothed Lady's-mantle	49	49	25	49%
Clustered Lady's-mantle	74	81	14	83%
Rock Lady's-mantle	27	34	15	56%

*In the 2000–07 survey neither species were found to be as frequent in any of the fields as they were in the original survey, nor were either of them frequent along contiguous lengths of road verge. Occurrences in these places were recorded as 'dots'.

and re-seeded following a relaxation of Environmental Impact Assessment (Agriculture) (England) Regulation 2006 that had previously protected fields of less than two hectares (about five acres).

It is fortuitous that the early survey was made at the beginning of a period of considerable post-war changes in farm management and mobility of all kinds. Post WWII, the government-supported drive for more home-produced food required the meadows to produce more 'grass'. This was aided by the application of the now readily available artificial fertilizers (*e.g.* ICI 'Nitram') and in some places herbicides to kill the buttercups and docks. This forcing of the meadows led to a fairly rapid decline in the best quality meadows (Grade 4 and 3b) and concurrently a decrease in the frequencies of the lady's-mantle species. The Clustered and Rock Lady's-mantles were, or are, found usually as single plants thinly scattered in calcareous grassland, stream banks, flushes, rock-ledges and even on the fell-top grasslands. Single plants are extremely vulnerable to destruction. Many have gone, yet it is surprising to find some individuals still there after 60 years. In recent years, all five species have been found in places and fields not visited in the original survey. Clustered Lady's-mantle in particular has been found in more meadows. This is the result of the author's efforts to encourage field recorders to identify the individual species of the Common Lady's-mantle group by providing identification courses and a back-up service, and also the more intensive survey of meadows in the NPAONB Hay Time Project 2006–09. John O'Reilly (*Hay Time Project* 2006–08) has shown that a further decline in quality of the meadows has taken place in the last two decades. Of 20 meadows graded the highest quality (grade 4) in the 1980s, only 20% remained, and only 12% of 67 good quality (Grade 3b) meadows remained as species-rich grasslands in 2008 (see Fig. 3 *opposite*).

In the whole of this period, many meadows were designated as SSSIs and a large number entered into the first agri-environment scheme, the Pennine Dales Environmentally Sensitive Area (ESA). Today there is a greater level of awareness of the conservation importance of these meadows. This is shown by their designation as a **UK BAP Priority Habitat** and an **Annex 1 Habitat of European Importance.** The five lady's-mantle species are themselves **UK BAP species** and all are on the **Vascular Plant Red Data List for England** (Stroh *et al.*, 2014). Natural England is the UK BAP Leader Partner, but today no fields have been entered into the Agri-environment Higher Level Scheme (HK15) primarily on the grounds of the presence of one or more UK BAP lady's-mantle species.

Fig. 3 | The state of upland hay meadows in the North Pennines (from O'Reilly, 2010)

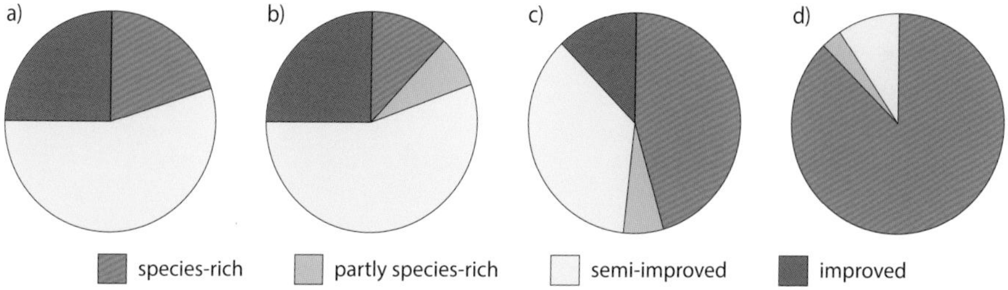

a)   b)   c)   d)

☒ species-rich   ☒ partly species-rich   ☐ semi-improved   ■ improved

a) 2010 state of 20 meadows, which were all of the highest quality (grade 4) in the 1980s
b) 2010 state of 67 meadows, which were all of good quality (grade 3b) in the 1980s
c) 2010 state of 33 SSSI meadows designated for their upland hay meadow vegetation
d) Natural England's condition assessment of the same 33 meadows as in (c)

Case Study 7: Hybrid Teesdale Violet × Common Dog-violet (*Viola × burnatii*) on Widdybank Fell

Although there are several populations of the hybrid Teesdale Violet × Common Dog-violet on Widdybank Fell, only the population at Site 3 (NY 8164 2970) has been recorded at each of the two plots since 2003. One of these plots (Plot 3ss2) started as a more or less closed habitat with a very dense population of violet shoots, probably from one original seedling and few grasses; the other (Plot 3pp3A) is more open, on exposed sugar-limestone with a rendzina soil and more floriferous vegetative units. The lower numbers in 2003 was preceded in 2002 by low sunshine totals and similarly the lower population number in 2006 had been preceded by low sunshine totals in the summer months of 2005. Coincidentally the summer sunshine and temperatures in 2003 and 2004 were high, probably boosting the formation of buds on the roots and hence leading to the increase in numbers in the following year. Admittedly this is a small sample.

The size of the sheep flock was reduced to about one-third (250 ewes and followers) *c.* 1995 and it continued at this level until 2012, rising gradually to 350 until 2015, when the number was reduced to 250 ewes again, and in 2016 the numbers were increased towards 450. The Rabbit population – at a maximum in 2003 – had been controlled and was virtually nil within the NNR by 2009, since when there has been a fluctuating increase. The low numbers of sheep and Rabbits have failed to maintain the short sward height required by the majority of the rare species. During this time Plot 3ss2 was completely invaded by grasses and mosses and the hybrid violet population reduced to only six plants, whereas plot 3pp3A, always a more open habitat, maintained 19 plants despite being subject to scratching disturbance by Rabbits that appear to enjoy the roots.

In 1976, the hot, dry conditions that hit the south of England in June did not affect Upper Teesdale until mid-July and continued into August, to be followed by a very wet September that produced a good growth of autumn grass. The populations of three species illustrated in the following charts each behaved differently before and after the drought, and therefore need to be considered separately.

Case Study 8: Dwarf Milkwort and Spring Gentian

These two species are short-lived perennials, with a half-life of six years dependent on a regular supply of fertile seed but, like an annual, can be subject to population fluctuations. Individual

239

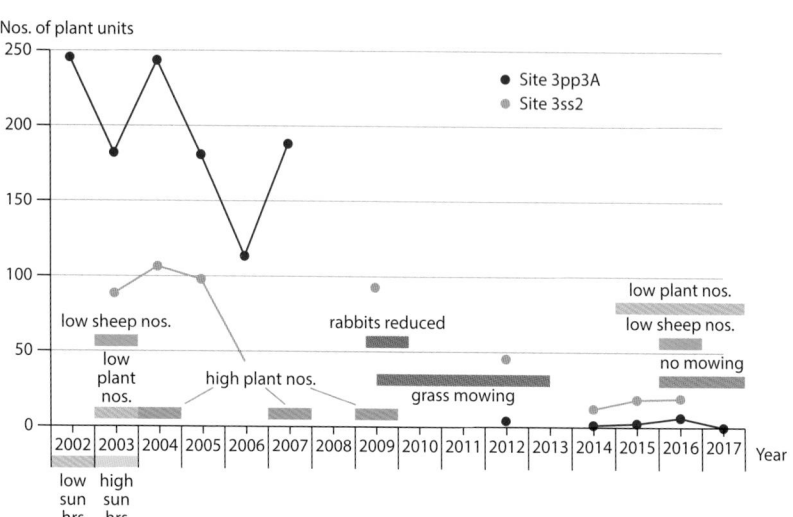

Fig. 4 | Hybrid Teesdale Violet × Common Dog-violet (*Viola × burnatii*) on Widdybank Fell

plants were not entered into the population records until after a year. The habitat management on Widdybank Fell was stable with approximately the same level of grazing, whilst on Cronkley Fell the grazing has been more variable.

When the populations of Spring Gentian at six sites and Teesdale Violet at four sites are summed separately, the graphs show that the number of gentian propagules increased in the wetter September and autumn, while the number of violets reduced, starting after the dry winter of 1975, followed by the drought of July/August 1976, and continued into 1977; the violet was clearly unable to respond.

Case Study 9: Bird's-eye Primrose

As a species of damp communities, the dry winter of 1975–76 and drought of the following July/August reduced the number of seedlings and young plants. It did not respond to the 1976 September rains as did Spring Gentian and remained at about the same population size until 1981.

The effect of over- and undergrazing in the 21st century

a) Population dynamics of Teesdale Violet in seven plots on Widdybank Fell

The Teesdale Violet occurs in the CG9b Blue Moor-grass–Limestone Bedstraw sub-community on the metamorphosed Melmerby Scar limestone. At the beginning of the 21st century the Rabbit population was at a maximum, whilst the sheep flock on the fell was at a minimum of 250 ewes and followers (compared with nearly 600 for much of the 20th century). By then, parts of the limestone grassland were so closely grazed they resembled a 'thread-bare carpet'. Eventually, English Nature and the Raby Estate started to control the Rabbit population at the beginning of 2005 by shooting and gassing; this continued (with a few lapses) until the population was virtually eradicated by December 2009. A long period of deep snow in the winter of 2009–10 reduced the Rabbit numbers in the whole of the dale, when the thousands that attacked the farmers' stored bales of haylage or silage

Fig. 5 | Effect of the unusual very low rainfall over winter/spring 1975/76 and high temperature of July/August 1976 and high rainfall in September on selected Teesdale rarities.

a)

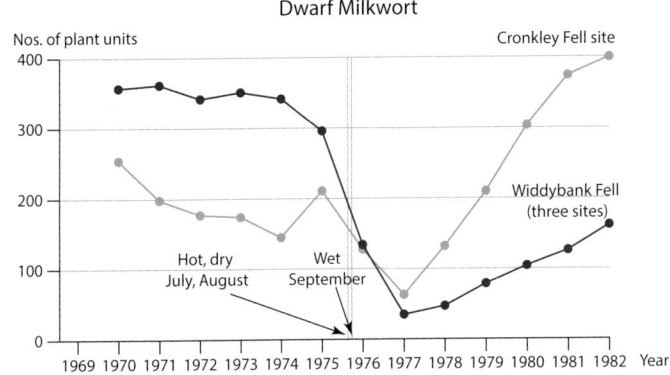

Dwarf Milkwort

b)

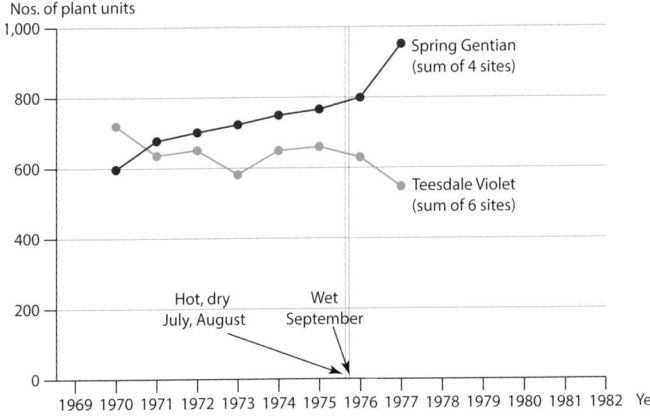

Spring Gentian and Teesdale Violet

c)

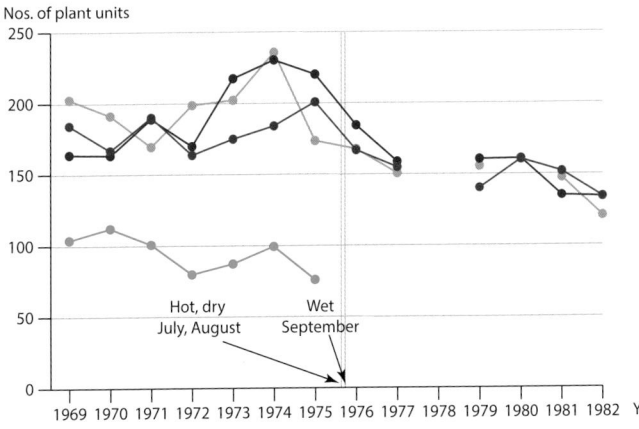

Bird's-eye Primrose

died as they could not digest the fermented herbage. The vegetation of all seven Teesdale Violet sites is open, with exposed limestone, and the plots are of various sizes with different numbers of 'plant-units' (vertical axis of graph *opposite*) in each. Recording commenced in 2002 when Rabbits were ubiquitous.

Only significant events are mentioned on the graph *opposite*: at Site 6 when the terminal rosettes had been eaten many dormant buds along the woody stem produced new rosettes (plant-units); at Site 2 blown sugar-limestone sand from the shore of the nearby reservoir covered the Site in 2006, but the plants soon grew through this; as the Rabbit numbers decreased, the short Blue Moor-grass turf became longer and longer, producing shade that smothered the light-requiring violets and caused this and other rare species to be

Bagged mown grass ready for removal, Natural England staff, 2013 *MEB*.

shaded out. Following a farmer's suggestion, NE commenced to mow and rake off the long grass in the expectation that the sheep would graze the calcareous turf again (neither sheep nor Rabbits will eat the mature, silica-filled leaves of Blue Moor-grass or Glaucous Sedge). Mowing commenced in 2013 with the response of the plants showing in the following year. The areas of mowing were increased in the following years and included more of my recorded plots; by 2016, good increases had occurred in Sites 7 and 8, but only a modest one in Site 1. But alas, changes in the staffing on the NNR, along with the weather, have combined to interrupt the mowing; there was no mowing in 2016 and only areas of Sites 1, 2 and 3 in autumn 2017. Plots 2 and 6 are both overgrown and the populations have decreased; Site 8 was mown in 2014 and 2015 and a small increase occurred, but there was no mowing in 2016 or 2017. See also Spring Gentian (Case Study 4, *p. 236*)), where both Sites 7 and 8 were mown in 2013 and 2014 and increases in gentians followed, but when there was no mowing in 2016 or 2017 these increases were lost.

b) Results of mowing plots of Spring Gentian in recent years

Mowing commenced in 2013 at Site 1 (a year I was unable to record), and the following year Sites 1, 7 and 8 were mown, as well as additional grassland. By 2016, the number of gentian rosettes had increased at Sites 7 and 8, but not at Site 1 as there were few plants in or near the plots from which plants could spread. No mowing was carried out in 2016, and the gains made at Site 8 were lost, numbers falling from 34 to six. However, mowing was possible in 2017 and 2018 and all populations increased, apart from the mere two rosettes at Site 1. The number of gentian rosettes at the sites had become so small by 2009 that recovery has been very slow, except in Site 7 which started with 24 rosettes and has been regularly mown since 2013. Although Site 1 started with 12 rosettes, it dropped to three in 2016 and in 2018 had only two. The vegetation here, and probably the soil, may have become more acidic; it is very dense and contains much Red Fescue and little Blue Moor-grass.

So, the issue for the Teesdale flora is to foster a mosaic of factors that assist the different constituent parts of it to flourish to their best ability, and to retain the integrity of the ecosystem as a whole while being mindful of the range of requirements.

Fig. 6 | Population dynamics of Teesdale Violet in seven plots on Widdybank Fell

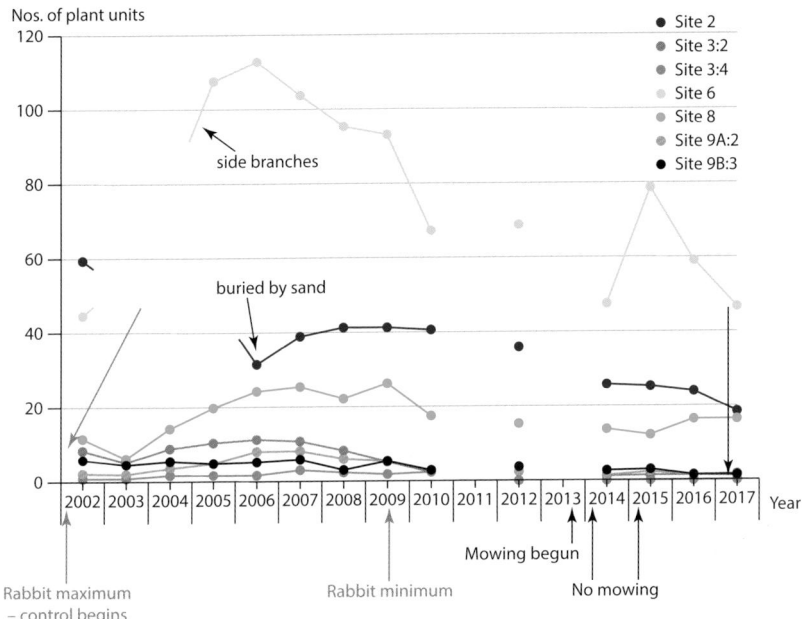

Fig. 7 | Results of mowing plots of Spring Gentian in recent years

Land management and social change

I arrived in Co. Durham from the Yorkshire Wolds in 1950, just in time to witness and absorb the traditional way of farming in Upper Teesdale. Even the greater demand for food production during WWII only lightly touched the upper dale and, where it did, profitability was so uncertain and low that the growing of any new crops such as potatoes, barley and oats was soon discontinued.

Background

Farms, including those in the Raby and Strathmore Estates, were small: 20–30 acres of meadow, adjacent pasture and a number of sheep stints for grazing on the moorland. Most of the farm work was done by the farmer, his wife and children; often the farmer had a second job in the whinstone quarries or on the roads. Each farm would have a number of red or roan Northern Dairy Shorthorn cows and sheep and one or more Dales ponies or Clydesdale horses; tractors were only just coming into the upper dale in the 1950s. Fertility of the land was maintained by dressings of farmyard manure (FYM) and the occasional applications of lime (subsidized by the Government); basic slag was also favoured, especially for the upland pastures and was readily available from the Teesside steel works. This traditional management of the meadows – mown in summer, grazed with cattle and lambs (hogs) in the autumn, rested in the winter, grazed by the ewes at lambing-time, mucked and fertilized (FYM) in the spring, then 'shut-up' to produce the next crop of hay – would have maintained the large variety of plant species of the herb-rich meadows, formerly characteristic of the north Pennines.

Herb-rich meadow (MG3), the Tatty Field, Baldersdale, 2007 *J'OR*.

During the next two decades, the march of agricultural and social progress spread through the Tees catchment; the little grey Fergie tractor arrived, others followed. There were more cars, farm and quarry-related transport on the roads. On the farm, artificial (bag) fertilizer (Nitram or other Nitrogen-Phosphorus-Potassium fertilizers (NPK)) together with FYM was used to boost the hay crop and, occasionally, meadows were treated with herbicides to remove the buttercups and, of course, other broad-leaved plants disappeared too. The monthly milk cheque of the Milk Marketing Board (started in 1933) provided the farmer with a regular income. In order to increase production, the red/roan dual-purpose Northern Dairy Shorthorn (NDS) cows were replaced by the more milk-producing black-and-white Friesian breed. Later, the lane-end milk churns went when the milk-tankers arrived, except in situations where the farm road was too narrow, hilly or twisty. To keep the milk cool and germ-free, an expensive on-farm cooler-tank was needed for the once-a-day milk collection. At this time, many farms decided to let the calf milk the cow and so the suckler-herds became the norm along with a change to producing store beasts to be matured elsewhere for the butcher. The farmer's harvest from his cows (their calves) was sold at the autumn and winter 'cattle markets' and thus the regular monthly milk-cheque was replaced by the lottery of the annual market for the store cattle and store lambs, along with the four-year-old and caste ewes. On the estates, as the small farms became vacant, the land was amalgamated with that of an adjacent farm, or several, making a larger and more viable unit.

On the farms, beef bulls, such as the heavy Charolais (that caused much poaching of wet, rare plant communities) and the lighter Limousin, were hired from a local Bull Centre to produce calves, which were then sold as stores, of the type required by the butcher. This increase in the numbers of livestock required more home-produced hay and thus more fertilizer was applied; some fields on the flood-plain were ploughed and re-seeded with Rye-grass, Timothy and Cock's-foot grasses. More sheds were built (supported by the Hill Farming Allowance) to house the cattle in winter. These required straw for bedding purchased from outside the area; the resulting FYM was different from the earlier, almost pure, cow dung. The straw and dung mix was often less well composted and more acidic, taking nitrogen from the soil for decomposition. Some arable field weeds arrived this way. The sheep were mainly Swaledales and usually a small flock was crossed with the Blue-faced Leicester ram to produce the North Country Mules, the popular dame of lowland flocks. A few farms began to make silage in pits; silage towers were rare in Teesdale. Later, bales of green grass were placed in black plastic bags that were sealed and usually stacked near the cattle shed(s); much later, wilted hay meadow grass in large round bales was bandaged with thin plastic and stored while it matured into haylage. Hill farms with sheep continued to make some small bales of hay, convenient for carrying on the quad-bike that had replaced the Dales pony.

Agricultural support

Changes in land management were influenced by national and European Policy. The Treaty of Rome, signed in 1957, established the European Common Market and created the Common Agricultural Policy (CAP) that regulated agricultural production in the member states. The UK did not join until 1973, and then gained access to farm subsidies, while contributing to the common purse. These payments were for the numbers of sheep, cattle and goats held on the farm (known as headage payments). As a consequence, on a national basis, some farmers over-stocked, particularly if market prices were low. This was not so prevalent in Teesdale where a high proportion of the farms had tenancy agreements with the estates that stated the number of stints that could be kept on each farm and grazed on the moorland. In 1987, some selected areas were designated as Environmentally Sensitive Areas (ESAs). One such area included most of Teesdale. In return for payment, the management of the farm had to be environmentally friendly. In Teesdale, for example, hay meadows received reduced quantities of FYM and fertilizer, and the numbers of sheep per farm were reduced and also kept off the fell for a longer period. Planting hedges and trees and making ponds were also encouraged, although these were mostly not viable in the upper part of Teesdale.

In 1991, the Countryside Stewardship Scheme was introduced, replaced by Stewardship in 2005. In 1992, the McSharry report recommended taking land out of production for corn and milk, because of the corn and butter 'mountains'. Milk was limited by farm quota, and in arable areas wide headlands and even whole fields went into fallow – this became known as 'set-aside' – an unexpected by-product of these was an increase in farmland bird populations. It was the limitation of the milk quota that affected the farms in Teesdale.

In 1999, 'Agenda 2000' split the money from the Common Agricultural Policy, CAP, into two: Pillar 1: Agricultural Production and Pillar 2: Rural Development. Pillar 1 encouraged diversification and Agri-Environment schemes. In Teesdale, more restrictions were placed as to when the farmer could apply FYM and fertilizer, harrow and roll the meadows, the date when the field gate was closed to allow the grass to grow for hay, and even the dates before which the grass could not be cut. These controls were intended to improve the breeding success of the birds (especially waders and Black Grouse); the low nutrient input in the meadows was to increase the floristic diversity of the meadows. But, a 'one prescription' for England did not 'fit' the meadows and pastures of the north Pennines. In this area of high rainfall and excessive leaching the nutrient input proved to be insufficient to maintain a herb-rich sward and to produce an adequate crop of hay for viable farming.

Although emanating from the Common Market via CAP, these schemes were designed partly by the UK and driven by what the environmentalists thought best. Attached to the farm subsidies this approach controlled how a large part of the north Pennines within the SSSIs could be managed by land owners and farmers affecting the survival of the plants, birds and other wildlife.

Conservation development

An interest in wildlife conservation was revived and took root, developing into the Wildfowl and Wetlands Trust and the Worldwide Fund for Nature (WWF). In the UK, the 1949 National Parks and Access to the Countryside Act recognized the importance of maintaining wildlife for the 'health of the nation'. Conservation areas allowing wildlife to flourish were recognized as national assets; earning tourist business, encouraging exercise and health, preserving culture and beauty. The Act also set up the statutory nature conservation organization, the Nature Conservancy (NC), which recognized the need for research to aid effective habitat management and thus wildlife conservation. Later, the research arm of the NC was split off to become the Institute of Terrestrial Ecology (ITE, now the Centre for Ecology & Hydrology (CEH)) leaving the NCC without its scientific base – believed by some to be a retrograde move. Concurrently there was an upsurge of County Naturalists' Trusts – now the Wildlife Trusts – an increased membership of the Royal Society for the Protection of Birds (RSPB) and other bodies concerned with countryside protection such as the former Council for the Protection of Rural England (CPRE, now named CPRE, the countryside charity) and the National Trust (NT)).

The first five National Nature Reserves (NNRs) in England were jointly announced on 19th May 1952 and included the Moor House NNR. The Moor House site comprised 7,400 hectares of the North Pennine uplands above 490 m, centred on an existing Shooting Lodge at 550m. Moor House became a Scientific Research Centre, which was later aligned with Abisko in Arctic Sweden in the International Biological Programme (IBP) 1964–74. Additional areas in Teesdale were designated as Sites of Special Scientific Interest (SSSIs). Later in 1963, the Upper Teesdale NNR (in North Yorkshire) was created specifically because of the *great geological interest and the high number of rare plant species*. Later still, the corresponding area of high geological and botanical attributes on the Durham side of the Tees was recognized and included in the Teesdale NNR in the early 1970s.

The NNR is a European 'Natura 2000' area by virtue of being formally declared under European Community (EC) legislation, the 'Habitats Directive', as a Special Area of Conservation (SAC) in 2005, and under the 'Birds Directive' as a Special Protection Area (SPA) at the earlier date of 1995. It was, and is, the statutory duty of the Nature Conservancy (now Natural England) to conserve the natural features and wildlife within the NNR and SSSIs. The decision of the UK to leave the European Union has resulted in legislation being developed to continue protection of these sites.

On both sides of the Tees the upland blanket bog and heaths are the home of the game birds – Red and Black Grouse. In 1995, the total numbers of sheep were reduced and they were, and still are, kept off the uplands for an extra month in the winter. The consequence of this is that the sheep have to be kept on the grassland pastures nearer the farm buildings and the species-rich meadows. By now, a greater variety of breeding sheep were in the dale – more North Country Mules, North Country Cheviot and smaller numbers of Texel, Beltex, Jacob, Herdwick and Suffolk: the valley-bottom farms aim to have butcher-ready lambs straight off the farm; the Limousin breed had become the favoured beef sire and one farm had Aberdeen Angus, although a few farms retained the traditional suckler herds of black, dun or Belted Galloways and Blue-grey cows, the product of a White Shorthorn bull and a Galloway cow. These are very scarce in Teesdale nowadays, being replaced with the un-missable Belted Galloways.

Belted Galloways in Widdybank Pasture and (INSET) bull *MEB*.

Threats

In recent times, the greatest scourge in the middle altitudes of Teesdale has been the Rabbit. Formerly, at the higher altitudes, say >300 m, when deep snow lay on the ground for several weeks, the Rabbit population was kept in check and any serious damage to the rare flora was not evident. Each summer, myxomatosis gradually moved up the dale and added a further check on Rabbit numbers. But winters have become warmer: for example in 1992–3 and 1993–4 there was no snow on Widdybank or Cronkley Fells. As the furry predators of Rabbits are controlled rigorously, in the interests of the preservation of grouse and ground-nesting birds such as waders, the Rabbit population expanded farther up the dale to breed in the boulder screes and make warrens in the soft metamorphosed limestone.

By the early 21st century, their numbers expanded to 'plague' proportions, reaching a peak in 2004. In August that year, a newly fenced exclosure on Thistle Green had as many Rabbits inside as out, and on both fells the species-rich sugar-limestone turf was reduced to the appearance of a thread-bare carpet. After I had expressed strong concerns about the damage they were doing to the sugar-limestone vegetation in 2003, English Nature (EN) and the Raby Estate began, in January 2005, to gas and shoot the Rabbits to reduce the numbers. By 2009, there was no evidence of Rabbits on Widdybank Fell or in the exclosures on Cronkley Fell that surround the large quantities of species-rich grassland. In the wider area of Teesdale, the prolonged snow cover in winter 2009–10 severely reduced the Rabbit population. Although many found a ready supply of food in the farmer's silage and haylage, this fermented grass proved fatal to thousands of Rabbits. But, the Rabbit populations soon recovered when the winters were milder again, as in 2013–14. Since then, their numbers have fluctuated, but never reached those of the beginning

A Rabbit warren that resulted in the destruction of violet habitat at The Rods *MEB*.

of the century. The huge snowdrift created by the 'Beast from the East' weather event in 2018 covered many holes in the sugar-limestone, thus sealing Rabbits in their burrows and reducing the population on the southern arc of the sugar-limestone on Widdybank Fell. At the higher altitudes of the blanket bog (about 610 m) the greater severity of the weather in most winters has always kept the Rabbit numbers low.

Although the higher parts of Teesdale seem remote, they have been populated by people from early times; for example, micro-flints have been found on the fells by the shore of Cow Green Reservoir (2015) and near Widdybank Farm. In 1663, there were eight settlements in Harwood and 33 by 1851. Mining for lead and other minerals from the 17th to the 20th century has left a disturbed landscape that is visible today in exposed veins and semi-bare spoil heaps. Most of the miners had a few acres on which to keep stock – a pig, a cow or goat, maybe a few sheep and one or more geese and hens; there would be a garden in which to grow vegetables and useful herbs. As the mines spread to higher altitudes so did the smallholdings – Grasshill at 610 m was the highest occupied farm in England until 1957. The last tenant started with the Northern Dairy Shorthorns cows, but soon changed to Galloways and used a White Shorthorn bull to produce the profitable Blue-grey heifers that he sold when 18 months old to become the popular suckler cows of the upland farms. The heavy metal-contaminated soil provided the opportunity for metal-tolerant plants to spread, for example to create the scarce Calaminarian flora with Spring Sandwort, Alpine Penny-cress and Thrift, the latter found in quantity in the outflow from Rod's Vein on Widdybank Fell before being flooded by the Cow Green Reservoir. These species are associated with lead mining throughout the Pennines and indeed England.

A Rabbit hole, excavated ground and the effect of a barbeque tray burn at Widdybank Fell *MEB*.

Protection

The plant communities most sensitive to farming practices are the herb-rich meadows and the lime-rich mires in some of the pastures, *e.g.* Widdybank and Cronkley Pastures. The colourful richness of the Teedale meadows was lost in 1950–60, some by ploughing and reseeding but mostly by the application of 'bag' fertilizer and sometimes herbicides in the drive to make the country self-sufficient in food and provide a living for the farmer. Today, only a small number of these traditional meadows (MG3) remain. Only a low level of FYM (in modern terms) and inorganic fertilizer is allowed and meadows may not be mown before a specified date, 8th July is the earliest – but, of course, the farmer's actions are influenced by the weather. The NPAONB initiated a detailed plant survey to identify the state of the dales' meadows. J. O'Reilly produced a map in the Report NECR 069 (p. 11) showing the occurrence of the MG3, MG6, MG7 and MG8 NVC types. A high percentage of Teesdale meadows are MG8, characterized by a high proportion of Marsh-marigold – a plant of damp/wet habitats indicative of the high rainfall and high water tables. Recently, meadow restoration is being done by spreading green-hay from neighbouring species-rich meadows on to those meadows deemed to be worth improving the floristic diversity.

Species-rich mires of the M10 short sedge-marsh type are full of rare species, including Alpine Bartsia, False Sedge and the newly identified Northern Deergrass and its hybrid with Common Deergrass (*Trichophorum ×foersteri*). These are pastures grazed by cattle for most of the year and sheep in the winter. Before 1995 there would be 900–1,000 sheep in the Lower Pasture about one month before lambing, from early April onwards; by mid-May the ewes and lambs would have been moved to hill grazing, of these 600 on to Widdybank Fell. In the Lower Pasture the sheep grazed the remains of last year's growth so there was no accumulation of leaf-litter as there has been in the last 20 years. For a few years since 1995 the pasture was grazed by heavy Charolais-cross cows and their robust calves, which severely poached the mires and disturbed the drainage systems. Recently, lighter traditional Galloway and Blue-grey cows and calves have grazed the Lower Pasture, whilst mixed breeds occupy the Upper Pasture. Unfortunately, the free movement of water through the mires has not recovered and elsewhere in the pastures species of tall rushes have taken over.

Calcareous grasslands occur at two altitudes: >610 m and at approximately 520 m. The latter include the grasslands on the metamorphosed and unchanged limestones on Herdship Fell and High Hurth, while the former are on Cronkley and Widdybank Fells, and are very species-rich. Unlike most of the uplands in the UK, those in the north Pennines were not so overgrazed, because in much of Upper Teesdale the dominant interest of the land-owners is to maintain a good habitat for game birds – Red and Black Grouse. By tradition, the sheep numbers were limited by the 'stints' agreed between the tenant and landlord. In the SSSIs, EN/NE caused the sheep numbers to be reduced and kept off the Heather moors for an additional four weeks. These sheep spent more time in the in-bye pastures and meadows or were housed often in additional newly constructed sheds. Meanwhile the moorlands are now said to be undergrazed. Cattle are still grazed on the lower slopes of Meldon Hill near Birkdale and a few Dales ponies graze the north side of the dale near Langdon Beck, and there was a breeding herd on the moor north of Middleton-in-Teesdale.

At the higher altitudes, the combinations of sheep and a short growing season had produced a very short turf with few rare species such as Alpine Forget-me-not being recognized. When the sheep were removed because of the Foot-and-mouth Disease outbreak in 2001 the vegetation expanded several inches, so that two years later new species were identified – two sedges, Water

Sedge and Sheathed Sedge, and more populations of Alpine Foxtail. Subsequently in the Moor House NNR, where the land had been purchased by the Nature Conservancy, many of the grazing rights have now been bought by NE, so a much smaller number of sheep graze in that part of Upper Teesdale. Now, 21 years later, how well are these two sedges, the grass and other smaller rarities faring?

On the lower limestones the grazers are sheep and Rabbits. On Widdybank Fell this combination of a small number of Rabbits and 600 ewes and followers kept the sward to about 5 cm high and the rare species, mostly low-growing, had adapted to this condition and had flowered and mostly produced seed; an exception was the Spring Gentian, whose 15–20 cm-tall fruits were usually grazed but which maintained its populations successfully by vegetative reproduction, with a turnover of about 33% of its rosettes each year. This balance was upset when the sheep flock was reduced by over half to 250 ewes in 1995. For a while their removal was not noticed as the milder winters in the new century allowed the Rabbits to multiply to catastrophic proportions, reaching a peak in 2003; in places, the species-rich turf on the sugar-limestone looked like a threadbare carpet. Again, the balance changed when the Rabbit population was reduced to almost nil on Widdybank Fell and in the exclosures on Cronkley Fell by 2009 and the prolonged deep snow of winter 2010/11. With only the reduced number of sheep as grazers, the vegetation on Widdybank Fell and in the exclosure on Cronkley Fell grew to 15–25 cm and some rarities such as Spring Gentian failed to flower or produce new rosettes. Thus, this and other rare species, for example Teesdale Violet and Dwarf Milkwort, are struggling to survive in the undergrazed vegetation.

It is the opinion of some botanists working in Upper Teesdale, that most rare of the perennials can survive overgrazing for many years possibly due to their deep root systems, but they soon fail and die in the shade produced by taller vegetation (even from pasture grasses) because most rarities are 'light-demanders'.

A recording plot illustrating the effect of undergrazing *MEB*.

A modern-day photo of High Force, with an ancient Common Juniper *MR*.

Teesdale: past and present

Today, an inventory of the rare flora of the catchment area of the Tees is excitingly greater than when J. G. Baker wrote his much-quoted words in 1868:

> *"There is probably no piece of ground in Britain that produces so many rare plants within a limited space as Widdy Bank Fell."*

However, a closer look provides the saddening truth that even in the 60 years that I have known Teesdale, these species are now much more thinly spread in the dale, and two or maybe more are presumed to be extinct. Those species that are now much more thinly distributed include Mountain Everlasting and Spring Gentian.

Threats: Causes of decline

The botanists

The end of the 18th century and early part of the 19th were the periods of exploration and discovery of the flora of Britain. The characteristics of each new species were made known by the distribution of sheets of specimens. Some of these sheets were filled with complete plants, *e.g.* seven plants of Bog Orchid from Eggleston Moor, many large pieces of Hoary Rock-rose from Cronkley Fell, and more flowering shoots of Horseshoe Vetch are currently in herbaria than grow in Teesdale today. Were the five shoots of the presumed Shining Lady's-mantle, complete with rhizome, on one sheet collected by Druce (1928) near Langdon Beck the whole of a surviving population? It has not been found in Teesdale since. The best-known assumed extinction is that of the Oblong Woodsia. Undoubtedly, this little fern was over-collected by botanists and Victorian fern-hunters, for the last sighting of the indigenous plant was in 1950.

Fig. 8 | Changes in the numbers of fields containing three meadow-flowering plants between 1967 and 2003/4 in Upper Teesdale (Bradshaw, 2006)

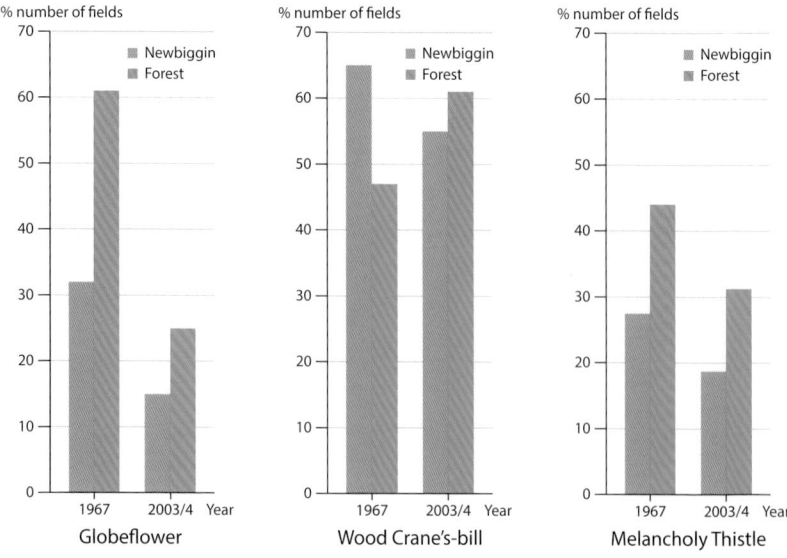

Climate change

To date, we do not have any relevant records of the performance of individual species in relation to the climate. The survivors of the late-glacial flora have withstood many fluctuations in the climate of the last 10,000–12,000 years, initially colder, then warmer and later wetter than today. However, over the last 2,500 years, and particularly 60 years, the role of humans has had an overriding influence on the vegetation during a period of relatively stable climatic conditions, but the evidence is that a definite climatic change is now taking place. How this will affect these rare species, mostly at the edge of their climatic range, only time will tell.

In 2019, baseline sites (or new plots) were established for ten species at or near the limit of their northern or southern range in Britain, or centred in northern England, in addition to five species first recorded in 1969 or 1970. The species are: Mountain Everlasting, Alpine Bartsia, False Sedge, Scottish Asphodel, Bird's-eye Primrose (stemless form), Mountain Avens and Hoary Rock-rose. These are in addition to: Spring Gentian, Bird's-eye Primrose (stalked form), Rare Spring-sedge, Dwarf Milkwort, Alpine Cinquefoil, Teesdale Violet, Teesdale Violet × Common Dog-violet and Hoary Whitlowgrass.

Atmospheric pollution

There is evidence that atmospheric pollution from the industrial developments in Lancashire and the West Riding of Yorkshire caused a rise in the acidity of the soils of the Pennines. But there is no proof that can be directly linked to the decline of any rare species considered in this book, although the increase in more acidic-type vegetation could be having an indirect effect.

Birds

It is my opinion that the decline of two relic *Sphagnum* mosses (*S. austinii* and *S. fuscum*) was initiated at a time (1960–70) when a colony of Black-headed Gulls roosted and defecated on the prominent hummocks of these mosses. Scarce hummocks of two rare mosses have survived in the very wet mire that had too little Heather to warrant burning for grouse food (!). At the lower altitudes of the meadows, Pheasants are now quite common. It is not known if the active scratching with their long toes will damage the soft, marsh communities.

Two *Sphagnum* mosses affected by breeding Black-headed Gulls: Imbricate Bog-moss (LEFT) and Austin's Bog-moss (RIGHT) *MEB*.

Shore erosion in the Slapestone Sike area by Cow Green Reservoir *MEB*.

Thistle Green, species-rich sugar-limestone vegetation covered with gale-blown calcareous sand *MEB*.

Thistle Green erosion of soil has exposed glacial erratics on the bed-rock of sugar-limestone that continues to erode due to weathering and wind *MR*.

Thistle Green colonization after controlled sheep grazing, mainly in autumn *MR*.

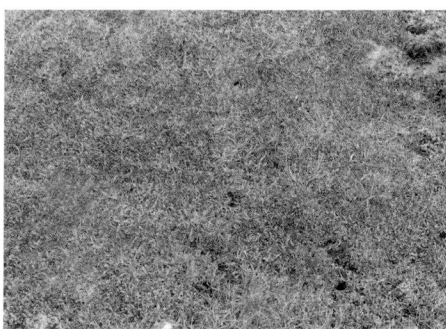

(LEFT) Mat of Mountain Avens under-run by voles at White Well in 2017; (RIGHT) the same area in 2019 with vole runs collapsed *MEB*.

Loss of land

Rare species-rich plant communities have been, and continue to be, lost due to flooding and soil erosion.

a) Construction of the Cow Green Reservoir – see *p. 224*.

b) Erosion of soil on the summit of Cronkley Fell, known as Thistle Green. This summit consists today of areas of more or less bare rock and of soil to the depth of 60 cm. I believe that the exceptionally deep (60 cm) soil in the eastern portion of the plateau has been augmented by wind-blown sugar-limestone sand from the area that is now almost bare limestone and sandstone rock to the SW, *i.e.* erosion and accretion. This may have been initiated at the time in the 18th and 19th centuries when the Green Trod over Cronkley Fell was a drove-route between Alston, via Birkdale and Holwick, into Teesdale and farther south for cattle, sheep and ponies from Scotland, as well as a passage from Teesdale to Appleby and the west. The passage of feet and hooves, and those of pack-ponies laden with lead-ore would have broken the protecting cover of turf exposing the friable 'sandy' soil to the destructive elements of rain, frost and high winds. I have experienced a 10 cm-deep blast of sugar-limestone 'sand' that almost completely buried the plants in the turf. Additional erosion was created by sheep rubbing their itchy backs on the vertical face of the eroding soil. Today, Thistle Green is surrounded by a sheep- and rabbit-proof fence, but destruction of the soil continued for many years. In the 1950s, the turf-covered soil was adjacent to a large boulder on Thistle Green; wind erosion and sheep rubbing have caused the considerable loss of soil and vegetation during the following 50 years. This century, a new fence, better control of the Rabbits and sheep grazing have allowed some stabilization of the edge and colonization by plants to take place.

Moles and netting

In the 1950s, the late Ken Park concluded that molehills in the sugar-limestone on Cronkley Fell were initiation loci for a type of erosion when the sandy soil of the hill dried and was blown away by the frequent strong or gale-force winds. This left a disk of bare ground that was subject to further erosion, but some sand accumulated on the front edge of the disk that was colonized by the adjacent vegetation forming a crescent of raised vegetation. In 1970, the then EN fixed horticultural cotton netting over the more or less bare limestone and isolated plants on Thistle Green with a view to stabilizing the vegetation and increasing the accretion of loose limestone. Unfortunately, this has not been maintained, although remnants of the netting could be found recently.

Rabbits

Rabbits join the domestic sheep in being the major grazers in the upland parts of Teesdale. The numbers of both determine the height of the grassland vegetation, including the base-rich grassland over the sugar-limestone that supports so much of the rarer flora. Most of these are 'light-demanders', meaning that they cannot thrive in shade such as that created by tall associated vegetation. Prior to 1995, the sheep maintained a short turf rich with many species. At the turn of the century, first the sheep flock on Widdybank Fell was reduced to less than half, and then an outbreak of Foot-and-mouth Disease caused more sheep to be removed from the higher fells; meanwhile, the Rabbit population in the dale exploded. The changing levels of grazing on Widdybank Fell are described in Land Management (*below*). Near the Pennine ridge the absence of grazing on the vegetation has had the dramatic effect of allowing rare species, such as Sheathed Sedge and Water Sedge, to flower and be identified there for the first time.

Land management

a) For grouse rearing

Heather is the staple for grouse – providing food for young to eat and shelter for older animals, a mixture of which is maintained by rotational burning. Although there is no actual proof, it is possible that species such as the Lesser Twayblade, Bog Bilberry, Stag's-horn Clubmoss and maybe Dwarf Birch have all suffered. However, vigorous control of the furry predators of grouse – Fox, Stoat, Weasel and Common Rat – has indirectly had the very serious effect of allowing the Rabbit population to grow without restraint. Hard-core access roads through the moorland are destroying drainage patterns. Unless access is controlled, these provide easy access for motorcyclists, mountain bikers and fell walkers to higher ground.

b) Farmers' livestock

Cattle, sheep, horse/ponies and geese have been grazed on the fells for well over two centuries. Small Highland-type cattle (kylies) were summered on the south-west of Cronkley Fell, at Birkdale, a drovers' stop-over and Meldon Fell, on Cow Green and on the north side of the valley above Valence Lodge Fells as recently as the beginning of the 20th century. Geese were summered in the area of the now-flooded Weel. In much of the area, the numbers of stock were regulated by the number of stints attached to each holding. But sheep in particular are very selective grazers and would concentrate on the limestone and more species-rich bent–fescue grasslands.

In Teesdale, in the places where the vegetation comprises a mosaic of common and rare plant communities, the latter is made-up of many rare and exacting species. The management of the correct level of grazing is a nightmare – one species requiring only light grazing, the next cannot tolerate the shade that is created! In the period 1950–95, the level of grazing on the top of Widdybank Fell appeared to allow most of the rare species to survive satisfactorily, although a few did not produce ripe fruit, but did have effective vegetative reproduction. In 1995, EN reduced the number of sheep on Widdybank Fell to less than half, coincidentally at this time the Rabbits were increasing. Rabbits are much closer grazers than sheep and, together with their scrapings and burrows, caused many rare species to suffer (*e.g.* Hoary Whitlowgrass has almost disappeared and other species are still at low levels – see Case Study 5, *p. 237*). Hoary Whitlowgrass is a short-lived perennial (2–3 years), dependent upon the annual production of abundant seed that would have been halted when the Rabbits grazed off the inflorescences. Conversely, only the inflorescences and not the leafy shoots of most sedges were eaten, allowing them to become taller and denser in the sugar-limestone grassland

and in some short sedge-marsh communities to the detriment of species such as Alpine Meadow-rue with its prostrate leaves. Now that the Rabbit population has been controlled, undergrazing is creating a different threat to the rare species, most being light-demanders, which are now weak and flowerless, although some can propagate vegetatively. Since 2013, additional sheep have been bought onto Widdybank Fell and the flock will be further increased to 400 by retaining ewe lambs (I would prefer 450). Unfortunately, once the

Short turf outside exclosure, Little Dun Fell *FJR*.

vegetation has become this tall (12–18 cm) it is coarse and the sheep will not eat it if there is some short grass, such as the bent-fescue, available. As an experiment, in 2013 some small areas of the Blue Moor-grass/Red Fescue/Glaucous Sedge-dominated community were mown to encourage the sheep to graze the short, formerly species-rich grassland. Mowing of these and larger areas has been continued, intermittently at first, then more regularly each year to the present. Occasionally, sheep have been seen grazing, or droppings found in the mown areas.

The montane heaths and grasslands (>610 m)
The intensity of the sheep grazing was only revealed by the erection of exclosures, as on Little Dun Fell. The event of Foot-and-mouth Disease in the north Pennines in 2001 was devastating for farmers, but it provided a bonus for the botanists, as has been shown in several species' accounts. It has revealed the existence of unexpected 'new' species, including 'meadow' plants, such as Globeflower. As a result of new agreements with NE the sheep numbers will now be kept low.

The lower pastures
In the lower pastures of Widdybank and Cronkley Pastures there are mosaics of other rare plant communities, mostly fed by base-rich drainage. Today, these are mainly grazed by suckler cows and their calves. For a number of years, heavy continental-cross cows did much damage in the soft ground in Widdybank Pasture, reducing the unique habitat of the gravelly flushes to a muddy, silty soup. In Cronkley Pasture, the slopes below the Scar have been severely overgrazed by cattle and sheep; Heather has almost disappeared; a relict thicket of Shrubby Cinquefoil some distance from the present bed of the Tees has completely died out and several of the rare species in the many, scattered flushes recorded in 1973 are now, almost 50 years later, very scarce indeed, *e.g.* Hair Sedge and Spring Gentian.

The meadows
The quantity of hay that could be made determined the number of cows and heifers that could be kept on a holding. Much changed during the middle of the 20th century. Initially stung by war-time food shortages, the government aimed at self-sufficiency for food for the nation, and, among other things, to raise the productivity of the hills. Subsidies were offered to modernize or replace old buildings and increase the number of cattle, which required more hay and artificial fertilizer (ICI Nitram) and imported straw for bedding and feed. Lime to reduce the soil acidity was subsidized and basic slag was the favoured treatment for the poorer pasture. Tractors and cars, milk- and other lorries all became more numerous in the dale than before or during the war.

This forcing of the meadows to grow more 'grass' started the decline in the species richness of the 'herby' meadows and of the associated iconic species – Globeflower, Wood Crane's-bill, Melancholy Thistle and several rare lady's-mantles recorded by myself. This decline was demonstrated convincingly by J. O'Reilly in his survey of over 500 meadows in the NPAONB between 2006 and 2008, with significant losses being detected in 48% of them, despite agri-environment management agreements being in place. Yet, in a recent NE condition assessment 80% of these fields were rated as satisfactory.

People

Other than those who earn their living or work on the land of the area (*e.g.* farmers, gamekeepers, NE and AONB employees), there are those who use the area for recreation. This takes many forms:

- Motorcycles, mountain bikes and quad bikes being driven across and through species-rich flushes, destroying both these and the natural drainage patterns in Open-Access land.
- Skiers.
- Climbers.
- Paddlers, including kayakers and tubes/doughnuts. The Tees is one of the top ten rivers for paddlers in England, especially the Low Force area. The river's south bank is species-rich meadow-type vegetation where several square metres have been destroyed by trampling and some characteristic rare rock-face plants reduced in number, *e.g.* Shrubby Cinquefoil and Mountain Everlasting. NE/NPAONB and the Paddler's Association have attempted to mitigate the damage by producing a guide and painting the boundaries of the accepted route out of the water onto the river's south bank, but kayakers in particular prefer to climb the cliff on the north side. But, there is no policing to ensure the agreed route is taken and not the more species-rich one up the cliff under Wynch Bridge, where Shrubby Cinquefoil and rare hawkweeds are being destroyed.
- Serious walkers, *e.g.* along the Pennine Way; many feet have eroded the path:
  a) over the blanket bog that is now covered with 'duck-boards'; or
  b) on mineral soil now paved with stone slabs. Elsewhere on slopes paths are deepened or become braided.
- Other walkers, strollers and picnickers – recent incidents have been of 'tin-tray instant-BBQs' burning vegetation on the riverbank and the fell – one narrowly missing a long-term research plot on in the NNR on Widdybank Fell.

Peace and Tranquillity in the countryside

Apart from the normal rural **noises** – that should be accepted as part of the countryside – there is noise pollution from:

- High-powered motor bikes.
- Passenger planes.
- Small 'pleasure' planes.
- Air Force jets.
- Helicopters.
- Microlights.
- Hang gliders.

From these one cannot hide.

Alpine Foxtail Flush damaged by trail bikes, Great Dun Fell *FJR*.

Tubers, Tees entry demo. over rare Lady's-mantle plants *MEB*.

Braided Pennine Way path near High Force (LEFT) and the same path paved with flag-stones (RIGHT) *MEB*.

Kayakers climbing rare species-rich cliff site on north side under Wynch Bridge *MEB*.

Competition fly-fishing, Wynch Bridge *MEB*.

Teesdale: The future

In *The Natural History of Upper Teesdale* (Gater, 2018), Stephen Trotter wrote an excellent chapter on conservation which illustrates that the subjects of this book are but part of the whole natural fabric of Upper Teesdale. I agree with Stephen when he writes:

"So, we should conserve Upper Teesdale for two reasons, for:
Its own sake and its intrinsic interest; and
What it provides for society – a home and livelihood, food, tourism, carbon [capture], biodiversity,
clean water and air."

Following publication of that book, a three-year survey of over 100 plant species was launched on Widdybank Fell. The results were shocking: 19 of the rare species had decreased (see *Table 8*). The results were published as a promotional leaflet by the Teesdale Special Flora and Conservation Trust in 2020. It was written by John O'Reilly and part-funded by the Teesdale Research Trust.

During 1968–75, teams of volunteers were organized to map the locations of some 24 of the rare plant species on the whole of the sugar-limestone grassland on Widdybank Fell; 50 years later, 2017–19, a large part of this same area has been re-surveyed by John O'Reilly using a grid of 10 m × 10 m squares.

A comparison between the baseline data of 1968–75 and the recent records, matching 10 × 10 m squares of the earlier and later periods for each of 19 species, revealed that all 19 species have declined in population extent (not plant numbers). On average, these species are now present in fewer than half of the areas they occurred in 45 or so years ago (*Table 8*).

Shocking as it is that the top three species have decreased by 100%, 98% and 85% respectively, it was the **decrease by 80%** in the area covered by Mountain Everlasting (photo *opposite*) that was the greatest surprise. This plant, once a common species on Widdybank Fell, is now present in only 20% of the area it formerly occupied. Even the iconic Spring Gentian now occupies less than half the area it covered in 1970. On a bright, sunny day following several dull days, the display of gentians will look as good as ever, but, as has been shown above, that is deceptive. Will the Spring Gentian still manage to light up the fells in spring with its electric blue stars in 50 years' time, or will one have to search for the elusive flower?

There is a glimmer of hope (although governments are fickle) in the change of financial support, so vital to the farmer in the hills, in the Government's *25 Year Environment Plan* and the Agriculture Bill that will enable the promises of the EP to be activated. The emphasis will be on 'public money for public goods'. By 2028, the direct payment and agri-environment schemes will be phased out and replaced by the Environmental Land Management Scheme (ELMS); the higher level Tier 2 includes payments for:

TREE/SHRUB AND/OR HEDGE PLANTING

- Habitat creation/restoration/management (including woodland, wetlands, freshwater, peatlands, heathland, species-rich grassland…).
- Species management (*e.g.* introduction, translocation and/or recovery and invasive species prevention/control).

Table 8 | A comparison of the number of plants recorded for 19 species between 1968–75 and 2017–19

English name	Page	1968–75	2017–19	Decline
Variegated Horsetail	74	95	44	54%
Alpine Meadow-rue	90	454	225	50%
Yellow Saxifrage	94	28	7	75%
Dwarf Milkwort	103	24	18	25%
Alpine Cinquefoil	108	97	2	98%
Teesdale Violet	124	353	295	16%
'Hybrid' Violet	126	48	32	33%
Hoary Whitlowgrass	138	22	0	100%
Thrift	141	9	3	67%
Alpine Bistort	143	829	423	49%
Teesdale Sandwort	145	62	35	44%
Bird's-eye Primrose	149	607	363	40%
Northern Bedstraw	152	605	230	62%
Spring Gentian	156	638	349	45%
Sea Plantain	160	362	174	52%
Mountain Everlasting	173	829	154	81%
Scottish Asphodel	177	278	163	41%
Three-flowered Rush	185	128	19	85%
Rare Spring-sedge	200	64	24	63%

Mountain Everlasting, Widdybank Fell 2018 *MEB*.

Blue with Spring Gentian, Teesdale *MR*.

Pink with Bird's-eye Primrose, Teesdale *MR*.

As the whole of the Teesdale Special Flora R&C Project area is managed land, and viable farms are closely linked, the welfare of the special flora through the uptake of ELMS should be beneficial. ELMS is designed primarily to benefit farmers who make environmentally positive changes to their businesses. Productivity grants are also being introduced to help farmers invest in these changes, including purchasing new equipment and technology.

The 'Tees–Swale naturally connected' project encompasses almost the whole of the Special Flora area. The aims include: '*Upland hay meadow and species-rich grassland*'. Hopefully, these can be expanded to include species-rich flushed vegetation as in Widdybank Meadow and Widdybank and Cronkley Pasture, and the high-altitude habitats mostly above the blanket bog at 600 m (2,000 ft).

A Teesdale herb-rich meadow, Holwick *MR*.

The Carrifran Project

In 1956, searching for lady's-mantle species, I walked down the treeless (well, almost) Carrifran valley in the Southern Uplands of Scotland. Fifty years later a transformation is underway by Philip and Myrtle Ashmole.

Carrifran Wildwood was the brainchild of local people who mourned the lack of natural habitats and decided to act. It was the first large land-based project of Borders Forest Trust (BFT) and after 20 years' work, the Wildwood has become an inspirational example of ecological restoration.

Removal of sheep and goats, together with planting 700,000 trees launched the return of native woodland and moorland, transforming degraded hill land into something akin to its pristine, vibrant, carbon-absorbing state, teeming with plants, animals and fungi, alive with birdsong and the sound of the wind in the trees.

After a tremendous day visiting the Carrifran and Talla-Gameshope BFT projects, Lord Harry Barnard wrote:

> "One couldn't help make comparisons on our return to the North Pennines, with clear differences in landscape scale, altitude, wildlife and farming practices but still with possibilities of establishing native woodland areas even if on a much smaller scale."

Teesdale Special Flora, if not valued for its own sake, should then be seen as a 'public good' (*i.e.* the focus used by the tourist trade to attract business to Teesdale) – something wanted by the public – fell grassland blue with Spring Gentian and pink with Bird's-eye Primrose; species-rich meadows, riversides and verges colourful with Globeflower, Wood and Meadow Crane's-bills and Red Campion.

Experience has shown, as by the Carrifran Project, that a strong voluntary body that is passionate to care for Teesdale's Special Flora – gentians, Bird's-eye Primrose and Globeflower, *etc.* – and hence the welfare of the Upper Dale is the best guarantee for the future survival of its Special Fora. The Green Recovery Challenge Fund round 2 awarded funding to Dr Margaret Bradshaw's Special Flora Trust in July 2021 to enable detailed recording to be continued, requisite management to be carried out, and for this work and the place to be made known more widely.

Roadside verge in Harwood-in-Teesdale, 2020 *MR*.

It is **our Heritage**, *this unique assemblage of plant species,* **mine and yours**.

In spite of trying, I have failed to prevent its decline, now it is up to you. You, who will inherit less than I started with, as I inherited less than Isaac Tarn before me. It is for you, readers of this book, and all to care for the survival of Teesdale's Special Flora, to ensure your children and theirs do not inherit less.

Please do not let them down.

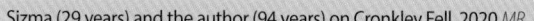

Sizma (29 years) and the author (94 years) on Cronkley Fell, 2020 *MR*.

References

Entries highlighted in green relate to legislation, regulations and policy instruments relevant to England that were in place as of December 2022, with a brief explanation of their aim.

Andrews, C. B. (ed.) 1936. *The Torrington Diaries containing the Tours through England and Wales of the Hon. John Byng (later Fifth Viscount Torrington) Between the Years 1781 and 1794.* Eyre & Spottiswoode.

Babington, C. C. & Wilmott, A. J. (ed.) 1922. *Manual of British botany, containing the flowering plants and ferns arranged according to the natural orders, 10th Edn.* Gurney and Jackson, London.

Backhouse Jr., J. 1842. *Soft Hawksbeard, Alpine Saxifrage.* In Horsman, 1998.

Backhouse Jr., J. 1843–1844. Notes of a botanical ramble in Yorkshire, etc. in the summer of 1844. *The Phytologist* Vol. 1: pp 1,065–1,069, 1,089–1,093, 1,126–1,128.

Backhouse Jr., J. 1884. Teesdale botany: historical and personal recollections. *The Naturalist*, 10–1. Biodiversity Heritage Library.

Backhouse Sr., J. 1810. *Small White Orchid.* In Horsman, 1998.

Backhouse Sr., J. 1821. *Rock Whitebeam: 1st record near Cauldron Snout, 1810.* In Horsman, 1998.

Backhouse Sr., J. & Backhouse Jr., J. 1844. An Account of a Visit to Teesdale in the Summer of 1843. *The Phytologist* Vol. 1: pp 892–895.

Backhouse Sr., J. & Backhouse Jr., J. 1852. *Alpine Forget-me-not, Dwarf milkwort.* In Horsman, 1998.

Backhouse Sr., J. & Binks, J. 1811. *Horseshoe Vetch.* In Horsman, 1998.

Baker, J. G. 1863. *North Yorkshire, studies of its botany, geology, climate and physical geography.* (Published 2018 by Franklin Classics.)

Baker, J. G. 1903. Biographical Notes on the Early Botanists of Northumberland and Durham. *Transactions of the Natural History Society of Northumberland, Durham and Newcastle upon Tyne* Vol. 14: pp 69–861.

Baker, J. G. & Tate, G. 1868. A New Flora of Northumberland and Durham. *Hist. Trans. of Northumberland and Durham* 11.

Binks, J. 1801. *Mountain Saxifrage.* In Horsman, 1998.

Binks, J. & Oliver, Revd. W. 1798. *Bearberry, Small Cowwheat, Alpine Cinquefoil.* In Horsman, 1998.

Boydell, P. 23 Nov. 1966. *Evidence given to the Select Committee of the House of Lords on the Tees Valley and Cleveland Water Bill.*

Bradshaw, M. E. 1962. The Distribution and Status of Five Species of the *Alchemilla Vulgaris* L. Aggregate in Upper Teesdale. *Journal of Ecology* Vol. 50(3): pp 681–706.

Bradshaw, M. E. 2006. The Survey of Three Meadow Plants in Teesdale Revisited. *Teesdale Record Society Journal* 3rd Series, pp 25–30.

Bradshaw, M. E. 2009. The decline of Lady's-mantles (*Alchemilla vulgaris* L. agg.) and other hay-meadow species in Northern England since the 1950s. *Watsonia* Vol. 27: pp 315–321.

Bradshaw, M. E. 2011. Four Centuries of Plant Hunting in Upper Teesdale. *Teesdale Record Society Journal.*

Bradshaw, M. E. & Doody, J. P. 1978. Plant population studies and their relevance to nature conservation. *Biol. Conserv.* Vol. 4: pp 223–242.

Camden, W. 1722. *Britannia, Ed. 2.* Edmund Gibson.

Cheffings, C. M., Farrell, L. (eds.), Dines, T. D., Jones, R. A., Leach, S. J., McKean, D. R., Pearman, D. A., Preston, C. D., Rumsey, F. J. & Taylor, I. 2005. *The Vascular Plant Red Data List for Great Britain (Species Status No.7).* JNCC, Peterborough.

Clapham, A.R. (ed.) 1978, *Upper Teesdale, The Area and its Natural History*. Collins, London. [Reviewed in **Tinker, J.** 4 May 1978. Cow Green Twelve Years On. *New Scientist*, pp 311–312.]

Clapham, A.R., Tutin T.G. & Warburg, E.F. 1959. *Excursion Flora of the British Isles*. Cambridge University Press.

Convention on International Trade in Endangered Species of Wild Fauna and Flora (CITES). 1973. [Aims to ensure that international trade in wild animals and plants does not threaten their survival.]

Cope, T., Gray, A., & Ashton, P. (ed.) 2009. *Grasses of the British Isles.* BSBI Handbooks Vol. 13.

Corner, R., Roberts, F.J. & Robinson, L. 2006. Sheathed Sedge, *Carex vaginata*: an update on its status in the Northern Pennines. *BSBI News,* part 101: pp 6–8.

Council Directive 92/43/EE, Convention on Biological Diversity. 21 May 1992. [Objectives are "the conservation of biological diversity, the sustainable use of its components, and the fair and equitable sharing of the benefits arising out of the utilisation of genetic resources".]

Countryside and Rights of Way Act (CROW Act), 2000. [Normally gives a public right of access to land mapped as "open country" (mountain, moor, heath and down) or registered common land.]

Cranston, D.M. & Valentine, D.H. 1983. Transplant experiments on rare plant species from Upper Teesdale. *Biological Conservation* Vol. 26(2): pp 175–191.

Dallas W.G., *et al.* 1984. Environmental Audits and Research Needs. [In **Roberts, R.D. & Roberts, T.M. (eds.)** *Planning and Ecology*. Springer, Boston, MA. [Available at: https://doi.org/10.1007/978-1-4899-3045-3_8.]

Davis, P.S. and Graham, G.G. 1981. The authorship of Plantae rariores agro Dunelneneo indigine. *Archives of Natural History* Vol 10(2): pp 335–340.

DEFRA. 2021. *Green Future: Our 25 Year Plan to Improve the Environment.* [Sets out what we will do to improve the environment, within a generation.]

Department for Levelling Up, Housing & Communities. July 2021. *National Planning Policy Framework (NPPF).* [Searchable version available at: https://www.gov.uk/government/publications/national-planning-policy-framework--2.]

Dickson, J. 1799. Visited Teesdale in 1799 and discovered the False Sedge; cited by **Horsman, 1998** and in Botanical RBGE.

Dines, T. 2008. *A Vascular Plant Red Data List for Wales.* Plantlife.

Druce, C.G. 1928. *British Plant List.* T. Buncle & Co.

Durkin, J.L. 2016. *County Durham Rare Plant Register 2016.* Self-published. [Cites T.J. Foggitt's first record of 'Hybrid' Deergrass, collected in 1905.]

Durkin, P. 2009. *The Oxford Guide to Etymology.* Oxford University Press.

Eddy, A., Welch, D. & Rawes, M. 1969. The Vegetation of the Moor House National Nature Reserve in the Northern Pennines, England. *Vegetation* **Vol. 16**: pp 239–284.

European Union (EU). 1992. *Council Directive 92/43/EEC on the conservation of natural habitats and of wild fauna and flora* ('The Habitats Directive'). [Ensures the conservation of a wide range of rare, threatened or endemic animal and plant species. Aims to promote the maintenance of biodiversity, taking account of economic, social, cultural and regional requirements.]

European Union (EU). 2020. *Biodiversity Strategy for 2030: Bringing nature back into our lives.* COM/2020/380 final. [Aims to put Europe's biodiversity on the path to recovery by 2030 for the benefit of people, climate and the planet. Aims to build our societies' resilience to future threats such as the impacts of climate change, food insecurity and disease outbreaks – including by protecting wildlife/fighting illegal trade.]

Fearn, G. M. 1971. *Biosystematic studies of selected species in the Teesdale flora.* Thesis submitted for the degree of Doctor of Philosophy in the Department of Botany, Sheffield University.

Fitter, R. Fitter, A. & Farrer, A. 1984. *Grasses, Sedges, Rushes & Ferns of Britain and Northern Europe.* HarperCollins.

Garland, R. J. 1803. *A Tour in Teesdale.* A Bartholoman. [Facsimile edn. (2011), British Library, Historical Print Editions.]

Garland, R. J. 1813. *A Tour in Teesdale: Including Rokeby, and Its Environs.* [Facsimile edn. (2016), from Patala Press.]

Gater, S. (ed.) 2018. *The Natural History of Upper Teesdale, 5th Edn.* Durham Wildlife Trust.

Gibson, G. S. 1844. *Alsine uliginosa,* Widdybank. *Botanical Society of Edinburgh,* Session X11, 1879.

Godwin, H. 1975. *History of the British Flora, 2nd Edn.).* Camb Science Classics, Cambridge University Press.

Graham, G. G. 1988. *The Flora and Vegetation of County Durham Watsonian Vice County 66.* Durham Flora Committee.

Gregory, A. 1971. *The Price of Amenity, Five Studies in Conservation and Management.* MacMillan, London. [Includes Cow Green, River Tees.]

Halliday, G. 1978. *Flowering Plants and Ferns of Cumbria.* Centre for North-West Regional Studies, Lancaster University.

Halliday, G. 1997. *A Flora of Cumbria.* University of Lancaster.

Harriman, W. & Oliver, Revd. W. 1796. *Spring Gentian.* In Horsman, 1998.

Harriman, W. & Oliver, Revd. W. 1798. *Lily-of-the-Valley.* In Horsman, 1998.

HM Government, Office of the Deputy Prime Minister (ODPM). 2005. *Circular 06/05 Biodiversity and Geological Conservation – Statutory Obligations and their impact within the Planning System.*

HM Government. 2018. *A Green Future: Our 25 Year Plan to improve the Environment.* [Updated May 2019 to set out what the government will do to improve the environment within a generation.]

HM Government. 2018. *The Conservation of Habitats and Species and Planning (Various Amendments) (England and Wales) Regulations.* [To align with EU Directives: Regs. 2018, No. 1307.]

HM Government. 2021. *Environment Bill.* [Aims to improve air and water quality, protect wildlife, increase recycling and reduce plastic waste. Part of legal framework for environmental protection, post-Brexit.]

Holden, J. & Adamson, J. K. 2001. Gordon Manley and the North Pennines. *Journal of Meteorology* **Vol. 26**: pp 329–333.

Holmes, N. T. H. & Whitton, B. A. 1977. The Macrophytic Vegetation of the River Tees in 1975: Observed and Predicted Changes. *Freshwater Biology* **Vol. 7(1)**: pp 43–60.

Hollingsworth, P. M. & Swan, G. A. 1999. Genetic differentiation and hybridisation among subspecies of Deergrass (*Trichophorum cespitosum* (L.) Hartman) in Northumberland. *Watsonia* pp 235–242.

Horsman, F. 1990. Some Backhouse Discoveries in Upper Teesdale. *Naturalist* **115**: pp 89–96.

Horsman, F. 1995. Ralph Johnson's notebook. *Archives of Natural History* **22(2)**: pp 147–167.

Horsman, F. 1998. *Botanising in Linnaean Britain: a study of Upper Teesdale in Northern England.* Thesis submitted for the degree of Doctor of Philosophy in the Dept of Philosophy, University of Durham.

Horsman, F. 1999. Plant distribution patterns: the first British map. *Archives of Natural History* **Vol. 26(2)**: pp 279–286.

Horsman, F. 2005. *William Oliver (ca. 1761–1816) Surgeon Apothecary and Botanist of Middleton in Teesdale.* The Teesdale Record Society.

Horsman, F. 2021. *Early Botanising in Upper Teesdale.* Royal Botanic Gardens, Edinburgh.

Horsman, F. 2021. *Who discovered the "Teesdale rarities?"* Self-published.

Howarth, E. Y., Lund, J. W. G. & Turner, J. (eds.) 1984. *Pollen diagrams from Cross Fell and their implications for former tree-lines in Lake Sediments and Environmental History.* Leicester University Press, pp 317–357.

Hulme M. & Jenkins, G. J. 1988. *Climate change scenarios for the UK: Scientific report. UKCIP Technical Report No 1*, Climate Research Unit, Norwich, p 80.

Hutchinson, T. C. 1966. The occurrence of living and sub-fossil remains of *Betula nana* L. in Upper Teesdale. *New Phytol.* **Vol. 65**: pp 351–357.

Intergovernmental Science-Policy Platform on Biodiversity and Ecosystem Services (IPBES). 2019. *Global Assessment Report.* [Examines the state of nature, its ecosystems, and its contributions to people. The Global Assessment aims to empower policy makers with the knowledge and evidence to make better informed decisions when developing policies and taking actions for the benefit of both people and nature.]

International Union of Conservation of Nature (IUCN). 2022. *Guidelines for using the IUCN Red List Categories and Criteria.* IUCN Species Survival Commission, IUCN, Gland, Switzerland and Cambridge, UK.

Jalea, J. & Suoetenon, J. (eds.) 1976. *Atlas Florae Europaeae: Distribution of Vascular Plants in Europe.* Helsinki.

Jeffrey, D. W. 1971. The Experimental alteration of a *Kobresia*-rich sward in Upper Teesdale. In Duffey, E. & Watt, A. S. (eds.) *The Scientific Management of Animal and Plant Communities for Conservation. Br. Ecol. Soc. Symp.* **11**. pp 78–89.

Jermy, A. C., Simpson, D. A., Foley, M. J. Y. & Porter, M. S. 2008. *The Sedges of the British Isles.* BSBI Handbooks, **Vol. 1**: p 97.

Johnson, G. A. L. & Dunham, K. C. 1963. *The Geology of Moor House.* Nature Conservancy Monograph No. 2. HMSO, London.

Lightfoot, Revd. 1777. *Flora Scotica,* **Vol. 2**, 2nd Edn. London.

Lloyd, P. S. 1963. *Poa alpina* L., found in Upper Teesdale in 1962. *Note included in BSBI Exhibition meeting 1963*, p 375.

Louseley, J. E. 1927. *Pale Forget-me-not.*

Manley, G. 1942. Meteorological observations on Dun Fell, a mountain station in northern England. *Quarterly Journal of the Royal Meteorological Society* **Vol. 68**: pp 151–265.

Manley, G. 1980. The northern Pennines revisited: Moor House, 1932–78. *Meteorological Magazine* **Vol. 109**: pp 281–292.

Marrs R. H., Rawes, M., Robinson, J. S. & Poppit, S. D. 1987. Long-term studies of vegetation change at Moor House NNR: research note. In: Bell, M. & Bunce, R. G. H. (eds.) *Agriculture and conservation in the hills and uplands.* Grange-over-Sands, NERC/ITE, 139. (ITE Symposium, 23.)

Matthews, J. R. 1955. *Origin and distribution of the British Flora.* London.

Merryweather, J. 2020. *Britain's Ferns – A field guide to the clubmosses, quillworts, horsetails and ferns of Great Britain and Ireland.* Princeton WILD*Guides.*

National Trust. 2019. *State of Nature 2019 – UK's wildlife losses continue unabated.* [Available at: https://www.nationaltrust.org.uk/features/state-of-nature-2019-uks-wildlife-loss-continues-unabated.]

Nichol, R. & Gledhill, T. 2003. Charcoal-making Pits in Teesdale. *Teesdale Record Society Journal 3rd Series* **Vol. 11**: pp 8–13.

O'Reilly, J. 2010. The state of upland hay meadows in the North Pennines. *British Wildlife,* **Feb 2010**: pp 184–192.

O'Reilly, J. 2020. *The Roles of Different Sphagnum Species in Bogs.* North Pennines

AONB webinar 20th April 2020. [Available at: https://www.northpennines.org.uk/what_we_do/peatland-programme/pennine-peatlife/webinars.]

Oliver, Revd. W. 1789. *Hoary Whitlowgrass, Hoary Rockrose.* In Horsman, 1998.

Oliver, Revd. W. 1794, *Mountain Everlasting, Birdseye Primrose.* In Horsman, 1998.

Oliver, Revd. W. 1796. *Thrift, Alpine Bartsia, Mountain Avens, Hairy Stonecrop.* In Horsman, 1998.

Oliver, Revd. W. 1798. *Roseroot.* In Horsman, 1998.

Oliver, Revd. W. & Binks, J. 1810. *Chickweed Willowherb.* In Horsman, 1998.

Oliver, Revd. W. & Harriman, W. 1796–1797. *Bog Orchid, Spring Sandwort.* In Horsman, 1998.

Pearman, D. A. 2017. *The Discovery of the Native Flora of Britain & Ireland.* Botanical Society of the British Isles.

Perring, F. & Farrell. 1977, 1983. *Red Data Book for vascular plants in Great Britain.* JNCC.

Pigott, C. D. 1956. The Vegetation of Upper Teesdale in the North Pennines. *Journal of Ecology* Vol. 44(2): pp 545–586. [Available at: https://doi.org/10.2307/2256835#.]

Pigott, C. D. 1958. *Polemonium caeruleum* L. Biological Flora of the British Isles. *Journal of Ecology* Vol. 46: pp 507–525.

Pigott, C. D. & Walters, S. M. 1954. On the Interpretation of the Discontinuous Distributions shown by certain British Species of Open Habitats. *Journal of Ecology* Vol. 42(1): pp 95–116.

Plantlife. *Important Plantlife Areas: Moor House to Upper Teesdale IPA (Grid Reference: NY 73 33).* [Available at: https://www.plantlife.org.uk/uk/nature-reserves-important-plant-areas/important-plant-areas/moor-house-upper-teesdale.]

Preston, C. D. 2007. Which vascular plants are found at the northern or southern edges of their European range in the British Isles? *Watsonia* Vol. 26: pp 253–269.

Preston, C. D. & Hill, M. O. 1997. The geographical relationships of British and Irish vascular plants. *Botanical Journal of the Linnean Society* Vol. 124(1).

Preston, C. D., Pearman, D. A. & Dines, T. D. (eds.) 2002. *New Atlas of the British and Irish Flora.* Oxford University Press.

Ramsar Convention. 1971. *The Ramsar Convention on Wetlands of International Importance especially as Waterfowl Habitat.* [International treaty for the conservation and sustainable use of wetlands.]

Proctor, H. G. 1972. *Carex aquatilis* Walhenb. in Upper Teesdale. *Vasculum* **57**, pp 17–24.

Ramsden, D. M. 1947. *Teesdale.* Museum Press, London.

Ratcliffe, D. A. & Eddy, A. 1960. *Alopecurus alpinus* Sm. in Britain. *Proceedings of the Botanical Society of the British Isles* Vol. 3: pp 389–391.

Rawes, M. (ed.) 1978. *Moor House 19th annual progress report.* Nature Conservancy Council (Unpublished).

Rawes, M. 1981. Further Results of Excluding Sheep from High Level Grasslands in the Northern Pennines. *Journal of Ecology* Vol. 69: pp 651–669.

Ray, J. 1677. *Catalogue of English Plants, 2nd Edn.* A. Clark, London.

Rich, T. C. G. & Jermy, A. C. 1998. *Plant Crib.* Botanical Society of the British Isles.

Richards, A. J. 1972. The *Taraxacum* Flora of the British Isles. *Watsonia: Journal and Proceedings of the Botanical Society of the British Isles,* Supplement to Vol. 9: pp 1–141.

Roberts, F. J. 2002. After Foot and Mouth, Cross Fell in Bloom. *Carlisle Naturalist* Vol.10(2): pp 33–40.

Roberts, F. J. 2009. Northern Deergrass in Upper Teesdale. *BSBI News* No 111: pp 22–26.

Roberts, F. J. 2010. *Marsh Saxifrage, Saxifraga hirculus, status of English sites in 2009.* Unpublished report for Natural England.

Roberts, F. J. 2010. *Moor House & Cross Fell SSSI: Review of Vascular Plant Scoring Species 2009.* Unpublished report to Natural England.

Roberts, F. J. 2010. *Pale Forget-Me-Not. NE report 18/44; 21/48*, p 182.

Roberts, F. J. 2011. The Northern Deergrass *Trichophorum cespitosum* (L.) Hartm., new to Cumbria, with comments on its habitats. *The Carlisle Naturalist* Vol. 19(1): p 27.

Roberts, F. J. 2013. Identification of *Viola rupestris*, Teesdale Violet. *BSBI News* No. 122: p 29.

Roberts, F. J. & Amphlett, A. 2018. *Three Trichophorum taxa – ID and ecology.* [Available at: https://bsbi.org/wp-content/uploads/dlm_uploads/Deergrass-Id.pdf.]

Roberts, F. J. & Halliday, G. 1979. The altitudinal range of *Catabrosa aquatica* (L.) Beauv. *Watsonia* Vol. 12: pp 342–343.

Roberts, R. D. & Roberts, T. M. 1984. *Planning and Ecology.* Chapman Hall, London. [Includes chapter 8.3: **Bines, T. J., Doody, J. P., Findlay, H. & Hudson, M. J.** *A retrospective view of the environmental impact on Upper Teesdale of the Cow Green Reservoir.*]

Robinson, R., Corner, R. & Roberts, J. 2006. Damage to the vegetation of the Northern Pennines by the use of motorcycles and quad-bikes. *BSBI News* No. 103 (September).

Robson, E. 1793. *Downy Currant.* Privately published.

Robson, E. 1794. *Catalogus Plantarium rariorum circa Darlington sponte nascentium.* Privately published.

Robson, E. 1798. *Plantae rariores agro Dunelmensis indigenae.* [Davis & Graham (1981) wrote "Stephen Robson wrote a short list of local plants; the longer and more critical list was produced by his more knowledgeable nephew Edward.]

Robson, S. 1777. *The British Flora.* W. Blanchard.

Rodwell, J. S. 2006 (2012). *National Vegetation Classification Users' Handbook.* JNCC, Peterborough. Cambridge University Press (Pelagic Publishing).

Rodwell, J. S. (ed.) 1991. *British Plant Communities, Volume 1: Woodlands and scrub.* Cambridge University Press.

Rodwell, J. S. (ed.) 1992. *British Plant Communities, Volume 2: Mires and heaths.* Cambridge University Press.

Rodwell, J. S. (ed.) 1992. *British Plant Communities, Volume 3: Grassland and montane communities.* Cambridge University Press.

Rodwell, J. S. (ed.) 1995. *British Plant Communities, Volume 4: Aquatic communities, swamps and tall-herb fens.* Cambridge University Press.

Rodwell, J. S. (ed.) 2000. *British Plant Communities, Volume 5: Maritime communities and vegetation of open habitats.* Cambridge University Press.

Sarker, F. 2015. Field Meeting, Upper Teesdale 3rd–4th July 2014. *BSBI Year Book* pp 79–80.

Sayers, C. D. & Gaman, J. H. 1972. Gene banks: a case-study with Teesdale species. *J. R. Hort. Soc.*, **97**: pp 478–481.

Sell, P. & Murrell, G. 1997. *Flora of Great Britain and Ireland: Volume 5, Butomaceae – Orchidaceae.* Cambridge University Press.

Sell, P. & Murrell, G. 2006. *Flora of Great Britain and Ireland: Volume 4, Campanulaceae – Asteraceae.* Cambridge University Press.

Sell, P. & Murrell, G. 2009. *Flora of Great Britain and Ireland: Volume 3, Mimosaceae – Lentibulariaceae.* Cambridge University Press.

Sell, P. & Murrell, G. 2014. *Flora of Great Britain and Ireland: Volume 2, Capparaceae – Rosaceae.* Cambridge University Press.

Sell, P. & Murrell, G. 2018. *Flora of Great Britain and Ireland: Volume 1, Lycopodiaceae – Salicaceae.* Cambridge University Press.

Smith, J. E. & Sowerby, J. (illus.) 1808. *English Botany, or, Coloured Figures of British Plants, with Their Essential Characters, Synonyms, and Places of Growth, Vol. 26*. R. Taylor and Co., London.

Stace, C. A. 2019. *New Flora of the British Isles, 4th Edn.* C&M Floristics.

Stroh, P. A., Leach, S. J., August, T. A., Walker, K. J., Pearman, D. A., Rumsey, F. J, Harrower, C. A., Fay, M. F., Martin, J. P., Pankhurst, T., Preston, C. D. & Taylor, I. 2014. *A Vascular Plant Red List for England.* Botanical Society of Britain and Ireland (BSBI). [Available at: http://www.bsbi.org.uk/england.html.]

Swan, G. A. & Walters, S. M. 1988. *Alchemilla gracilis* Opiz, a new species to the British flora. *Watsonia* **Vol. 17**: pp 133–138.

Tansley. A. G. 1939. *The British Islands and their Vegetation.* Cambridge University Press.

Taylor, K. & Rumsey, F. J. 2003. *Bartsia alpina* L. *J. of Ecology* **Vol. 19.**

Tennant, D. J. 1995. *Cystopteris fragilis* var. *alpina* Hook. in Britain. *The Naturalist* **Vol. 120**: pp 45–50.

Tennant, D. J. 2008. Small Cow-wheat *Melampyrum sylvaticum* L.; Scrophulariaceae in England. *Watsonia* **Vol. 27**: pp 23–36.

Tennant, D. J. 2010. The British records of *Cystopteris alpina* (Lam.) Desv. *Watsonia* **Vol. 28**: pp 57–63.

Tennant, D. J. & Rich, T. C. G. 2008. *British Alpine Hawkweeds: A Monograph of British Hieracium (Section Alpina).* Botanical Society of the British Isles.

Trevelyan, C. W. 1832. (Cited in Baker, 1903.)

Turner, D. & Dillwyn, L. W. 1805. *The Botanist's Guide Through England and Wales, Vol. 1.* Phillips and Fardon.

Turner, W. 1551, 1562, 1568. *A New Herball.* Part 1, Mierdman, London; Parts 2 and 3, Barckman, Cologne, Cambridge

University Press. [Known as being one of the first 'parson-naturalists' in England.]

United Nations (UN). 1992. *Convention on Biological Diversity.*

Valentine, D. H. 1965. *The Natural History of Upper Teesdale.* Northumberland and Durham Naturalists' Trust Ltd., Newcastle-upon-Tyne.

Walters, S. M. 1947. *Clustered Lady's Mantle, Rock Lady's Mantle.* Proceedings of the BSBI.

Walters, S. M. 1949. *Alchemilla vulgaris* L. in Britain. *Watsonia* **Vol. 1**: pp 6–18.

Walters, S. M. 1952. *Alchemilla subcrenata* Buser in Britain. *Watsonia* **Vol. 2**: pp 277–278.

Whitby, M. C. & Willis, K. G. 1978. A Cautionary Case Study. *Rural Resource Review,* Routledge; chapter updated 13 Dec 2018: pp 395–422.

Wigginton, M. J. 1999. *Red Data Book for vascular plants in Great Britain.* JNCC.

Wildlife and Countryside Act, 1981, as amended. [Available at: https://www.legislation.gov.uk/ukpga/1981/69.]

Wilmott, A. J. 1922. Manual of British Botany. *J. Bot.* **Vol. 60**: p 165.

Wilson, Revd. E. 1744. *Alpine Bistort.*

Winch, N. J. 1805. *Pyrenean Scurvy Grass.*

Winch, N. J. 1832a. [First] Addenda to the Flora of Northumberland and Durham. *Transactions of the Natural History Society of Northumberland* **Vol. 2(1)**: pp 137–146. And **Winch, N. J.** 1832b. Observations on the preceding flora (of Northumberland and Durham).

Winch, N. J. (ed.) 1805. *The Botanist's Guide through the Counties of Northumberland and Durham.* [Available from Gurney Creative Media Partners, LLC.]

Winch, N. J., Thornhill, J & Waugh, R. J. 1805. *Rosebay Willowherb.* Hodgson, Newcastle upon Tyne.

Glossary and abbreviations

BOTANICAL TERMS

adpressed	flattened against but not joined to
anther	the fertile, pollen-producing part of a flower
apiculate	having a short, sharply pointed tip
apomixis; *adj.* apomictic	asexual reproduction without fertilization
aril	an extra seed covering, typically coloured and hairy or fleshy
awn	a stiff bristle, especially one of those growing from the flower of many grasses
axil	the upper angle between a leaf stalk and the stem
bract	a modified leaf with a flower or flower cluster in its **axil**
bulbil	a small bulb-like structure, often in the **axil** of a leaf, which may fall to form a new plant
calcicole	a plant that thrives in lime-rich soil
calyx	the **sepals** of a flower, typically forming a whorl that encloses the petals and forms a protective layer around a flower in bud
capitulum; *pl.* capitula	a dense, flat cluster of small flowers or florets arising from a platform-like base, as in plants of the daisy family
cleistogamous	self-pollinating within a flower which does not fully open
cordate	heart-shaped
corolla	the petals of a flower, typically forming a whorl which encloses the male and/or female reproductive structures
cotyledon	the seed leaf: the first leaf/leaves to appear from a germinating seed
crenate	having a round-toothed or scalloped edge
decumbent	lying along the ground, curving upwards at the end
deflexed	bent or curving downwards or backwards
dehisce; *noun* dehiscence	to burst open
dioecious	having the male and female reproductive organs on separate individuals
disjunct	discontinuous
epicalyx	an outer whorl of **sepal**-like structures, characteristic of certain families of plants
forb	a herbaceous flowering plant other than a grass
gamete	a reproductive cell
gemma; *pl.* gemmae	a small cellular body or bud that can separate to form a new plant without sexual reproduction
glabrous; *adj.* glabrescent	smooth, free from hair or down
glaucous	grey- or bluish-green
glume	each of two membranous **bracts** surrounding the **spikelet** of a grass, or one surrounding the florets of a sedge
hemiparasite	a parasitic plant that extracts water and mineral nutrients from its host, but still has functional green tissues
hermaphrodite	having male and female reproductive organs within the same flower
inflorescence	a head, or cluster, of individual flowers
internode	the portion of a stem between the attachment points of the leaves
lanceolate	long and narrow, tapering at both ends
monocarpic	flowering only once and then dying
mycorrhiza; *pl.* mycorrhizae	a fungus which grows in association with the roots of a plant in a symbiotic or mildly pathogenic relationship
obovate	an oval leaf which is narrower at the base
ovary	an enlarged basal portion of female flower parts which develops into seed(s) upon fertilization
palmate	a leaf with lobes that radiate from one point
papillose	covered in small fleshy projections

pappus	a structure made of scales, bristles, or feather-like hairs, attached to the seeds of, and aiding the wind-dispersal of, some plants
pedicel	a stalk of an individual flower
perennate; *noun* perennation	to survive a winter or dry season and grow again in one or more seasons
perennial	a plant that lives for more than two years
perianth	the outer part of a flower, consisting of the **calyx** (**sepals**) and **corolla** (petals)
petiole	a leaf stalk
pinna; *pl.* pinnae	the first-level segment of a fern frond
pinnate	having leaflets or primary divisions arranged on each side of a common stalk
pinnule	the second-level segment of a fern frond
proliferous	producing buds or side shoots from a flower
propagule	a structure that can give rise to a new plant, *e.g.* a bud, sucker, spore or seed
pubescent	covered with short soft hair; downy
raceme	an **inflorescence** in which individual flowers are attached by short stalks to central stem
rachis	(of a fern) the main stem of a frond
ramet	an individual plant from a genetically identical (clonal) colony
reniform	kidney-shaped
reticulate	with a net-like pattern
rhizome	a horizontal underground stem
ruderal	growing on disturbed ground; 'weedy'
scape	a long flower stalk coming directly from a root
sepal	one part of the **calyx** enclosing the petal, typically green and leaf-like
spikelet	the sub-units of a grass **inflorescence**
sporangium; *pl.* sporangia	a spore capsule
stamen	the male reproductive organ of a flower consisting of a filament (stalk) and **anther**
stigma	the pollen-receiving section of the female flower parts
stipule	a small leaf-like appendage typically at the base of a leaf stalk
stolon	a creeping horizontal plant stem or runner that takes root at points along its length to form new plants
style	the usually elongated structure that joins the **stigma** to the **ovary**
subacute	moderately acute in angle
taxon; *pl.* taxa	a taxonomic unit of any rank, *e.g.* genus, species, subspecies or variety
tiller	a side-shoot that grows from a grass plant or similar
utricle	a small, one-seeded fruit usually not splitting at maturity

OTHER TERMS

adit	a horizontal mine-shaft
alluvium	the material deposited by running water
anthropogenic	originating in human activity
artesian	(of water) rising to the surface under internal hydrostatic pressure
base-rich	pH more alkaline than neutral
burn	a stream
Calaminarian	characterized by high levels of toxic metals
calcareous	containing calcium carbonate; chalky
closed	(of grassland *etc.*) without significant areas of bare ground
col	the lowest point of an upland ridge
dolerite	a type of volcanic rock containing large crystals
drumlin	an oval or elongated hill, formed during the last Ice Age
escarpment	the steep slope of a hill
eutrophic	(of a water body) excessively rich in nutrients
flush	a ground-water spring
friable	crumbly
gill	a ravine
gley	sticky waterlogged soil lacking in oxygen, typically grey-to-blue in colour

GLOSSARY AND ABBREVIATIONS

grip	a drain
gryke	a fissure in limestone pavement
half-life	the time taken to decrease by half
hushes	gullies formed by water used in mining to reveal mineral veins
igneous	having solidified from lava or magma
issue	a spring
marl	rock containing clay and calcium carbonate
mesotrophic	having a moderate amount of dissolved nutrients
micaceous	containing mica
moraine	a mass of rocks and sediment carried down and deposited by a glacier
mull	soil comprising a mix of rich organic matter and mineral earth
open	(of grassland *etc.*) with significant areas of bare ground
poaching	(by cattle) trampling
podsol	infertile acidic soil characterized by a white or grey subsurface layer resembling ash
rendzina	fertile lime-rich soil with dark humus above a pale soft **calcareous** layer, typical of grassland on chalk or limestone
rill	a small stream
rip-rap	large boulders protecting underlying soft material from strong wave action
runnel	a small drainage channel
schist	a flaky rock often formed from mudstone or shale
scree	a mass of small loose stones that form or cover a slope on a mountain
serpentine	hydrated magnesium silicate occurring in winding veins
shake-hole	the depression or crater formed when the underlying rock has collapsed
sike	a small stream
solifluction	the gradual movement of wet soil down a slope
spate	a sudden flood in a river
stint	a grazier's entitlement to graze a specified number of animals
talus	a pile of rocks that accumulates at the base of a cliff
till	unsorted glacial sediment
tufa	porous rock composed of calcium carbonate and formed by precipitation from water, *e.g.* around mineral springs

ABBREVIATIONS

BSBI	Botanical Society of Britain and Ireland
CGE	Botany School, University of Cambridge
DHM	Botany Department, University of Durham
ESA	Environmentally Sensitive Area
FYM	Farmyard manure
herb.	herbarium
ITE	Institute of Terrestrial Ecology
IUCN	International Union for Conservation of Nature
JNCC	Joint Nature Conservation Committee
NE	Natural England (pre-2006 English Nature (EN), pre-1991 Nature Conservancy Council (NCC) and pre-1973 Nature Conservancy (NC))
NERC	Natural Environment and Rural Communities
NNR	National Nature Reserve
NPK	Nitrogen-phosphorus-potassium fertilizers
RBGE	Royal Botanic Garden Edinburgh
RBGK	Royal Botanic Garden Kew
SAC	Special Area of Conservation
SPA	Special Protection Area
sp.; *pl.* spp.	species
ssp.; *pl.* sspp.	subspecies
SSSI	Site of Special Scientific Interest
vc	vice-county

Gazeteer: places in Teesdale mentioned in the text

Site name	OS Grid reference	Site name	OS Grid reference
Arn Gill	NZ 075 245	Hunt Hall Farm	NY 853 306
Baldersdale	NY 945 185	Knock Fell	NY 725 305
Barnard Castle	NZ 045 170	Knock Ore Gill	NY 705 305
Bellbeaver Rigg	NY 765 355	Langdon Beck	NY 853 312
Birkdale	NY 804 278	Little Dun Fell	NY 705 335
Blackton Reservoir	NY 945 185	Little Fell	NY 784 218
Blea Beck	NY 875 278	Long Crag	NY 845 255
Bowes Close	NY 835 324	Low Force	NY 903 279
Bowlees Visitor Centre	NY 907 282	Lunedale	NY 925 215
Brignall Banks	NZ 055 115	Marshes Gill	NY 825 325
Brockers Gill	NY 925 275	Meldon Hill	NY 775 295
Burnhope Seat	NY 785 375	Mickle Fell	NY 806 245
Cauldron Snout	NY 815 285	Middleton-in-Teesdale	NY 947 254
Cow Green Reservoir	NY 806 301	Nether Hearth	NY 758 330
Cronkley Fell	NY 845 275	Newbiggin	NY 914 277
Crook Burn	NY 775 345	Noon Hill	NY 859 273
Cross Fell	NY 685 345	Outberry Plain	NY 937 330
Dine Holm Scar	NY 867 283	Park End Wood	NY 925 265
Dodgen Pot	NY 765 325	Ravelin	NY 925 274
Dubby Sike	NY 795 318	Rough Sike	NY 756 315
Eggleston	NY 995 235	Sand Sike	NY 835 305
Ettersgill	NY 885 295	Selset Reservoir	NY 915 215
Falcon Clints	NY 825 285	Skyer Beck	NY 865 275
Fendrith Hill	NY 877 333	The Rods	NY 816 303
Forest-in-Teesdale	NY 866 298	Thistle Green	NY 845 285
Great Dun Fell	NY 715 325	Trout Beck	NY 745 325
Green Castle	NY 715 315	Wheysike House	NY 855 295
Green Hurth	NY 780 327	White Force	NY 855 275
Hard Hill	NY 735 335	White Well	NY 835 285
Harwood	NY 817 333	Widdybank Fell	NY 827 295
High Cup Nick	NY 745 265	Widdybank Meadow	NY 839 301
High Force	NY 885 285	Wynch Bridge	NY 905 275
Holwick Scar	NY 905 265	Yad Moss	NY 785 355
Hunder Beck	NY 905 165		

Species mentioned in the text

English names are used throughout this book when referring to plant species. Although the scientific name is included for species that are the subject of a species account, to make the text more accessible to most readers and to save space, English names only are used for other species that are mentioned. For the benefit of readers who are more familiar with scientific names, however, these are included in the following alphabetical list of all the plant species mentioned in the text. The nomenclature, both English and *scientific* names, follows Stace (2019).

Alder *Alnus glutinosa*
Anemone, Wood *Anemone nemorosa*
Angelica, Wild *Angelica sylvestris*
Apple-moss, Fountain *Philonotis fontana*
Apple-moss, Thick-nerved *Philonotis calcarea*
Arrow-grass, Marsh *Triglochin palustris*
Ash *Fraxinus excelsior*
Aspen *Populus tremula*
Asphodel, Bog *Narthecium ossifragum*
Asphodel, Scottish *Tofieldia pusilla*
Avens, Mountain *Dryas octopetala*
Avens, Water *Geum rivale*
Bartsia, Alpine *Bartsia alpina*
Beak-sedge, Brown *Rhynchospora fusca*
Bearberry *Arctostaphylos uva-ursi*
Bedstraw, Heath *Galium saxatile*
Bedstraw, Lady's *Galium verum*
Bedstraw, Limestone *Galium sterneri*
Bedstraw, Marsh *Galium palustre*
Bedstraw, Northern *Galium boreale*
Bellflower, Giant *Campanula latifolia*
Bent, Brown *Agrostis vinealis*
Bent, Common *Agrostis capillaris*
Bent, Creeping *Agrostis stolonifera*
Bent, Velvet *Agrostis canina*
Betony *Betonica officinalis*
Bilberry *Vaccinium myrtillus*
Bilberry, Bog *Vaccinium uliginosum*
Birch, Downy *Betula pubescens*
Birch, Dwarf *Betula nana*
Birch, Silver *Betula pendula*
Bird's-foot-trefoil, Common
    Lotus corniculatus
Bistort, Alpine *Bistorta vivipara*
Bitter-vetch *Lathyrus linifolius*

Bladder-fern, Alpine *Cystopteris alpina*
Bladder-fern, Brittle *Cystopteris fragilis*
Bladderwort, Intermediate
    Utricularia intermedia
Blinks *Montia fontana*
Bluebell *Hyacinthoides non-scripta*
Bogbean *Menyanthes trifoliata*
Bog-moss, Austin's *Sphagnum austinii*
Bog-moss, Compact *Sphagnum compactum*
Bog-moss, Cow-horn *Sphagnum denticulatum*
Bog-moss, Feathery *Sphagnum cuspidatum*
Bog-moss, Flat-topped *Sphagnum fallax*
Bog-moss, Flexuous *Sphagnum flexuosum*
Bog-moss, Golden *Sphagnum pulchrum*
Bog-moss, Imbricate *Sphagnum affine*
Bog-moss, Magellanic
    Sphagnum magellanicum
Bog-moss, Papillose *Sphagnum papillosum*
Bog-moss, Red *Sphagnum capillifolium*
Bog-moss, Russow's *Sphagnum russowii*
Bog-moss, Rusty *Sphagnum fuscum*
Bog-rosemary *Andromeda polifolia*
Bog-sedge *Carex limosa*
Bog-sedge, Tall *Carex magellanica*
Bracken *Pteridium aquilinum*
Bramble, Stone *Rubus saxatilis*
Brome, False *Brachypodium sylvaticum*
Buckler-fern, Broad *Dryopteris dilatata*
Buckler-fern, Northern *Dryopteris expansa*
Buckler-fern, Rigid *Dryopteris submontana*
Burnet, Great *Sanguisorba officinalis*
Burnet, Salad *Poterium sanguisorba*
Burnet-saxifrage *Pimpinella saxifraga*
Bur-reed, Unbranched *Sparganium emersum*
Buttercup, Bulbous *Ranunculus bulbosus*

Buttercup, Meadow *Ranunculus acris*
Butterfly-orchid, Lesser *Platanthera bifolia*
Butterwort, Common *Pinguicula vulgaris*
Cat's-ear *Hypochaeris radicata*
Cat's-tail, Alpine *Phleum alpinum*
Celandine, Lesser *Ficaria verna*
Cherry, Bird *Prunus padus*
Cinquefoil, Alpine *Potentilla crantzii*
Cinquefoil, Marsh *Comarum palustre*
Cinquefoil, Shrubby *Dasiphora fruticosa*
Cinquefoil, Spring *Potentilla verna*
Cleavers *Galium aparine*
Cloudberry *Rubus chamaemorus*
Clover, Red *Trifolium pratense*
Clover, White *Trifolium repens*
Clover, Zigzag *Trifolium medium*
Clubmoss, Alpine *Diphasiastrum alpinum*
Clubmoss, Fir *Huperzia selago*
Clubmoss, Lesser *Selaginella selaginoides*
Clubmoss, Stag's-horn *Lycopodium clavatum*
Club-rush, Floating *Eleogiton fluitans*
Cock's-foot *Dactylis glomerata*
Comb-moss *Ctenidium molluscum*
Corncockle *Agrostemma githago*
Cottongrass, Broad-leaved
  Eriophorum latifolium
Cottongrass, Common
  Eriophorum angustifolium
Cottongrass, Hare's-tail
  Eriophorum vaginatum
Cowberry *Vaccinium vitis-idaea*
Cow-wheat, Common *Melampyrum pratense*
Cow-wheat, Small *Melampyrum sylvaticum*
Crack-willow, Hybrid *Salix × fragilis*
Cranberry *Vaccinium oxycoccos*
Crane's-bill, Meadow *Geranium pratense*
Crane's-bill, Shining *Geranium lucidum*
Crane's-bill, Wood *Geranium sylvaticum*
Crisp-moss, Frizzled *Tortella tortuosa*
Crowberry *Empetrum nigrum*
Cuckooflower *Cardamine pratensis*
Currant, Black *Ribes nigrum*
Currant, Downy *Ribes spicatum*
Currant, Red *Ribes rubrum*
Daisy *Bellis perennis*

Daisy, Oxeye *Leucanthemum vulgare*
dandelions *Taraxacum* spp.
Dandelion, Teesdale
  Taraxacum pseudonordstedtii
Deergrass, Common
  Trichophorum germanicum
Deergrass, 'Hybrid' *Trichophorum × foersteri*
Deergrass, Northern *Trichophorum cespitosum*
Ditrichum, Bendy *Ditrichum flexicaule*
Dock, Broad-leaved *Rumex obtusifolia*
Dog's-tail, Crested *Cynosurus cristatus*
Dog-violet, Common *Viola riviniana*
Elm, Wych *Ulmus glabra*
Everlasting, Mountain *Antennaria dioica*
Eyebright, Arctic *Euphrasia arctica*
Eyebright, Common *Euphrasia nemorosa*
Eyebright, Confused *Euphrasia confusa*
Eyebright, Montane
  Euphrasia officinalis monticola
Eyebright, Ostenfeld's *Euphrasia ostenfeldii*
Eyebright, Rostkov's
  Euphrasia officinalis pratensis
Eyebright, Scottish *Euphrasia scottica*
Eyebright, Slender *Euphrasia micrantha*
Feather-moss, Wrinkle-leaved
  Rhytidium rugosum
Fern, Beech *Phegopteris connectilis*
Fern, Lemon-scented *Oreopteris limbosperma*
Fern, Oak *Gymnocarpium dryopteris*
Fern, Parsley *Cryptogramma crispa*
Fescue, Red *Festuca rubra*
Fescue, Tall *Schedonorus arundinaceus*
Flat-sedge *Blysmus compressus*
Flax, Fairy *Linum catharticum*
Fleawort, Field *Tephroseris integrifolia*
Forget-me-not, Alpine *Myosotis alpestris*
Forget-me-not, Pale *Myosotis stolonifera*
Forget-me-not, Wood *Myosotis sylvatica*
Fork-moss, Broom *Dicranum scoparium*
Foxglove *Digitalis purpurea*
Foxtail, Alpine *Alopecurus magellanicus*
Foxtail, Marsh *Alopecurus geniculatus*
Foxtail, Meadow *Alopecurus pratensis*
Fragrant-orchid, Heath *Gymnadenia borealis*
Fragrant-orchid, Marsh *Gymnadenia densiflora*

Fringe-moss, Woolly *Racomitrium lanuginosum*
Gentian, Autumn *Gentianella amarella*
Gentian, Field *Gentianella campestris*
Gentian, Spring *Gentiana verna*
Globeflower *Trollius europaeus*
Goldenrod *Solidago virgaurea*
Golden-saxifrage, Alternate-leaved *Chrysosplenium alternifolium*
Golden-saxifrage, Opposite-leaved *Chrysosplenium oppositifolium*
Gorse *Ulex europaeus*
Grass-of-Parnassus *Parnassia palustris*
Haircap, Common *Polytrichum commune*
Hair-grass, Crested *Koeleria macrantha*
Hair-grass, Tufted *Deschampsia cespitosa*
Hair-grass, Wavy *Deschampsia flexuosa*
Hard-fern *Blechnum spicant*
Harebell *Campanula rotundifolia*
Hart's-tongue *Asplenium scolopendrium*
Hawk's-beard, Marsh *Crepis paludosa*
Hawk's-beard, Northern *Crepis mollis*
Hawkbit, Autumn *Scorzoneroides autumnalis*
Hawkbit, Rough *Leontodon hispidus*
Hawkweed, Mouse-eared *Pilosella officinarum*
Hazel *Corylus avellana*
Heath, Cross-leaved *Erica tetralix*
Heather *Calluna vulgaris*
Heather, Bell *Erica cinerea*
Heath-grass *Danthonia decumbens*
Helleborine, Broad-leaved *Epipactis helleborine*
Helleborine, Dark-red *Epipactis atrorubens*
Herb-Paris *Paris quadrifolia*
Herb-Robert *Geranium robertianum*
Holly-fern *Polystichum lonchitis*
Hook-moss, Curled *Palustriella commutata*
Horsetail, Field *Equisetum arvense*
Horsetail, Great *Equisetum telmateia*
Horsetail, Marsh *Equisetum palustre*
Horsetail, Shady *Equisetum pratense*
Horsetail, Variegated *Equisetum variegatum*
Horsetail, Wood *Equisetum sylvaticum*
Iris, Yellow *Iris pseudacorus*
Jacob's-ladder *Polemonium caeruleum*
Juniper, Common *Juniperus communis*

Knapweed, Common *Centaurea nigra*
lady's-mantle agg. *Alchemilla vulgaris* agg.
Lady's-mantle, Clustered *Alchemilla glomerulans*
Lady's-mantle, Garden *Alchemilla mollis*
Lady's-mantle, Hairy *Alchemilla filicaulis* ssp. *vestita*
Lady's-mantle, Large-toothed *Alchemilla subcrenata*
Lady's-mantle, Pale *Alchemilla xanthochlora*
Lady's-mantle, Rock *Alchemilla wichurae*
Lady's-mantle, Shining *Alchemilla micans*
Lady's-mantle, Silky *Alchemilla glaucescens*
Lady's-mantle, Slender *Alchemilla filicaulis* ssp. *filicaulis*
Lady's-mantle, Smooth *Alchemilla glabra*
Lady's-mantle, Starry *Alchemilla acutiloba*
Lady's-mantle, Velvet *Alchemilla monticola*
Lady's-slipper *Cypripedium calceolus*
Lady-fern *Athyrium felix-femina*
Lettuce, Wall *Mycelis muralis*
Lily-of-the-valley *Convallaria majalis*
Loosestrife, Tufted *Lysimachia thyrsiflora*
Lousewort, Marsh *Pedicularis palustris*
Male-fern *Dryopteris filix-mas*
Male-fern, Golden-scaled *Dryopteris affinis*
Male-fern, Mountain *Dryopteris oreades*
Marsh-marigold *Caltha palustris*
Marsh-orchid, Early *Dactylorhiza incarnata*
Marsh-orchid, Northern *Dactylorhiza purpurella*
Marshwort, Lesser *Apium inundatum*
Mat-grass *Nardus stricta*
Meadow-grass, Alpine *Poa alpina*
Meadow-grass, Glaucous *Poa glauca*
Meadow-grass, Rough *Poa trivialis*
Meadow-grass, Smooth *Poa pratensis*
Meadow-rue, Alpine *Thalictrum alpinum*
Meadow-rue, Lesser *Thalictrum minus*
Meadowsweet *Filipendula ulmaria*
Melick, Mountain *Melica nutans*
Melick, Wood *Melica uniflora*
Mercury, Dog's *Mercurialis perennis*
Milkwort, Common *Polygala vulgaris*
Milkwort, Dwarf *Polygala amarella*

Milkwort, Heath *Polygala serpyllifolia*
Mint, Water *Mentha aquatica*
Moonwort *Botrychium lunaria*
Moor-grass, Blue *Sesleria caerulea*
Moor-grass, Purple *Molinia caerulea*
Moschatel *Adoxa moschatellina*
Moss, Golf-club *Catoscopium nigritum*
Mouse-ear, Common *Cerastium fontanum*
Nettle, Common *Urtica dioica*
Oak, Pendunculate *Quercus robur*
Oak, Sessile *Quercus petraea*
Oat-grass, Downy *Avenula pubescens*
Oat-grass, False *Arrhenatherum elatius*
Oat-grass, Meadow *Helictochloa pratensis*
Oat-grass, Yellow *Trisetum flavescens*
Orchid, Bog *Hammarbya paludosa*
Orchid, Early-purple *Orchis mascula*
Orchid, Frog *Coeloglossum viride*
Orchid, Small-white *Pseudorchis albida*
Orpine *Hylotelephium telephium*
Pansy, Mountain *Viola lutea*
Parsley *Petroselinum crispum*
Pearlwort, Knotted *Sagina nodosa*
Penny-cress, Alpine *Noccaea caerulescens*
Pignut *Conopodium majus*
Pine, Scots *Pinus sylvestris*
Plait-moss, Cypress-leaved
   Hypnum cupressiforme
Plantain, Ribwort *Plantago lanceolata*
Plantain, Sea *Plantago maritima*
Pond-sedge, Lesser *Carex acutiformis*
Pondweed, Red *Potomageton alpinus*
poplars *Populus* spp.
Primrose, Bird's-eye *Primula farinosa*
Quaking-grass *Briza media*
Ragged-Robin *Silene flos-cuculi*
Ragwort, Common *Jacobaea vulgaris*
Ramsons *Allium ursinum*
Rannoch-rush *Scheuchzeria palustris*
Rock-rose, Common
   Helianthemum nummularium
Rock-rose, Hoary *Helianthemum oelandicum*
Roseroot *Rhodiola rosea*
Rowan *Sorbus aucuparia*

Rush, Alpine *Juncus alpinoarticulatus*
Rush, Bulbous *Juncus bulbosus*
Rush, Heath *Juncus squarrosus*
Rush, hybrid *Juncus* × *surrejanus*
Rush, Jointed *Juncus articulatus*
Rush, Sharp-flowered *Juncus acutiflorus*
Rush, Three-flowered *Juncus triglumis*
Rustyback *Asplenium ceterach*
Rye-grass, Perennial *Lolium perenne*
Sage, Wood *Teucrium scorodonia*
Sandwort, Spring *Sabulina verna*
Sandwort, Teesdale *Sabulina stricta*
Saw-wort *Serratula tinctoria*
Saxifrage, Alpine *Micranthes nivalis*
Saxifrage, Marsh *Saxifraga hirculus*
Saxifrage, Meadow *Saxifraga granulata*
Saxifrage, Mossy *Saxifraga hypnoides*
Saxifrage, Rue-leaved *Saxifraga tridactylites*
Saxifrage, Starry *Micranthes stellaris*
Saxifrage, Yellow *Saxifraga aizoides*
Scabious, Devil's-bit *Succisa pratensis*
Scabious, Field *Knautia arvensis*
Scabious, Small *Scabiosa columbaria*
Scurvygrass, Pyrenean *Cochlearia pyrenaica*
Sedge, Bottle *Carex rostrata*
Sedge, Carnation *Carex panicea*
Sedge, Common *Carex nigra*
Sedge, Dioeceous *Carex dioica*
Sedge, False *Carex simpliciuscula*
Sedge, Flea *Carex pulicaris*
Sedge, Glaucous *Carex flacca*
Sedge, Hair *Carex capillaris*
Sedge, Oval *Carex leporina*
Sedge, Pill *Carex pilulifera*
Sedge, Sheathed *Carex vaginata*
Sedge, Slender *Carex lasiocarpa*
Sedge, Stiff *Carex bigelowii*
Sedge, String *Carex chordorrhiza*
Sedge, Tawny *Carex hostiana*
Sedge, Water *Carex aquatilis*
Sedge, White *Carex canescens*
Selfheal *Prunella vulgaris*
Shaggy-moss, Little *Rhytidiadelphus loreus*
Sheep's-fescue *Festuca ovina*

Sheep's-fescue, Viviparous *Festuca vivipara*
Shoreweed *Littorella uniflora*
Sneezewort *Achillea ptarmica*
Soft-grass, Creeping *Holcus mollis*
Soft-rush *Juncus effusus*
Sorrel, Common *Rumex acetosa*
Sorrel, Sheep's *Rumex acetosella*
Spear-moss, Giant *Calliergon giganteum*
Spear-moss, Pointed *Calliergonella cuspidata*
Spearwort, Lesser *Ranunculus flammula*
Speedwell, Germander *Veronica chamaedrys*
Speedwell, Wall *Veronica arvensis*
Spike-rush, Few-flowered
　　Eleocharis quinqueflora
Spleenwort, Green *Asplenium viride*
Spleenwort, Maidenhair
　　Asplenium trichomanes
Spotted-orchid, Heath *Dactylorhiza maculata*
Spring-sedge *Carex caryophyllea*
Spring-sedge, Rare *Carex ericetorum*
Squinancywort *Asperula cynanchica*
St John's-wort, Slender *Hypericum pulchrum*
Star-of Bethlehem, Yellow *Gagea lutea*
Stonecrop, Hairy *Sedum villosum*
Strawberry, Wild *Fragaria vesca*
Sundew, Round-leaved *Drosera rotundifolia*
Sycamore *Acer pseudoplatanus*
Thistle, Creeping *Cirsium arvense*
Thistle, Marsh *Cirsium palustre*
Thistle, Melancholy *Cirsium heterophyllum*
Thrift *Armeria maritima*
Thyme, Wild *Thymus drucei*
Timothy *Phleum pratense*
Tormentil *Potentilla erecta*
Tufa-moss, Hook-beaked
　　Hymenostylium recurvirostrum
turf-mosses *Rhytidiadelphus* spp.
Tussock-sedge, Fibrous *Carex appropinquata*
Twayblade, Common *Neottia ovata*
Twayblade, Lesser *Neottia cordata*
Valerian, Common *Valeriana officinalis*
Valerian, Marsh *Valeriana dioica*
Vernal-grass, Sweet *Anthoxanthum odoratum*
Vetch, Horseshoe *Hippocrepis comosa*
Vetch, Kidney *Anthyllis vulneraria*

Vetch, Wood *Ervilia sylvatica*
Violet, Marsh *Viola palustris*
Violet, Teesdale *Viola rupestris*
Violet, Teesdale × Dog-violet, Common
　　Viola × burnatii
Wall-rue *Asplenium ruta-muraria*
Water-milfoil, Alternate
　　Myriophyllum alterniflorum
Water-purslane *Lythrum portula*
Whitebeam, Common *Sorbus aria*
Whitebeam, Rock *Sorbus rupicola*
Whitlowgrass, Common *Erophila verna*
Whitlowgrass, Hoary *Draba incana*
Whitlowgrass, Wall *Drabella muralis*
Whorl-grass *Catabrosa aquatica*
Willow, Bay *Salix pentandra*
Willow, Creeping *Salix repens*
Willow, Eared *Salix aurita*
Willow, Goat *Salix caprea*
Willow, Grey *Salix cinerea*
Willow, Tea-leaved *Salix phylicifolia*
Willowherb, Alpine
　　Epilobium anagallidifolium
Willowherb, Chickweed
　　Epilobium alsinifolium
Willowherb, Marsh *Epilobium palustre*
Willowherb, Rosebay
　　Chamaenerion angustifolium
Woodruff *Galium odoratum*
Wood-rush, Field *Luzula campestris*
Wood-rush, Great *Luzula sylvatica*
Woodsia, Oblong *Woodsia ilvensis*
Wood-sorrel *Oxalis acetosella*
Yarrow *Artemisia millefolium*
Yellow-rattle *Rhinanthus minor*
Yellow-sedge, Common *Carex demissa*
Yellow-sedge, Long-stalked *Carex lepidocarpa*
Yellow-sedge, Small-fruited *Carex viridula*
Yew *Taxus baccata*
Yorkshire-fog *Holcus lanatus*

Acknowledgements and photographic credits

This project began when Jill Sutcliffe, then employed at English Nature, the predecessor of Natural England, said that she didn't have the money to clone me but wondered whether I would consider writing a book about the botanical riches of Teesdale. It has had a long gestation, not helped by the pandemic, during which I was unable to meet up with key contributors and had to liaise with many people over Zoom!

Given the changes to the status of the UK as it detached from the European Union, the changes in the names of plants and the new results from monitoring work, additional inputs were required to finalize the text and to locate the wonderful extra photographs.

I would like to thank Dr Chris Gibson, former Natural England Principal Adviser based in Essex, and his wife Judith, for contributing much in the way of extra support and enthusiasm for this project; they provided wider botanical expertise, and spent hours editing and proof reading the text. Frances Abraham, Susie Daniels, Martin Greenfield, Bruce Middleton, John O'Reilly, Keith Spurgin and Nick Wilcox-Brown gave particular assistance at key points, reflecting their interests and expertise; and Dr Mark Howarth helped on site and provided photographs, and was a great support behind the scenes.

Permission was kindly given by Ian Findlay to use his report and data included in the section on Climate and Weather, which he had worked on with John Adamson. Permission was also given by Frank Horsman for me to draw on his research into the Teesdale flora that formed the basis of his PhD thesis, and is included in his book *Who Discovered the "Teesdale Rarities?"*, self-published in 2021.

There are also the many people who have perhaps assisted unknowingly! These are the numbers of volunteers who help in the UK

The author, Dr Margaret Bradshaw, demonstrating the identification of species of lady's-mantle *MWH*.

John O'Reilly, expert botanist working in Teesdale, demonstrating the identification of eyebrights to visiting botanists *MWH*.

by making wildlife records, supplying the local Biodiversity Records Centres with up-to-date information, running our local wildlife groups and producing invaluable reports and maps. They are a vital asset contributing much to the UK's conservation knowledge.

In particular, I wish to record my heartfelt thanks to Rob Still and Andy Swash at Princeton WILD*Guides*/Princeton University Press, and to their families who must have seen much less of them as they worked tirelessly to translate my words and the accompanying photographs into the wonderful volume that this is.

Photographic credits and key to initals

I am also very grateful to the many photographers who have generously allowed their work to be featured in the book. The following is a complete list of the contributing photographers, presented in alphabetical order by surname and showing the code (initials) used in the image captions to credit the photographer: Dr Margaret Bradshaw [*MEB*], Geoffrey Chaytor [*GC*], J. R. Crellin [*JRC*], Dr Chris Gibson [*CG*], Stuart Hedley [*SH*], G.S. Herbert [*GH*], Dr Mark Howarth [*MWH*], Richard Laidler www.middletonphotos.co.uk [*RLai*], Richard Lansdown [*RLan*], Tim Laurie [*TLa*], Trevor Lowis [*TLo*], R. Lowe [*RL*], David Mitchell [*DM*], John O'Reilly [*JO'R*], J. Parkin [*JP*], Elizabeth Pickett [*EP*], Mike Porter [*MP*], Dr Chris Proctor [*CJP*], Quaternary Research Association [*QRA*], Jeremy Roberts [*FJR*], Martin Rogers [*MR*], Linda Robinson [*LR*], F. Sarker [*FS*], Cameron Sharp [*CS*], Ann Skinner [*AS*], T. Snaith [*TS*], Peter Stroh [*PS*], Sarah H. Watts [*SHW*] and Gordon Young [*GY*].

Natural England

The production of this book was supported by Natural England (NE), the government's adviser for the natural environment in England, which focusses on wildlife conservation and landscape protection. In 1949, it was the National Parks & Access to the Countryside Act that first made nature conservation part of the law, setting up the Nature Conservancy to implement it. NE is the latest incarnation of such an organization and was established in 2006. Its purpose is to help conserve, enhance and manage the natural environment for the benefit of present and future generations, thereby contributing to sustainable development. NE's aim is to foster:

● a well-managed Nature Recovery Network across land, water and sea, which creates and protects resilient ecosystems rich in wildlife and natural beauty;

● people connected to the natural environment for their own and society's wellbeing, enjoyment and prosperity;

● nature-based solutions contributing fully to tackling the climate change challenge improvements in the natural capital that underlies sustainable economic growth, healthy food systems and prospering communities;

● evidence and expertise to protect and strengthen the needs of habitats and species particularly in view of both the biodiversity and climate emergencies.

Contact: Head Office: Foss House, Kings Pool, 1-2 Peasholme Green, York YO1 7PX; and 24 Local offices. See: www.gov.uk/natural-england.

Index of people

This index includes all the people referred to in the text (excluding references and contributors to this book mentioned in the Acknowledgements and photographic credits on *p. 283* and *opposite*).

Index of plants

This index includes the English and *scientific* (in *italics*) names of all the plant species that are the subject of a species account. Every species that is referred to in the text is listed in the section *Species mentioned in the text* (*p. 278*), together with its scientific name, but those that are not the subject of a species account are not specifically indexed here.